THE T

ABOUT R

Critical Studies

LIVERPOOL ENGLISH TEXTS AND STUDIES

General Editors: JONATHAN BATE and BERNARD BEATTY

*

**A full list of available titles can be obtained from
Liverpool University Press.**

THE THING
ABOUT ROY FISHER

Critical Studies

*

Edited by
JOHN KERRIGAN and
PETER ROBINSON

LIVERPOOL UNIVERSITY PRESS

First published 2000 by
LIVERPOOL UNIVERSITY PRESS
Liverpool, L69 3BX

British Library Cataloguing-in-Publication Data
A British Library CIP record is available

ISBN 0–85323–515–5 (hardback)
0–85323–525–2 (paperback)
Set in Monotype Garamond by
Wilmaset Limited, Birkenhead, Wirral
Printed and bound in the European Union by
Bell & Bain, Glasgow

Contents

Notes on Contributors

Ian F. A. Bell is Professor of American Literature at the University of Keele. His books include *Critic as Scientist: The Modernist Poetics of Ezra Pound* (1981) and *Henry James and the Past: Readings into Time* (1991).

Simon Jarvis is Gorley Putt Lecturer in English Literary History in the University of Cambridge. Co-founder of the journal *Parataxis: Modernism and Modern Writing*, he is the author of *Scholars and Gentlemen: Shakespearean Textual Criticism and Representations of Scholarly Labour, 1725–1765* (1995), *Adorno: A Critical Introduction* (1998) and a number of articles on contemporary poetry. He is currently completing a study of Wordsworth.

James Keery teaches English at Fred Longworth High School, Tyldesley, near Leigh. His first collection of poems, *That Stranger, The Blues*, was published by Carcanet in 1996. In 1995 he was invited by the British Council to give a series of readings and talks at six Japanese universities, and he attended the Kyoto Modern Poetry Seminar. He is a regular contributor to *PN Review* and has edited the poetry of Burns Singer.

John Kerrigan (co-editor) is a Fellow of St John's College, Cambridge and University Reader in English Literature. He is the author of many literary essays, and of *Revenge Tragedy: Aeschylus to Armageddon* (1996), which won the Truman Capote Award for Literary Criticism. Among the works he has edited are *Shakespeare's Sonnets and 'A Lover's Complaint'* (1986) and an anthology of laments, *Motives of Woe: Shakespeare and 'Female Complaint'* (1991). His reviews of recent poetry have appeared in *The Sunday Times*, *The Times Literary Supplement*, *Thumbscrew* and the *London Review of Books*.

Meriel Lland is a practitioner who teaches Creative Writing and Live Art at Manchester Metropolitan University. She has written on Willa Cather and on narratives of female identities in Frida Kahlo, Madonna Ciccionne, Cindy Sherman and Helen Chadwick.

John Lucas is publisher/editor of Shoestring Press and Research Professor of English at The Nottingham Trent University. He is the author of many books, including *England and Englishness: Ideas of Nationhood in English Poetry, 1688-1900* (1991), and, most recently, *The Radical Twenties* (1997), *William Blake: New Essays*, edited and introduced (1998), and *Robert Bloomfield: Selected Poems*, edited with John Goodridge (1998). He has published a number of volumes of poetry including *Studying Grosz on the Bus* (1989), and plays cornet with various jazz groups in the Nottingham area, especially the Burgundy Street Jazzmen.

Michael O'Neill is Professor of English at the University of Durham. As well as editing numerous works on Romantic period literature, he is the author of *The Human Mind's Imaginings: Conflict and Achievement in Shelley's Poetry* (1989), *Percy Bysshe Shelley: A Literary Life* (1989), *Auden, MacNeice, Spender: The Thirties Poetry* (with Gareth Reeves) (1992) and *Romanticism and the Self-Conscious Poem* (1997). A founder and for many years co-editor of *Poetry Durham*, he regularly reviews contemporary poetry for the *London Magazine* and *The Times Literary Supplement*. His book of poems, *The Stripped Bed*, was published in 1990.

Marjorie Perloff is Sadie Dernham Patek Professor of Humanities at Stanford University and the author of ten books. The two most recent are *Wittgenstein's Ladder: Poetic Language and the Strangeness of the Ordinary* (1996) and *Poetry On and Off the Page: Essays for Emergent Occasions* (1998).

Ralph Pite lectures in the Department of English at the University of Liverpool. He has published *The Circle of our Vision: Dante's Presence in English Romantic Poetry* (1994) and has edited Henry Carey's 1814 translation of *The Divine Comedy* for Everyman (1994). He is currently working on a study of regionalism in the nineteenth- and twentieth-century novel.

Peter Robinson (co-editor) is Visiting Professor of English Literature at Tohoku University, Sendai, Japan. His four books of poetry are *Overdrawn Account* (1980), *This Other Life* (1988), which won the Cheltenham Prize, *Entertaining Fates* (1992) and *Lost and Found* (1997). He has edited the poems of Adrian Stokes, a collection of essays on Geoffrey Hill, and an anthology, *Liverpool Accents: Seven Poets and a City* (1996). His translations include *Selected Poems of Vittorio Sereni* (1990). A volume of critical writings, *In the Circumstances: About Poems and Poets*, was published by Oxford University Press in 1992. He co-edited with Robert Sheppard *News for the Ear: A Homage to Roy Fisher*, published by Stride in 2000 to mark the poet's seventieth birthday.

Ian Sansom is writing a book about W.H. Auden and is a regular contributor to the *London Review of Books*, *Poetry Review* and the *Guardian*.

Robert Sheppard is Senior Lecturer in English and Writing Studies at Edge Hill University College, Lancashire. He has published many articles and reviews on contemporary British poetry and poetics, which have appeared in journals such as *PN Review*, *New Statesman* and *The Times Literary Supplement*. A selection of these pieces is published as *Far Language: Poetics and Linguistically Innovative Poetry 1978–1997* by Stride Publications. He also co-edited the anthology *Floating Capital: New Poets from London* (1991). His own poetry, from the long project *Twentieth Century Blues*, is published in *The Flashlight Sonata* (1993) and *Empty Diaries* (1998), both from Stride.

Derek Slade is Head of A Levels at Bexley College.

Clair Wills is a Reader in English at Queen Mary and Westfield College, University of London. She is the author of essays on the innovative poetries of Fanny Howe, Denise Riley and Lyn Hejinian, of *Improprieties: Politics and Sexuality in Northern Irish Poetry* (1993) and *Reading Paul Muldoon* (1998). She has edited the Contemporary Writing section of the forthcoming *Field Day Anthology of Irish Writing*, vol. IV.

Acknowledgements

Grateful acknowledgement is made to Roy Fisher for permission to use quotations from his works, and for the use of quotations in *The Dow Low Drop: New and Selected Poems* (1996) to Neil Astley at Bloodaxe Books. The editors would like to thank Robin Bloxsidge of Liverpool University Press for his support and understanding at all stages of the work, and the individual contributors to our volume for their sustained work and patience. We are grateful to Rachel Coldicutt, who helped us eliminate errors and inconsistencies in the completed typescript. Roy Fisher did not read any of these essays before their publication and was not involved in any editorial decisions. He was, however, generous in providing information when requested. Our work has been made more enjoyable by the poet's equanimity, and we should like to thank him.

JOHN KERRIGAN
PETER ROBINSON

Abbreviations

BR	*Birmingham River* (Oxford: Oxford University Press, 1994)
CP68	*Collected Poems 1968: The Ghost of a Paper Bag* (London: Fulcrum Press, 1969)
Cut (1971)	*The Cut Pages* (London: Fulcrum Press, 1971)
Cut (1986)	*The Cut Pages* (London: Oasis Books/Shearsman Books, 1986)
DLD	*The Dow Low Drop: New and Selected Poems* (Newcastle upon Tyne: Bloodaxe Books, 1996)
F	*A Furnace* (Oxford: Oxford University Press, 1986)
JS	*The Thing about Joe Sullivan: Poems 1971–1977* (Manchester: Carcanet New Press, 1978)
M	*Matrix* (London: Fulcrum Press, 1971)
P55–80	*Poems 1955–1980* (Oxford: Oxford University Press, 1980)
P55–87	*Poems 1955–1987* (Oxford: Oxford University Press, 1988)

Introduction

PETER ROBINSON

I

Roy Fisher's 'The Making of the Book' begins with this quoted advice: 'Let the Blurb be strong, / modest, and true.' The reason given for this policy is firmly defensive: 'Build it to take a belting; / they'll pick on that.'[1] It has become the practice now to place alongside the blurb on poetry books some plea-bargaining quotations from earlier reviews, and, in Fisher's case, lines exerpted from a piece by John Ash seem the poet's and his publishers' choice, for they appear on the back of his three most recent gatherings of poems: 'In a better world, he would be as widely known and highly praised as Seamus Heaney and Ted Hughes...'[2] This is a sentence that could, as Fisher's poem has it, 'take a belting', and from a number of angles. The first might be that while the late Poet Laureate is undoubtedly more widely known than Fisher, his work is not as consistently praised, though it is true that Hughes's status means that he has attracted more than the advocacy or silence reserved for the less prominent. Secondly, though the Nobel prize winner is both more highly praised and more widely known, Fisher could not be described as having anything like an over-pitched reputation that stands in need of considered correction, a situation that may have arisen for Heaney's work, and one not within the poet's control. Finally, it is by no means clear where or what such a 'better world' might be, and, while the aim of the critical studies gathered here is to make Fisher's work more widely known in this world, among the many virtues of his poems engaged in transforming the

1

perception and understanding of life is their having little time for wholly imaginary, alternative places.

Our title, *The Thing about Roy Fisher*, alludes to one of the poet's more unusual works. As Derek Slade's invaluable chronology (published here for the first time) tells us, 'The Thing about Joe Sullivan' was written over three days at the end of July 1965. Despite its eventual appearance as the title poem of a 1978 collection, this 62-line homage remained unpublished for over six years. Fisher may have been prompted to let it see the light of day in September 1971 by the death of its subject, the jazz pianist Joe Sullivan (1906–1971). This enthusiast's poem borrows some of its style from the fulsome encomia published by cognoscenti on the sleeve notes to jazz records. Sullivan is picked out for being 'in his time almost the only / one of them to ignore / the chance of easing down, / walking it leisurely, / he'll strut'. The poet has explained that he did not publish it in the 1960s, when there were occasions, because of the work's eccentricity among his writings at that time—an eccentricity manifested, perhaps, in its crescendoing clauses of amateur music criticism. Praise for Sullivan's playing, however, soon turns into an aesthetics by analogy, when Fisher points to the pianist's 'running among stock forms / that could play themselves / and moving there with such / quickness of intellect / that shapes flaw and fuse'. What Sullivan uses as impetus for his style embeds these transformative notions in a common life. Thus, the 'thing' that 'drives him' is described as 'his mood: / a feeling violent and ordinary'. That last word is repeated eight lines later at the poem's close, where Sullivan's 'invention, wakefulness' are described as 'the rapid and perverse / tracks that ordinary feelings / make when they get driven / hard enough against time' (*P55–87*, pp. 52–54). This, in short, is the thing about Roy Fisher too: his work is wakefully inventive, has a quickness of intellect and remains vitalized with ordinary feeling and mood.

Fisher has been writing now for nigh on half a century, and has plainly managed to keep doing 'his thing'. Yet, as the essays brought together here underline, his inspiration has required him to attempt many and various things. Indeed, the variousness of Fisher's work is evident in his first pamphlet publication, *City* (1961). This text—a collage of poems, a prose-poem, and paragraphs of prose—assembles separate pieces of work composed at intervals between January 1957 and February 1961. While some of the prose passages are close to social documentary, others are hallucinatory and surreal. The poems can be autobiographical narratives ('The Entertainment of War'), brief imagistic lyrics ('North Area' and 'By the Pond'), or they can be frankly lyrical songs with metre and rhyme ('A Lullaby . . . for the Unwilling Hero', 'The Hill Behind the Town', and 'The Wind at Night'). Most heterodox of all is 'Starting to Make a Tree', a work with an adapted prose lineation but a poetic presentation and ordering of perceptions which combines details from what look like an ordinary communal urban life with others that make the tree and the business of making it resemble the assemblage of a pop art junk-sculpture by Robert Rauschenberg.

The heterogeneous character of *City*, still probably Fisher's best-known work, set its author to one side of the writers who gain recognition for the achievement of a single characteristic style, or for finding their own voice. While the poet has developed far beyond the uneasily exploratory results of his début, its variety and lack of conviction about there being any one best way to proceed have continued to make themselves felt through subsequent publications. His formal procedures have been astonishingly varied and strikingly successful: he has written a neo-cubist, prose-poem-like 'novel' (*The Ship's Orchestra*), a set of long-lined poems with various prose lineations (*Ten Interiors with Various Figures*), sequences of short-lined, free verse lyrics such as 'Matrix' or 'Handsworth Liberties', and works that vary in size from the haiku-like third part of 'Three Ceremonial Poems' to the book-length short epic *A Furnace*. Fisher's syntax can be acutely disjunctive and fragmentary as in 'The Cut Pages', or as continuously logical and directly communicative as in 'The Lesson in Composition' or his burlesques about the literary world such as 'The Making of the Book' or 'Paraphrases'. He can use utterly traditional range-left lineation for poems, and, equally, set indentations for stanzaic patterns and refrains, or the expressively adjusted various indentations introduced by the old masters of modernism. While there are readers who find themselves at home with the vast majority of Fisher's work, it is perhaps inevitable that an oeuvre of this kind will have been disconcerting in different ways to readers who, under the rubric 'poetry', expect a certain kind of thing and bristle or turn off when something else comes along appearing to fly that particular flag. Just why Fisher's work has needed and taken this variety of forms is a complex question involving his individual history, the cultural history of English provincial and metropolitan culture and the history of twentieth-century art. The essays gathered here help in their different ways to fill out the details of this complex question and to suggest various kinds of answer to it.

The sceptical might remark that Fisher has hardly put himself and his work about in such a way as to gain a large audience and high praise. However, a poet's access to publication is not something that allows for high-percentage control. Nor indeed is the production of poetic texts that deserve to be published. Fisher was neither a child prodigy nor equipped by birth or education even to want a metropolitan media career. Although, like many a poet, he began publishing poetry while at university, it was not until he was in his thirties that his work achieved even pamphlet publication, and not until the second half of his third decade that he found himself with a publisher who issued substantial, well-made volumes that caught the attention of reviewers in visible places. This was Stuart and Deirdre Montgomery's Fulcrum Press, which published four of his books before winding up its operations in the early 1970s. Fulcrum was also instrumental in bringing to attention the work of the neglected Northumbrian modernist Basil Bunting, and a flurry of neo-experimental writers from Britain and America in his wake. Fisher emerged blinking into the light of some slight media attention as one of this loosely knit group.

When the Montgomerys' press withdrew, that might have seemed to be that: Fisher found himself still being invited to publish in fugitive magazines, limited editions and ephemeral pamphlets. He has never shown much relish for the usual habit of sending out batches of poems to literary newspapers and journals in the hope that one or two will catch the eye of the poetry editor. The scattered followers of Fisher's work—and he had found quite a few through his

Fulcrum publications—would have to wait until 1978 for the chance to appreciate in one available place what he had been doing for much of that decade. *The Thing about Joe Sullivan*, published by Carcanet Press, was a Poetry Book Society Choice, a fact which may have helped him secure a contract to collect up his work for the Oxford University Press volume *Poems 1955–1980*. However, if to some this event might have signalled the poet's absorption into a supposed mainstream canon, to others it signalled his exit from the avant-garde. Fisher's audience, such as it was, seemed to be factionalizing along the entrenched dualistic lines of the British poetry scene's affiliation politics—a crude mapping that survives by the trade-mark patenting or prejudicial labelling of certain style-features like the use of ampersands, rhyme, punctuation, or page layout, while turning a blind eye to the innumerable exceptions which do not begin to prove this much-applied rule. The fact that Fisher's most discontinuous text, 'The Cut Pages', did not appear in the Oxford edition could only suggest to some, incorrectly as it turned out, that the poet's work had been carefully trimmed along consumerist lines.

Fisher's subsequent publishing hardly suggests any strategy at all. Six years would go by before the poet followed up his Oxford volume, and he did so with a book that worried its prospective publishers enough to have them ask for an explanatory preface. This was the long poem *A Furnace*, for some readers undoubtedly Fisher's masterpiece, yet, for others who had savoured his oblique and discontinuous styles, curiously discursive and straight-talking. Though the long poem was a Poetry Book Society Recommendation, Fisher's associations with Oxford seem to have begun to unravel. While his writing over more than forty years has meant that the poet's entire collected poems would make a substantial volume, he has experienced periods of creative silence, and never been prolific. In the early 1980s, his output of shorter poems was such that, rather than a new collection, his recent texts appeared in a thirty-page section added near the end when *Poems 1955–1980* was reissued in paperback as *Poems 1955–1987*, ensuring that the majority of his work remained in print for some more years. Though Fisher published *Birmingham River* with the same firm in 1994, when Oxford allowed the collected

volume to go out of print he was able to respond to an offer from
Bloodaxe Books to publish a selection of unavailable texts.
The Dow Low Drop: New and Selected Poems came out in 1996, with a
jacket blurb that, if nothing else, drew attention to the scattered and
discontinuous nature of the poet's actual and possible readership:
'The reputation he gained in the 60s and 70s as a difficult poet is
wrong: this book shows that he is one of the funniest, most open and
liberating writers of his generation'. This is a fine example of letting
'the Blurb be strong', and it too might invite a 'belting'. Were those
readers of Fisher's work as it emerged in small press editions and
magazines wrong in thinking that it was of value to them exactly
because it challenged and troubled them, wrong to go back and reread it because it provided them with difficult insights and ways of
experiencing life unavailable elsewhere? While a long-time reader of
Fisher's work could agree that it can be amusing and is often covertly
witty, the idea that this aspect of his writings might be pushed at the
expense of others seemed partial. Nevertheless, its attempt to
package Fisher for a less specialist market points to one more reason
why, to cite another jacket quotation, his poetry and prose 'is something altogether rare in contemporary British poetry'.[3] With its many
varieties of style and tone, Fisher's work has seemed so incon-
veniently hard to place.

II

Probably conceived 'during those days in late 1929 when Wall Street
was falling in ruins',[4] Roy Fisher was born on 11 June 1930 in
Handsworth, Birmingham. He lived at 74 Kentish Road, the house
in which he was born, until the age of 23, a period that included the
Blitz and his local streets falling in ruins. He was born into a re-
spectable but straitened upper-working-class family, his father being
a craftsman jeweller. He won a scholarship to the local grammar
school, later securing a place at Birmingham University where he
read English and first published poems in the student magazine. To
earn a living and support a family, Fisher went into teaching, first at a

grammar school in Newton Abbot, Devon, in the 1950s; he then returned to Birmingham and a job in a college of education. From 1963 to 1971 he was principal lecturer and head of the department of English and Drama at Bordesley College of Education in Birmingham, when he became a member of the department of American Studies at Keele University. Through these three decades he pursued a second career as a semi-professional jazz musician, from time to time producing and publishing the works in poetry and prose that, despite various resistances, have constituted his lifelong vocation. In 1982 Fisher took early retirement and has since survived as a freelance. His early retirement also allowed him to settle in the Peak District, an area to the north of Birmingham which has come to hold for him equal poetic fascination.

These biographical details fixing him in or around the English industrial midlands are occasionally offered by the poet himself as explaining why his work is centred so intensively on those provincial urban and, more recently, rural landscapes. Yet such a biography is hardly unique among people from Fisher's social and generational origins, most of whom have not gone on to become poets, and they cannot thus explain the peculiarly compulsive grip that minutely specific locations have had on his imagination. Nor could those facts serve to predict the kinds of writing that this landlocked local product would go on to produce. Fisher's work is occasionally described as 'paradoxical',[5] a word gesturing towards the fact that while his apparent subjects tend to come from a fairly strictly bounded territory, his styles and influences are fetched from much further afield. For example, a chance contact through small-magazine publication with the poet Gael Turnbull would introduce him, in 1956, to many of the then barely known poets of second- and third-generation American modernism. Perhaps the most overwhelming of these international influences came from jazz. Fisher has described how hearing Meade Lux Lewis's 1936 piano solo 'Honky Tonk Train Blues' changed the direction of his life, and how two books, Wilder Hobson's *American Jazz Music* and Hugues Panassié's *Le Jazz hot*, were 'the first developed writings about any of the arts I ever encountered'.[6] He taught himself to play jazz piano, well enough to perform in pick-up bands backing American stars on tour. However, while Philip Larkin's interest in early New Orleans jazz seems to provide the exception to his dislike of the foreign in culture and life, Fisher's is continuous with his well-informed awareness of developments in all the arts. So, for example, *The Ship's Orchestra* was set off by staring at Picasso's *Three Musicians*, and the poet has commented that 'The Return' section of *A Furnace* was inspired by, among other things, the music of Shostakovich. Fisher has also collaborated on projects with a number of artists including Derek Greaves, Ronald King, Tom Phillips and Ian Tyson.

Indeed, as his work gained a certain prominence in the mid-1960s, it was just such supposedly far-fetched modernist allegiances that were taken up to position him. The poet has described how in a letter to Edward Lucie-Smith, a ringmaster in the poetry circus of that decade, he described himself as a *'1905 Russian Modernist'*, a remark that Lucie-Smith repeated on Radio 4, and later elsewhere, adding that it was 'a wry summary which has a good deal of truth in it'. Fisher clearly liked this mysterious formula enough to allow its quotation on the inside dustjacket flap of *Collected Poems 1968*, where it did appear to have come straight from the horse's mouth. What the poet had in mind, it seems, is that in 1905 such Russian modernism as there was had a faintly provincial air, shaken up by distant war and abrupt social change, but a little behind the times, not the state-of-the-art modernism in, say, the Paris or Munich of that year.[7]

When Donald Davie took up this remark in his study of the poet, he revised it to suggest that Fisher has 'set himself to school to the Russian modernists of the '20s',[8] an idea that Lucie-Smith himself then used in his biographical outline of the poet for the 1975 edition of the *Contemporary Poets* reference volumes.[9] Thus Davie was able to ignore any imagined affinities Fisher's work might show with Bely and Blok in favour of Mandelstam or Pasternak. He could also concentrate his sense of Fisher's experimentalism on the Russian formalist 'making strange' techniques identified by Shklovsky. While Fisher was aware of and has acknowledged an interest in such strategies, this sense of him as primarily a defamiliarizing formalist has become a received idea of the critical literature, with distortions and mischaracterizations inevitably following. That Fisher was so labelled has also contributed to the definition of his work as 'paradoxical', for while being located almost exclusively in the English Midlands, it seemed to be written by an imaginative cosmopolitan, yet one who had been constrained to a stay-at-home existence far more thorough than even that enemy of foreign travel, Larkin. Yet this paradox evaporates outside the straitening conceptual boxes of centre and periphery, home and abroad, provincial and metropolitan, rooted or cosmopolitan, further dualisms which evaluatively constrain cultural understanding and debate.

III

Writing in 1975, Fisher was able to paraphrase an imaginary, or perhaps real, letter from a desperate student who admitted to having 'articles by Davie, D., / and Mottram, E., / but not your Books...' (*P59–87*, p. 130). Though by no means the only writing on the poet in existence at that time, Davie's discussion of Fisher's work in *Thomas Hardy and British Poetry*, and Mottram's essay in *Stand*, were the only substantial studies more or less readily available. They helped to perpetrate, and, being taken up, perpetuate, the image of an oeuvre split in two. For Davie, advancing his polemic about a social democratic English poetry of consciously reduced scope, the pre-eminently important text was *City*, and more precisely its prose sections. While having time for such early pieces as 'Toyland', 'The Entertainment of War' and 'For Realism', works in which a recognizable scene or series of events is described in a relatively straightforward language, Davie drew the line at 'Three Ceremonial Poems' in which he insisted that the substance did not merit the stylistic elaboration. Mottram, on the other hand, presented Fisher as the English exponent of an international modernism whose lineaments he gestured at by listing an extensive number of writers and artists, including Tony Hancock, whom the poet resembled. Whereas Davie appeared to be trimming and recuperating Fisher for a notional mainstream, Mottram was launching him as nothing if not a well-read, neglected experimentalist.

Two decades later, though the number of available critical studies has increased, the binarism is still in place. Characterizing Fisher's position, Sean O'Brien describes the poet as: 'the modernist (and postmodernist) the non-modernists enjoy and to some extent understand; the acceptable face of what is still seen, by detractors and some supporters alike, as *avant-gardisme*.'[10] Readers inclined towards the 'modernist' version of Fisher could begin by consulting Derek Slade's exhaustive bibliography of primary and secondary sources, where they will find the publication details of John Matthias's wide-ranging 'The Poetry of Roy Fisher', perhaps the best single introduction to the poet's work to date, or, for its theoretical ramifications, Andrew Crozier's authoritative 'Signs of Identity: Roy Fisher's *A Furnace*'. Postmodernism is broached in the writings of John Ash, and extended in Ian Gregson's 'Music of the Generous Eye', while the non-modernist account is perhaps best represented by O'Brien's own lucid and commendatory study, 'A Polytheism with No Gods', in *The Deregulated Muse*. Yet into this various, but still plainly dualistic picture, the 1996 'Roy Fisher Reviews Roy Fisher' in which the poet characterizes himself as 'a Romantic' fails to fit this stubbornly ephemeral divide—as, differently, does Jeremy Hooker's indication, in 'Magician of the Common Place', that Fisher's affinities with the novelist John Cowper Powys extend beyond the dedication to him and brief quotations from his writings in *A Furnace*.

In a sense, Fisher's work does not occupy a position in contemporary poetry, for 'occupying a position' supposes some collaboration between the poet constructing and maintaining one, and the critics describing the work in a collaborative fashion. Like the Bartleby in Melville's story, Fisher, it appears, would rather not. Though he has spoken frequently and at length about his work in interviews, Fisher has sought, by maximizing room for manoeuvre in its inception and reception, to avoid the straitjacketing of either aesthetic self-assertion or cultural positioning or both. This has allowed the work to find its own allegiances among those who want to explore it, without bullying them about how it should be approached or responded to—allegiances that may, as in Fisher's case,

Introduction

11

occur at quite different locations in the spaces allotted to poetry in a culture at any given moment. The poet was quick to respond implicitly to Davie's use of his work as representative of a social democratic poetry with reduced ambitions, objecting to the way 'people take a little bit of poetry, a little bit of literature, and if there's a moral in it, however crude, it will be taken, it will be coarsened still further'.[11] Yet if some of his work has been the victim of such usings, it has also been seen by others as inviting that approach. In a more recent interview Fisher remarks: 'There are writers to whom I am "Le Douanier" Rousseau among the Cubists: I'm the simple-minded guy who writes simple moral pieces.' When asked about being 'dogged by the "difficult" label', he replied that his comic poems were not hard to get; but then again, 'If I were to read a burlesque about the Arts Council in a school it wouldn't connect. A joke only goes as far as its constituency. In so far as it finds its constituency, it is absolute. It either works or it doesn't.'[12]

Fisher's poetry has not only found a variety of constituencies, it has demonstrated how a plurality of approaches, a freedom from over-determined aesthetic and thematic constraints, can generate a flexibly responsive oeuvre open to creative use by different sorts of readers with various artistic needs. This oeuvre has been produced during decades in which the issue of where a poet stands, what position he or she takes up, been intensified by a caricatural account of poetic literary history as a sequence of palace intrigues between generations for the claims of the next important writer, style, grouping or movement. It is supposed that the most successful of these takeovers was that performed in the mid-1950s by poets associated with the Movement, supplanting the Apocalyptics, in their turn plotted against but not overthrown—so the story goes—by neo-experimentalists in the 1960s, who were kept in the wilderness by the Martians and new narrative poets of the late 1970s and early 1980s, followed by the New Generation poets, and the post-New Generation, and so on and so forth.

Such a sense of cultural history as a series of 'next best things' has, equally polemically, been described by the philosopher and art critic Arthur C. Danto as coming to an end at more or less the moment when Fisher began to emerge into the relative visibility of small-press print. Danto describes how young artists arriving in New York in the mid-1960s found an environment of competitive puritanical exclusivities: certain ways of producing art were proscribed. This atmosphere has survived in the talk and behaviour of many poetry circles. But alongside it, poets themselves have practised, like their contemporaries in the visual arts, what Danto believes is a form of '*deep* Pluralism'.[13] The appearance of Julian Schnabel and the neo-expressionists allowed some to believe and claim at the beginning of the 1980s that art history was back on track, the next best thing had arrived. A similar function was performed by the Martians and their allies in English poetry, as emblematized by the introduction to Motion and Morrison's anthology *The Penguin Book of Contemporary British Poetry* (1982), a work in which Roy Fisher's name does not appear. Yet few believed at the time, and very few now, that this was indeed the grand new historical direction.

'The Poplars', an early poem, has a speaker who thinks he is 'afraid of becoming / A cemetery of performance' (*P55–87*, p. 24). Fisher's reluctance to be placed, in or on the ground, is a form of staying creatively alive. Somewhat removed from the poetic and literary 'wars of feeling' (23) outlined above, he has written with an eye to responding and staying aesthetically alert to what is 'new, never to be defined',[14] as his recent 'Last Poems' puts it. Such purposes are not taken much account of in the journalistic account of 'new voices' and the like. Fisher has simultaneously maintained a certain distance from the various gangs it is said with irony to be necessary to belong to in 'The Making of the Book', and from the 'civilization: or just / the dirtiest brawl you ever saw' (*P55–87*, p. 106) in 'Sets', by, for instance, not confecting a signature style. This is by no means to say that Fisher's work has no styles, and no characteristic traits, but that these retrospectively identifiable qualities arise from specific tasks and developed processes of writing in plural 'Englishes' (*P55–87*, p. 143)—a word he put into a mid-1970s poem, 'Style', some years before multiculturalism had emerged on the literary and wider stage.

The essays that follow are inevitably touched by the embattled dualisms sketched above. Some, such as Marjorie Perloff's and

Robert Sheppard's, address Fisher's contributions to the modes of avant-garde writing over the last four decades. Simon Jarvis brings to his searching study of Fisher's writing block a conceptual scheme with its own perspectives on the two-party system of contemporary poetry. John Lucas qualifies the poet's commitment to experiment by describing his forms as improvisational—linking his literary work to his favoured styles of jazz piano. In a similar fashion, Ian Sansom examines Fisher's frequently surrealist contributions to the popular vein of comic writing in contemporary verse, and Michael O'Neill provides a close reading of poems which is at times sceptical about the self-reflexivity of Fisher's techniques. Others, such as James Keery, have undertaken careful research which significantly revises the assumption that the 1950s was the story of the Movement or that the Apocalyptics of the 1940s simply expired without offspring once their decade was done. Indeed, Slade's bibliography reveals how much of a non-aligned independent in his publishing Fisher has been. Similar revisions of received ideas are conducted by Perloff in her questioning of the poet's supposed relations to William Carlos Williams and the Black Mountain College poets, or by John Kerrigan in his study of Fisher and the poetry of place, an essay where the poet's own doubts concerning 'The "place" tag'[15] are analysed and pursued into his poems about the perceptual and epistemological complexities of location as such.

The co-authored essay by Bell and Lland describes Fisher's work as actively engaged in cross-border and cross-party forays, suggesting by the poet's freedom of movement a likely blurring to disappearance of the divides through which he passes. The essays focussing on *A Furnace* by Ralph Pite and Clair Wills find the short epic engaged in an unpredictable series of interventions related to the different materializations of which life forces are capable, and the power of the dead to make themselves manifest in and around us—both incidentally revealing how that work's polemic against binary divisiveness exfoliates into a poem whose bearings and directions serve to set it free from partisan pigeon-holing. The usual terms of contemporary poetry's map are, from either side, resolutely formalistic. In my closing essay I concentrate on Fisher's lifelong engagement with the time-honoured themes of mortality and literary finality, and the frequently explicit ethics that his formally various treatments of them display.

Roy Fisher's work is alive with an awareness that the one position worth occupying in contemporary poetry is in the hearts and minds of present and future readers. What all the essays in *The Thing about Roy Fisher* share is a conviction that his writings have been rather a well-kept secret for too long. In their different ways, the critical approaches brought together here contribute to an understanding of why these poems have found enthusiastic readers, why they deserve to find many more, and why we believe they will continue to find such readers—not necessarily in a better world, but in the only one that, for better or worse, we find ourselves inhabiting.

NOTES

1. *Poems 1955–1987* (Oxford: Oxford University Press, 1988), p. 69. Subsequent references in text.

2. This quotation, in ever shorter excerpt, appears on the covers of *Poems 1955–1987*, *Birmingham River* (Oxford: Oxford University Press, 1994) and *The Dow Low Drop: New and Selected Poems* (Newcastle upon Tyne: Bloodaxe Books, 1996).

3. David Sexton, 'Tact and Tenderness', *Sunday Times*, 6 July 1986, p. 46. This quotation appears on the front of *Poems 1955–1987* and the back of *Birmingham River*.

4. 'Roy Fisher 1930– ', *Contemporary Authors (Autobiography Series)*, vol. 10 (Detroit, New York, Fort Lauderdale, London: Gale Research Inc., 1989), p. 79.

5. Sean O'Brien, *The Deregulated Muse: Essays on Contemporary British and Irish Poetry* (Newcastle upon Tyne: Bloodaxe Books, 1998), p. 112.

6. 'Roy Fisher 1930– ', pp. 91–92.

7. The original remark from the radio broadcast is cited on the inside front flap of the dustjacket to *Collected Poems 1968* (London: Fulcrum Press, 1968). It is elaborated in Lucie-Smith's headnote to a selection of Fisher's work in *British Poetry since 1945* (Harmondsworth: Penguin Books, 1971), p. 236. Fisher 'goes back beyond the modernism of America to the sources in Europe: he has at times been described as "a Cubist poet" and "a 1905 Russian Modernist". These descriptions are accurate, in so far as they demonstrate an interest in simultaneity, and an affinity with certain kinds of Symbolist poetry.' This explanation of what he intended by a '*1905 Russian Modernist*' is given in a letter of Roy Fisher's to John Kerrigan, 26 November 1997.

8. Donald Davie, 'Roy Fisher: An Appreciation', *Thomas Hardy and British Poetry* (London: Routledge & Kegan Paul, 1973), p. 167.

9. Edward Lucie-Smith states that Fisher 'once aptly described himself as "a 1920s Russian modernist"'. Entry on Roy Fisher, *Contemporary Poets*, ed. J. Vinson and D. L. Kirkpatrick (London: St James Press, 1975), p. 496.

10. *The Deregulated Muse*, p. 112. O'Brien plays up antipathy between the contemporary poetry scene's opposed camps when, in the headnote to Fisher's selection for an anthology, he states that 'what is less often remarked is that he is a rare *avant-gardiste*: one who can write as well as theorize'. *The Firebox: Poetry in Britain and Ireland after 1945* (London: Picador, 1998), p. 129.

11. Jed Rasula and Mike Erwin, 'An Interview with Roy Fisher', in Roy Fisher, *Nineteen Poems and an Interview* (1975; Pensnett, Staffs: Grosseteste, 1977), p. 16.

12. Roy Fisher Interviewed by Ra Page, 'People who Can't Float', *Prop*, 2 (Bolton, Lancs., 1997), p. 30 (twice).

13. Arthur C. Danto, 'Learning to Live with Pluralism', *Beyond the Brillo Box: The Visual Arts in Post-Historical Perspective* (New York: Farrar, Straus and Giroux, 1992), p. 229.

14. *CCCP 8*, Programme and Anthology of the Eighth Cambridge Conference of Contemporary Poetry, 24–26 April 1998.

15. Robert Sheppard, *Turning the Prism: An Interview with Roy Fisher* (London: Toads Damp Press, 1986), p. 22.

1

Roy Fisher on Location

JOHN KERRIGAN

Documentaries about writers rarely make good cinema. In Tom Pickard's inventive *Birmingham's What I Think With* (1991), however, the usual traps are avoided. The star of the show is Roy Fisher, improvising jazz piano and talking his verse to the cameras, but also on location, introducing viewers to the packed housing, dusty walkways, furnaces, wrecked factories, noisy roads, silent canals and dead brick walls of his native city. Fisher has always been a keen collaborator with visual artists, and the poetry he wrote for this film is a natural successor to texts produced for Tom Phillips and others. Much less experimental than, say, the Fisher / Ian Tyson *Cultures* (1975)—which consists of disjoined phrases radially arranged on paper discs—'Six Texts for a Film'[1] can be interpreted as being in retreat from the neo-modernism that made Fisher's reputation in the 1960s and 1970s, but it also shows us a writer always too versatile to rest with one style finding a documentary idiom.

It is an idiom that makes tractable some long-standing concerns, several of them announced in the lines that give the film its title. 'Birmingham's what I think with', Fisher tells the cameras: 'It's not made for that sort of job, / but it's what they gave me.'[2] This catches with such downbeat elegance the poet's grudge against the authorities who limited his youthful world-view that it secures what it implies about place becoming cognitively effective. Still more striking, because so humdrum, is the instrumental relationship it asserts with Birmingham. A surprising range of recent poetry, from the occult urbanism of Iain Sinclair to Seamus Heaney's *Seeing Things*, has sought

16

to re-enchant home ground, but Fisher happily adopts the utilitarian briskness of a Brummie, looking for a tool to do a job and using place because it comes to hand. 'As a means of thinking', he says of his city,

> it's a Brummagem
> screwdriver. What that is,
> is a medium-weight claw hammer
> or something of the sort, employed
> to drive a tapered woodscrew home
> as if it were a nail.
>
>   It's done
> for lack of a nail, a screwdriver, a drill,
> a bradawl, or the will to go looking.[3]

Imagine R. S. Thomas saying that he lives in Aberdaron for want of somewhere better, or Tom Leonard confessing that he writes about Glasgow because he lacks the will to travel. Fisher, by contrast, admits that he remained in Birmingham for decades for the reason that most people live where they do: because it's there.

Does it have to be there? As historical geographers point out, the site of Birmingham has few natural advantages, and it was for centuries a one-street town. Though settled early by Celts and Saxons, the 'dwelling of Beorma's people' had to wait until the Industrial Revolution before it began to grow. Birmingham is a quintessentially modern city in that it developed once the power of technology could overcome the accidents of place. This 'city of a thousand trades', full of forges, nailshops, jewellers, car plants and, latterly, electronics factories, has accumulated piecemeal, in minor spasms and often disastrous large-scale redevelopment. Something of its workshop ethos has plainly rubbed off on Fisher, who delights in made and dismantled things and composes with an eye to what language immediately and often minimally needs to perform a task. But there is a larger congruence: by seeking to register the contingency of what one geographer calls 'a city of process and dynamic change',[4] Fisher has developed a writing-field which is often exploratory and metamorphic, even when the topics he addresses are not the Birmingham that he thinks with. The poetry which results can seem difficult—not least when compared to Fisher's lively forays into light verse—but it could be enjoyed by a wider readership than it currently reaches because it is so often mobilized by the sights and rhythms of a city which is exceptional only by virtue of being so extensively representative of post-war urbanization.

It is a sign of the importance of Birmingham to Fisher that his most ambitious poems have been precipitated by dislocations in its fabric (redevelopment is almost his muse) or by changes to where he lives. His first major sequence, *City* (1961), which was stimulated by—and begins by describing—demolition, was written after a period of teaching in Devon: 'I found that returning to Birmingham after an absence had given me an artist's distance from it.'[5] By moving to Staffordshire in 1971, and then in the 1980s to Derbyshire, Fisher enablingly detached himself from a conurbation which was, in any case, shedding much of its thereness as its heavy industries were dismantled. In 'Handsworth Liberties' (1978), his home district is a scene of memory and musical evocation, while in 'Wonders of Obligation' (1979) the poet becomes newly explicit about the injustices endured by 'the poor of Birmingham / the people of Birmingham,/ the working people of Birmingham'[6]—an iteration which is the more potent because Fisher for the first time feels able to *name* his city in verse. His longest poem, *A Furnace* (1986), makes a virtue of the movements now necessary for contact with Birmingham by structuring itself on a double spiral, coiled but centreless: venturing into and out of its urban material, it intercuts the historical geography of Birmingham with that of Staffordshire and Derbyshire, factoring Fisher's past and present into the relationship between a megalopolis and its environs.

With so much going on, it is tempting for the poet to be reductive in *A Furnace*, to 'evolve' (as Fisher puts it in 'Six Texts')

> Book City, just
> as it evolved itself: rock, water,
> forest, settlers, trade. Then
> property, sewage, architects, poets.

But *A Furnace* is Fisher's greatest achievement partly because it keeps in touch with the question which is set against 'Book City':

> Interesting. But what is it
> when you're first set loose in it, with only
> your nostrils, fingertips, ears, eyes
> to teach you appetite and danger?[7]

It is crucial to understand what is being asked. Though Fisher's urban texts take their bearings from high modernism, rather than from the postmodernist 'city of signs' elaborated by such poets as Ciaran Carson,[8] he does not imagine that place can be experienced apart from the semiotic[9] and he is alert to what nostrils, fingertips, ears and eyes tell him, not as neutral receptors but as filters on what we can know, as organs which construct space.

This is a major reason why his writing became technically extreme during the 1970s: he was setting location in perceptual and psychological spheres, exploring as close-in as possible how sensory and cognitive processes interact with the stuff of culture—music, the visual arts, language—to constitute spatial experience, and trying to think beyond three dimensions. Put like that the enterprise sounds abstruse, but the writing is frequently appetitive and involvingly injured. By that I mean that it confirms what biography might lead one to expect: Fisher ranges questioningly around perceptual and psychological limits not least because he has been afflicted by spatial phobias, eyesight problems, and a disease of the inner ear which deranged his sense of balance.[10] I am not about to present Fisher as a pathological poet. What interests me is how his somatic and cognitive preoccupations lead this locationally obsessed writer to insist that 'The "place" tag is not very meaningful to me.'[11]

Fisher's early association with magazines and presses hospitable to American modernism has led many to assume that his books about Birmingham have behind them William Carlos Williams's *Paterson*, a patchwork epic about his home town in New Jersey (1946–58), and Charles Olson's *Maximus Poems* (1960–75), centred on Gloucester, Massachussetts. Those works did encourage 'alternative' British poetries, from early J. H. Prynne to the diffuse books on London, called *Place*, written during the 1970s by the poet's namesake, Allen Fisher. The inception of *City*, however, was rather different. The prose in the sequence, for instance, started life as 'diary observations, private, not intended for publication', and it got into print via the draft of 'a preposterously apocalyptic *bildungsroman*'.[12] The poet Michael Shayer assembled the first text of *City*, and it is clear from his *Persephone* (1961), a sequence about Worcester, that—unlike Fisher, at this date—he had read *Paterson*.[13] But the touches of socio-political zealotry and open-form composition which recall W.C. Williams in the Migrant Press *City* (1961) were swiftly removed; by 1963, Fisher had cut, tonally subdued and relineated the text to produce a consistently dense array of prose blocks and lyric measures.[14]

The contrast between the versions is particularly clear in the situation of the 'I'. As a layered contrivance, pieced out of Fisher's 'diffused zone' of selfhood and already processed as both a diary persona and the 'voyeuristic, alienated' *Bildungsroman* protagonist,[15] the subject could hardly be consistent. The 1961 'I', however, is almost randomly the sum of its functions. When the pronoun first appears in prose, it is to float a piece of loco-descriptive autobiography so low pressure (though typical of Fisher in dealing with an 'edge') that it was cut in revision: 'Where I was born, on the edge of the city a narrow road runs north from the main westward road into the small triangle of farmland that still separates the city from two of its neighbouring townships.'[16] At other points, however, the 'I' displays the antisocial excesses of the abandoned novel persona. Encountering on 'the pavement outside the Listowel' a woman whose neck 'was encased in a support of plastic or leather, ridged like the tubing of an [e]normous gas-mask', he speculates about what he would say to her, 'had we then possessed any common language', about his 'own disease, which is hereditary, complete in its domination of me, progressive, so slow as to be barely perceptible' (pp. 13–14). The phobic mix of the passage is as striking as its locational detail,[17] but the 'I's obtrusive aloofness frustrates the achievement, stylistically, of the deadpan morbidity of *The Ship's Orchestra* (written 1962–63).

The 'I' of the revised *City* is altogether more discreetly febrile. An added section introduces him thus:

> Brick-dust in sunlight. That is what I see now in the city, a dry epic flavour, whose air is human breath. A place of walls made straight with plumbline and trowel, to dessicate and crumble in the sun and smoke. Blistered paint on cisterns and girders, cracking to show the priming. Old men spit on the paving slabs, little boys urinate; and the sun dries it as it dries out patches of damp on plaster facings to leave misshapen stains. I look for things here that make old men and dead men seem young. Things which have escaped, the landscapes of many childhoods.
>
> Wharves, the oldest parts of factories, tarred gable ends rearing to take the sun over lower roofs. Soot, sunlight, brick-dust; and the breath that tastes of them.[18]

This atmospheric scene has been moralized by Donald Davie[19] and astutely characterized by Sean O'Brien as 'minutely detailed but somehow hard to contextualise—spatial rather than thoroughly pictorial'.[20] What neither critic notes is the animation brought to the text by the 'I's neurasthenic propensity to taste human breath in the air, to zoom in on body secretions and scrutinize decay: as in *The Ship's Orchestra*, indirectly authorial hang-ups achieve a workable elegance. Less specifically located than the 'I' of the Migrant *City*, the revised protagonist is also more subtly preoccupied with his own detachment.

How far the sequence succeeds in creating what Fisher calls 'psychological environments'[21] is open to debate, but it matters that the revised 'I' first appears in the phrase 'what I see now'. Seeing is an inspected activity in this oeuvre (the eye on the cover of *Poems 1955–1987* draws attention to that), not just because the poet's sight was formatively problematic—'between the ages of about 12 and 29, when I had a corrective operation, I had very defective 3D vision'— but because of his early interest in psychoanalysis.[22] At one point the revised *City* reads: 'I have often felt myself to be vicious, in living so much by the eye, yet among so many people. I can be afraid that the egg of light through which I see these bodies might present itself as a keyhole' (p. 28). The voyeurism and alienation inherited from the *Bildungsroman* protagonist are eventually so inseparable that knowledge depends on withdrawal:

> To know these tall pointers
> I need to withdraw
> From what is called my life
> And from my net
> Of achievable desires.[23]

This 'I' is not quite the poet, yet it is hardly surprising that Fisher advanced beyond *City* into writer's block. Looking back, he has seen the text as bound up with the block's development: *City* projected Birmingham as a 'huge image or symbol for a very elaborate *stasis* of mind', and that inner seizure was reinforced by the attention to 'appearances and products' which the projection required.[24] Having written out of this perplex, in such impending-block poems as 'Seven Attempted Moves' (1964), Fisher lost himself in almost total silence and only broke free in 1970. The writings which followed are, as he points out, 'much concerned with processes of loosening, slackening and psychic mobility and relativity' which is why 'the ostensible subject-matter of those poems is so often art'.[25] Fisher turned, in fact, to Picasso and to Klee, finding in cubism and the swirling cityscapes of Kokoschka an antidote to inertia. He produced random-looking texts—most spectacularly in *The Cut Pages* (1971)—which were therapeutic because deliberative. Yet if calculation made for freedom, there was a risk of poems being too purposively concerned with the loosening which made them possible. This weakens such lyrics as 'In the Black Country', which superficially de-Anglicizes England by saying that 'Dudley from the Castle keep / looks like a town by Kokoschka'.[26]

Elsewhere, reflexive mobility lends the Birmingham-writing of this period a rewarding dynamism. Take the first lines of 'Handsworth Liberties', a sequence based on the images evoked in Fisher by listening to certain pieces of music (mostly jazz):[27]

Open—
and away

in all directions:
room at last for the sky
and a horizon;

for pale new towers in the north
right on the line.

It all
radiates outwards
in a lightheaded air
without image;

there is a world.[28]

As often, the external cue is demolition and redevelopment. To that
extent the sequence deals with what one geographer has called 'the
most profound social dislocation ... in the country's urban history,
and Birmingham was a prime example'.[29] In the verse, however, the
social is in abeyance and the command, or statement, 'Open—',
marks both the start of the poem and a creative dislocation, a dash out
from the speech act into the 'liberties' of mental space. If the first line
opens a door, the second carries us through it, and that movement is
reinforced by a stanza-break that provides a landing-place which can
only accelerate dispersal—'in all directions'—followed by a colon
which points beyond.

Fisher says in the Pickard film that, as a child, he was excited by
street-maps of Birmingham ('the feeling that you could, in fact, get
up above the thing and know the story of it') and he has recently
declared 'I live a good deal in maps—some of my favourite
reading'.[30] 'Handsworth Liberties' is not cartographic in the sense
that its layout is emblematic of the city; its 'Open—' disposition has
less to do with imitative form than with achieving a (strictly articulated) syntax which gives words room to float. Fisher has complained
that English is too facile in movement, too 'slithery';[31] the cleared
spaces of 'Handsworth Liberties' slow language and enhance its yield
without depending on heavy figuration or metrically determined

stress. Yet the effect of placing 'horizon' at a strophe-end, and of straggling 'pale new towers in the north' along an extended verse, while reducing syntax to order at 'right on the line', where another line, and strophe, ends, is undeniably location-suggestive. There is the conceptual pressure of a limit, though no attempt at concrete poetry. Meanwhile, Fisher marshals his syntax: if it resolves at 'line', there is still no subject in the initial sentence, leaving a displaced latency where reader and poet touch open ground. A subject comes, firmly but too late, in another short line, balancing the first, where 'It all' claims summary force ('it' is often a keyword: more often Fisher's subject than 'I'); being verbless, for its moment, this phrase readily dilates into the radiance, lightheadedness and imagelessness which make the apparently blunt truism, 'there is a world'—already oblique because tagged on, like an afterthought—mysterious.

Fisher's achievement would be less formidable if everything written in the wake of his block were so palpably reactive against it. In fact the dynamic outwardness of 'Handsworth Liberties' is complemented by a number of rich accounts of inner-geography. The title-poem of *Matrix* (1971) is a case in point. Like 'In the Black Country' it draws on art: late Monet, an oriental souvenir, a little drawing of a fisherman's hut (probably by Dürer), as well as Thomas Mann's *Doctor Faustus*. Above all it was sprung by Arnold Böcklin's *Isle of the Dead*.[32] This sombre late nineteenth-century painting, which shows a sinister boat being rowed with a shrouded coffin to an island of mausoleums, chimes with the poem in more than one respect, because it 'was initially devised in response to a request ... for a picture to induce dreams' and Fisher has said that 'Matrix' had oneiric origins.[33]

By observing and manipulating half-awake dream-processes, Fisher brought to light a set of associations which was in the mind but shot through with bodily data. When discussing 'Matrix' with Eric Mottram, Fisher wrenched the interview to stress 'that what I talk about has got body analogues all over it'.[34] His passion for 'referring EVERYTHING to bodily existence'[35] brings hearing into view, as section 5 of 'Matrix' bears in on the impacted structure where the stasis of a writing block might lurk:

Spiralling from the shore
in blocked paths and on dropped
or jutting levels,
the stations of the thing
face over one another,

inseparable, interfolded,
wall-face into roof-angle,
catwalks over the garden-clefts
hung with valerian:

variants on cochlea,
invisibly thin
stone ear in the sky;

on how to get down
in through the horn
of the gold snail-shell
and not grow small.[36]

These lines use images from Monet's water-garden and elsewhere to
trace within the mind-matrix a version of the spiral which will later
shape *A Furnace*. As in the long poem, the motif is registered in
stone, sky and the animal kingdom, but most intimately in the ear,
where it is both the external whorl of cartilage and the cochlea.

This multi-scale congruence is satisfying but destabilizing because
the lymphatic disease that damaged Fisher's sense of balance from his
late teens into his thirties made his inner ear a locus of instability and
nausea. Hence section 9 of the poem, with its account of 'Doctor
Meinière' and his tilting cabin:

the floorboards opposite
heave up, keep coming,
silent dog attack—
spreadeagle as the floor
becomes a roof
to slide off—
the whole room
falling betrayals

always the same way,
insatiable axis.

For the victim of Ménière's disease 'there is a world' only in giddiness. This mimetically vigorous writing (not the poet's usual mode) works on our eyes and ears—as in the sudden line-breaks and end-prominent sound-reversals of 'floor . . . roof . . . off'—to internalize vertigo and achieve the 'subversive' aim that Fisher looks for in a poem: 'some kind of potentially new dislocative effect in the minds of some readers'.[37]

Those terms are worth putting under pressure. Interviewed in 1977, Fisher described a line from 'Seven Attempted Moves'—'Beside the soft earth steps'—as 'dislocative' on the grounds that 'Steps are occasionally made out of earth, but not for long.'[38] Can such a gentle shock really be called 'subversive'? To judge from interviews, the poet would reply out of Blake, citing 'the bit in *The Marriage of Heaven and Hell*, where the angel quietly says, "How do you know but ev'ry Bird that cut[s] the airy way / Is an immense world of delight, clos'd by your senses five?" That proposition is always present to me', he explains, 'even when I'm just muttering and messing around with tiny tricks of perception.'[39] By means of dislocative tricks, poetry can point up the limits of the human perceptual machine, and show the world of experience to be as physiologically dependent as the reality that fills the head of a sufferer from Ménière's disease. This process is subversive because it goes against the work that culture does when it naturalizes expectations in politically interested ways into what Fisher (following Blake) calls 'Newton's sleep'.[40] One of the least moralizing of poets,[41] he confesses to a 'didacticism' born of his belief that

the world is made particularly in its social manifestations, in its economics, by mental models. That's not an unfamiliar view. And it's probably in Blake, who's about as near to the political position that I have as anybody. The human mind makes the world. The examination of this organism that makes the world is of paramount interest. If we do not know how our minds work, and how our appetites work, and how our senses and our rationalizations are interactive ... we're very poorly equipped to interpret the forms by which we live, i.e. the political dimension of the world.[42]

How useful is it to construe contemporary perception and cognition through Blakean/idealist arguments? To put 'Handsworth Liberties' or 'Matrix' next to, say, the restlessly deflected writing of John Wilkinson's 'Book of Birmingham', *The Interior Planets*,[43] is to be reminded that, in the information-flux and cyborg knowledge-state of advanced capitalism, it can be doubted how far any single or collective 'human mind makes the world'. Wilkinson's is a poetry invaded by advertising verbiage, media chat, psychotherapeutic discourse and the black dialects of Handsworth, and driven as though in flight from itself by a consciousness which has no place to speak from, but is flung clear in a sullied flow of graphic lyricism, intermittently fixated on the hard objects of consumerism:

> Semi-conscious, double-glazed, & nothing came
>   between us, we who *were*
>   mirror dizziness, whose lack—
> balance, noticing out of the cold
> granite's hurtful breath its glints of mica,
>   struck this old claim like a knife's
>   gothic ivory, just as a saint's
> leg, cased & stuck with mirrors & gems,
>   blunts in the kiss & touch, off-balancing
>   its erstwhile cabinet, its array.

Wilkinson's fragmenting modernism is limited in what it can say by its very immediacy, but this glancing, ironic foray into the ontology of sex-'n-shopping (the reliquary is a boutique window) probes the make-up of the post-industrial, shopping-mall Birmingham that Fisher walks through in the Pickard film but which figures in his poetry only as the 'glassy metaphysical void' to which the world of satanic mills is said to have been reduced, in section v of *A Furnace*.[44] In 'Varnishing' Wilkinson persuasively looks into the glazed void to find selves subject to the display-power of fetishes.

It would be wrong to conclude, however, that Fisher's liking for
Blake makes his understanding of psychology two centuries out of
date. On the contrary, his poetry shadows so closely recent research
in the field (no doubt through cultural osmosis) that it is not surprising to find him becoming perplexed, in an interview of 1984,
about the fact that 'talking about perception ... makes it sound as
though I'm conducting exercises in experimental psychology'.[45] He is
of course right to insist that his poetry has its own procedures, but it
is suggestive to compare his middle-period verse with, for instance,
the classical work of Ungerleider and Mishkin on how different brain
systems perceive the 'what' and the 'where' of things,[46] or with what
John O'Keefe and his followers have maintained about Kantian *a
priori* space conforming to a spatial framework hard-wired into the
hippocampus. O'Keefe is particularly keen to insist that science can
now demonstrate the falsity of what we see in 'Newton's sleep'. We are
programmed to perceive three dimensions and to have a false confidence about the place of things: 'The existence of a serious
mismatch between the Euclidean spatial representations of the brain
and the physical world is strongly pointed to by recent experiments
in quantum physics.'[47]

Roy Fisher's interest in such conjunctions of psychology and
physics can be detected in section 7 of 'Matrix', which reworks a
passage in *Doctor Faustus* about an imaginary descent into the ocean
depths using a quartz-windowed bathysphere. Vividly afflicted
by syphilis, the composer Adrian Leverkühn sees luminous sea-
creatures—beasts which become, in the poem,

> quartz-fires
> in the under-vault,
> scattered through softer globes,
> their spiral trails
> chasing and merging,
>
> to form an uneasy field ...

Fisher's 'globes' and 'spiral trails' may be more somatically suggestive
(of eyes, nerves, the cochlea) than the 'circling will-o'-the-wisps' seen

by Leverkühn, but they also recall, as in the novel, the 'whirling disk' of our spiral galaxy and the relativities of particle physics—traced as though in a cloud-chamber along 'trails / chasing and merging, / to form an uneasy field'.[48] At this point, moreover, the passage's reflexivity is almost as loaded as its imagery because it has digested (more happily than the Migrant *City*) the influence of what American modernists call 'composition by field'. Fisher would no doubt be sceptical of the wilder claims that have been made for a relationship between modernism and post-Einsteinian science, as when W. C. Williams writes:

> poems cannot any longer be made following a Euclidean measure, 'beautiful' as this may make them . . .
>   A relative order is operative elsewhere in our lives. Even the divorce laws recognise that. Are we so stupid that we can't see that the same things apply to the construction of modern verse . . . ?[49]

But a fascination with physics has shaped how Fisher thinks about the way non-metrical writing can free language to respond to relativities and indeterminacies not simply in the 'field' of its subject-matter but among its own resources of sound and meaning.

The fruits of this are apparent in 'Without Location' (1975):

> A life without location—
> just the two of us
> maybe, or a few—
>
> keeping in closeup:
> and the colours—
> and just the colours
>
> coming from the common source
> one after the other
> on a pulse;
>
> and passing around us,
> turning about and
> flaking to form a world,

patterning on the need for a world
made on a pulse.

That way we keep the colours,

till they break and go
and leave no trace; nothing
that could hold an association.[50]

This lyric has been valuably related to a train of thought about experience which runs from Emerson through William James: 'Man lives by pulses; our organic movements are such; and the chemical and ethereal agents are undulatory and alternate.'[51] As his title indicates, however, Fisher is not trying to capture what everyday consciousness feels like: it is as though, in Ungerleider and Mishkin's terms, 'where' information had been experimentally blocked for the better investigation of 'what'—producing a loss of solidity, as objects are revealed as the waves and electric impulses which physics knows them to be. The poem seeks to uncouple experience from the allocentric framework which is built into human minds (into the limbic system, if O'Keefe is right) and which misconstrues the nature of the space-time continuum.

Certainly, when asked about the lyric, Fisher pointed to post-Einsteinian physics: ' "Without Location" arose from its title, which is a phrase from, I think, some such venerable explainer as Eddington. I can't now place it. I just started wondering what such a concept was like as an affect.'[52] Almost any work of popular science could have stimulated this poem because it draws on standard insights, but A. S. Eddington summarizes these with his usual grace when he explains, in *The Nature of the Physical World*, that the dependence of location on speed and point of view destroys it in the conventional sense:

> Having any number of ... systems of location, or frames of space, we can no longer pretend that each of them indicates 'just where things are'. Location is not something supernaturally revealed to the mind; it is a kind of conventional summary of those properties or relations of objects which condition certain visual and tactual sensations.

Does not this show that 'right' location in space cannot be nearly so important and fundamental as it is made out to be in the Newtonian scheme of things?[53]

Undecidability does not just hold for swiftly moving large objects: it applies all the way down to Schrödinger's observation that 'as the position of a wave-group becomes more defined the energy . . . becomes more indeterminate'. Nor is this version of the uncertainty principle a fact to be isolated from perception and cognition (if it were, it would be less interesting to Fisher, and there would be a sharp break between the 'concept' and the 'affect' of dislocation). 'The principle of indeterminacy is epistemological', Eddington notes: 'It reminds us once again that the world of physics is a world contemplated from within, surveyed by appliances which are part of it and subject to its laws' (p. 225).

So 'Without Location' draws on the relationship between perception, cognition and a post-Einsteinian vision of the cosmos to develop the 'dislocative' gambits found in a poem like 'Seven Attempted Moves'. In doing this, however, it confronts a problem identified in the very interview (from 1977) which discusses 'the soft earth steps':

Space is part of our mental life . . . We haven't a language for space–time. We haven't a four-dimensional language at all. I suppose a lot of what we're talking about here is my perhaps rather small but insistent attempt to assume that a four-dimensional perception is somehow necessary for us to have . . . the moral at last![54]

Fisher's didacticism can switch with ease from Blake to modern physics because both seek to wake us up from 'Newton's sleep'; but it sets the stakes for poetry awesomely high. Beyond the phenomenology of the early work, the aim is now for verse which would register the mental contours of space while transcending the limits of language in order to present a place 'Without Location'.

That poem fails as it must, but to beautiful effect, using glancingly non-specific deictics to establish a situatedness which remains indeterminate, and melting its own architecture in a flux of participles. There is a psychologically adroit interplay between syntactical spontaneity and structure, as the poem hypostatizes in its tercets that 'patterning on the need for a world' which it attributes to the sort of organism ('just the two of us ... or a few') that has written and is reading the poem. Phrasal repetition—starting with the title which recurs in line one—does much to create decorum, but it is striking that each tercet except the first and the last (which rhyme on the poem's only polysyllables, 'location' and 'association') gives a leading role to one of the present participles which initially space out the poem but then accumulate in the four climactic lines that redisplay the text's keywords—colours, pulse, world—in reverse (i.e., unravelling the pattern as it coheres, from the solidity of 'world' through 'pulse' to 'colours'). Fisher has complained that, in translations of Brodsky, 'There's a great deal going on, and it's not quite systematised so as to show its inner form, the way in which ideas hang as planets hang in the sky. I can't see the three- or four-dimensional relationships of the ideas, because I'm seeing a very active single surface.'[55] 'Without Location' achieves that sort of depth, that hint of an extra dimension, partly because of its placing of keywords at line-ends, where they radiate into silence, open to contemplation.

To read any book on Einstein is to find blunt confirmation that 'We haven't a language for space–time.' Yet a poem may intimate what it cannot say, and 'Without Location' models some relevant complexities between the space of its disposition and the times of its reading. A full analysis of this would take pages, but Fisher most obviously energizes the field by fusing the minute, the vast, the fleeting and the constant. 'Pulse', for instance, is both stellar and somatic, evanescent and steady, and it alludes to the rhythms which sustain the poem's organic form as well as the life of the reader. At a cosmic pitch 'the colours // coming from the common source ... on a pulse' suggest a pulsar, emitting bursts of light, X-rays and gamma radiation—particles and/or waves which ripple across space to earth where they are scrutinized by spectroscopy, measured for redshift and the like. Yet the poet remains aware that 'whatever one talks about has got body analogues ... all over it', and the 'pulse' in space is inextricable from that of the perceiver, who internalizes its flashes as rhythm, constructs reality blood-beat by blood-beat, and tries to hang on to colour.

The fleetingness of those flaking impressions can be glossed out of Eddington, who invokes the insubstantiality of colour to highlight the role of mind and body in the constitution of 'reality': many attributes of substance, he explains, are 'projections of our sense-impressions . . . Thus the colour which is so vivid to us is in our minds [and] no part of the essential nature of substance' (p. 273). None of this is unique to *The Nature of the Physical World*, but the book does show how post-Einsteinian physics can lead to views compatible not just with philosophical idealism but with a degree of mysticism. When Eddington declares that 'the solid substance of things is another illusion . . . Illusion is to reality as the smoke to the fire [and] it is reasonable to inquire whether in the mystical illusions of man there is not a reflection of an underlying reality' (pp. 318–19), he might be writing about *A Furnace*, described by Fisher in his Preface as 'an engine devised . . . to persuade obstinate substances to alter their condition and show relativities . . . Some of the substances fed in are very solid indeed' (*F*, p. vii). Eddington provides no master key to unlock the matrix of Blakean politics, general relativity and mysticism out of John Cowper Powys which goes into Fisher's grandest poem, but he does help one see how the oeuvre developed from the phobic phenomenology of *City* to *A Furnace*, where the landscapes of Birmingham and the rural North Midlands are mutually dislocated and space–time is curved around a double spiral.

In 1981 Peter Riley published *Lines on the Liver*. Impressive in its own right, this assemblage of verse and prose was calculated to attract Roy Fisher because it focussed on a windswept part of Derbyshire which he was exploring in the early Eighties and which would be his home by the time *A Furnace* was published in 1986. By a fruitful coincidence, the occasion of Riley's book was itself a house-move, one that took him twelve miles across the 'pendant pearl' of the southern tip of the Peak District, traversing an area which 'hovers over the magno-industrial parks and wastelands of a false and hollow centrality'.[56] It matters to *Lines* that its location should be temporally as well as spatially paradoxical: 'Moving east, then, and setting up house well up an eastern valley-side, just off the limestone, facing west. What is behind me is then in front of me and I walk backwards into the future.' Even more important, however, is the conjunction of rural beauty with the grime of industrial parks: Riley maintains in 'Spitewinter Edge' that these poles are so interdependent that to divide them is to break up 'the continuous human agency that we are' and to succumb, not just in art, to the 'short-circuited dreamwork, leafy parabolas, ontological egotism' of pastoral. For him, poetry has to be altogether more engaged and situated. It must be tied to the 'totally inhabited . . . space' which he decisively (but with scare marks) calls ' "here" ', and which he also describes as 'the furnace'.

Those familiar with *A Furnace* will already have spotted many points of contact with *Lines*, and Fisher has conceded that 'the spitewinter prose piece was influential in giving me a single image for holding the elements of my land-maze'.[57] At least in the abstract, Riley's vision of the urban/rural Midlands as a 'labyrinth of pre-waste', orientated by a sky that is no longer Newtonian, sounds very like the 'land-maze' that Fisher sets under the 'star-fields' of his cosmology (*F*, p. 41). It is true that the Preface of *A Furnace* attributes to John Cowper Powys the poem's root idea of layering North Staffordshire onto Birmingham, citing from 'his novel *Atlantis*, a description of a lost poem which gains its effects by the superimposition of landscape upon landscape' (*F*, p. vii). In some respects, though, this clinches the Riley connection because Powys also figures in *Lines*:

> Such a commotion in the grass!
> Can't you see all the little mortifacts
> running around, can't you see
> John Cowper Powys
> bending over a bracken pit
> and striding off again
> to the nearest stationers
>
> Now is the future to any past, *upon us*!

Can't you hear the music of the garden of the earth,
running screaming from the nearest box office

The tone and texture of this short poem define, however, a difference between Riley and Fisher. *Lines* is driven by the founding ethical priorities of the 'Cambridge school': it traces 'harm' in the social order with startling confidence. The impatience of 'Can't you see . . . Can't you hear' (with no question marks, for surely we can) and the exhortation 'Now is the future . . . *upon us!*' could hardly be more assured. We should learn from Powys to recognise the fulness of the present, and rush off to the shops for writing materials: that's the way to flush the deluded out of the constraints (box/office) of the pastoral theatre. *A Furnace* is more explicit than early Fisher about social damage (it is, by his standards, a heavily *peopled* poem), but its denunciations of injustice are caught up in an involved poetic structure of seven internally divided and laterally interactive sections (plus an 'Introit') in which no position is static. The symphonic amplitude built up by this means is fed by a sense of the past which came late to Fisher. *City* occasionally contrasts the demolitions of the present with Victorian industrial grandeur; 'Wonders of Obligation' deals movingly with the Blitz; but *A Furnace* takes permission from the space-time continuum of physics[58] to modulate several phases of history through the 'headless / relativity of zones' which the poem self-descriptively finds in North Staffordshire/Birmingham (*F*, p. 27). Riley's feeling of vanguard responsibility—which makes even the present a future to any past—would strike Fisher as too forward: in the vortex of *A Furnace*, the past might be the future to any present.

This is so because the figure of the double spiral on which the poem is based allows the movement of time to flow back from its advance. Like the early Stephen Hawking,[59] Fisher seems attracted to the idea that in a 'no boundary' (i.e. post-Einsteinian) universe time will eventually go into reverse. As the example of 'Matrix' has suggested, it isn't possible to give just one reason for the structuring of *A Furnace* on a double spiral: influenced by the shape of our galaxy, and that of those starry neighbours which have (as Eddington notes) 'the form of a double spiral',[60] the poem concatenates its whorls through snail-shells and megalith inscriptions to the remembered presence of what the sequence 'New Diversions' (written during the gestation of *A Furnace*) calls 'a glistening inflamed ear. Cochlea, / balance, half-circles of canal.'[61] But Fisher has said that his poem is 'a thing in which I am trying to describe the affect of . . . space, time and other dimensions if you like being warped and subjectively bent',[62] and such physics must lie behind the comment, in his Preface, that *A Furnace* is 'based on a form which enacts, for me, the equivocal nature of the ways in which time can be thought about' (*F*, p. vii).

What is equivocal, by its nature, cannot be approached directly, and that is in itself a reason for the poem's spiralling progress, which is always oblique in relation to its advance, even though the writing follows Fisher's long-standing habit of creating 'a long line without anything / you could call repetition'. A double spiral tends to maximize linearity within constriction, while finding an appropriate geometry for what 'Releases' identifies as Fisher's typical movement through urban as well as poetic space: 'My whole tortuous track warps into a single advancing line.'[63] Above all, the warping movement avoids establishing a determinate centre. This is attractive to Fisher because he regards centres as dictatorial, unstable, fake, or a combination of all three. His campaign against them runs from the abstractions of *The Cut Pages* ('They brought a centre and set it up here, but it wouldn't take')[64] to the documentary mode of 'Six Texts for a Film', which warns against trusting the centres of cities because they enshrine the deceptions of authority. The official centre of Birmingham thus resembles the Forum of Augustus, which sat 'firm and new, / drawing centrality to itself', in front of 'a massive / curtain wall', set there to 'mask / slum tenements behind'.[65]

A dislike so intense must have its impact on form, and Fisher has said 'I'm not interested in making a structure which has got . . . an authoritarian centre, a rule or mandate somewhere in its middle which the work will unfold and will reach.'[66] This relates to time and how it is thought about because of the kind of knowledge an elusive core facilitates. The loop of the double spiral connects opposites (out/ in, up/down) and abolishes antitheses in the act of displacing authority. In this it contributes to one of the most significant attempts of *A Furnace* to 'dislocate' the minds of readers. The effect is sought by means which are necessarily *ad hoc* and irregular, and these are self-definingly associated by the dissident, heterodox, somewhat autodidactic Fisher with the figure of the charlatan: 'Grown man / without right learning; by nobody / guided to the places' (*F*, p. 8)— guided, that is, neither to the culturally approved commonplaces nor to the sites where these are inculcated. In sections II and III of *A Furnace*, Fisher implies that John Cowper Powys would be one such man, seeing him, in the manner of Peter Riley, as a searcher of bracken pits, but not as a confidently striding moralist:

> pacifist mystics, self-chosen,
> who would be driven by private
> obsessions to go looking
> among slurries and night-holes
> for what might be accidentally
> there, though not instituted; having to be
> each his own charlatan.   (*F*, p. 23)

These provincial-eccentric mystics are admirable because their obsession with the accidental and the counter-institutional protects them from the 'antinomies' that culture will impose on people,

> Unless

> thrown. And again
> and repeatedly thrown
> to break down the devil
> his spirit; to pull down
> the devil his grammar school,
> wherein the brain
> submits to be
> cloven, up,
> sideways and down
> in all of its pathways;

> where to convert
> one term to its antithesis

> requires that there be devised
> an agent with authority—
>
> and they're in. That's it. Who
> shall own death? Spoken for,
> and Lazarus the test case. Only Almighty
> God could work that trick . . .   (*F*, p. 16)

This is a strong example of the phrasally syncopated verse which characterizes parts of *A Furnace*. The writing advances conceptually instead of following musical or formal cues, and the differential positioning of keywords within lines ('thrown', 'down', 'to . . .') opens the concepts to scrutiny and strikes a relativistic note. Those shifts are particularly bracing in this passage because it enacts the breaking down of binaries. With Nietzschean vehemence Fisher deconstructs the desiccating antitheses that are educated into members of a competitive society (he did not enjoy being at grammar school), and that are secured by religion when it exploits the human intuition that there is a continuum between states of existence by installing the categories of 'life' and 'death' and using fear to establish God as the gatekeeper between them. Lazarus becomes the exception to prove the antithetical rule.

So the warp at the centre of the double spiral has philosophical implications for those who think equivocally about time. It connects Fisher's antinomian determination to break antithetical ideology into relativities to the Einsteinian thesis that the universe is finite but has no bound, folds into itself. The beliefs of that heroic charlatan J. C. Powys can contribute to this heady brew because he espoused (as Fisher's Preface notes) 'the idea that the making of all kinds of identities is a primary impulse which the cosmos itself has' (*F*, p. vii). The word to notice is hidden in 'impulse'. At the start of *A Furnace*, Fisher returns to the matter of *City* (his 'Introit' is dated 12 November 1958) but rewrites the decay of Birmingham through the 'pulse' of 'Without Location':

> Something's decided
> to narrate

in more dimensions than I can know
the gathering in
and giving out of the world on a slow
pulse, on a metered contraction
that the senses enquire towards
but may not themselves
intercept. All I can tell it by
is the passing trace of it
in a patterned agitation of
a surface . . .

•

And the biggest of all the apparitions,
the great iron
thing, the ironworks,
reared up on end into the bright
haze, makes quiet burning
if anything at all.

When the pulse-beat for it comes
it is revealed, set
back a little way, arrested,
inward, grotesque, prepared for.

Then gone by,
with the shallowing of the road
and the pulse's falling away
cleanly through a few more
frames of buildings, noise,
a works gate with cyclists;
the passing of it quite final, not a tremor
of the prospect at the crossroads; . . .   (*F*, pp. 3–4)

This wonderfully alert and supple verse is, if anything, even more
accomplished than the 'Brick-dust . . .' section of *City*, yet it shares
with it a receptiveness fed by detachment. Now, though, the
powerlessness of the vigilance is less the product of individual
alienation and more a function of the nature of the cosmos, as the

building and demolition of an ironworks pass as easily as a scatter of colours.

The calm of the passage is not without its tensions—process-related and pitched against 'quite final'. Similar energies pester the heart of *A Furnace*, in 'Core', which probes dark spaces, tombs and the like and finds them strangely vital. The section starts from one of Fisher's versions of a cloud chamber ('its place / plotted by every force' (F, p. 28)), but it then makes legible the double spiral which structures the poem in depth (there is an analogy with the double helix of DNA). Writing of 'sky-trails' that 'merge with earth-trails', Fisher alludes to the marked liths on the solar-orientated Celtic burial site at Newgrange.[67] 'We're carving the double spiral / into this stone', he declares: 'Write sky-laws into the rocks; draw / the laws of light into it and through it' (F, p. 29). This is light being drawn from the sky into the clock of ancient liths and the cosmic mystery-map inscribed on them, but the light is drawn not merely as a Celt of *circa* 2500 B.C. would draw it because it is both drawn into a curve by the earth's gravitational field and drawn around the space–time whorl of the spiral, which, at this point, resembles a diagram in a physics textbook. Somewhere hereabouts the poem starts to return upon itself, as it modulates through an account of a warehouse nightclub in Birmingham, where the ageing Coleman Hawkins is doing one of his last gigs, to an unglossable 'polished black basalt / pyramid, household size' (F, p. 31)—a model necropolis, with the opacity of death. The cloud-chamber which opens the section finds its equivalent in a closing passage about a burial site in Brittany which is made to sound like the 'Core' of a nuclear-power station: 'their buried radiance / variable, heavily shielded, / constantly active' (F, p. 32).

The scope for religious musing about returns of all sorts is considerable, but it would be false piety to confuse the circularity of 'Core' and the looped formation of *A Furnace* as a whole with, say, T. S. Eliot's 'In my beginning is my end ... In my end is my beginning.' More than the Lazarus polemic stands between *A Furnace* and 'East Coker': once its obsession with space–time is grasped, Fisher's poem comes into focus as an ambitious attempt to think beyond religious schema about mysteries which have been enlarged rather than resolved by the advance of scientific knowledge. Yet although *A Furnace* is informed by science, its aims and understandings are poetic, often speculative and intuitive. Fisher writes as one whose wonder has been awakened by subatomic particles and multi-dimensionality, much as a Christian poet's would be by angels or the incarnation: he is not trying to write a treatise on physics. And because 'We haven't a four-dimensional language', his approaches to the inexpressible are coloured by the Christian beliefs ingrained in the language that we do have, even though his predicates are not those of the later T. S. Eliot.

When he writes about huge, slow-moving clouds, for instance, in the closing section of *A Furnace*, he describes his

> Relief at the sight of them
> even though they seem to mean
> irrevocable dislocation. Creatures
> of the Last Days, coming to the muster.   (*F*, p. 45)

By this stage in the poem, and, indeed, in Fisher's career, 'irrevocable dislocation' is the weightier for remaining non-explicit: it signifies a subversion of mindsets incident on the opening up of the space (as in 'Without Location') which the clouds ostensibly occupy—hence, as the passage moves on, their being 'perfect to themselves / in some other dimension' (*F*, p. 46). But the clouds are also apocalyptic figures, Goyaesque giants who might illustrate the Book of Revelation:

> Apocalypse
> lies within time; as these beings
> may or may not so lie; if they do,
> their demeanour could equally match
> the beginning of all things. It's the same
> change. There's a choice of how to see it.   (*F*, p. 45)

This tonally remarkable passage offhandedly gives us the chance to escape time by associating the teleology of the universe—which emerged out of clouds of gas and vapour and is heading back in that direction—with that relief which Fisher finds in the apocalyptic but 'equivocal' thought ('lies' can mean telling lies) that time can be abolished.

There is a trauma here which presumably goes back to Fisher's never-published 'apocalyptic *bildungsroman*', and it gives a final twist to his writing on location. Eddington remarks that 'time seems to us so much more mysterious than space' because we can never escape it: 'When I close my eyes and retreat into my inner mind, I feel myself *enduring*, I do not feel myself *extensive*.'[68] This is one version of a truth which appals Fisher—the 'psychological torment' of the fact that time 'doesn't come apart from me. I'm never a yard away from it';[69] and it runs so strongly through his work that it is tempting to conclude that the sickness which afflicts the 'I' of the Migrant *City* ('hereditary, complete ... progressive, so slow as to be barely perceptible') is the mortality of being in time. Certainly, both texts of the sequence declare: 'Once I wanted to prove the world was sick. Now I want to prove it healthy ... Where there is no time there is no sickness.'[70] So it may be that *A Furnace* is Fisher's most astonishing exploration of space and place because it is also his grandest attempt to prove the world healthy, to redeem it for us by alleviating death-anxiety and managing what is fearful in our having time pulse inside us. From this point of view, it is not just the locational intricacy of Birmingham but the rapidity of its industrial decline—its manifestation of temporal process—which has made it such a rewarding place for Roy Fisher to think with; and he emerges as a poet rightly suspicious of 'The "place" tag' because his attraction to the topographical is inextricable from anxieties attached to quite another part of the space–time continuum.

NOTES

1. Extracts are spoken in the film by Fisher; the full sequence was published in *Birmingham River* (Oxford: Oxford University Press, 1994).

2. 'Talking to Cameras', *BR*, pp. 11–16, at p. 11.

3. *Ibid.*

4. Gordon E. Cherry, *Birmingham: A Study in Geography, History and Planning* (Chichester: John Wiley, 1994), p. 229.

5. 'Roy Fisher 1930–', *Contemporary Authors (Autobiography Series)*, vol. 10 (Detroit, New York, Fort Lauderdale, London: Gale Research Inc., 1989), pp. 79–100, at p. 98.

6. 'Wonders of Obligation', *Poems 1955–1980* (Oxford: Oxford University Press, 1980), pp. 155–64, at p. 155.

7. 'Talking to Cameras', *BR*, p. 13.

8. See Carson's *The Irish for No* (Dublin: Gallery Press, 1987) and *Belfast Confetti* (Loughcrew, Co. Meath: Gallery Press, 1989).

9. See, e.g., Andrew Crozier, 'Signs of Identity: Roy Fisher's *A Furnace*', *PN Review*, 18:3 (January/February 1992), pp. 25–32.

10. ' "Come to Think of It, the Imagination" ': Roy Fisher in Conversation with John Kerrigan' [24 September 1998–20 February 1999], in *News for the Ear: A Homage to Roy Fisher*, ed. Peter Robinson and Robert Sheppard (Exeter: Stride Publications, 2000).

11. Robert Sheppard, *Turning the Prism: An Interview with Roy Fisher* (London: Toads Damp Press, 1986), p. 22. Cf. Jed Rasula and Mike Erwin, 'An Interview with Roy Fisher', in Roy Fisher, *Nineteen Poems and an Interview* (1975; Pensnett, Staffs: Grosseteste, 1977), pp. 12–48, at pp. 17–20.

12. Paul Lester and Roy Fisher, *A Birmingham Dialogue* (Birmingham: Protean Pubs, 1986), p. 22; Roy Fisher, letter to John Kerrigan, 9 May–14 October 1997.

13. Cf. *Birmingham Dialogue*, pp. 21–22.

14. See the text in *Living Arts*, 1 (1963), pp. 64–79. A few additional changes were made before publication in *Collected Poems 1968* (London: Fulcrum Press, 1969), but the *City* which appears there and in subsequent collections had cohered by 1963.

15. 'Roy Fisher 1930–', *Contemporary Authors*, p. 97; *Birmingham Dialogue*, p. 22.

16. *City* (Worcester: Migrant Press, 1961), p. 8.

17. Fisher tells me (e-mail, 4 February 1999) that 'The building . . . was a rather good old Gothic hotel called the Cobden. Playing by the rules I was using, I simply changed the name to something else in period.'

18. *City, P55–80*, pp. 14–30, at p. 20. The revised text is quoted throughout from this collection, which here diverges from the *Living Arts* text by removing an article from 'dries out the patches', substituting an adjective in 'of countless childhoods' and dividing the passage with a break.

19. 'Roy Fisher: An Appreciation', in his *Thomas Hardy and British Poetry* (London: Routledge & Kegan Paul, 1973), pp. 152–72, at p. 159. In some respects his diagnosis was more prescient than merely wrong, because the avoidance of moralism in such early Fisher poems about civic infrastructure as 'For Realism' and 'The Memorial Fountain' (1965) now coexists with writing which defines the ethical topography of scenes rather plainly—e.g., 'The Burning Graves at Netherton' (1981) or 'The Sidings at Drebkau' (1990).

20. 'Roy Fisher: A Polytheism with No Gods', *The Deregulated Muse: Essays on*

Contemporary British and Irish Poetry (Newcastle upon Tyne: Bloodaxe Books, 1998), pp. 112–22, at p. 114.

21. Rasula and Erwin, 'Interview', p. 12.
22. ' "Come to Think of It, the Imagination" ', pp. 92–93.
23. Revised *City*, p. 24; Migrant *City*, p. 16 (with different layout).
24. Jonathan Roper, 'An Interview with Roy Fisher' [27 September 1989], *Disclaimer*, 2 ([early 1990]); *Birmingham Dialogue*, p. 27 (cf. Rasula and Erwin, 'Interview', p. 21).
25. *Birmingham Dialogue*, p. 28.
26. *P55–80*, p. 106.
27. 'A Note on the "Handsworth Liberties" ' in *P55–80*, p. 193; 'Handsworth Compulsions', *Numbers*, 2:1 (Spring 1987), pp. 24–28.
28. 'Handsworth Liberties', *P55–80*, p. 117–24, at p. 117.
29. Cherry, *Birmingham*, p. 174.
30. ' "Come to Think of It, the Imagination" ', p. 91.
31. Valentina Polukhina, 'A Noble Quixotic Sight: An Interview with Roy Fisher' [5 March 1990], in her *Brodsky through the Eyes of his Contemporaries* (London: Macmillan, 1992), pp. 292–308, at p. 300.
32. Eric Mottram, 'Conversation with Roy Fisher' [22 January 1973], *Saturday Morning*, 1 (Spring 1976), unpaginated [pp. 2ff.]; 'A Tuning Phenomenon: An Interview with Roy Fisher', *Sad Traffic*, 5 (1971), pp. 31–34, at pp. 32–33.
33. Elizabeth Clegg, 'Arnold Böcklin', in *The Dictionary of Art*, ed. Jane Turner, 34 vols. (London: Macmillan, 1996), vol. 4, pp. 203–07, at p. 205; ' "Come to Think of It, the Imagination" ', p. 98; cf. blurb of *Matrix* (London: Fulcrum Press, 1971).
34. 'Conversation', [p. 6].
35. Rasula and Erwin, 'Interview', p. 20.
36. 'Matrix', *P55–80*, pp. 87–94, at p. 90.
37. Rasula and Erwin, 'Interview', p. 23; cf. p. 29.
38. 'Roy Fisher Talks to Peter Robinson', *Granta*, 76 (June 1977), pp. 17–19, at p. 18, where the poet misquotes 'Beyond . . .' for 'Beside . . .'.
39. 'Interview: Roy Fisher by Helen Dennis' [9 May 1984], University of Warwick, typescript, pp. 126–40, at p. 138, quoting *Marriage*, plate 7.
40. 'Interview: Roy Fisher by Helen Dennis', p. 139, quoting Blake's letter to Thomas Butts, 22 November 1802.
41. See Rasula and Erwin, 'Interview', p. 16.
42. *Turning the Prism*, p. 13.
43. 'How Many Voices You Got?': The John Wilkinson Interview, Part 2' [remarks gathered by Andrew Duncan, August 1992], *Angel Exhaust*, 9 (Summer 1993), pp. 60–78, at p. 71; *The Interior Planets*, subscribed '*Birmingham 1986–1990*', can be found in Wilkinson's *Flung Clear: Poems in Six Books* (Brighton: Parataxis, 1994).
44. *A Furnace* (Oxford: Oxford University Press, 1986), p. 35.

45. 'Interview: Roy Fisher by Helen Dennis', p. 139, noting the scramble which ensues: 'I don't mean to hog tie myself with that although I know very well that that's present but again I don't—I suppose I could equally say that I go into the imagination because my reaction to what looks like a moment, an event, a chartable, plottable, timeable event, in which a thing like that little thunder storm happens . . . my immediate reaction to that is that of a cat being put on a lead or put in a basket—rather than a dog: "How the Hell can I get out of this?".'
46. Leslie G. Ungerleider and Mortimer Mishkin, 'Two Cortical Visual Systems', in *Analysis of Visual Behavior*, ed. David J. Ingle, Melvyn A. Goodale and Richard J. W. Mansfield (Cambridge, MA: MIT Press, 1982), pp. 549–86. For a current overview see Melvyn A. Goodale, 'One Visual Experience, Many Visual Systems', in *Attention and Performance XVI: Information Integration in Perception and Communication*, ed. Toshio Inui and James L. McClelland (Cambridge, MA: MIT Press, 1996), pp. 369–93.
47. John O'Keefe, 'Kant and the Sea-Horse: An Essay in the Neurophilosophy of Space', in *Spatial Representation: Problems in Philosophy and Psychology*, ed. Naomi Eilan, Rosaleen McCarthy and Bill Brewer (Oxford: Basil Blackwell, 1993), pp. 43–64, at p. 44.
48. Thomas Mann, *Doctor Faustus: The Life of the German Composer Adrian Leverkühn as Told by a Friend*, tr. H. T. Lowe-Porter (London: Secker & Warburg, 1949), 269–70.
49. 'On Measure—Statement for Cid Corman' (1954), *Selected Essays of William Carlos Williams* (New Directions: New York, 1969), pp. 337–40, at pp. 337–38. This piece first appeared in 1954, in the magazine *Origin*, where Fisher published poetry in 1953 and 1955. Cf. Williams, 'The Poem as a Field of Action' (1948), *Selected Essays*, pp. 280–91, at pp. 282–83, 286.
50. *P55–80*, pp. 115–16.
51. Quoted from Emerson's essay 'Experience' by Ian F. A. Bell and Meriel Lland, in 'Osmotic Investigations and Mutant Poems: An Americanist Poetic', below, p. 110.
52. ' "Come to Think of It, the Imagination" ', p. 95.
53. A. S. Eddington, *The Nature of the Physical World* (Cambridge: Cambridge University Press, 1928), p. 18. Reprinted frequently, well into the 1950s.
54. 'Roy Fisher Talks to Peter Robinson', p. 18.
55 Valentina Polukhina, 'A Noble Quixotic Sight: An Interview with Roy Fisher', p. 306.
56. Peter Riley, 'Spitewinter Edge Lookout Prose' (a), *Lines on the Liver* (Cambridge: Ferry Press, 1981), unpaginated.
57. ' "Come to Think of It, the Imagination" ', p. 111.
58. 'I'm not very good at separating space–time . . . how anybody after Einstein can separate history from geography puzzles me somewhat', *Turning the Prism*, p. 22.

59. *A Brief History of Time: From the Big Bang to Black Holes* (London: Bantam, 1988), p. 150.

60. *Nature of the Physical World*, p. 165.

61. 'New Diversions', *Poems 1955–1987* (Oxford: Oxford University Press, 1988), pp. 173–80, at p. 175.

62. 'Interview: Roy Fisher by Helen Dennis', p. 138.

63 'Linear' (1957) *P55–80*, p. 2; cf. 'Conversation with Eric Mottram', [p. 12]. 'Releases', *P55–80*, pp. 149–50, at p. 49.

64. *The Cut Pages* (London: Fulcrum Press, 1971), p. 48.

65. 'Talking to Cameras', *BR*, p. 16.

66. Rasula and Erwin, 'Interview', p. 13.

67. ' "Come to Think of It, the Imagination" ', p. 110. For an erudite and contemporaneous instance of what 'New Diversions' calls 'a book of / marked megaliths, the spirals / of the snail shells', p. 177 (cf. *F*, section VII) see Michael J. O'Kelly, *Newgrange: Archaeology, Art and Legend* (London: Thames & Hudson, 1982). Cf. the 'emptied tombs of Bronze Age chieftains' in Fisher's part of rural Derbyshire: 'Roy Fisher 1930–', *Contemporary Authors*, p. 99.

68. *Nature of the Physical World*, p. 51.

69. Valentina Polukhina, 'A Noble Quixotic Sight: An Interview with Roy Fisher', p. 300.

70. Migrant *City*, p. 18; revised *City*, p. 27.

2

'Menacing Works in my Isolation': Early Pieces

JAMES KEERY

Derek Slade's bibliography changes the shape of Roy Fisher's poetry. The impression of a body of mature work with its origins in the early 1960s proves to be mistaken.[1] The addition of previously uncollected pieces brings the total for the 1950s to around forty. The output of an entire decade in the career of a major poet is now on the record, most of it for the first time.

In 1973, Fisher observed that 'my periods of writing have been on the whole separate'; he distinguished 'about three periods over the twelve years ... between 1958 and 1970 ... [with] spaces in between'.[2] In the light of the bibliography, both periods and spaces are identifiable, though 1957, a prolific year, might be a better point of departure than 1958, a lean one. The years 1950–55 might also be considered as a distinct if sporadically productive period, followed by a barren year. The years 1950–73 might therefore be broken down as follows:

First period   1950–55 (1956: no recorded work)
Second period   1957–61 (1961–62: one poem between February 1961 and July 1962)[3]
Third period   1962–65 (1966–70: nine 'false starts')[4]
Fourth period   1970–73[5]

Andrew Duncan's unpublished summary of the 1950s as experienced by Fisher is exemplary in its emphasis on inhibition and reaction; in its refusal to be distracted by 'Russian Modernism' of any vintage; and in its scrupulous account of 'the English literary scene'.[6] In particular, Duncan accepts Eric Homberger's assessment of the impact of Harvard formalism, epitomized if not originated by Richard Wilbur and imported to Oxford by Donald Hall.[7] Locating Fisher amongst 'the poets of formalism, with rhyme and strict metre', against whom he was 'reacting . . . at the outset of his career', Duncan makes an ironic suggestion:

> while Fisher's American influences turned English con-
> servatives against him (but got him published in *Origin* in the
> 1950s), the *chefs de file* of the formalism around him were also
> American . . . Perhaps we could, by inversion, consider him as a
> product of the 1950s, a mysterious decade of formalism . . .[8]

It is indeed illuminating to consider Fisher's work as 'a product of the 1950s', but the process is not a simple 'inversion' of prevailing formalism. I intend to read the early poetry on its own terms and in the light of statements made by the poet, and to explore its context and interrelations, moving outwards to develop a perspective on the period. I shall employ the shorthand of reference to various move-ments and schools, considered rather as allotropic states through which poets may pass than as pigeon-holes into which they may be placed. The bibliography begins tidily in 1950, and the finest work in the second period falls within the 1950s. However, I shall also deal with certain later works, in pursuit of themes arising out of the 1950s.

Four of Fisher's earliest poems appeared in *Mermaid*, the Bir-mingham University magazine, which, in 1951, he also edited. His editorial is a well-informed and highly sophisticated piece:

> Time was, when editors in search of editorials could fall to and
> compose the furious, or the admonitory, manifesto; this has
> been done often enough in *Mermaid* in the past; and it must be
> confessed that it is what we, too, had intended to do. But we
> find to our dismay that such things are quite out of fashion:
> those little magazines which remain, and those which are still
> stillborn from time to time stoutly affirm that they have no axes

to grind, and demonstrate their truthfulness by grinding exceeding small. A university magazine, before the war, could have a heavy political, ideological, and aesthetic bias, while at the same time doing no more than reflect the corresponding tendencies in the body it represented; but the keyword seems now to be, in all fields save one, 'Liberal'—a word which, after the first few pages of this number, will probably be hanging in fiery letters before the eyes of every reader, imprinting itself across libraries and lecturers and everything in sight. In one of the most recent attempts to pin down the Zeitgeist, these words occur:

> More and more people, exhausted by the demands of liberal thought, are searching for a congenial group to assume, or at least to share, their responsibilities. And so the great dogmatic machines—Catholicism and Communism in the first place—have gained an immediate advantage.

Yet while the individual members of a university are free to find their congenial groups, the organism as a whole—and the magazine which should reflect some part of the organic life that is supposed to exist in it—cannot afford to submit to an exhaustion brought on by the demands of liberal thought. Our magazine cannot enjoy the partisan but fevered vitality it might have, were this a seminary or a doctrinaire college of political science; instead, it has to live with the drawbacks, as well as the advantages, of a photograph of The Ideal Girl, produced by superimposing those of The Six Most Beautiful Girls. In our case there are always about twenty, and the risk of blurring the outlines is so much greater . . . We, bearing the burden of that immaculate composite Face, and making no speculations for profit, cannot take sides; but we invite you to rage overhead and all around us . . .[9]

The witty conflation of Franklin's axe with the mills of God, the deft allusion to the re-election of Churchill and the mocking image of 'fiery letters before the eyes' for the ubiquity of the new 'keyword' would have graced the *Times Literary Supplement*, though it would be difficult to determine whether it is 'furious' dogmatism or blurry liberalism that is the more cuttingly ironized. The editorial might be interpreted as a single elaborate sarcasm, from the parodic opening narrative gesture and vignette of the time-serving hack to the facetious closing fantasy and invitation.

What is clear is that Fisher's own attempt 'to pin down the Zeitgeist' is more accurate than the one he cites. His account of 'liberal thought' and its freedom from 'political, ideological, and aesthetic bias' anticipates the tone and import of three key documents of the emergent Movement. Anthony Hartley's *Spectator* review, 'Poets of the Fifties', commends 'a liberalism distrustful of too much richness or too much fanaticism'; D. J. Enright observes, in his introduction to *Poets of the 1950s*, that '[o]ur new poets are ... "moderate", and of course moderation lacks the immediate popular appeal of the extremes'; and Robert Conquest's more polemical introduction to *New Lines* champions poetry which 'submits to no great systems of theoretical constructs', remaining 'free from both mystical and logical compulsions and . . . empirical in its attitude to all that comes'.[10]

By this time, the 'fevered vitality' of Apocalyptic poetry, together with its 'furious' manifestos, had already been 'out of fashion' for some years. The term 'Apocalyptic' has had almost exclusively pejorative connotations, so I had better define my own usage. A sliding signifier in post-war criticism, it has been polemically extended 'to indict a whole poetic decade'[11] and narrowed to exclude even contributors to the Apocalyptic anthologies such as Norman MacCaig and Dylan Thomas. I shall use the term to denote poetry written in the 1940s and subsequently in the mode of high rhetorical modernism on the 'grander themes'[12] proscribed by Kingsley Amis and in particular on the theme of (im)mortality. Poetically politicized in the 1950s, the themes, as well as the style, of Apocalyptic writing went into critical eclipse, but with hindsight can be seen to have informed both the poetry of the decade and that of the subsequent apparent reaction. What was attacked and repressed as a decadent culmination can now be considered in the context of an unbroken romantic-modernist tradition, with its own disturbing features. As summary evidence for these assertions, one might point to the influence of Thomas on Ted Hughes, avatar of the 'new' poetry of the 1960s,[13] and on W. S. Graham, an exemplary figure for the Cambridge poets, and to an Apocalyptic preoccupation with (im)mortality on the part of Hughes's alleged antithesis, Philip Larkin.

A detailed submission might begin with the derivative sublimities of the earliest extant poem by Fisher, 'Old Man in a Shower of Rain' (October 1950):

> I, lion and lord of the womb am passed,
> Manhood and manhood's pride are gone from me
> With garments of light on limbs, river's creation;
>   The god in me walks naked,
> And now I could stalk like a prophet through those fields
> Crying my truth to men digging in the rain
> Who, listening a moment, with the lovers there under the tree,
> Would see me, a crazed but harmless old man and turn
> To earth's more urgent speech.[14]

Fisher has made a significant assessment of his early poems:

> What is interesting ... is that it was reading Thomas that enabled me to start. It was like one of those astronomical events where a body is struck by another and kicked out of its familiar orbit into a new one, by way of a violent wobble. I came across *The Burning Baby*, then read, along with the gang of surrealist and neo-romantic things I was hunting out, the first two collections of poems and *The Map of Love*. It was simply the spectacle of something apparently quite primal (allowing for the obvious tropes and tricks), a sort of linguistic/imaginative magma, unsuspected innards, the breaking of taboos one hadn't known existed, that shook up my innocence. That was all. I've not returned to those Thomas texts for years, but they remain an extraordinary phenomenon which won't quite factorize out into the visible elements—Welsh, the Bible, drink, testosterone and so forth—there's still something that resists explanation, however difficult it may be to find a place for it.[15]

Such excitement was scarcely characteristic of the contemporary poetry scene, which had yet to recover from the collapse of the market after the wartime boom. In March 1950, the *Times Literary Supplement* observed robustly that 'Poetry is suffering from one of its periodic fits of depression', associating this 'slump' with the 'encircling financial gloom', but drawing some comfort from the latest volume of *Poetry from Oxford*, 'much of it more than promising' (in the words of Professor Bonamy Dobrée, 'an attestation of the vigour of poetic life').[16] However, the section on 'Poetry in England' in a comprehensive survey of British writing in August 1950 is acutely pessimistic, lamenting 'the deficiency in motive power among contemporary poets', taking 'the youngest generation' sharply to task ('Oxford and Cambridge, once nurseries of talent on the edge of new achievement, now display little more than drawing room precocity, and this has been so for nearly a decade . . . a time of woolly romantic nostalgias and sheer bad writing among younger poets') and concluding that 'the economics and profession of poetry could hardly be more discouraging than today'.[17] The section on 'Literary Periodicals' is resonant in its despair: 'After this holocaust, what survives? . . . There is . . . still room, indeed a crying need, for a magazine . . . that will devote itself to the furtherance of what is best and most vital in English letters today'.[18] *Horizon*, *Penguin New Writing* and the magazines most sympathetic to Apocalyptic poetry in the 1940s, J. M. Tambimuttu's *Poetry (London)* and Charles Wrey Gardiner's *Poetry Quarterly*, were among the numerous early casualties of the 1950s. Survivors such as *Mandrake*, and the newly 'stillborn', such as the Oxford and Cambridge magazines, *Departure*, *Trio* and *Delta*, tended to favour the astringently demure. In his 'Retrospect 1950', F. R. Leavis had summed up the years since the publication of *New Bearings in English Poetry* (1932) in a one-liner: 'Yeats has died, and Eliot has gone on.' He refers his reader to *Scrutiny* for 'placing reference' to or 'dismissal' of all of the major 'new reputations' of the 1930s and 1940s.[19] Poetry itself, then, appeared to be in recession; and editors, in Fisher's withering phrase, were 'grinding exceeding small'.

Meanwhile, Hall had commenced operations in Oxford, his 'evangelism' on behalf of Wilbur acting as a catalyst to the crystallizing Movement and informing the publication from 1952–54 of 26 modest nine-penny pamphlets in Oscar Mellor's remarkable Fantasy Poets series.[20] Mellor published six of the nine contributors to *New Lines*, alongside transatlantic formalists such as Adrienne Cecile Rich, Richard Selig, F. George Steiner and Hall himself, and numerous younger Oxford poets such as Anthony Thwaite, Martin Seymour-Smith, J. E. M. Lucie-Smith and Adrian Mitchell, all at this stage dutiful formalists. It is fitting that the inauguration of the Movement by Hartley should have taken the form of a review of these Fantasy Press pamphlets.

Fisher's alertness to this context is established by his editorial. Its aplomb is shared by the single poem recorded for 1952, which appeared in a later number of *Mermaid*. Anything less like 'Old Man in a Shower of Rain' would be hard to find:

HOUGH! HOUGH!

Home from the funeral, the horses and gilded cars,
Prince Androgyno, searching for almonds, found
A frog and a ferret asleep in a jasper vase.
It was surely a portent; already mourning-dim
His ecstatic eyes blossomed in tears, which falling like stars,
Caused the oblivious pair to be deftly drowned,
Engulfing the pointed head and each furry limb,
And all of the frog, who knew perfectly well how to swim.[21]

Exquisite formalism makes a virtue of virtual nullity of import. Some of the properties might recall Stevens, perhaps Ransom, but the cruelly polished decadence, the androgyny and motif of drowning are reminiscent of Eliot.[22] The point is the analogy between the impeccable regularity of the only 'perfectly' anapaestic and consecutively rhyming line in the poem, and the expert technique of the frog, despite which it is overwhelmed by a portentous cataclysm. Fisher's metaphor may be compared with a simile of Wilbur's:

And has this simile a like perfection?
The mind is like a bat. Precisely. Save

> That in the very happiest intellection
> A graceful error may correct the cave.[23]

Like 'Hough! Hough!', 'Mind' is constructed on the basis of an impeccably regular but paradoxical final line; both poems turn ostentatious technique against itself in order to question its supposed 'perfection'. It is not necessary to allege any direct influence by Wilbur: as often with Fisher, it is the analogue that is intriguing, not the source.[24] And the poems are implicitly antipathetic. Wilbur's final conceit implies belief in the constitutive power of the imagination, but in a corrective role as opposed to the radical divergence adumbrated by Fisher in *Turning the Prism*.[25] The 'cave' is Plato's; the 'graceful error' the poetic equivalent of a Popperian approximation such as those of Copernicus, Newton and Einstein: each, pending falsification, a reigning orthodoxy. In contrast to Wilbur's implicit claim to poetic hegemony, 'Hough! Hough!' might be seen as a baroque gesture of self-contempt, originating in stylistic angst and parodied in the simian ruttishness of the title.[26]

The finest of the *Mermaid* poems, 'A Vision of Four Musicians', dates from August 1951:

> The village will soon forget them, and how they came
>   wandering
> As if by chance through the crowd, in clothes the colour of
>   earth;
> Stopping unasked, and playing tenuous music
> That rose in the heat-haze, suspended, hovering
> Fragile as an echo from the journey they came or the path
> They had yet to travel; ancient measures, wavering,
> Drawn by lean hands from the weathered strings and wood . . .
>
> To see them then in fields where the blissful vision
> Is undisturbed; pursue that land where the mild heraldic
> Creatures sport, free of their myths: the ghostly musician,
> Gryphon, and the unicorn – lost his Avenger and Maiden,
>   dissolved
> In a friendly sky; to abandon these formulae, learn the hieratic

Art: but here are avenger and maiden, dancing, prepared;
Become them, but offer no victim; never hear music.[27]

The 'tenuous music' articulates a tenuity of meaning that culmi-
nates in a mysterious series of increasingly peremptory injunctions.
There is an admirable nicety in the deployment of 'wavering'
anapaestic and dactylic 'measures' and, with two contrasting effects,
of the full-dress hexameter. In line 14, in which the 'fading voices' of
the musicians remain 'High in the air behind them, striving still to be
heard', the paronomastic repetition of the aspirate and long vowel of
the opening syllable has an echoic poignancy; in the final line, music
is repudiated in a paradoxically musical sequence of disjunct
but assonantal disyllables ('Become'; 'victim'; 'music'). Including
approximate and pararhyme, seven rhymes are used in the three
seven-line sentence-stanzas. Yet the formal pattern is expressively
asymmetrical: the rhymes occur with different frequency in an irregular scheme (abcabad edafged gcgfcdc); and there is a sharp contrast
between the elegiac syntax of the first two stanzas and the paralogical
infinitives and imperatives of the third. Steeped in *Four Quartets*, the
former might be described as *Burnt Norton* i and *East Coker* i re-
written in the mode of *The Dry Salvages* ii, with its enervated rhythms
and feminine rhymes. In the latter, however, the evanescent Eliotic
'music' is curtly proscribed.[28] If nothing else, the poem vindicates
Fisher's technique in the face of Donald Davie's uninformed asper-
sions: 'the attempt at rhyme and metre (those enabling constrictions
so invaluable to Hardy) is quite plainly an embarrassing obstruction
and impediment to Fisher'.[29]
    A many-faceted, hermetic structure, the last stanza might be con-
strued as the self-communings of the 'mind', perhaps that of another
'lion and lord of the womb', in which the 'anonymous faces / Remain',
as distinct from the minds of the villagers; a resolution to study in the
Apocalyptic 'singing-school' without becoming a 'victim' of its siren
'music' (or sharing the fate of the accomplished frog).[30] Fisher
appears to commit himself to 'the hieratic / Art', the bardic phrase at
an acute angle to the elegiac style with its abrupt enjambement, 'Art'
issuing anagrammatically from its defining adjective. However, in

speaking of the influence of 'hieratic' modernism, Fisher is as insistent as Larkin on an 'undramatic, complete and permanent' reaction:[31]

> Starting to write, in my ignorance, I taught myself to do all kinds of continuity structures with rhythm. I taught myself to go on like Wallace Stevens, or to carry on tramping with Yeats. It was a pleasant moment when I could abandon metre, about which I do know something, and write a-metrical language, which in those days always had to be called prose.[32]

Again like Larkin, Fisher oversimplifies. The meagre harvest of the next two or three years, during which he married a fellow-student (contributor of artwork to *Mermaid*) and became a school teacher in Devon, includes free verse and stanzaic verse and prose-poetry; but it is the stanzaic verse that is most impressive, including one of the poems that later 'got him published in *Origin*'. In 'The Military Graveyard in France' (February 1953), ten thousand crosses function as an academic chorus:

> 'We live for paint, and theorems to suppose
> Among our pleasant rows, and here are stuck
> As life or art, autonomous decoration
> In this good ground, eliminating luck.
>
> 'For Chance it was that laid our boys below,
> Through her malign intention here we perch
> From love of order gravely to consider
> This true career of posthumous research.'
>
> They speak; and their immaculate conclusion
> Is told in paint and gravel all around,
> Correct and paradigmatic for such women
> As hush their skirts in consecrated ground;
>
> Though always arrives some one insane Arachne
> Who spins down every column her black wheel,
> Under which skirt her moving legs are anger
> Striding that slice of time, to her, unreal.[33]

The American influences on this poem, if any, are those of Ransom and Wilbur, rather than those of the Black Mountain poets with whom Cid Corman's *Origin* is primarily associated. As in 'Hough! Hough!', an 'immaculate conclusion' is contemptuously ironized; and as in 'A Vision of Four Musicians', elegiac formalism is consummately disrupted. The poem might be interpreted as an attack on careerism and on the 'posthumous research' by which a unique 'life or art' is 'consecrated' and homogenized. Both 'Avenger and Maiden', Arachne expresses the poet's own 'anger'. Yet, in contrast to the demure widows, 'their sex tucked up inside them' (stanza 2), she is also imagined as a black widow spider, a 'black wheel' with 'moving legs', suggesting both mariticide and castration.

In contrast, *Three Early Pieces*, exercises in 'verbal automatism',[34] represent the young poet as a delirious surrealist. 'Piano' (November 1953), the only poem, is the feeblest of the three ('sea-brine saps his banded legs, / though to his candy tunes / sad parasols revolve'). In the malarial hallucinations of 'The Doctor Died' (*circa* March 1954), delirium is itself grounded in literal content: 'A bad fly bit him. There in the soft hillocks through the olive arch behind his breast, that gold-and-green angular fly from the laughing parrot-woods laid its own chuckle with a jab and a pinch...' The only moment of significance occurs in 'Pharoah's Dream' (*circa* March 1954), in which a parodic Freudian liturgy reveals a Ruskinian revulsion from pubic hair, anticipating the poet's later work: 'Foetus is central, a nexine; where nexus is, let no man show, Amen, hairs...'

I would propose Fisher's first published poem as a more authentic point of departure. It also dates from March 1954, two years before its appearance in *The Window*. Edited by John Sankey, proprietor of a London printing business, this obscure little magazine ran to nine issues between 1951 and 1956, gaining a reputation for openness to 'experimental' writing.[35] Consisting of 50 quarto pages and featuring, besides Fisher, Gael Turnbull, Christine Brooke-Rose and Patricia Beer, the final issue bears out the editor's sense of a direction 'counter to ... the current movement in poetry' and signals the emergence of (what might have been) a significant forum, in the barren middle of the decade, for indigenous, continental and transatlantic 1950s modernism. *Artisan* aside, there is nothing of the kind before *Migrant* at the decade's end.[36] Turnbull was 'so struck' by Fisher's contribution that he 'wrote to him c/o the magazine' and proceeded to introduce him to the transatlantic avant garde.[37] It is the most compelling of the early poems, 'a bitter and perfect fruit'. The pressure on its watertight construction is intense, allowing neither pathos nor eroticism to seep through, and subjecting narrative and figurative meaning to Apocalyptic overdetermination:

THE LEMON BRIDE

She grew as child, a bitter and perfect fruit,
Her lemon-face, her bewildered goose-glances
Closing on grimy tears, while painfully
Sounded the round bells of her querulous voices.

A time of urine, sunlight and shaking cold,
The dull hair curving like knives about her ears;
Her mind was metal, a power come in too soon,
Ringed thoughts breaking inwards on stumbling fears.

Acid burn iron, lemon to rind-in grief;
So she was perfect, having no world for wrath,
Uncut unharmed, enclosed: in that early pity
So she was child, shaped like a waiting death.

This waxen man, cold as the melon moon,
Ranging abroad, from fire and salt tide free,
Mere thought and earth, in stillness watched by her
And stood about her as a weather tree,

But she was hardened far, beyond his comfort,
No outside weather could nettle or soothe that skin
Nurtured in frost and damp; nor might caresses
Make any path for calm love to come in.

Smooth as a creamy stone or a sea-worn bough,
He stayed impassive, his first forcings gone;
And, stealing her vacant youth, became for her
A wax thought for all pains to fasten on.

And when she knew him with her, the shuddering girl
Clenched on the bough through hatred; her grief and rage,
For ever now unleashed from the clinging fruit,
Lashed at the strong master of her undreamed age.

She kept under savage daylight her still-blind womb,
Still lemon womb; and a scattered soundless rain
Opened her shifting world, where a dark sky shadowed
Great figures, ominous, comforting, tall beyond pain.

I intend to compare 'The Lemon Bride' with a paradigm of 'the current movement' by Larkin, written in February 1950, an analogue rather than a source.[38] 'Deceptions' too excludes eroticism, but allows pathos the duration of 'the unhurried day' and of a nine-line stanza (the extra unrhymed second line a startling formal mimesis of an intrusive 'gulp'). Larkin's epigraph from Mayhew is a direct quotation of a rape-victim's own words. Her shame is exposed by the forbidding and implacable figure of 'light', a personification of patriarchal retribution; and her alienation from the precisely defined environment of 'bridal London' is absolute.

In contrast, 'The Lemon Bride' is a linguistic and mythopoeic construct in a minimally defined environment. The bride's world of protean compulsions and impingements is more akin to that of Blake's 'Visions of the Daughters of Albion'. A 'lemon' is bitter even when ripe, and 'a perfect fruit' might imply ripeness, or, in a girl, puberty; however, there are implications of younger childhood in the images of 'grimy tears', 'urine' and 'shaking cold'. In a different context, the phrase 'Nurtured in frost and damp' would carry angry and empathetic irony, as in Larkin's simile of the 'drawer of knives'. The contrasting simile in 'The Lemon Bride', 'dull hair curving like knives', is a blunting and deflecting of pathos, one of several images of ambiguous self-sufficiency and force that qualify, or outweigh, the images of vulnerability. The relationship between 'fruit', 'bough' and 'tree' is obscure, but whatever is meant by the unidiomatic (and unbiblical) phrase, 'she knew him with her', it would appear that a sexual violation has taken place. What is unambiguous is the force of the girl's retributory 'rage' (a surplus to shared 'grief'). If 'savage daylight' is a personification of authoritarian male aggression, as in 'Deceptions', it is in no sense 'unanswerable'. Far from (passively) 'suffering' or being 'buried', the violated 'Maiden' becomes her own 'Avenger', an active and empowered protagonist.

Larkin's passive rape-victim is also, however, a transhistorical symbol of 'suffering', allotted a role in a dynamics of identification that is critical for the poet. 'Deceptions' insists on extending its consideration from victim to rapist, its climax an intense evocation not of the violence of male desire, but of its futility. The strained comparison depends on the shift of focus from the act of rape to the prior deception involved in drugging the victim. As a piece of special pleading, or as a presentation of rape as paradigmatic of male desire, the poem would be indefensible.[39] In fact, the deeper identification is with the victim, in spite of the generalization forced on the protagonist by the transfer of the original title, expanded by the definite article, to the collection, and the currency of the transferred title as a metonym for the Movement sensibility: 'The phrase stands on its head Ophelia's remark in *Hamlet* that she is "more deceived" than the Prince ... Larkin intended that his adaptation should summarize the book's mood of restrained self-awareness...'[40] There are good grounds for questioning Motion's account of what 'Larkin intended'. Decontextualization could hardly go further than to transmute the traumatization of a rape-victim into 'restrained self-awareness'. On the contrary, complicity conceals an agonized repudiation of desire and a self-dedication to 'suffering'. The victim of rape is vouchsafed an 'exact' apprehension of reality. 'Slums, years have buried' her, but in and as text she is agonizingly alive. The implication is that such apprehension exacts a degree of suffering for which rape is not an excessive metaphor. Larkin associates male sexuality with violence, self-deception and futility; female sexuality with suffering, intensity of vision and immortality. Identifying with the latter, he presents the poetic vocation as a kind of martyrdom.[41]

'Deceptions' is central to the journalistic phenomenon of the Movement, supplying its posture of aggressive yet complacent scepticism with a defining phrase. Yet it is also at the heart of a personal poetics of immortality through suffering and of the

contemporary conversation about sex, violence and poetic achievement to which Fisher's early poetry is a significant, if hitherto
unheard, contribution. Larkin's partial repudiation of Yeats in favour
of Hardy is the outcome of a complex negotiation, hinging on a
willingness to redefine but a refusal to relinquish his conception of
artistic immortality. The crucial nexus is 'Leda and the Swan', an
erotic fantasizing of Leda's reaction to divine rape, which is implicitly
condoned: how can she—and why should she want to—resist a
god?[42] Yeats focusses, like Larkin, on the male orgasm, the 'shudder
in the loins' and 'that white rush'; and, unlike Larkin, on the 'brute
blood' and 'burning... tower' of the male organ. He implies no sense
of post-coital desolation, however; the sonnet climaxes in an an-
nunciation of sexual and esoteric 'knowledge', knowledge, in fact, of
immortality, of deliverance from the state in which sex 'engenders'
only death. For Yeats, 'his knowledge' is exclusively masculine,
except as vouchsafed to the 'mastered' female, a medium to be
subdued by and imbued with the power of immortal art. Yeats's
identification with predatory divinity contrasts with Larkin's identification with the victim of rape.

If 'Deceptions' and 'Leda and the Swan' are contrasting allegories
of poetic inspiration, an allegorical reading of 'The Lemon Bride'
might also begin with its dynamics of identification. The 'waxen man'
is the antithesis of the girl, 'melon' a bland anagram of 'lemon'. Their
incompatibility is graphed by a series of binary oppositions ('inward'
/ 'abroad'; 'stumbling' / 'ranged'; 'enclosed' / 'free'; 'hardened' /
'waxen') and he is constituted almost entirely by words which
connote passivity. A shadow of 'the brute blood of the air' by which
Leda is 'mastered', he is described as 'the strong master' only at the
moment of his disappearance, having been onomatopoeically flayed
alive ('unleashed . . . Lashed'). His 'forcings' find no image, while his
phallic 'bough' bears the brunt of the girl's hatred, 'shuddering', as
contrasted with an involuntary 'shudder in the loins', denoting active
strength, intensified in 'Clenched', as in fist, but also as in teeth or the
misogynistic image of the *vagina dentata*.

Yet, despite the deflection of pathos, it is hard to resist a sense of
identification with 'The Lemon Bride'. This is most nearly explicit in

the last stanza: 'She kept under savage daylight her still-blind womb, /
Still lemon womb . . .' The lingering soft-consonantal quality of the
last phrase has connotations of repose; of a painterly still-life (though
the title might sardonically suggest a floating figure of Chagall's); of a
paradoxical fruitfulness; and of admirable persistence or defiance. If
'still-blind' carries suggestions of 'still-born', recalling 'shaped like a
waiting death', its main implication seems to be that the child's
'lemon womb' has survived her violation. Still sexually immature,
she is neither infertile nor pregnant; nor, specifically, the gestating
source of the antithetical 'Great figures'.

'The Lemon Bride' differs from 'Deceptions' and 'Leda and the
Swan' in that the violation of its protagonist is not a metaphor for
inspiration, but rather for its opposite. The 'girl' is not only a realistic
child from a 'tough Birmingham primary school' such as the one
attended by Fisher,[43] but also an immature poet who suffers English
culture as an infliction. The 'waxen man' is a cipher for the culture of
the 1950s. He is clearly akin to the 'absorbent, malleable selves' constituted by the kind of 'speciously democratic' authority of which
Fisher is mistrustful,[44] and to the blurred 'Ideal Girl' produced by
'democratic' superimposition. If he were to take on a definite identity
and rewrite 'The Lemon Bride' in his own style, he might produce
something not unlike 'Swan Village (*Birmingham—Wolverhampton New
Road*)':[45]

> Did it turn out a goose? Did some loose liver,
> Teetering homewards, run into a sheet?
> Or was it some conurban Bernadette, who met
> That white display of where the road would never stray . . . ? . . .
>
> Or did some fierce and backward god, mad
> For a female hand, land with lashing feathers and,
> Finding Lemnos but no Leda, leave a
> Noun generic to a dismal field, a file of houses, and a derrick?

As editor of *Mermaid*, Fisher had printed Enright ('The Dead
Egyptian Cat', vol. xviii no. 1, Autumn 1951), but might have
resented this sustained sneer of a poem, so close to home. It isn't even

funny, just a blurry superimposition of one condescending image on another. The 'dismal' pedantry of 'Lemnos but no Leda' finds an echo in the charmless affectation of internal rhyme. This is Oxford formalism (the 'Noun generic' which numbers Enright in its Cambridge contingent) at its emptiest. As for 'some conurban Bernadette'. . .

The closest analogue to 'The Lemon Bride' is by Geoffrey Hill (like Fisher, Larkin and Enright, a native of the Midlands). Fisher could not have known 'Metamorphoses' 5 in 1954,[46] yet its four quatrains contain over a dozen lexical parallels: 'he'; 'she('d)'; 'path'; 'love'; '(out)weather'; 'sun(-clouded)'; '(marsh)world'; 'sea'; 'tide'; 'gone'; 'stone'; 'dark(ness)'; 'clenched'; 'salt'; 'burn(ed)'; an inventory of the elements of an archetypal family romance. Hill's protagonist might also be described as a linguistic and mythopoeic construct in a minimally defined environment. In both poems, there is an association between oppressive love and prevailing weather, and an oxymoronic contrast between unilluminating light and revealing darkness. Revulsion against 'love' results in sexual violence that results in turn in a dramatic change of perspective.

The difference is in the dynamics of identification. Hill's protagonist is male and the poem is a plea on behalf of the 'extremities' to which he is 'pitched'. His violence is self-inflicted but nevertheless vitriolically misogynistic: 'he tore his flesh-root and was gone, / Driven by sulphurous blood and a clenched heart'. Self-castration bears the connotative weight of ascetic Christianity. 'His love', on the other hand, is associated with the middle-'ground' of temporal property and commitments, and sunlight is symbolically female rather than male, belonging to Blake's (and Yeats's) world of generation. One is enjoined to 'grant' that the 'spirit' liberated from the 'flesh' will be able to plumb the depths and aspire to the heights of a love beyond the limits of mortality.

Nevertheless, the affinity is striking. Here are firm grounds for one of Fisher's more enigmatic pronouncements: 'I could have come out, as it were, like Geoffrey Hill.'[47] Like Fisher and Larkin, Hill is deeply implicated in the Apocalyptic obsession with martyrdom and (im)mortality. His conclusion fuses a number of potent images: the 'flesh' as a drowned body washed ashore for cremation, but also clothing cast off by the 'spirit' to be 'bleached' in the sun. An immediate point of reference within *For the Unfallen* is 'The Death of Shelley', which is seeded with tropes of immortality, Shelley's own perennial theme, and which fuses the myths of Leda and Europa: 'The bull and the great mute swan / Strain into life with their notorious cries'. 'The Death of Shelley' is an oxymoron: in 'Metamorphoses' 2 the poet invokes the 'shrines' of his sainted precursors and adjures himself to 'make the sun your pedestal'. Hill's early poetry might be described as a recital of the Apocalyptic litany (or identikit) of 'miracles', 'immortality', 'saint', 'martyr', 'sacrifice', 'angels', 'Pentecost', 'Christ's blood', 'Orpheus and Eurydice', 'Time's betrayal', etc. Throw in 'holocaust' and 'Auschwitz', and you are in business. In 1940s London, at any rate. In 1950s Oxford you might be in trouble . . .

In fact, far from catching a chill in the prevailing weather, Hill was a precociously successful undergraduate poet, with a Fantasy pamphlet to his name at the age of twenty.[48] 'By the autumn of 1953, [he] was sufficiently distinguished a figure in Oxford literary circles to merit a personality profile in *Isis* as one of a series of "Isis Idols" '!'[49] He co-edited *Oxford Poetry 1953* with Hall and the sixth and final issue of Hall's own magazine, *New Poems*, with Jonathan Price. The appreciation of Hill by 'the *chefs de file* of . . . formalism' is a healthy complication, a warning against a crude account of the interrelations between the Apocalyptic 1940s and the subsequent decade.

The New Poetry, edited by A. Alvarez (yet another Fantasy pamphleteer), offers just such a crude account. Alvarez famously divides his contributors into poets of 'gentility' and of 'a new seriousness'; whilst the 'followers' of Thomas in the 'drum-rolling forties' are identified as a 'negative feedback . . . against intelligence'.[50] Yet the epitome of the 'new seriousness', as far as British poetry is concerned, is 'A Dream of Horses', a textbook example of a viciously (and literally) Apocalyptic poem, by Fisher's exact contemporary, Ted Hughes. On the publication of *The Hawk in the Rain* in 1957, Hughes was acclaimed as something explosively new, rather than as an exciting development of the mode of Thomas (itself indebted to Lawrence, whose direct influence on Hughes is equally significant). How much of Hughes's 'supercharged' reworking of English nature poetry is implicit in a single poem (or line) such as 'The Force that Through the Green Fuse Drives the Flower'?[51] Critical blindness to the continuity between the energies and ambition of Hughes and those of the occulted Apocalypse is so powerfully typical of the epoch that it has remained difficult, for forty years, to see Hughes in his true context. Both Hughes and Plath, like Larkin and like Fisher, emerge out of a matrix of influences in which those of modernism, the Apocalyptic 1940s, the Harvard formalism of Wilbur and the Oxford formalism of the Fantasy pamphleteers can all be discerned.

Thus the intertextuality of 'The Lemon Bride' situates it, despite itself, at the heart of 1950s English poetry. The most interesting of the three poems written in the following year, 1955, emphasizes the extent of Fisher's implication in that culture. 'Double Morning' appeared in the Cambridge cousin of the little magazines of Oxford formalism. Founded by Peter Redgrove in 1953, *Delta* was the cradle of the Group, which has been described as 'a deliberately antithetical response to the supposedly tame, formalist poetics of the Movement',[52] a description not even the presence of Hughes can justify. Under the editorship of Philip Hobsbaum, and subsequently of Christopher Levenson, *Delta* acquired a sub-Leavisite character to go with its Downing College address. Hobsbaum's editorial to no. 3 is comically conscious of the reader over his shoulder: 'The editor realises that he has nothing distinctively major; he has rather aimed at poems interesting in a minor way. Cloudy pseudo-philosophizing and decaying romanticism will, it is hoped, not be found here'. It is ironic that the cloudy romanticism of 'Double Morning' should find itself so much at home:

> This long inconstant waking to a day
> Hung round with clouds, fouled with dark smears of rain
>   On passive walls of grey
> That spent-out gusts obscurely trouble,
> Makes a contented window, whose wide pane
> Looks two ways on a world made double;
> Uncertain day, uncertain dream.

I wake under wings, among such wraps
As yield to dawn's murk imperceptibly;
   My limbs succeed to histories that lapse
Slow-fingered into the giant holes of night,
From their persuasions loosing me,
Comforted in this ashen world to remember them:
Dreams of an unknown freedom and appetite.

For I have been through and still am moist from it
Some place of birth in that last untroubled plain of sleep:
   A misted, populous marl-pit
   Where the body's made whole;
And countless human limbs lie folded deep,
Growing in ease under a silvered rain,
In dream-earth's strange and common bowl
Denuded of identity and pain.[53]

Fisher's 'place of birth' is a bizarre composite of dream, womb and mass grave, but the binary opposition between the waking world's 'dark smears of rain' and the 'silvered rain' of the 'dream-earth' is a reassuring device. It is more than coincidence that the poem immediately following Fisher's, 'Other Times' by Robert Nye, hinges on a similar antithesis between Tennysonian lyricism ('Midsummer's liquid evenings linger even . . .') and 'this ashen world' ('oily rags . . . And executed dolls . . . precipitant to ash'). However, there are deeper parallels with Larkin's 'Waiting for breakfast . . .': compare 'Uncertain day, uncertain dream' with 'Featureless morning, featureless night'; and the collocation of 'love' and a 'fallow . . . field' with Fisher's 'love' that 'rests as winter soil.'[54] Both poems are ironic aubades in which 'love' is subordinated to art and both adopt a solemn Apocalyptic formalism.

The bibliography records nothing at all for 1956, the year in which Turnbull had made contact:

> He was then living and working in Newton Abbot. We kept in touch and later met a few times when he had moved back to Birmingham . . . Exchanged poems & general buzz. When I

began *Migrant* magazine, he was naturally on my list of possible contributors and had poems in a couple of issues (1959–60).[55]

Fisher gives his own account of the 'general buzz':

> in about '56, '57, when I made contact with people like Gael Turnbull, Denise Levertov, Cid Corman, Bill Price Turner, I was given a lot of encouragement and a lot of feedback. Things were read, things were published. There was very much a feeling in the air of people willing to listen and share ideas . . .[56]

The auspicious period appears to have been brief, more or less confined to the year 1957. Something of its flavour may be gauged by the relative sunniness of 'Toyland' ('a pleasant thing I did when I was feeling quite good about learning to write'),[57] which completes by far the most prolific single month in the bibliography (more distinct lyrics than in any other *year* except 1960 and 1975).[58] Its mood is so different from the other (nevertheless intimately related) poems as to be directly attributable to the access of fluency. 'Midlanders' (12 January 1957), the first in the series, is a sour edition of 'Toyland', the same scene without 'the paint of stillness and sunshine': 'Sometimes, for a moment, it humiliates the strong father before his children; / They don't see it, but they begin to learn its ways . . . If it stank, somebody would do something about it . . .' Similarly, it is necessary to contrast Fisher's pleasure in the 'buzz' with his firm repudiation of the same poets:

> the aesthetic surroundings were there for me to have . . . I would probably have hit a mode about as free as Denise Levertov and Cid Corman were doing at that time and stayed on it . . . I just felt pretty sick. I was in a very morose mood, very up against it. The surroundings were propitious in a direction which I didn't take . . . That cut me off from the ticket I'd got to run with the *Origin* crowd. I didn't really value that.[59]

In 'The Poplars' (February 1957), a disturbing development from 'The Lemon Bride', Fisher finds a symbol for what might be described as his solipsistic ambition.[60] The poplars are figures of potent but celibate masculinity, oxymoronically freed by 'capture' from the 'net of achievable desires' and from the implicitly feminine world of 'obligation'; they fulfil the phallic function of a transcendent signified. The poet's fear is of imprisonment not in stasis but in action, living, chillingly imaged as a 'cemetery of performance'. Another in the series of funerary images in Fisher's early poetry, this recalls the description in the first Futurist manifesto of art galleries and libraries as 'cemeteries of empty exertion, calvaries of crucified dreams, registries of aborted beginnings'.[61] By a concealed oxymoron, the 'stiff' poplars '[r]elax' the 'iron templates' of experience considered as a state of obligatory 'becoming' (momentarily isolated, by enjambment, as a noun). The poet's unachievable desire is for immortality, conceived in terms of the 'permanent', almost priapic stasis of male art (non-consummation is inherent in the poplars' 'virginity'). In a companion poem, 'The Lover', the sexual revulsion is more explicit:

> To cleanse the gross involvements
>   Of my thick fancy
> Where everything I loved
>   Was spoiled, made heavy
>   With my possessing it . . .
>   My choice was flawed,
> And now, everywhere in my mind,
>   That sullen weight, that naked flavour
> Hector and madden me.[62]

The ascetic glory of 'The Poplars' is the transfiguration of 'what is called my life' into the human-divine 'Man'. This exalted absolute is an avatar of the '[g]reat figures' of 'The Lemon Bride', 'tall beyond pain' in their male aloofness from 'the shuddering girl'; and symbolic of great but oppressive precursors such as Yeats, from the 'shifting world' of whose 'ominous' verse they might appear to have stalked, perhaps in the form of 'figures' of speech or tropes. The antonyms 'ominous' and 'comforting' become synonymous (each a dactylic foot in that superb hexameter) in a context in which 'his comfort' is insufferable, another metonym for the 'outside weather' of the Movement sensibility (comfort is often subject to disdain in Fisher's work).[63] In 'Silence', dating from the week before 'The Poplars', in which he considers his 'solitudes' both singly and in the plural, a comparable image occurs:

> Each of my solitudes
> Should be, as some of them are,
> A cylinder of decision

The 'cylinder of decision' is an echoing Léger-like variant of the 'tall pointers', of which the final trope—'Giant legs of stone / Can become old men's / Crumpled trousers'—is a surreal parody. 'Silence' is reminiscent of Magritte's 'Le Puits de la Verité' (1963), as regards both its title ('The Well / Shaft of Truth') and its image of a grey concrete trousered leg, immaculately tailored and unsettlingly serene, symbolic of an inhuman permanence.

The only poem recorded for the second half of 1957 is 'A Debt for Tomorrow', in which 'this day' is personified as a friend whose 'coarseness jostles, / his heavy beauty disappoints and drags' (like that of the woman in 'The Lover'). Only three poems, none of which has been collected, are recorded for 1958. Yet this is a crucial year. Fisher returned to Birmingham in 1958 to become a lecturer at Dudley College of Education,[64] but his description of 'a grim period' suggests a return not only to the Black Country but also to the 'black and . . . clenched' mood of 'The Lemon Bride':

> when I went back to Birmingham . . . the mood of the work dropped. I became quite fixed with the idea of working over archaic models. I certainly didn't want to go along with the freewheeling American thing, whatever you want to call it. I wasn't being reactionary in the ordinary English way . . . But I was doing things which were written in a black and cool aesthetic . . . black and obviously clenched and strangely self-regarding poems . . . certainly there was a grim period—the *City* period—where the noise I wanted to make was an extra injection of blackness, an extra darkness of the aesthetic, so that I actually wanted to make menacing works in my isolation . . .[65]

The intention to make 'menacing works' appears to have been immediately and spectacularly fulfilled in 'While the Young

Hero . . .', cited in full below. However, Fisher's specific reference is to 'Five Morning Poems from a Picture by Manet' (August 1959), 'very morbid, I think, in their way'.[66] In this sequence, the numerous painterly images in Fisher's poems of the 1950s, particularly in those selected for *Poems 1955–1980*, culminate in 'an extra darkness of the aesthetic'. They go beyond sensuous apprehension of colour and light to the physicality of layers of pigment in a vocabulary of texture (thinness and thickness; application and erosion) that ranges from the bold brushwork of 'a leaning fence-post daubed with rain' to the viscous defilement of 'thought, an uneven slime'.

Manet's 'Boy with Cherries: Study of Alexandre' dates from 1858–59. A century separates painting and poem, aptly for a meditation on (im)mortality, which is what is at stake in a centenary. Unlike Larkin, Fisher does not aim at 'exact' response, either to the painting or to the experience of its subject, despite his subsequent death by hanging in Manet's studio and Fisher's own recollection of the accidental death by hanging of a 'schoolmate'.[67] The bitter kernel of the poem consists of an attack on 'the fiction of understanding', precisely in the imagery of 'Deceptions'. Larkin's tact in apportioning degrees of deception on the basis of 'splinters of fact' extracted from Mayhew might well be considered presumptuous by the 'dead', whose 'knives' are weapons rather than metaphors. His confidence that he 'can taste the grief' contrasts with 'the troubling taste of an alien mouth'. Fisher refuses to be misled into such a 'fiction', describing the fourth section in Apocalyptic terms:

> That, of course, is a very theatrical moment . . . a savage and black turn . . . their death is given ceremony on an almost Yeatsian level. But they're certainly portrayed as dead who have been tricked . . . As if the principles of the world are illusory . . . In which case poetry would have no function but to complain and make sardonic or very highly romantic statements . . .[68]

City apart, 'To the Memory of Wyndham Lewis', together with two uncollected sonnets, brings Fisher's writing of the 1950s to a close.[69] I now intend to take an overview of 'the *City* period', in which I include *The Ship's Orchestra* (1962–63). Within the four distinct periods specified above, I would identify a single extended major period, comprising the second and third, 1957–65.

Consideration of the work of the late 1950s and early 1960s as a continuum goes against the grain of the documentation and of the poet's own distinction between 'composed works' such as *The Ship's Orchestra* and 'assemblages' such as *City*.[70] However, it respects what he has himself described as the 'fluid medium of my inner life'.[71] Fisher's account of 'The Citizen', 'the ghost-text which lies under *City*',[72] reveals the continuity with *The Ship's Orchestra* and substantiates the connection between solipsism and immortality that impels 'The Poplars' with an explicit allusion to Yeat's 'artifice of eternity':

> The 'I' in it was, it must be said, wholly voyeuristic, alienated, de-politicised and a-social: and the text petered out at the point where, after a couple of hundred pages, I decided I'd better make him have a conversation with another human being. He couldn't get a single word out. So that was the end of him. In *The Ship's Orchestra* . . . I did a much crisper run-down of this whole matter . . . taking an 'I' character out of the city and sending him to sea . . . One of the compulsive fantasies of the 'I' in 'The Citizen' was the wish to become, gradually, an area at a time, an inscribed black statue, perennial, imperishable and, of course, well out of it all. Not so much in the manner of a reified travesty of a human being . . . but grandly, more like Senator Yeats contemplating the satisfaction of turning into a metal bird . . .[73]

Fisher has written illuminatingly on his relationship with his 'central occupation':

> For while my relations with other people are—or so they seem to me—extremely simple for the most part, and certainly not likely to generate much paperwork, my relations with my own inner life are complex, shifting and bulky, and over several decades they've produced a great heap of notebooks and journals. Although this mass of observations, sensations, introspections is inchoate, and undeveloped except by move-

ments of its own tides, I've come to think of it, rather than the poems, as my work, my central occupation.[74]

The description of his 'own inner life' as 'shifting' is an echo of the 'shifting world' of 'The Lemon Bride', itself 'inchoate, and undeveloped'; and its association with 'tides' strengthens the sense of alienation from the 'waxen man ... from fire and salt tide free'. Fisher's solipsistic 'relations with other people' are the subject of a sardonic joke in a later poem, 'Of the Empirical Self and for Me / for M. E.' (1975), where the identity of the dedicatee and the eponymous 'Me', together with the image of 'two invisible ghosts', combine to attenuate to vanishing point the quirky sense of intimacy with 'Mary' and to imply that as far as he, too, is concerned, 'My life is for me. / As well ignore gravity'.[75] His description of his own mentality as 'haunted and phobic' is a neat summary of the less whimsical implications both of this poem and of 'The Lemon Bride'.[76]

Fisher has referred drily to a series of 'very manic, very hairy epics', 'my prose masterpieces like *The Fog at Birmingham* and *The Image* which one or two people have seen in past years and have retired ashenfaced from'.[77] There seems no reason to question this, since one might well retire 'ashen-faced' from the hairier sections of *City* and *The Ship's Orchestra*. I would argue that the primary precursor text of *City* is not *Paterson* but *The Waste Land*. The sexuality of the poem is a fusion of a Larkinesque sense of the male climax as self-expenditure and waste (the vagina imagined as 'that dark drain') with 'shivering' Eliotic dread. There is also a strong relationship between Eliot's early prose-poems, such as 'Hysteria', with its disorientation and ironic implication that the hysteric is the male narrator rather than the woman ('I was aware of becoming involved in her laughter ... I was drawn in by short gasps; inhaled at each momentary recovery, lost finally in the dark caverns of her throat') and *The Ship's Orchestra* ('The mouth. Fills the area of vision ... the lips part, widen ... he peers forward; then ... steps carefully over the lower teeth and into the mouth, ducking his head' (*P55–80*, p. 179)).[78]

Fisher acknowledges the 'personal' quality of *City*: 'I was coming

back to the city in my late twenties at a time when it was being rebuilt
... my father was dying, and he was very closely associated with the
city ... over a period of forty years ... my own lifetime was extended
through his ...'[79] Not, however, that of *The Ship's Orchestra*: 'I have no
knowledge of maritime matters at all ... I wanted to be writing about
something ... which was not entailed to any sort of reality.'[80] Yet it is
in the later work that consciousness of his father's death is made
explicit: 'There was a little old man I helped to nurse while he was
dying. His paralysed legs grew soft and feminine, his whole body coy.
In the coffin he was rouged and decked out in satin frills and ribbons'
(*P55–80*, p. 188).[81] Fisher may never have been to sea, but he is, after
all, like the narrator, a white English male jazz pianist.[82]

Every 'hairy' image in *City* can be paralleled with a hairier one
from *The Ship's Orchestra*, often trawled from the 'inchoate' material: 'I
can move about in it, guided by its skeins of metaphors, elliptical
jargon and obsessively acquired images'.[83] The most obsessive is that
of hair itself (hence its adjectival power for Fisher), the central term of
a complex comprising images of rubber tyres, webs, nets and fogs.
Any of these is likely to drag others in its wake: 'the dry, porous grey
fog, webbed with black net. Caked carbon of burnt hair' (*P55–80*,
p. 188). *City* (1961) is explicit about the significance of the complex:
'Sex fuses the intersections of the web where it occurs into blobs that
drag and stick'. In *The Ship's Orchestra*, scarcely a single female figure
escapes degradation. In particular, there are recurring images of an
old woman in a 'black net dress' and with 'desiccated hair', which the
narrator imagines pulling out 'in handfuls' and which proliferates
from 'her scalp, legs, belly' before catching fire in a fantasy incinera-
tion of the 'net / Of achievable desires' ('Pouflam!') (pp. 167–76). The
black humour is remarkable for its wry malevolence: 'If she were
really to go bald her breast would become beautiful ... I have to be
sentimental about her, for her own safety' (p. 177). At one point
the grotesque figure is installed in a chair on wasteground: 'Angry
brown eyes, pasty skin in folds down to the dewlaps and scrawny
neck ... Apart from the slippers, the dishcover and a pair of baggy
pink drawers, she wears nothing' (p. 175). *The Ship's Orchestra* stops
short of the implied climax, which has already found expression in a

mock-heroic sonnet (August 1958), a 'menacing' example of the 'working over' of 'archaic models':

WHILE THE YOUNG HERO . . .

While the young hero, white and generous,
Athletic, yet sufficiently refined,
His matt skin glistening softly from love's labours
Borrows a way of things from farmyard neighbours
And takes his pleasure on her from behind,
The grimed old woman, peg-toothed, brown, half-blind,
Dulled in each sense and hoarily lascivious,
Chatters and coughs, and wanders in her mind.

All she can want so dimly still, he gives,
And lets his own lust ride into the sun
Among her black skirts, fusty as a tomb;

Then, as his seed drips out of her like rheum,
He sees his love of woman where it lives,
And for the first time likes what he has done.

'While the Young Hero', one of six poems by Fisher to appear in *Migrant*, was deliberately selected by Turnbull as his magazine's defiant last word.[84] Like this sonnet, *The Ship's Orchestra* is an allegory not only of sexual disgust but also of despair of the saving formalism of art. Immortality is profaned in a surreal charade of the humiliation and martyrdom of 'a man with a giant orange for a head', associated by implication both with 'the actor who must be going to take the part of me in the immortalisation of these days' and with the narrator. The epistemological explorations of *The Ship's Orchestra* have borne the weight of commentary, but these are surely subordinate to its obsession with the grossness and violence of sex and to its visceral destructiveness. Fisher's observation that 'the central intelligence . . . is at liberty to think in metaphoric terms without standing on any kind of pedestal . . . but his libido moves among his thoughts quite freely' is a sanitizing understatement.[85]

In view of all this, there is great significance in Fisher's account of 'Interiors' as 'an emanation from the writer's progress *towards* the human middle ground *en route* from a spell of experiencing his own psyche as undergoing petrification'.[86] In this respect, his 'progress' parallels Larkin's. As Davie has argued, 'lowered sights and patiently diminished expectations' together with the partial surrender of 'the proudest claims traditionally made for the act of the poetic imagination'[87] (including that of immortality) are characteristic of both poets. They are Hardyesque in this but also in a different sense. Both undertake a programmatic disennobling of the soul of romanticism. Larkin attributes his rejection of Yeats to a reading of 'Thoughts of Phena, at News of her Death', which entertains the possibility of the disennoblement suffered and conscientiously reported but never directly manifested by Hardy.[88] Larkin makes a poetic virtue of it, investing in ignobility as his stock-in-trade. His love of the commonplace has to struggle against a contempt for the Bleaneyesque that is also self-contempt. A similar ambivalence may be discerned in Fisher, whose own ignobility takes darker forms but whose evocations of 'the human middle ground' are less distorted and self-pitying.

Larkin could never bring himself to express the satisfaction of having done a day's work, about which 'After Working' (1964) is so memorably straightforward. The poem is a literal enactment of 'lowered sights', but also a more complex negotiation. Squatting by the 'zoo patch / fed with dog dung', Fisher also *raises* his eyes to 'the petrol haze / that calms the elm-tops': the familiar pollutants are accommodated in an urban lyricism that bears out his wry claim to a 'Tennysonian streak', a 'desire to be lyrical, despite all the evidence' (*P55–80*, p. 49).[89] Those 'sunset shadows I sit among' might seem excessively poetical, 'a very good Birmingham industrial sunset . . . well worth doing',[90] were it not for the rhyme with 'dung'. Fisher's mood has more in common with wariness and weariness than glorious summer pleasure-leisure, a kind of happiness probed and defined by Edward Thomas, for whom 'elm-tops'[91] are equally fetishistic: 'But if this be not happiness,—who knows? / Some day I shall think this a happy day'.[92] 'After Working' is less rueful but no less guardedly moved and moving than Larkin's evocation, in 'Toads Revisited', of how it feels 'When the lights come on at four / At the end of another year' ('year' a weighty yet almost vertiginous substitution for 'day').

Another of Larkin's workaday touchstones—'Half-past eleven on a working day, / And these picked out of it' ('The Building')—is troped in the 'Introit' ('12 November 1958') to *A Furnace*, which, according to the 'Preface', 'identifies the poem's preoccupations in the sort of setting in which they were forcing themselves on me at the time I wrote the pieces which were to be published as *City*'. In other words, during the 'grim period' of 'menacing works in my isolation': 'And in the sun's ray through the glass / lifting towards the low noon, I / am bound; / boots on the alloy / fenders that edge the deck, / lost out of the day / between two working calls ...'[93] It must be around 11.30 a.m., 'towards low noon', an exact notation of the winter zenith ('November light low and strong') and an ironic variation on upper-case 'High Noon', the 'flawless weather' (and noble standards) of which we are so conscious of 'falling short' (Larkin's 'To the Sea'). There is a similar feeling of dislocation, yet of being within another stint of lunch, but no sense of cowering in the 'working day' as a refuge from ill health and death, rather a 'sensation as of freedom' that is nevertheless entailed to a complex reality.

The most beautiful of Fisher's later poems is a reply to 'The Poplars' from 'the human middle ground'. Dating from 1987, the year of the poet's second marriage, 'Near Garmsley Camp' begins with the poet and a companion 'searching ... for antiquities', conscious of 'a need / between us to discover something.' They fail to find it in the 'young plantation' of poplars, 'straight pale poles' which strike them as 'stage trees'. However, 'at the bottom of the wood', they come across a 'translucent patch set into / what seems the opaque ground':[94]

> a field-gate chained shut
> and an unmarked meadow, thickly
> hedged round, and floating above itself,
> floating a foot above its own grassy floor
> as a silky, flushed
> level of seed-heads ...   (*P55–87*, pp. 194–95)

In a 'measurable depth of clear air', 'winged creatures swim ... through the stems.' Then the 'strange descent' is counterpointed by another perspective-shift upwards 'into infinite / distance', in which, 'visible for miles', 'a man stands sunlit and hammering / high on Edvyn Loach church steeple'. The 'entire man standing / upright in the sky' is a parodic White Man with a comically crude erection, as well as 'simply Man', theatrical like 'stage trees', 'giving / the game away' by his blatant 'trespassing'. Appropriately, the illustration by Caroline Hands (in the Hereford card-poem edition) depicts not a workman but a 'towering' figure the height of the steeple, something like 'The Angel of the North'. In contrast, the vision of low ('a foot above its own grassy floor'), enclosed ('chained shut') and finite ('measurable') fecundity is an ironic plenitude. Hands's illustration of the meadow is as delicate and suffused, yet also as amusing, as the text. One might interpret the poem as an epithalamium.

NOTES

1. *Collected Poems 1968* (London: Fulcrum Press, 1969) begins with a section entitled 'Early Poems', containing six undated poems, followed by the revised text of *City*. *Poems 1955–1980* (Oxford: Oxford University Press, 1980) is unsectioned, with 11 poems preceding *City* (Slade reveals that the contents of this volume are arranged, with one or two exceptions, in exact chronological order). *Poems 1955–1987* (Oxford: Oxford University Press, 1988) is an identical reprint of *Poems 1955–1980*, with an additional section. *The Dow Low Drop: New and Selected Poems* (Newcastle upon Tyne: Bloodaxe Books, 1996) begins with *City* and includes only four of the eleven. None of these volumes makes any reference to *Three Early Pieces* (London: Transgravity Advertiser, 1971), which includes a poem and two prose-poems dating from 1953–54.

2. Jed Rasula and Mike Erwin, 'An Interview with Roy Fisher', in Roy Fisher, *Nineteen Poems and an Interview* (Pensnett, Staffs: Grosseteste Press, 1975), p. 22.

3. 'Chirico' (22 November 1961) contains a definitive image of writer's block: 'I read a typewriter of stone' (*P55–80*, p. 32).

4. 'I had been almost completely blocked for four years … I even gave up adding to the file of self-strangulated false starts' ('The Cut Pages', *The Cut Pages* (London: Oasis Shearsman, reissue, 1986), p. 8). 'The Cut Pages' is a prose introduction to the reissue of the text and is dated June 1986.

5. '[T]he … inhibitors … had been burnt away and would probably never bother me again' (*ibid.*, p. 9).

6. Andrew Duncan, 'Roy Fisher', draft chapter of forthcoming book on con-

temporary British poetry. According to Fisher himself, the 'tag about my "Russian Modernism" is splendidly wrong and devilishly adhesive' (letter to John Kerrigan, 26 November 1997).

7. Eric Homberger, *The Art of the Real: Poetry in England and America since 1939* (London: Dent, 1977), pp. 86–95.

8. Duncan, 'Roy Fisher'.

9. *Mermaid*, 18:1, ed. Roy Fisher (Birmingham, Autumn 1951), pp. 1–2.

10. Anthony Hartley, 'Poets of the Fifties', *Spectator* (27 August 1954), pp. 260–61; 'Poetry in England Today: An Introduction', *Poets of the 1950s: An Anthology of New English Verse*, ed. D. J. Enright (Tokyo: Kenkyusha, 1955), p. 13; 'Introduction', *New Lines: An Anthology*, ed. Robert Conquest (London: Macmillan, 1956), p. xv.

11. ' "It is impossible to indict a whole poetic decade", wrote Kenneth Allott in 1948, but he was surely wrong. The decade in which he wrote this . . . has popularly become the decade dominated by the punch-drunk Apocalypse [and] by a wartime hysteria which could only have produced such rubbish' (Ian Hamilton, 'The Forties' (1964), *A Poetry Chronicle: Essays and Reviews* (London: Faber & Faber, 1973), p. 55). Hamilton re-enacts the double-bluff whereby the Apocalypse could be denied intrinsic interest yet identified with an entire decade (his only purpose is to retrieve a few uniformed poets from the débâcle). See Arthur Edward Salmon, *Poets of the Apocalypse* (Boston: Twayne Publishers, 1983), p. 23, and Andrew Crozier's seminal article, 'Thrills and Frills: Poetry as Figures of Empirical Lyricism', in *Society and Literature, 1945–70*, ed. Alan Sinfield (London: Methuen, 1983), pp. 199–233.

12 Kingsley Amis, untitled contributor's note in *Poets of the 1950s*, p. 17. Amis's 'grander themes' are those with which, according to Enright, the good poet is 'far too modest, or too wise, to deal directly' ('The Significance of *Poetry London*', *The Critic*, 1, ed. Wolf Mankowitz, Clifford Collins and Raymond Williams (Mistley, Essex: Spring 1947), p. 8). This article is the earliest 'wholesale dismissal' of the 1940s by a Movement writer, albeit also an orthodox Scrutineer (A. T. Tolley, *The Poetry of the Forties* (Manchester: Manchester University Press, 1985), p. 277).

13. 'Introduction: The New Poetry, or Beyond the Gentility Principle', in *The New Poetry*, ed. A. Alvarez (Harmondsworth: Penguin, 1962). Anthony Thwaite, perhaps the last poet one would associate with Thomas, has testified to 'my conviction that the way of Dylan Thomas was the only hope for poetry' ('A Few Memories in Homage', *Poetry Dimension 2: A Living Record of the Poetry Year*, ed. Danny Abse (London: Abacus/Sphere, 1974), p. 234); and Thom Gunn writes as follows: 'One morning I read in the *News Chronicle* of Dylan Thomas's death . . . I went round to Karl [Miller]'s room and . . . left a solemn little note on his mantelpiece: "This is a black day for English poetry" ' ('My Cambridge', *Poetry Dimension Annual 5: The Best of the Poetry Year*, ed. Danny Abse (London: Robson Books, 1978), p. 169).

14. *Mermaid*, 18:3, ed. R. A. Foakes (Birmingham, June 1951), pp. 9–10; lines 34–42 (of 55) are cited.

15. Letter to James Keery, 1 June 1998. Compare the implications of a previous apology: 'The first poem I wrote, when I was nineteen, was a cheap trip through Dylan Thomas's stage properties. Nobody who's read me in print since would believe that . . . I've never revealed it to anybody' ('John Tranter Interviews Roy Fisher', *Jacket* (http://www.jacket.zip.com.au./jacket01/fisheriv.html), 29 March 1989, p. 3).

16. 'Poet and Public' (leader), *Times Literary Supplement*, 24 March 1950, p. 185. The *Times Literary Supplement* carried a regular leader in the 1950s.

17. 'Poetry in England', *A Critical and Descriptive Survey of Contemporary British Writing for Readers Overseas*, *Times Literary Supplement*, 25 August 1950, pp. xiv–xv. This writer has a sharp line in rhetorical questions: 'What critic of eminence has recommended a single living poet in the last year or so? Or reviewed him? Or discussed his work on the BBC?'

18. 'Literary Periodicals', *Times Literary Supplement*, 25 August 1950, p. xxxvii. Cf. Wolfgang Gortschacher, *Little Magazine Profiles: The Little Magazines in Great Britain, 1939–1993* (Salzburg: University of Salzburg, 1993), p. 101.

19. F. R. Leavis, 'Retrospect 1950', *New Bearings in English Poetry: A Study of the Contemporary Situation* (London: Chatto & Windus, 1950), pp. 166–67.

20. See Homberger, *Art of the Real*. Ironically, Hall had been anticipated in his mission to the British by none other than Thomas: 'I well remember, in 1947, the excitement of a reading by Dylan Thomas in Oxford . . . he started a great many budding poets reading John Crowe Ransom, Allen Tate, Wallace Stevens, Karl Shapiro, Richard Wilbur . . . and a dozen more . . . united in being *conscious craftsmen*' (my italics; John Wain, *Sprightly Running: Part of an Autobiography* (London: Macmillan, 1962); cited in Blake Morrison, *The Movement: English Poetry and Fiction of the 1950s* (Oxford: Oxford University Press, 1980), pp. 36–37).

21. *Mermaid*, 19:1, ed. James Heron (Birmingham, January 1953), p. 8. The poem was retitled 'The Moral' for broadcast on *Signature* (BBC Western Region, 13 July 1955).

22. Compare the opening of *The Waste Land* II, which has unmistakable affinities with an inferior poem in the same issue of *Mermaid* (p. 8), 'A Conceit for the Empress' (written December 1951).

23. 'Mind', *Mandrake*, 2:10, ed. Arthur Boyars (London, Autumn/Winter 1954–55), p. 317.

24. Northrop Frye, *Fearful Symmetry: A Study of William Blake* (Princeton: Princeton University Press, 1947), p. 12: 'In the study of Blake it is the analogue that is important not the source.'

25 Robert Sheppard, *Turning the Prism: An Interview with Roy Fisher* (London: Toads Damp Press, 1986), pp. 5–6.

26. 'Hough! Hough!' is 'a coupling remark' © the monkeys of London Zoo, as

recorded in a research study by a friend of the poet's (Fisher, letter to James Keery, 15 April 1998).

27. *Mermaid*, 18:1, (Autumn 1951), p. 31. The first and last of three stanzas are cited.

28. The final stanza might be viewed as a cubist reinterpretation of the rose or blue period lyricism of the first two. Fisher remarks that 'the actual starter' for *The Ship's Orchestra* was 'Picasso's picture, *Three Musicians* . . . and who is to say there are not four musicians?' in Eric Mottram, 'Conversation with Roy Fisher', *Saturday Morning*, 1 (London, Spring 1976), unpaginated [p. 5].

29. Donald Davie, 'Roy Fisher: An Appreciation', *Thomas Hardy and British Poetry* (London: Routledge & Kegan Paul, 1973), p. 154.

30. W. B. Yeats, 'Sailing to Byzantium', *Collected Poems* (London: Macmillan, 1973 reprint), p. 217.

31. Philip Larkin, 'Introduction', *The North Ship* (London: Faber & Faber, 1966 reissue), p. 10.

32. 'Roy Fisher Talks to Peter Robinson', *Granta*, 76 (June 1977), pp. 17–19, at p. 17.

33. *Origin*, 20, ed. Cid Corman (Ashland, Mass., Winter 1957). The last three of seven stanzas are cited. The irony goes deeper: 'Gael Turnbull was collecting material for a guest-edited number of . . . *Origin* . . . One of the people he chose . . . along with me, was Larkin . . . Larkin was sent a complimentary copy of the magazine, to see what kind of magazine he was going to be in. He opened it and . . . sent by registered post a countermand to withdraw all his material . . . our paths were close together for a little while there' ('John Tranter Interviews Roy Fisher', p. 5). The 'material' included 'Church Going' (Turnbull, letter to James Keery, 9 January 1999). The meagre harvest includes 'La Magdalena' (November 1953), five stanzas of four two-beat lines about a 'white witch', evidence of the interest in Graves to which Fisher refers in 'John Tranter Interviews Roy Fisher'.

34. Mottram, 'Conversation with Roy Fisher' [p. 3].

35. See, for example, *Chanticleer*, 1, ed. Patrick Galvin and Gordon Wharton (London, Autumn 1952), which describes *The Window* as a 'stimulating periodical' featuring 'experimental work by young writers, and more traditional work, also by young writers; the standard is high'. Contributors include T. E. F. (Thomas) Blackburn, Corman, Nicholas Moore, Philip Oakes and Harold Pinta (Pinter). A valuable piece by Turnbull outlines a context: 'When I returned to England in 1955, I was excited and challenged by the energy of a whole world of poetry that no one here knew about or wanted to know. Or so it often seemed. In fact, I was far from being entirely alone. There was the almost forgotten editor and publisher in Liverpool, Robert Cooper, and his magazine, *Artisan* . . . There were George Fraser's soirées in London, in the winter of 1955–6, where I took Robert Duncan on one memorable occasion . . . There was W. Price Turner and *The Poet* in Glasgow. Even John Sankey's *The Window* in London' ('Charlotte Chapel, the Pittsburgh Draft

Board and *Some Americans: A Personal Memoir*', *PN Review*, 28, ed. Michael Schmidt (Manchester, 1982), p. 11). *The Poet* was reputed to be less experimental, but its final issue alone (no. 15, 1957) includes work by Cummings, Williams, Corman, Turnbull, Fisher ('Why They Stopped Singing'), MacCaig and Burns Singer.

36. Edited by Robert Cooper in Liverpool, *Artisan* ran to seven issues between 1951 and 1955. No. 4 (Winter 1953–54) is an extraordinary anthology of nine American poets, including Charles Olson, Robert Creeley, Denise Levertov and Robert Duncan; and no. 6 (October 1954) was devoted to Canadian poetry, including Turnbull, who also co-edited the final issue (a year before encountering Fisher). The magazine was a forerunner of *Migrant*, in which eleven contributors to *Artisan* appear.

37. Turnbull, letter to James Keery, 11 March 1997. Fisher refers in passing to 'The Lemon Bride' as 'a very late romantic poem' (Mottram, 'Conversation with Roy Fisher', [p. 9]).

38. By 1954 'Deceptions' had appeared in *XX Poems* (Belfast: privately printed, 1951); and in *Springtime: An Anthology of Young Poets and Writers*, ed. G. S. Fraser and Iain Fletcher (London: Peter Owen), 1953, pp. 60–61), which Fisher is more likely to have seen. *Springtime* features forty-eight writers, including six of the *New Lines* poets, but also several little-known contributors to *The Window*, such as Anthony Borrow, Margaret Crosland, Jane Lunt and Iris Orton. At this date, Larkin himself was little-known, even, apparently, to the editors, who refer to 'Irish poets, like Mr Larkin' ('Editors' Introduction', p. 12).

39. Steve Clark observes that 'Larkin has often been criticized for equating the suffering of the victim with the self-delusion of her assailant' ('Larkin's Sexual Politics', *Philip Larkin: Contemporary Critical Essays*, New Casebooks, ed. Stephen Regan (London: Macmillan, 1997), p. 127, n. 25).

40. Andrew Motion, *Philip Larkin: A Writer's Life* (London: Faber & Faber, 1993), p. 262. Untitled in *XX Poems* (Belfast, 1951) and in *Springtime* (where it is headed 'IV', the second of six 'Poems Selected from a Set of Twenty'), the poem is entitled 'Less Deceived' in *Poets of the 1950s* (p. 81). The addition of the definite article tilts the phrase towards the plural and arguably towards the programmatic. The point of the original allusion is not 'to stand on its head Ophelia's remark' ('I was the more deceived') but to endorse it and thus to identify with her. It is she, not Hamlet, who is 'less deceived' as a result of his taunting declaration. Outside the poem, however, Motion's version of the phrase had passed into critical discourse by 1957: 'All of us owe a great deal to semantic philosophy for having taught us to talk sense . . . So far, so good: we are less deceived than we used to be' (Kenneth Tynan, 'Theatre and Living', in *Declaration*, ed. Tom Maschler (London: MacGibbon & Kee, 1957), p. 115).

41. See 'Waiting for breakfast, while she brushed her hair' (December 1947): 'Will you refuse to come till I have sent / Her terribly away, importantly live / Part

invalid, part baby, and part saint?' The bride in 'Wedding Wind' (September 1946) expresses her 'joy' in images of (implicitly male) violence and responses more suggestive of traumatization, yet also in a proleptic reversal of the 'salted shrunken lakes' of 'Dry-Point': 'Can even death dry up / These new delighted lakes . . . ?' In an uncompleted poem of 1948, Larkin contrasts himself with Amis, who 'seems to live at the centre of gratified desire./ But when my desire is for the past, or for immortality,/ Who can gratify that?' (Motion, *Philip Larkin*, p. 182).

42. Compare Davie's 'England', *A Winter Talent and Other Poems* (London: Routledge & Kegan Paul, 1957), in which 'the girls from the nearest college / of Further Education / spread their excited thighs' (Homberger, *Art of the Real*, notes the sour echo of Yeats); and Amis's 'The Choice' (*Poets of the 1950s*, p. 27, uncollected), a coarser 'Deceptions', featuring another 'bewildered' rapist. The best attempt to 'pin down the Zeitgeist' is probably *Springtime*, in which startling contributions to the conversation are made by Alvarez ('The Muse rapes what the sun can only see', 'Poetic Licence', p. 14), Blackburn ('The spirit carnal in a panting bull . . . Straddles her body with its heavy thighs', 'Pasiphae', p. 20), Gunn ('Hers was the last authentic rape', 'Helen's Rape', p. 47) and others too numerous to cite (Blackburn's image of Pasiphae '[b]lasted and burnt out like a terminal' is a striking prolepsis of Hughes). Also included is a translation by Ruth Speirs of the first of Rilke's *Duino Elegies*, perhaps the *locus classicus* of the romantic-modernist combination of solipsism, immortality and misogyny (pp. 133–35).

43. 'Roy Fisher Reviews Roy Fisher', *The Rialto*, 35, ed. John and Rhiannon Wakeman and Michael Mackmin (Norwich, Autumn 1996), p. 30.

44. *Ibid.*

45. D. J. Enright, *The Laughing Hyena and Other Poems* (London: Routledge & Kegan Paul, 1953), pp. 3–4.

46. The second and third of four stanzas are cited. 'Metamorphoses' 5 appeared as 'A Metamorphosis' in 1958, giving its name (in the plural) to the sequence in which it was collected as one of two untitled sections in *For the Unfallen* (London: André Deutsch, 1959). See Philip Horne, 'Bibliography of Works by and about Geoffrey Hill', in *Geoffrey Hill: Essays on his Work*, ed. Peter Robinson (Milton Keynes: Open University Press, 1985), p. 239.

47. *Turning the Prism*, p. 2.

48. *Geoffrey Hill*, The Fantasy Poets, no. 11, Oxford, 1952.

49. 'Editor's Introduction', *Geoffrey Hill: Essays on his Work*, p. ix. Squarely behind *For the Unfallen* stands 'The Quaker Graveyard in Nantucket' by Robert Lowell, as doubtless Hall recognized. There are direct parallels ('The tough pigheaded salmon strove, / Ramming the ebb' in 'Genesis' with 'Where the heelheaded dogfish barks its nose') but the influence of Lowell's potent and portentous concoction of 'the whale's viscera' and 'Our Lady of Walsingham' is diffused throughout Hill's poetry.

50. *The New Poetry* pp. 28ff., 23.

51. 'A jaguar . . . is a supercharged piece of cosmic machinery': 'Ted Hughes and Crow', interview with Egbert Faas, *London Magazine*, ed. Alan Ross (London, January 1971), cited in Keith Sagar, *The Art of Ted Hughes* (Cambridge: Cambridge University Press, 2nd edn, 1978), p. 18.

52. Neil Powell, entry on 'The Group', in *Oxford Companion to Twentieth-Century Poetry*, ed. Ian Hamilton (Oxford: Oxford University Press, 1994), p. 201.

53. Roy Fisher, 'Double Morning', *Delta*, 10, ed. Christopher Levenson (Cambridge, August 1956). The first three of five stanzas.

54. December 1947; but first published in the 1966 reprint of *The North Ship*; thus another 'analogue'.

55. Turnbull, letter to James Keery, 11 March 1997.

56. *Turning the Prism*, p. 2.

57. 'Roy Fisher Talks to Peter Robinson', pp. 17–19.

58. The uncollected poems of 1957 include 'Variations', a series of impressions of '[t]he city's eye' (and a stylistic forerunner of the recognizable Fisher poem of the 1960s): 'Inside this / shining vastness / men / walk, their steps rustling / around quick stabs of talk . . .'

59. *Turning the Prism*, p. 2.

60. The poem appeared in *Migrant*, 5, ed. Gael Turnbull (Worcester, March 1960), p. 1, with a pattern of indentation and a variant reading; also, thanks to Turnbull, in the 'remarkably compendious and catholic *Combustion*' (no. 4, ed. Raymond Souster, Toronto, October–December 1957), 'a privately-circulated, cyclostyled occasional magazine which included Beats, Black Mountain poets, Californians, first-timers and assorted Old Guys' (Mottram, 'Conversation with Roy Fisher').

61. 'The Founding Manifesto of Futurism', *Le Figaro* (February 1909), cited by Edward Lucie-Smith, *Art Today* (London: Phaidon Press, 1995), p. 8.

62. Written in January 1957, earlier in the same briefly prolific period, 'The Lover' is printed, with a similar pattern of indentation, immediately after 'The Poplars' in *Migrant*, 5.

63. 'Certainly a poem can, if you like, comfort, it can glorify the culture to which it belongs. I'm not at all interested in this' (Rasula and Erwin, 'Interview', pp. 23–24); 'Provision' considers 'the irritations of comfort': 'It won't do. It beckons'; and in 'Unravelling' (28 January 1957), 'My mind is full of images of comfort: / would you like a few? . . . Now / how about a gas-mask? / That's baleful . . .'

64. Fisher has described himself at this period as 'a twenty-eight-year-old teacher . . . sulking my way back down through the levels of the meritocracy' (Paul Lester and Roy Fisher, *A Birmingham Dialogue* (Birmingham: Protean Publications, 1986), p. 23). In fact, he was upwardly mobile, retiring in 1982 as Senior Lecturer in American Studies at the University of Keele.

65. *Turning the Prism*, p. 2.

66. *Ibid.*

67. See 'from The Dow Low Drop', *The Dow Low Drop*, p. 193 ('My schoolmate, D., / forty-seven years hanged'); Ian Gregson, *Contemporary Poets and Postmodernism: Dialogue and Estrangement* (London: Macmillan, 1996), chapter 10, pp. 170–91.

68. Rasula and Erwin, 'Interview', pp. 22–23.

69. 'To the Memory of Wyndham Lewis' commemorates another creator of 'menacing works in . . . isolation', its misanthropic exaltation of a 'white mare' also reminiscent of Lawrence and Hughes. 'Anecdote' takes drainage 'holes' in a flooded garden as a metaphor (and rhyme) for 'poor brief inchoate souls'. 'The Check' forces a portentous rhetoric ('Pain, / Worshipping me, rubs off humanity') on a finely realised experience: 'a crushed finger / Keeps me awake with pain: a spoon-shaped weight / Lolling steady and dull like old flood-water. / I switch on lamps; it will not drown in light.'

70. ' "The Ship's Orchestra" and "The Cut Pages" are composed works . . . "City" and some of the other prose pieces in "Cut Pages" . . . are assemblages . . .' Rasula and Erwin, 'Interview', p. 34. John Matthias compares shrewdly chosen passages from *City* and *The Ship's Orchestra* in *Contemporary British Poetry: Essays in Theory and Criticism*, ed. James Acheson and Romana Huk (New York: State University of New York Press, 1996), chapter 2, 'The Poetry of Roy Fisher', pp. 40, 61.

71. 'Poet on Writing', *Poets on Writing: Britain, 1970–1991*, ed. Denise Riley (London: Macmillan, 1992), p. 273.

72. *A Birmingham Dialogue*, p. 22. The 1961 Migrant version was assembled by Michael Shayer, an ex-student of Leavis, whose influence on the poetry of the 1950s thus extends to Fisher (*A Birmingham Dialogue*, pp. 21–22).

73. *A Birmingham Dialogue*, pp. 22, 26.

74. 'Poet on Writing', p. 273.

75. *P55—80*, p. 125; Larkin, 'Love' (December, 1962), *Collected Poems* (London: Faber & Faber, 1988), p. 150.

76. 'Roy Fisher Reviews Roy Fisher', p. 30.

77. *Turning the Prism*, p. 7.

78. See also 'The Engine': 'The engine hammered and hummed. Flat faces of American business men lay along the tiers of chairs in one plane, broken only by the salient of a brown cigar and the red angle of a sixpenny magazine. The machine was hard, deliberate and alert; having chosen with motives and ends unknown to cut through the fog, it pursued its course . . .' (*Inventions of the March Hare: Poems 1909–1917 by T. S. Eliot*, ed. Christopher Ricks (London: Faber & Faber, 1996), p. 90).

79. Rasula and Erwin, 'Interview', p. 19. According to an advertisement in *Satis*, 2, ed. Matthew Mead (Newcastle upon Tyne: Spring 1961), the projected title of *City* was *Birmingham Poems*.

80. Rasula and Erwin, 'Interview', p. 12.

81. Similar images of narcissism and transexuality occur in 'As He Came Near Death' (July 1964).

82. 'The tones and saying and outlooks and attitudes, particularly of white mid-

western jazz musicians . . . were very familiar to me' (*Turning the Prism*, p. 10). Fisher recalls how 'jazz music came in . . . through a hole in the wall . . . I was 13 or so, and it obviously was perverse, perceptively, not just sexually . . . it was more or less banned in the family', Rasula and Erwin, 'Interview', p. 30.

83. 'Poet on Writing', p. 273.

84. *Migrant* ran to eight issues between July 1959 and September 1960. See *Poetry Information*, 17, ed. Peter Hodgkiss (Summer 1977) for an index, compiled by Hodgkiss and Glyn Pursglove. It was a source of inspiration to the Cambridge magazines of the later 1960s and 1970s. A 'brief survey of the present artistic whereabouts' of the *Migrant* poets, including Fisher, Turnbull, Shayer and Hugh Creighton Hill, appeared in *Grosseteste Review*, 1:2 (Autumn 1968).

85. 'Roy Fisher Talks to Peter Robinson', pp. 17–19.

86. *A Birmingham Dialogue*, p. 27.

87. Davie, 'Hardy Self-Excelling', *Thomas Hardy and British Poetry*, p. 62.

88. 'Introduction', *The North Ship*, p. 10.

89. *Turning the Prism*, p. 7.

90. *Ibid.*, p. 4.

91. 'Thaw', *Collected Poems* (London: Faber & Faber, reprinted 1981), p. 31. See Fisher's appreciation of the 'recurring fetishes of treetops' in Dennis Potter ('Talking to *Staple*: Roy Fisher', *Staple*, 18, ed. Don Measham and Bob Windsor (Mickleover, Derbyshire, Summer 1990), p. 44).

92. 'October', *Collected Poems*, p. 76.

93. *A Furnace* (Oxford: Oxford University Press, 1986), pp. viii, l.

94. Such a 'translucent patch set into . . . opaque ground' may be found in 'July 1960' by Roger Hilton, reproduced in Martin Craiger-Smith, *Roger Hilton*, (London: South Bank, 1993), plate 38.

3

The Work of a Left-Handed Man

JOHN LUCAS

When jazz musicians tune up they commonly ask for an A. I have a pianist friend who, on any occasion he's confronted by this question, balances a pair of lens-less horn-rimmed spectacles on the end of his nose, stares severely over them, and in a Herr Doktorish way barks 'Any particular key?' The friend isn't Roy Fisher though I imagine he will be familiar with the joke. For all I know, he may have started it. Jazz jokes tend to become shared property, as endlessly and unquestioningly repeated as the two-bar tag on 'Buddy Bolden's Blues' or the ordering of themes in 'Panama Rag' (or any other rag, come to that). I suspect the underlying reason for this is that once you know the jokes and the routines—the rituals, even—you're considered part of the brother-and-sisterhood. This isn't to be compared to the masonic handshake, but only because jazzmen and women see themselves as either coming from or belonging to the wrong side of the tracks.

I am of course talking about jazz in the UK, and the kind of jazz I have in mind is usually dubbed 'New Orleans to mainstream'. Men (mostly) and women (a few) who began to play this music during and after the Second World War came from mostly provincial backgrounds and, with a handful of exceptions, were of working-class origin. Jazz became their music because, quite apart from its intrinsic merits, it exuded an enviable air of freedom, gaiety, of being un-English, unstuffy, above all, I suspect, unshackled from the snobberies of class. And in case this should seem to be a grotesque sentimentalization, we need to recall that post-war Britain was, not

86

surprisingly, a fairly depressing place in which to live, and that by contrast the USA, at all events as it appeared in versions supplied by technicolour Hollywood and other forms of popular culture, looked vivid with pleasures of the flesh. Jazz evoked such pleasures and in the UK it was therefore musically and, by implication, sexually, socially and politically transgressive. Jazz was the music of opposition. Jimmy Porter plays the trumpet.

Such opposition can be traced back to the 1920s, when jazz was associated with 'loose' living, with decadent bright young things, with drugs—especially cocaine, and with marches of the un-employed.[1] But twenties jazz often meant no more than the occasional 'hot' number as featured by society orchestras, or imported records played over and over again on wind-up gramophones. Very few indigenous bands played jazz. A generation later matters looked rather different. Most towns and cities now had their own jazz clubs. So, too, did most institutes of higher education. The clubs were kept going by local six- or seven-piece groups who did their best to sound like the bands with national reputations and recording contracts; from these semi-professional outfits the most gifted individuals were sometimes filched for the full-time and customarily London-based bands. These had their own bases—the 100 Club, Mac's, The Winning Post—but they also went 'on the road', playing to guaranteed full houses at clubs up and down England and even at town halls. Their movements and the comings and goings of 'personnel' were logged in the *Melody Maker*, which also carried regular reviews of new recordings and jazz concerts, often stretched to article length when concerts featured guest appearances by American jazzmen and women.[2]

Given all this, it might seem that in the 1950s jazz was a thriving business. For some, it must have been. But most of the musicians got by on comparatively little money. Moreover, the clubs themselves were usually either upstairs meeting-rooms in pubs, drill halls, or made-over hotel ballrooms. They were spartan places, often with an at best rudimentary stage, a poorly tuned piano and either a drinks licence which did not permit a late bar or, worse but by no means unusual, no licence at all. Hence the fact that jazz jokes seem for the most part hang-dog, wryly self deprecating, even defeatist. Alan Plater caught the note perfectly in his TV play *Doggin' Around*, when he has a singer tell a visiting American pianist that her retirement was 'widely reported in the *Methodist Times*'. Not only do jazz musicians tune to A, once they are in tune they announce that it's 'near enough for jazz'.

In the course of one of his entertaining and informative Radio 3 talks with the cornettist Mel Hill, Roy Fisher remarked that 'all my life I've been left-handed,' and he went on to recall that for this form of deviance he'd been caned at school.[3] Fisher was born in 1930, seven years earlier than me, but I too was caned at my midlands junior school for being 'cack-handed'. I was also made to sit on my left hand and practise writing with my other. Of course I couldn't do it. In those days we used steel-nibbed pens which had to be dunked in inkwells. My ink-globbed nib spiked and blotted each clean page, for which I received further canings. Mrs Levitt, the teacher who caned me, was convinced that if only I would persevere I would become ambidextrous. My brain would then develop on both sides and I would be a genius. Roy Fisher's teacher almost certainly shared this conviction. I am not about to claim that it turned him into a poet and jazz musician, but at the very least his early exposure to the absurdities of 'jobsworth' orthodoxy will have encouraged his recalcitrant wit. It also made him aware, as he says in the same interview, that as a left-hander he was using a pen 'against the grain', and that this valuable inhibition prevented fluency.

This may also have something to do with his lack of interest in regular metres. For although regular metres obviously enforce constraint and to that extent may hinder a fatal fluency, they can also permit an unthinking acceptance of the limits they impose, or of thinking within limits. To say this is merely to echo a twentieth-century commonplace, one which has its starting point in the Poundian injunction to break the pentameter. And although opposition to this has the American Yvor Winters as one of its most formidable spokesmen, and while there is no necessary connection between formalist poetics and a conservative or reactionary cast of mind, I hardly need to defend the statement that in the 1950s, when

Roy Fisher was starting out, English poetry appeared to be under the dominance of those formalists, most of them from Oxbridge, who were collectively known as the Movement. Some of them came from provincial England and for a time at least made much of their contempt for the tone of 'the centre', but in truth they were a pretty conformist lot. The fact they were genuinely interested in jazz of the 'classic' period—which covers mainstream—doesn't diminish their conformism, as Larkin's famous anathematizing of 'Pound, Parker and Picasso' makes clear. Fisher, with his early acquired and abiding interest in modern art and in 'redskin' American poetry, stands outside the Movement's fenced-off concerns.

Yet Larkin's passion for jazz can at least in part be explained as a way of licensing emotions and even a romantic yearning for extended horizons which elsewhere he mournfully or snarlingly repudiates. Hence the closing lines of his marvellous poem 'For Sidney Bechet':

> On me your voice falls as they say love should,
> Like an enormous yes. My Crescent City
> Is where your speech alone is understood,
>
> And greeted as the natural noise of good,
> Scattering long-haired grief and scored pity.[4]

The natural noise of good is both instinctive and improvisational. The double puns of the last line oppose Bechet's music to that of trained classical musicians (known as 'long-hairs' in 1950s jazz argot) and to the fully scored music they play—music which also suggests the deep-trenched lines of Niobe's forehead.

For Larkin the voyeuristic outsider, jazz 'licenses' the rioting imagination of his partly cod Englishman: in the New Orleans somehow evoked by Bechet's music, everyone is 'making love and going shares', while 'Mute glorious Storyvilles / Others may license'. The Storyville brothels, where many of the first great jazzmen played, lost their licences in 1917.[5] Renewing license enables sexual fantasy. ('License my roving hands to go.') Fisher's interest in jazz is very different, but it inevitably shares Larkin's Romantic belief in 'inspiration', which as far as jazz is concerned has to be found in improvisation. He touches on this in a long and fascinating interview with the Australian poet John Tranter, recorded in March 1989. Tranter remarks that jazz piano is an American art, and Fisher replies:

> Oh, yeah. Somebody once asked me in an interview years ago who influenced my writing and I said without thinking about it, Pee-Wee Russell, you know, the Chicago clarinet player. And I wasn't being smart. Because I learned that music, I learned it as outsider music, as music you had to go around corners to find. Music that was made *against* bourgeois traditions and academic traditions. I was studying the jazz of the twenties and thirties. And that appealed to me very much, and I could understand the way of thinking of people who didn't want to play the same thing twice ever, and who had for me—and I still admire it very much in musicians—a mixture of good old-fashioned, not too-worldly wise sense of Romantic creativity. You know, tonight may be the night, this number may be the number when I astonish myself, I may hit it this time. A combination of that with an honest artisan approach—yes, I know how to begin and end a number, I know how to play in time, I know how to get my fingers on the right notes, without any 'faff' about personality and fame. There's a basic artisan level in playing a tune in time and in the right key without failing, without scaling the impossible. But at the same time you're always pitching yourself against something—you've got to invent. So I like that combination.[6]

It is of the essence of jazz improvisation that unless someone happens to have a tape recorder handy you never know whether you did 'hit it this time'. (It is entirely possible that Armstrong's studio recording of 'West End Blues' may not be as good as some of those countless times he played the number live.) But Fisher's belief in 'not-too worldly wise' Romantic creativity goes hand-in-hand with his belief that as a poet he has to let the poem find its way. That is one reason 'Why They Stopped Singing', 'because / They remembered why they had started'.[7] It is why 'I saw what there was to write and I wrote it. / When it felt what I was doing, it lay down and died under me' ('Diversions', *P55–87*, p. 133). And it is why, in one of his most famous poems, he extols the pianist Joe Sullivan for striding 'over / gulfs of his own leaving' (p. 52). Jazz, like the poetry Fisher wants to write, is a way of risking the unknown. But unlike such poetry, jazz— the jazz Fisher plays—has clearly imposed limits. You have to play in the right key, in tune, in time. And if you play in a band you also have to rely on others. It is here that improvisational skills come up against the need to fit in with the overall structure of the tune you are playing and the band you are playing with. And as Fisher acknowledges, such contingent factors will inevitably (mis)shape intentions. Hence *The Ship's Orchestra*.

In his interview with Tranter, Fisher says that the poem came out of a combination of dreams and a reproduction of Picasso's *Three Musicians* which he owned:

> where there's a little monk-like figure holding a clarinet, and there's bits of a fourth musician, and I did a sort of you know 'What kind of musicians are these?' And I always sympathise—I mean, I make half my living by being a member of the band that turns up for a gig and say 'Who the hell have we got on bass?' The other night I played one where the bass player was really an accordion player, or a concertina player, and he played bass like a concertina, you know, what can you do? And you walk in, and you try to persuade the people to let you get out alive and pay you. I love this.

I doubt very much whether the subject of *The Ship's Orchestra* would have occurred to anyone who was not a jazz musician. Its deadpan prose is stiffened to comic resolve by the recognition that if things can go wrong for a hired musician then they almost certainly will. This ship's orchestra never even gets to play. Such comedy goes with, is sharpened by, that self-deprecatory manner which, to repeat, is endemic to jazz. It may also go with a self-conscious provincialism. Recalling in the interview with Tranter a reviewer who had claimed that the poet's 'subject matter is, I suppose, always "the provinces"', Fisher adds 'Which is everywhere else but London and Oxford and Cambridge, and one or two rather well-to-do spots around that way.

It doesn't mean much, but it affects the way you behave, and what you root for and what you snarl at.' One or two well-to-do spots around that way: now there's a jazzman's laconicism.

It therefore comes as something of a surprise to find that in *City* Fisher is prepared to adopt an almost Forsterian note of quizzical disdain:

> In this city the governing authority is limited and mean: so limited that it can do no more than preserve a superficial order. It supplies fuel, water and power. It removes a fair proportion of the refuse, cleans the streets after a fashion, and discourages fighting. With these things, and a few more of the same sort, it is content. This could never be a capital city for all its size. There is no mind in it, no regard. The sensitive, the tasteful, the fashionable, the intolerant and powerful, have not moved through it as they have moved through London, evaluating it, altering it deliberately, setting in motion wars of feeling about it. Most of it has never been seen.   (*P55–87*, pp. 22–23)

This is so strongly reminiscent of the cadences and indeed language of *Howards End* as to suggest that Fisher's account is, consciously or not, a pastiche of Forsterian effects. (To *Howards End* may be added 'the plucky, the considerate and the sensitive' of 'What I Believe'.) I mention this only because what feels like a lapse into the pose of long-haired grief and scored pity is, I think, momentary, although it may have lodged in Donald Davie's mind when he came to believe that *City* somehow reveals a desire for an anti-democratic, authoritarian politics, even though Davie concludes that these alternatives to 'social democracy on the British model—mean-spirited as that undoubtedly is—are too costly in terms of human suffering for any man of humane feeling, least of all a poet, to find them real alternatives any longer'.[8] In adding the last two words Davie plainly mourns the fact that late in the twentieth century it is not still possible to believe in the truly strong man. But there *are* still poets around whom I would not readily identify as men of humane feeling, even though Fisher isn't one of them. Nor would it be necessarily appropriate to substitute 'jazzman' for 'poet' in Davie's summing up.

On the other hand, Fisher's way of being a jazzman, his tolerance of contingency, is patently anti-authoritarian in its relish for the absurdities of happenstance, of bass-players who play the bass as though it's a concertina. After all, he was doing his best, and although I no more want to sentimentalize Fisher's regard for an 'honest artisan approach' than he himself does, he patently doesn't think it should be slighted. For once you have this artisanal approach—or to put it rather more vehemently—this mastery of craft, you can afford to welcome contingency. This is not to say that you will always be able to use it to best advantage, but if you turn your back on it you will be unable to find where it is you want to go. You will simply go 'Clanging along in A-flat' without ever 'letting the tenths look out/for their own chances' ('The Home Pianist's Companion' (*P55–87*, p. 168)).

And this of course is why Joe Sullivan is so important an exemplar to Fisher. In a deft review of *Poems 1955–1987*, John Mole remarks that 'the spirit of [Fisher's poetry], as it appeals to me, could be summed up by Earl Hines's comment (though I haven't traced a Fisher reference to Hines yet) that "every night I like to find a different harmonic route to a certain point, and when you see me smiling you know I'm lost." '[9] Fisher is in fact an admirer of Hines. He may even be invoking The Spirit of Earl 'Fatha' when he admits to Tranter that 'If I play ballads, or "Sophisticated Lady" or "Body and Soul", I make quite a meal of them. . . . I play piano in quite a juvenile, enthusiastic fashion'. On the other hand, he does not, as he here and elsewhere says, like what he describes to Tranter as 'any kind of go-go rhythm'. For a similar reason he is not especially interested in 'single-line melody', as he tells Mel Hill. And so even though he confesses that 'I play the piano more emotionally than I write', his interest in swing doesn't at all mean that he works within bar lines or accepts the clearly defined framework of, say, two- or four-bar units. He would rather go 'chasing the horns'.

So at least Fisher tells Hill, and this suggests why, to the best of my knowledge, he does not include Teddy Wilson among his pantheon of swing pianists. For Wilson, wonderful musician though he is, works within limits rather than pushing beyond them. This may be

not unconnected to the fact that Wilson is among the great accom-
panists, as anyone who has heard his recordings with the young Billie
Holiday would surely agree. Certainly 'Miss Brown to You' and
'What a Little Moonlight Can Do', recorded in New York in 1935, are
among the finest of the great singer's pre-war work, and Wilson's
immaculately crisp playing, together with the almost staccato effect
of his right hand, whether underpinning Holiday's voice or Roy El-
dridge's trumpet, seems to me about as good as swing piano can get.
But I can see that, assured, even perfect though, or perhaps because,
it is, such playing is definitely within limits. Nor does it feel in any
way cramped by them. You could never imagine Wilson 'perilously //
toppling octaves down to where / the chords grow fat again'. And
there is never a chance that his piano might seem 'at risk of being /
hammered the next second into scrap' (*P55–87*, p. 52). Larkin
thought of Armstrong as a kind of twentieth-century Chaucer; in
which case it might not be improper to think of Wilson in terms of
Popeian finesse, like the spider's touch which, 'exquisitely fine! / Feels
at each thread, and lives along the line'.

   Talking to Tranter, Fisher at one point remarks that critics of his
work have begun to elucidate and gloss 'things which I've blundered
into, habits I've blundered into, areas of material ... when I say
blundered, I'm not criticising myself—I intended 'to "blunder", I
wasn't doing anything else...' To 'Blunder', the *Oxford English
Dictionary* says: 'Move blindly; flounder, stumble.' To blunder is to
behave in an unpremeditated way; blundering is gauche behaviour.
We are back at left-handedness. More tellingly, perhaps, we can
deduce from Fisher's intention to blunder the reason for his shock at
Basil Bunting's reply to the younger poet's asking him whether
Briggflatts was finished. 'The music is,' Bunting assured Fisher. But
how could he have known?[10] Fisher, whose indebtedness to American
modernism is not in doubt, always wants to make for the open
ground. At the same time, he guards against the risk of falling into
romantic preoccupation with self (self-discovery, self-aggrandize-
ment) which this form of making can imply, may even require. Hence,
his poem-as-manifesto, 'Of the Empirical Self and for Me', which
begins 'In my poems there's seldom / any *I* or *you*' (*P55–87*, p. 125).

Poetry is therefore not so much concerned with selfhood as the happenstance of occurrence. The poem may draw attention to itself, the poet should not do so. Fisher is on record as saying that 'when I do readings in large halls, they have to turn the mike up. The monotone, the low conversation style is quite intentional.'[11] The poet effaces himself from his poem. Yet at the same time Fisher is characteristically the poet whose work is prompted by his readiness to honour the fortuitous. As 'A Poem to be Watched' (p. 182) puts it, a poem comes 'into the world / unprepared', and, 'driven to exhibit / over and over again / unpreparedness', it can become a kind of showpiece, 'habitually / unready to be caught / born' (there is no full-stop at poem's end).

Poems about poems and poetry, the art both reflecting and reflecting on itself, is, it almost goes without saying, a marked feature of much modern American poetry, from the early masters Stevens, Moore, Williams, through Levertov, Creeley, O'Hara, Ashbery, Duncan et al. There are probably quite enough of such poems in existence by now and it could be argued that, while at first they valuably endorsed ways of making it new, they have become so expected, not to say routine, as to look and feel only too well-prepared when they enter the world. For this reason, I much prefer 'On the Neglect of Figure Composition', Fisher's wildly funny fantasy about the exhausted possibilities of heroic representative/ tradition-sanctioned art. I would never dare to suggest that only a jazzman could have come up with anything at once so comic and—let us be honest—piss-taking, but I *can* report that I have jazzmen friends who think anyone interested in poetry must be due a visit by the men in white coats, but who have without exception loved 'Sketch for the First Exhibition of the New Heroic Art'.

Yet this comic masterpiece doesn't require us to identify Fisher with that most tiresome of postmodernist beliefs in the inevitable self-reflexivity of art. Although he accepts that his work is inevitably the product of what he told one interviewer is 'a rather complicated mentality', and although to the same interviewer he remarked that bad readers of a poem such as Eliot's ' "Prufrock" . . . can't float . . . can't just read the score, one note after another', he doesn't take the imagination to feed on itself. On the contrary Fisher is very much a poet to be identified with that modern, empirically verifiable phenomenon, the city.

Fisher's particular city, Birmingham, has, it is generally agreed, prompted much of his best work, from *City* itself through to *Birmingham River*. Yet talking to Tranter, Fisher as good as says that although he's lived in the city for forty years he doesn't necessarily feel of it. 'For some reason I never really swam in the city and was an urban person, although I lived in and around the town a great deal, and was in the pubs and in the jazz clubs and in the educational system of the same place for decades on end.' He ascribes this sense of not-quite-belonging to his parents: 'my family who were working people, who seemed to have not long been brought in from the country . . . they didn't know anything about the country, they didn't know where they'd come from, but there was a sort of strong moral air that it would be good to get back onto farm land again'.

The sense of being somehow a stranger in the city may almost be the defining experience of city existence. You can't know the city as you can the country, not only because it lacks the views by which the country is arranged—all those fixed prospects—but because its endlessly changing vistas, its streets, alleys, thoroughfares, are a kind of discomposition, a denial of orderly vision. All this is familiar to us now. The city as a place of atomistic lives, of disrupted and disorderly narratives has been addressed by writers from Baudelaire and Dickens onwards, and has more recently received much critical and scholarly attention, especially since the discovery of Benjamin's seminal essay on Baudelaire.[12]

All the more remarkable, then, that Fisher's *City* appeared in 1961, well before that attention began to be directed towards modern writing, at all events in England. It's a perfect example of where blundering can get you. (In the early 1960s *The Waste Land* was still typically written about in ways that granted it supreme authority for its evocation of spiritual malaise in the modern world, where 'world' was essentially an uninspected term. It wasn't however seen as a *city* poem. As for Dickens, the greatest novelist of city experience, he had famously nothing to offer 'the mature critical mind'.)

One of the tenets of writing about the city is that the spectator of its scenes is inevitably an invisible flâneur. Invisible because in all probability the spectator will be unknown to those he observes as they pass him by. Flâneur because while everybody else has what Engels called 'separate purpose', the lounger's only purpose is to observe and record. Still, the very fact that the flâneur *is* an outsider, one who recognizes no close kinship with others in the city, can be traced to his pathology, whether as an artist or a member of the bourgeoisie. This, at least, is a familiar enough tactic of reader/critics for whom realism is the predictable artistic mode adopted by those who take for granted the adequacy of their world view. Yet it would be difficult to argue that Fisher's registering of city experience in 'For Realism' is flawed by his spectatorial assumptions. It might, however, be said that at the poem's opening the narrator draws attention to the key word's problematic status by fencing it within quotation marks. The poem starts:

> For 'realism':
> the sight of Lucas's
> lamp factory on a summer night;
> a shift coming off about nine,
> pale light, dispersing,
> runnels of people chased,
> by pavements drying off
> quickly after them,
> away among the wrinkled brown houses
> where there are cracks for them to go; . . .   (*P55–87*, p. 54)

Yet at poem's end, when the word returns, the quotation marks have gone:

> A conscience
> builds, late, on the ridge. A realism
> tries to record, before they're gone,
> what silver filth these drains have run.   (p. 55)

'Realism' is, then, acknowledged to be literary artifice, and the flâneur's knowledge of what he records is initially a matter of random observation. Although he cannot help but know something about the shift workers, it is plain that he is an outsider. To him, such workers are reduced to the near-cliché of ant-like behaviour, scurrying to 'where there are cracks for them to go'. This in part re-visits a moment in *City* where the observer remarks that

> Lovers turn to me faces of innocence where I would expect wariness. They have disappeared for entire hours into the lit holes of life, instead of lying stunned on its surface as I, and so many, do for so long; or instead of raising their heads cautiously and scenting the manifold airs that blow through the streets.
>
> (*P55–87*, p. 26)

Such mournful acknowledgement of being outside the 'lit holes of life' is not a million miles from that occasion when Larkin hears 'The trumpet's voice, loud and authoritative, / Draw[s] me a moment to the lighted glass / To watch the dancers—all under twenty-five—/ Shifting intently, face to flushed face, / Solemnly on the beat of happiness' ('Reasons for Attendance'). It is also one of the few places in Fisher's oeuvre where the reader is bound to reflect that the empirical self can be found, all unguarded.

But guardedness soon sets in. Hence 'realism'. Yet a deeper sense of realism requires Fisher at the poem's end to acknowledge that he may be required at least to *try* to record 'what silver filth these drains have run.' Davie no doubt misreads the lines when he says that Fisher has in mind the

> social conscience of the confident demographer and humanitarian administrator who has demolished acres of the inner city and rehoused their denizens in high-rise apartment-blocks on the ridge above their old dwellings, at whatever cost to the human associations that these dwellings had for them.[13]

But he is right to see that Fisher is prepared to risk taking on the role of recording at a deeper and more responsible level than mere reportage: 'what silver filth these drains have run', by moving out of the present tense, acknowledges that the place has a knowable history.[14] And these are matters which engage him in *A Furnace* and *Birmingham River*.

I can't follow him in any detail into these book-length poems because to do so would take me too far from my subject. I will however note that in the 'Introit' to *A Furnace* Fisher makes himself very much the passive recipient of the scene. He blunders into the visible evidence of city living:

> And the road
> from Bilston to Ettingshall begins
> beating in. Whatever
> approaches my passive taking-in,
> then surrounds me and goes by
> will have itself understood only
> phase upon phase
> by separate involuntary
> strokes of my mind, dark
> swings of a fan-blade
> that keeps a time of its own,
> made up from the long
> discrete moments
> of the stages of the street,
> each bred off the last as if by
> causality.[15]

Such blundering goes with, cannot be dissociated from, the awareness of 'passive taking-in' which is yet actively alert to its own processes, those 'dark / swings of a fan-blade/ that keeps a time of its own'. At first glance this can look very near to a number of moments in *The Prelude*, as for example the one where Wordsworth recalls walking

> a steep ascent
> Where the road's wat'ry surface, to the ridge
> Of that sharp rising glittered in the moon . . .
>
> On I went
> Tranquil, receiving in my own despite
> Amusement, as I slowly passed along,
> From such near objects as from time to time

> Perforce intruded on the listless sense
> Quiescent, and disposed to sympathy...[16]

This too seems to be a passive taking-in, but with one crucial differ-ence. Wordsworth's mind is emptied out, laid to rest, so that it can be properly receptive to a moment of visionary, epiphanic significance. Much if not most of English poetry—and prose—since Wordsworth has been attuned to this idea of the epiphanic, that is to the reception of an image in which is embodied a pure concentration of meaning. Even 'silver filth' may be thought of as an epiphanic image, its con-centration of meaning including, as Neil Corcoran has remarked, great 'metaphoric and oxymoronic energies'.[17] These are inevitably predicated on the belief that there is a knowable, graspable world out there.

And this is so, both in *City* and any number of Fisher's poems. Yet having said this, I must at once add that Fisher's secular imagination requires him to register mental activity in a manner that queries the trust in purposiveness which is implicit—and sometimes explicit—in Wordsworth's egotistical sublime or for that matter in such later expressions of purposiveness as Hopkins's 'thisness'. To put it differently, and in a way that frees requirement from moral glumness, Fisher's cast of mind is, as he himself frequently avows, decidedly, if wryly, sceptical. Hence his disarming remark to Tranter, 'Apparently I do have a technique of describing bits of the world with loving care but in such language as to cast enormous doubt on whether there's anything there at all.' But, he all-importantly adds, 'I don't want to play mere language games.' And so while he avoids structuring poems in a manner that resembles 'realist' narratives, with a begin-ning, a middle and an end *and* in that order, he equally disavows the poem as existing within a closed circuit. Here, what he says of *A Furnace* is especially relevant. The poem, he tells Tranter, is 'accretive ... written in a sequence which to me is musical ... where you revisit themes at various times ... as if it were an orchestral work, certain instrument sounds, certain bell sounds...' And so, for all that it could be described as collagist, as he remarks, there is that which distinguishes *A Furnace* from other modern poems with which it apparently claims kinship. This has most markedly to do with capturing 'a cast of mind ... moods ... ways of reprocessing experience and joining new experience up to old experience', given that the cast of mind of this particular poet is also the cast of mind of a musician. To examine this claim apropos of *A Furnace* would take too long. There is, however, another, shorter poem that will serve my purpose, the 'The Home Pianist's Companion'.

For all its apparently freewheeling improvisatory air, 'The Home Pianist's Companion' is most subtly organized. To say this is not, however, to suggest that it is premeditated, let alone that it has a conventional narrative structure. As its use of participles indicates, the poem depends on a sure sense of blundering—if that oxymoron can be allowed—and its themes are discoverable through a kind of musical development: of statements, of phrasing, rephrasing, re-statement, modulation. It begins with what seems to be an account of dutiful piano practice: 'Clanging along in A-flat / correcting faults ... thinking of Mary Lou, / a lesson to us all, // how she will trench and / trench into the firmness of the music / modestly'. Even here, though, the poem modulates from the semi-automatic 'Clanging along' into self-awareness—'thinking of Mary Lou' (*P55–87*, p. 168). Mary Lou Williams (1910–81) is one of the less celebrated mainstream pianists, though Fisher's regard for her is entirely understandable. Not only did Duke Ellington call her 'perpetually contemporary', meaning that she was never content to settle into routine, but her rejection of the term 'jazz' came about because, for all her modesty, she regarded its use as 'fundamentally reductive'. In their vast, well-researched *Guide to Jazz on CD, LP and Cassette*, Richard Cook and Brian Morton note of her playing that, 'However swinging and jazz-based her solo and small-group output, Williams transcended the conventional bounds of jazz composition and performance.'[18] This is very like striding over gulfs of your own leaving.

Having introduced thoughts of Mary Lou, Fisher leaves her. The poem moves on:

> thinking,
> in my disorder of twofold sense,

or finding rather
an order thinking for me as I play,
of the look of lean-spoked
railway wagon wheels
clanging on a girder bridge,
chopping the daylight, black
wheel across wheel, spoke

over rim, in behind girder and out
revealing the light, withholding it,
inexorable flickers
of segments in overlap
moving in mean elongate
proportions, the consecutive
fourths of appearances,
harsh gaps, small strong
leverages, never still.   (pp. 168–69)

These lines provide a good instance of the kind of writing Barthes
called 'scriptible', 'where a co-operation between the reader and the
author is needed to attain a meaning', and which Fisher is happy to
agree with Ra Page defines his characteristic way of writing.[19] In the
passage just quoted we have to co-operate with Fisher's terse
notation in order to register his association of a certain style of jazz
piano with the flicker of repeated, clangorous wagon wheels (an
image redolent of the industrial cityscape) where 'segments in
overlap' is at once the stroboscopic effect of the wheels themselves
and of echoed and developing musical phrases. The lines are about
ways of playing, ways of seeing, and ways of thinking. And as the
poem goes on so other themes are picked up: the 'sour face / on that
kind of wheel' modulates into 'the eternal / mask of a narrow-faced
cat, / its cornered, cringing intensity / moving me to distraction
again.' And this distraction itself modulates by way of 'the calm / of a
time just after infancy' (p. 169) to a 'primal figure of the line, / pri-
mitively remembered, / just a posture of her, an apron' (p. 170). The
pianist follows a line of music which draws in the image of a railway
line, and *that* line then leads to a reverie where a washing-line recalls

an old woman 'gaunt, narrow-faced, closed in, / acceptable, / soon dead.' This then gathers up earlier, apparently abandoned scraps of theme, before modulating into the closing lines:

> Still in the air,
> haunting the fourths
> of A-flat major
> with wheels and a glinting cat-face;
>
> reminding me
> what it was like to be sure,
> before language ever
> taught me they were different,
> of how some things were the same. (p. 170)

Music is itself and yet makes possible a discovery of thought processes which are ultimately pre-linguistic. Pater thought all arts aspired to the condition of music and Fisher might agree. But he would not then agree that music is the perfect symbolist form of art. For symbolism is another expression of the epiphanic, its pure concentration depending on a Platonic belief in correspondence. 'The Home Pianist's Companion' is closer to Browning's 'A Toccata of Galuppi's', which is the greatest poem I know about what involvement in the act of playing means. And it is of course no accident that a toccata is a form of composition which has built into it a measure of improvisation. Browning, an accomplished pianist, spells out the means by which the man who plays Galuppi—he is very definitely not Browning himself—finds in the music's 'commiserating sevenths', 'dominant's persistence' and 'octave', sources for his own blundering into thought processes which take him a long way from the poem's beginning. Fisher is characteristically more oblique than Browning, or it might be better to say he is less explanatory. But no one who is not a musician could have written 'The Home Pianist's Companion'. And while the title jokily suggests a less than accomplished pianist who needs to have a 'Tutor' propped up in front of him, enabling him to follow basic chords and melodic patterns, the poem in fact pays sophisticated tribute to the power of music to get beyond the restrictions of language and contained and therefore constraining habits of thought. Fisher's way of writing is here and elsewhere closely linked to, might even be said to permit and be made possible by, his commitment to styles of jazz-piano and, thus, processes of imaginative thought that liberate him from intellectual and formal constraints within which post-war English attitudes to culture typically operate. 'The Home Pianist's Companion' is a properly recalcitrant poem, the work of a left-handed man.

NOTES

1. For more on this see John Lucas, *The Radical Twenties: Aspects of Writing, Politics and Culture* (Nottingham: Five Leaves Publications, 1997), chapter 4.

2. From the mid-thirties until 1956 the Musicians Union banned foreign bands from playing in the UK. Visiting musicians had to be accompanied by home grown musicians.

3. *The Fortunate Cat*, BBC Radio 3, 25–29 December 1995.

4. 'For Sidney Bechet', *Collected Poems*, ed. and intro. Anthony Thwaite (London: Faber & Faber and The Marvell Press, 1988) p. 83.

5. In 1917 the brothels of New Orleans lost their licences because the US government decided that the war effort would be harmed by soldiers and sailors making use of them.

6. The interview with John Tranter was recorded at Roy Fisher's Derbyshire house on 29 March 1989. It is available on Tranter's Internet magazine, *Jacket*, http// www.jacket/au/jacket01/fisheriv.html.

7. 'Why They Stopped Singing', *Poems 1955–1980* (Oxford: Oxford University Press, 1980), p. 1.

8. Donald Davie, 'Roy Fisher: An Appreciation'. *Thomas Hardy and British Poetry* (London: Routledge & Kegan Paul, 1974), p. 172.

9. John Mole, 'The Innovative Flicker of the Piano Player', a review of Fisher's *Poems 1955–1987* in the *Poetry Review*, 79:2 (Summer 1989), pp. 27–28, at p. 27.

10. Recalling this in interview with Mel Hill, Fisher adds that he now understands what Bunting means. This does not however diminish his sense that, as Theodore Roethke says, you learn by going where you have to go. (Though paradoxically Roethke said that in a villanelle, one of the most determined of poetic forms.)

11. In an interview with Ra Page, 'People Who Can't Float', *Prop*, 2 (1997), pp. 28–30, at p. 30.

12. There is no need to provide chapter and verse here, although attention should perhaps be drawn to Edward Timms and David Kelley's *Unreal City: Urban Experience in Modern European Literature and Art* (Manchester: Manchester University Press, 1985).

13. Davie, 'Roy Fisher', p. 163.

14. In his interview with Ra Page, Fisher remarks that he finds the kind of writing associated with Arnold Bennett impossible to do without appearing 'patronising and pedestrian', because it provides the reader with everything. See *Prop*, 2, p. 30.

15. 'Introit', *A Furnace* (Oxford: Oxford University Press, 1986), pp. 2–3.

16. Book IV, lines 370–80 (1805 text), in *William Wordsworth*, The Oxford Authors, ed. Stephen Gill (Oxford: Oxford University Press, 1984).

17. Neil Corcoran, *English Poetry since 1940* (Harlow: Longman, 1993), p. 171.

18. Richard Cook and Brian Morton, *The Penguin Guide to Jazz on CD, LP and Cassette*, new edition (Harmondsworth: Penguin, 1994), p. 1375.

19. See *Prop*, 2, p. 30.

4

Osmotic Investigations and Mutant Poems: An Americanist Poetic

IAN F. A. BELL and MERIEL LLAND

When Roy Fisher was commissioned to review his own most recent collection, *The Dow Low Drop*, for *The Rialto*, a review reprinted subsequently in the 1998 Bloodaxe catalogue, he created the persona of a writer frequently going 'to ground', operating from 'various positions of concealment' and moving 'from one patch of cover to another'. It is a persona which finds company with his earlier claim for a 'very irresponsible flirtation with the idea of language' as a calculated 'anarchic' (one of his favoured terms) gesture against the fixities of the 'language fetishists' and on behalf of an idea of fugitive style learned 'very much from translatorese ... a language I rather like'.[1] Such blending and bleeding, such transitional manoeuvrings which mix and mingle with no settled place, are the features of what Fisher has called his 'osmotic investigations'.[2] And this osmosis, this crossing of borders and boundaries of all kinds, demands the personae not only of the fugitive and the outlaw, but of the spy, as we are taught in 'The Lesson in Composition' where the spy's tactics of dissembling and obliquity are approved:

> What I have been doing in the world as long as I can remember
> is to witness and make conclusions. These are things
> you cannot learn unless you dissemble, especially
> if you start young. Like those of a spy
> my words and actions have leaned to the oblique, my troubles
> to the vague and hard-to-help.[3]

The 'oblique' and the 'vague' are major preoccupations in Fisher's stance against all forms of containment (literary, political, ideational), all issues that are seemingly salvageable from 'the whole rubble, the whole mass of tiny interlaced circumstances that carry you along, make the present in which you exist',[4] anaesthetized within the specious safety of an available discourse. The 'oblique' and the 'vague' become strategies to combat what he sees as the 'entailments'[5] of things, those transportable categories of perception and understanding which lead only to a 'sloganizing' of issues 'into an image' that would then be 'moralized' and hence 'coarsened' into a set counter or 'rallying point' where 'people stop reading, people stop attending'.[6] In terms of poetic practice, this means a double answerability: things in a Fisher poem owe allegiance both to a recognizable world and to the poem itself, and what is important to the poet is to 'make it fairly clear that the thing that's being written about is an artifact, is to do with the subjective'.[7] This alliance between the factitious and the subjective is a strange one, particularly since the anarchism of Fisher's permanently sceptical view extends to his deployment of the first person pronoun—the 'I' which may or may not be a 'truth'[-ful] indicator, as 'The Lesson in Composition' instructs:

> I have never chosen
> to speak about what I have
> myself said, seldom of what I have done.
> Though these things are my life
> they have not the character of truth I require.[8]

The instruction is pursued in the opening of the wittily and economically titled 'Of the Empirical Self and for Me', again notable for its rare use of the first person pronoun:

> In my poems there's seldom
> any *I* or *you*—
>
> you know me, Mary;
> you wouldn't expect it of me—[9]

So the 'I' is always located unlocatably: in 'The Lesson in Composition' it is 'where I once was,' awaiting the composition that has already started, and it is on that basis (in part a reflection of himself as 'a carrier of secrets' and a function of 'the location of my imagination' in a space cleared in distant childhood)[10] that the freedom to speak untainted by 'worldliness' is premised. One way of understanding this 'oblique' and 'vague' notion of subjectivity is to recognize its relation to Fisher's concern with 'referring EVERYTHING to bodily existence' which itself is problematical: 'while wanting to recreate, to assert the physicality of life, I also have to cope with a visual memory which is hallucinatory to a stupifying degree'.[11] It is here that William James is illuminating; and given the title of the poem cited above, an initial foray might enter that section of chapter 10 in *The Principles of Psychology* headed 'The Empirical Self or Me' where James argues for the objective nature of the self:

> To have a self that I can *care for*, nature must first present me with some *object* interesting enough to make me instinctively wish to appropriate it for its *own* sake, and out of it to manufacture one of those material, social, or spiritual selves which we have already passed in review ... certain *things* appeal to primitive and intuitive impulses of our nature, and ... we follow their destinies with an excitement that owes nothing to a reflective source. These objects our consciousness treats as the primordial constituents of its ME ... The *words* ME, *then, and* SELF, *so far as they arouse feeling and connote emotional worth, are* OBJECTIVE *designations, meaning* ALL THE THINGS *which have the power to produce in a stream of consciousness excitement of a certain peculiar sort*.[12]

James's linking of 'excitement' to the objects which constitute the self goes some way towards explaining Fisher's difficulties with the heaviness and immobility of sensations, 'a perceptual field which is just jammed solid with sensory data' that inhibits the freedom for 'simply SEEING things as they are in the world', for releasing them from a rendering that is either formalist or realist:

> I can sometimes have visual memory which looks like a colour slide. And the difficulty is sometimes simply to stalk up on it, to break it up, to find some way of realizing the subjectivity, the relative instability of the impressions, to stop them solidifying, turning into a collection of colour slides or a gallery of sensations.[13]

It is this immobility and solidifying that engages James in chapter 9 of *The Principles of Psychology*, 'The Stream of Thought', where he complains of our 'inveterate' habit of 'not attending to sensations as subjective facts, but of simply using them as stepping-stones to pass over to the recognition of the realities whose presence they reveal'.[14] Attending to sensations as 'facts' which are 'subjective' and not merely as temporary solidities comes very close to the kind of subjectivity that Fisher attempts to achieve; and for James, it is a matter not only of epistemology but of language:

> language works against our perception of the truth. We name our thoughts simply, each after its thing, as if each knew its own thing and nothing else. What each really knows is clearly the thing it is named for, with dimly perhaps a thousand other things. It ought to be named after all of them, but it never is.[15]

James's preference is for the 'transitive' aspects of thought and word as opposed to their 'substantive' aspects, their 'places of flight' rather than 'resting places',[16] because it is in the former we find the relational character of subjectivity. So caught up with the 'substantive' are words and thoughts that the 'thousand other things' become suppressed, and with wonderfully Fisheresque scepticism about 'existing language', James claims: 'We ought to say a feeling of *and*, a feeling of *if*, a feeling of *but*, and a feeling of *by*, quite as readily as we say a feeling of *blue* or a feeling of *cold*.'[17] His conjunctive lexicon resists the empiricist 'error' of 'supposing that where there is no name no entity can exist' where, consequently

> All dumb or anonymous psychic states have, owing to this error, been coolly suppressed; or, if recognized at all, have been named after the substantive perception they led to, as thoughts

'about' this object or 'about' that, the stolid word *about* engulf-ing all their delicate idiosyncrasies in its monotonous sound.[18]

For James the referential and representational stolidity and monotony of 'about' is inimical to the relational openness of con-junctive possibilities, as it is for the Fisher who wants a poetry that is 'not meaning to make a social point but to assume the social point',[19] that is interested in the 'actual bits' of anyone's body but exemplified by 'the back of their upper arm which may never need discussing in any context whatsoever'[20] or 'the back of the knee of the man who wasn't known to be there at the time of the event which didn't happen'.[21] There can be no 'image' of such 'actual bits' (and Fisher is firm on his view of the poet as 'image maker'):[22] what we are talking about is a perceptual proclivity that, as James recognizes, is a 'definite' and 'distinct' form of consciousness, is transitive, is unavailable to the comfort of substantive articulation. It sees 'psychic transitions' which are 'always on the wing' and, in Emersonian spirit, 'not to be glimpsed except in flight'; transitions which 'lead from one set of images to another', maintaining the 'feeling of direction' suppressed by 'full presence', and James asks:

> has the reader never asked himself what kind of mental fact is his *intention of saying a thing* before he has said it? It is an entirely definite intention, distinct from all other intentions, an abso-lutely distinct state of consciousness, therefore; and yet how much of it consists of definite sensorial images, either of words or of things? Hardly anything![23]

Both James and the Fisher of 'Without Location', who finds colours 'patterning on the need for a world / made on a *pulse*' (our emphasis), would be in sympathy with Emerson's essay on 'Experience' where he claims: 'Nature hates calculators; her methods are saltatory and impulsive. Man lives by pulses; our organic movements are such; and the chemical and ethereal agents are undulatory and alternate; and the mind goes antagonising on, and never prospers but by fits.'[24]

The project here, as for the 'radical empiricism' of James's thought more generally, is to give body, as it were, to this kind of 'mental fact', and the sensorial elusiveness of such facts, such 'tendencies', is, we will argue, what circulates around Fisher's preoccupations with the 'vague' of his subjectivity. James himself is quite clear about his ambition to enflesh 'these rapid premonitory perspective views':

> 'tendencies' are not only descriptions from without . . . they are among the *objects* of the stream, which is thus aware of them from within, and must be described as in very large measure constituted of *feelings* of *tendency*, often so vague that we are unable to name them at all. It is, in short, the re-instatement of the vague to its proper place in our mental life which I am so anxious to press on the attention.[25]

It is the experientiality of the vague that orchestrates to a great extent James's ideas of subjectivity which in turn underwrite his commitment to the relational character of things—a character neglected by the predilection for the substantive at the expense of the transitive, for the definite image rather than projective vagueness. With every image, he argues,

> goes the sense of its relations, near and remote, the dying echo of whence it came to us, the dawning sense of whither it is to lead. The significance, the value, of the image is all in this halo of penumbra that surrounds and escorts it.[26]

Within the Jamesian system, as he claims in a later essay, 'A World of Pure Experience', his 'experienced relations' must be accounted as ' "real" as anything else in the system'. The most important members of 'conjunctive relation' are the forms of 'continuous transition', and it is these which resist the substantive and the definite, the 'resting places' of thought which lead to the anaesthetizations of abstract thinking, 'involving words that drive us to invent secondary conceptions in order to neutralize their suggestions and to make our actual experience again seem rationally possible'.[27] James's 'resting places' match Fisher's 'rallying points' where 'people stop reading, people stop attending'.[28] When in the later poem 'At Once,' we find 'I say at once there's a light on the slope among the allotment huts. If I leave it a moment unsaid it'll set solid, and that only the beginning.

But, said, it has gone'[29] or in 'It is Writing' where we come across 'I mistrust the poem in its hour of success, / a thing capable of being / tempted by ethics into the wonderful',[30] we are in a place that is recognizably akin to Jamesian thinking. For the Fisher of *City*, just as much as for the conjunctive relations of James, 'The imaginary comes to me with as much force as the real, the remembered with as much force the immediate',[31] because for both the 'vague' warrants its particular place within the experientially relational.[32]

The hallmark of relations, conjunctions, and transitions is that simultaneously they are nominatively vague and experientially real. James's 'Is Radical Empiricism Solipsistic?' claims that while we 'live' in conjunctions, our state is literally transitional and that

> We can not, it is true, *name* our different living 'ands' or 'withs' except by naming the different terms towards which they are moving us, but we *live* their specifications and differences before those terms explicitly arrive.[33]

But more is involved here than a sustaining of a new reality and a questioning of stabilities and their legitimating boundaries, the means, in Fisher's phrase, to 'scramble the perceptive field'[34] (important as these are). Our cue is given by the metaphor of the 'mosaic' that James develops for his philosophy: 'In radical empiricism there is no bedding; it is as if the pieces clung together by their edges, the transitions experienced between them forming their cement.' He admits the partiality of the metaphor, but is keen to maintain that it 'serves to symbolize the fact that Experience itself, taken at large, can grow by its edges'.[35] These edges take boundaries and borders of conjunctive relations away from tropes of confinement and limit to the more open, and more vague, arena of liminality and perme-ability—the arena of Fisher's 'osmotic' investigations, and hence that alterability which may challenge the hierarchies and authorities of both traditional philosophy and rationalism (for James) and narrative and logic (for Fisher).[36]

Fisher's poetry, engaged with the difficulty of actual and imaginative joinings where, at its simplest expression in 'The Many', all landscapes are 'solid, and having transparency / in time, in state'

and the 'true gods' are 'known only | as *those of whom there is never news*',[37]
is sceptical—in 'Just Where to Draw the Line' for example—towards
the privileging capacities of perspective and the separating boundaries upon which it relies:

> —those Quattrocento paintings
> with a tiny peaceable city
> on every hilltop in the distance
> bobbing on the skyline in a rich
> luminous watery twilight. While
> near at hand huge imaginary personages
> slug out needless religious nastiness
> and mess up the view.[38]

It is to counter such privileging that he offers the liminality of
'osmotic investigations' where boundaries become permeable. This
form of inquiry is prompted by Fisher's resistance to representation
and its authority, to 'brute documentation'[39] which, in the language
of 'The Return', produces 'characters with certificates but no |
stories'[40]—a resistance he shares with that other James, Henry, who
admired Alphonse Daudet for being 'truthful without being literal'
and having 'a pair of butterfly's wings attached to the back of his
observation'.[41] It is not difficult to picture Fisher in the 'car' of the
deeply ambiguous 'balloon of experience' prescribed by James in his
'Preface' to *The American*:

> The balloon of experience is in fact of course tied to the earth,
> and under that necessity we swing, thanks to a rope of remark-
> able length, in the more or less commodious car of the imagin-
> ation; but it is by the rope we know where we are, and from the
> moment the cable is cut we are at large and unrelated: we only
> swing apart from the globe . . . The art of the romancer is, 'for the
> fun of it,' insidiously to cut the cable, to cut it without our
> detecting him.[42]

James's figure is a wonderful image for the kind of distance we find
in Fisher: it is not under the balloon itself that the writer swings but
under 'that necessity' of its being tied to the earth. Engagement and

disengagement interfere with each other remarkably here, and that interference dissuades us from that 'documentary' form of knowledge that may be associated with representation. The most revealing term of James's definition is 'fun', comparable to Fisher's sense of the 'anarchic', the 'fun' of the 'hocus-pocus' that he remembers as a version of the Hawthornesque 'latitude' in his composition of *The American*. In a particularly expressive simile, he fancifully differentiates the 'gambol' of 'frolic fancy' from the decision-making process of 'a board of trustees discussing a new outlay'[43]—a brilliant trope for subverting the forms of knowledge and authority which encourage encumbered representation and a faith in the 'substantive', which instigate 'rallying points' where 'people stop reading, people stop attending', and which suppress the permeable conjunctions of the 'transitive' and the relational.[44] 'Really, universally, relations stop nowhere' announced the 'Preface' to *Roderick Hudson*[45] on behalf of human intercourse as, in the fifth section of 'Matrix', material tracings are 'inseparable, interfolded'.[46] This is, perhaps, the greatest Jamesian lesson—his, in Bakhtin's phrase, 'dialogic imagination'[47]— which resists singularity, opens words and things to what is other, rather than freezing them into manipulable categories, which is sceptical of binaries and schismatic perception, of interpretation and fixed definition, is committed to the freedoms of alterability and which persuades a dispersive and mobile selfhood (however difficult and painful that may be) against the forms of totality and authoritarianism associated with autonomous selfhood, where the effort to construct a unified self depends always upon the suppression of others.[48] In both James and Fisher, being is fixed and objects or landscapes are solid only on a temporary and provisional basis, as a means of getting about, as points of departure.

'A Poem Not a Picture' is one amongst many of Fisher's graphings of the liminal world:

On a ground remarkable for lack of character, sweeps of direction form.

It's not possible to determine whether they rise from the ground's qualities or are marked on to it. Or whether, if the first, the lines suck the ground's force up, or are its delegates; or if the second, whether the imposed marks mobilize or defeat it; or both, in all cases.

Out of a scratch ontology the sweeps of direction form, and, as if having direction, produce, at wide intervals, the events.

These are wiry nodes made of small intersecting planes as if rendered by hatching, and having a vapid, played-out look. But they are the nearest the field has to intense features. Each has a little patch of red.[49]

That 'little patch of red' is meaningless in itself except as an un-designated sign which can honestly only ghost 'direction'—perhaps 'unmeaning', in Eric Mottram's sense,[50] is a better term in that it allows this splotch of colour its gesture towards otherness, its scope beyond direction. Biographically, constructions of the solidity and unity of the self (invariably dependant upon non-permeable boundaries) have been generatively troublesome for Fisher. His 'Autobiography' tells of his sense of 'exile' and of his discovery of American poetry in 1956, of writers who were 'behaving with all the freedom and artistic optimism of painters'. These instigated a 'new direction' which was not only liberating, but encouraged a fresh apprehension of selfhood out of a fuller appreciation of composi-tional method, using 'chance operations to begin poems I didn't think important', a method which relied upon a diversity of border-crossings:

The main effect of the method was to get me out of my own way. This was very necessary. I'd grown up with no trace of the compact self most other people seemed to have; instead I had a diffused zone in which *ad hoc* selves would be generated for temporary purposes, and then dissolve again. Establish-ing a usable, consistent self was later to prove a lengthy business, like growing a wind-break. The self I'd tried in those days to fix as a writing *persona* was just a kind of self-important bruise, a posture. It got in the way, and didn't ring true. Once rid of it, though, I could get at observations,

> memories, earlier selves, lost feelings, causal things—reality,
> in short—and my clotted language cleared like a cloudy
> liquid left to settle.

But settlement of any kind is only ever a temporary affair for Fisher. Despite the 'writer's block' following *City*, he started *The Ship's Orchestra* and *Ten Interiors with Various Figures* where 'I knew I'd found a tone and a way of relating to material I could feel at home with.' Again, however, even domicility is not comfortable: 'I'd also saddled myself with my troublesome inability to repeat formulae, which puts me to the bother of inventing a new form every time I start writing again.' With characteristically turning wit he concludes: 'sometimes I've been paid to give thoroughly egocentric talks on what it's like to be born without a self'.[51] Poetically the 'I' becomes scattered amongst the 'actual bits' of the body, in large part to negotiate border-crossings and liminal possibilities. His commitment to the 'commands of a rule of sensation', being 'driven' by 'daily and hourly rhythms of physical appetite and physical attention span' in order to 'recreate, to assert the physicality of life', is turned invariably by 'a visual memory which is hallucinatory to a stupefying degree'.[52] It is to work his way through the unsettlings of this turning that he engages with 'actual bits'—images we noted earlier of 'the back of their upper arm which may never need discussing in any context whatsoever' and 'the back of the knee of the man who wasn't known to be there at the time of the event which didn't happen'.[53] This is not to deny a straightforward pleasure in unproblematical physicality, registered, for example, in his memory of the piano with several malfunctioning keys at his childhood home as 'deeply sensual in that you couldn't just ripple over it; you had to prod about to find something that loved you and would answer you back',[54] where the pleasure is in the exploratory, the break with existing pattern. And, in part, the images of these 'actual bits' bespeak his appetitive sense of place as 'childlike' which, again, prompts their variousness understood geographically—'A matter of simple appetite. An idea that places may be rich in various ways. Bits of places may subdivide into further bits of places'—and allies appetite and the child's perspective on behalf of an egalitarian impulse for 'a levelling in language'.[55]

Fisher's 'actual bits' avoid the 'substantive' and, within another register, allow a particular physiology which is expressed through the transitive conjunction of flow, seepage, and permeability. He says of *The Ship's Orchestra*:

> For me the thing had to be grounded in sensations and in refinements of sensation, and indeed the book is written as an elaboration of almost hallucinatory sensory effects—tactile, olfactory, visual of course, auditory. And the book has a fairly simple base vocabulary of colours, substances, things like grey mucus, saline tastes, things which are body tastes, body sensations, and things in the world.[56]

And his brief appreciation of Pound concludes with an acknowledgement of his own aesthetic corporeality: 'In language my specialization is in the pathology of soft tissues, transient and perishable substances; when it comes to bone I'm out of my element. I'll still turn to Pound for a reminder of what hardness is.'[57]

This recuperation of the distinctions in Pound's own essay on 'The Hard and Soft in French Poetry' inverts Pounds hierarchy of poetic value to suggest again the new kind of materiality Fisher seeks—not the 'substantive' and containable, but the more expressive range of mucus, the 'transient and perishable'. It is in the conjunctive flow of the body's amorphous attributes that the possibilities for liminality and border-crossings become available, avoiding, in the language of *The Ship's Orchestra*, an 'attenuation of substance to concepts'.[58] Bits in this sense belong partly to byproducts—the byproducts of the long-dead cultural and economic ideas of a city's planners which are left now in the forms of street layouts or civic sites as 'an indecipherable script with no key',[59] as a trace which is material and immaterial, physical and hallucinatory simultaneously. But, more radically, the flows of the body, its perishable deposits, realign our expectations of the containable and push the ambition of the liminal to extremes. Fisher's 'attenuation' is a direct consequence of the containable, of the cleanliness of disposal:

All this disposal business, these basins, enamel buckets,
plunging tubes, embalming sluices, constant jets, sterile bins,
sealed incinerators, consideration of where the banjo-player
might have gone that night, of the abolition of words taped to
our memories, of the storage of one night under another night,
the earlier ones gradually fading as the multi-track builds up
beyond the bounds of desire . . .[60]

The Ship's Orchestra is filled with such machinery for disposal and
with the forms of flow they are designed to contain, channel and
cleanse—'Visceral pipes of white porcelain' whose 'Potential
fracture' reveals the world of 'debris', 'rubbish' and 'seepage',[61] where
an alternative cleansing agency, 'Great glycerine drops of water', is
immediately threatened by 'Corridor of grey mucus. A kidney bowl
of it behind each door.'[62] The ambiguity of both bodily flow, urine,
smells, 'cold fluids' and vomit,[63] and the pipes for their containment is
such as to take these images beyond an anxiety about mess towards
the risk of pursuing the osmosis of liminality to its full extreme, of
recognizing that the generative otherness of conjunctive relations
and abrasions is also a site of fear—a fear of all that is permeable,
uncontainable and cannot be separated fully from the body, idea, or
word. In short, to cross borders is simultaneously to engage
openness and to risk, following Julia Kristeva and, specifically,
Elizabeth Grosz, 'the conditions under which the clean and proper
body, the obedient, law-abiding, social body emerges, the cost of
its emergence'. Grosz's consideration of physical flow provides
pertinent access to what is at stake in the 'osmotic investigations'
conducted by Fisher's subjectivity:

> Body fluids attest to the permeability of the body, its necessary
> dependence on an outside, its liability to collapse into this
> outside (this is what death implies), to the perilous divisions
> between the body's inside and its outside. They affront a sub-
> ject's aspiration toward autonomy and self-identity. They attest
> to a certain irreducible 'dirt' or disgust, a horror of the
> unknown or the unspecifiable that permeates, lurks, lingers,
> and at times leaks out of the body, a testimony of the fraudu-

lence or impossibility of the 'clean' and 'proper.' They resist the determination that marks solids, for they are without any shape or form of their own.[64]

These fluids re-question borders to display them as both sites for transformation, for undoing the representational violence that suppresses otherness, and as anxious sites for dispersal. The radicalism of the subjectivity in Fisher's conjunctive relations, his illuminating erosions and 'osmotic' probings, is to acknowledge the egalitarian possibilities of the former and to face the literal uncontainability of the latter: the 'Great glycerine drops of water' which putatively refresh the woman (Joyce, we assume) in *The Ship's Orchestra* become 'a thin film of something slightly viscous' which originates outside her body from the fragility of the very instruments that are designed to contain flow but are seeping themselves—'It must be dropping from somewhere overhead. Cold sweat out of the metal.'[65]

At one of the rare moments of clear definition in *The Ship's Orchestra*, flow, in the form of dampness, is given a specific human value:

> A person is a white damp thing . . . greyish in some lights even when alive. You could inject salt water into the human body. An all-over emetic. Ha ha. Seminarist. Plankton. Bathyscape. Handkerchief.[66]

Fisher, thinking of Joyce, provides a local exegesis—'anybody who isn't in control of their own fate, is a bit of a drifter, is described as soggy and a bit moist, bit damp, a bit out of control' [67]—but the salt of the emetic serves also an aesthetic purpose, as 'The Only Image' testifies:

> Salts work their way
> to the outside of a plant pot
> and dry white.
>
>   This encrustation
> is the only image.

Against this singularity, all the rest is 'variable', enabling the poet to 'compare what I like to the salts' and compare the salts 'to anything there is'. It is the drying of the salts, their 'encrustation' out of moisture, that produces the enabling ground for treating the 'variable', the other material of a poem 'that shifts / in any part, or vanishes'.[68] The osmotic act that is graphed here in miniature assumes a larger scale in a poem like 'Linear', where the world and the body are conjoined:

> To travel and feel
> the world growing old on your body
>
> breathe and excrete
> perpetually the erosion that makes the world

Their conjunction gives attention to that complex of life and death through effluvia whereby the world is made not through 'encrustation' but through the 'erosion' of excrement, that which is made in and of the body continuously, and marking very clearly the dynamic of abjection within which order and entity always struggle. Movement through this world is slow and generous; the 'caravan' crosses 'patiently,' giving itself time to witness erosion's final condition, 'how each day's dust lay and shifted and lies again' where the possibility of deception in the shift to the present tense of 'lies' is simultaneously present and absent: 'no forgotten miles or kinks / in the journey other than cunning ones'. Its crossing is appropriative and tangential, 'to pass through many things acquisitively / and touch against many more'—the only material the poem offers for collection is the excrement and the dust of erosion itself, and its borders are now meaningless, can only be touched against rather than substantially transformed—and it becomes imaginable eventually, despite the patience of its efforts, only as a 'long line', written over, lacking in history, 'without anything / you could call repetition'. Its present condition can be one only of dry humour, 'amused by others and other worlds', because it acknowledges the impossibility of anything apart from 'eroded / country', and so the 'line' is given the simile of 'certain snail tracks / crazily long and determined'.[69] The simile re-introduces the slime and viscosity of the body's flow—not volitional or energetic in motion, but the sticky awkwardness of that which hovers between solidity and fluidity to mark the poem's struggle through erosion.

Fisher didn't need the form of the simile here (it is not one of his customary tropes in any case) but its literariness, underlined by the adjectival 'determined', echoes the more generative possibilities of border questionings by gesturing towards one of major modernist inquiries into the liminal—William Carlos Williams's 'The Rose'. Here, the 'edge' and the 'end' of the flower's petals are worked to produce a vacant place, 'The place between the petal's / edge and the　.' The poem pauses, and reverses itself from the immediately unknowable to engineer its 'line' which starts 'From the petal's edge' and 'penetrates' first the 'Milky Way' and then 'space' itself. Penetration is, with a compact pun, 'infinitely fine, infinitely / rigid' and it works 'without contact', is 'neither hanging / nor pushing'.[70] The cleanliness and clarity of Williams's 'line' is a powerful counter to the viscosity of the 'tracks' we see in Fisher's poem, but only putatively so: the vacancy of its initial site and the infinity of its ultimate placing leave such cleanliness and clarity literally untouched by the immediate world which concerns 'Linear'. Fisher is fond of eliding direct reference, inevitably at his 'hallucinatory' moments but also in his more formal exercises, of which 'The Trace'[71] is exemplary. This marvellously detailed tracking through the metamorphic movements of an 'it' which can never be identified is perhaps his clearest version of 'the back of the knee of the man who wasn't known to be there at the time of the event which didn't happen', and traces of people, events, ideas, are possibly his most achieved understandings as a poet. But traces themselves, as versions of the Jamesian subjectivity discussed above, are not allowed to remain content with their manoeuvrings: they are always at the prey of Fisher as 'the maker / of mutant poems' who 'overproduces' in 'Irreversible' to play with 'The Trace' itself:

> Here's
> my poem *The Trace*, that started
> to feed off itself, and breed:
>
> — *silky swallowed hair*
> *that dried and was*
> *flying in a fan*—

> Now it's *dined and was*
> *flying in a fan*—
>
> — *sulky squalid whore*
> *that dined and was*
> *frying in a fin*—[72]

Fisher's mutancy is a gritty analogue to his liminality: his literalisation of 'feed', with its gesture towards Richard Aldington's parodies of Pound's Imagist exercises, mutates upon mutation to transfer a strategically 'poetic' moment back to the awkwardness of the material world, to give a fresh shape to his own predilection for appetite as a poetic urgency.[73] But within all the fun[74] we remember not only that the poem is prompted by the death of Kokoschka but that it is appetite which occasions, ineluctably, excrement. Of 'The Six Deliberate Acts', two (sections 2 and 5) focus upon the emptying of the bowels and the view from 'the small outside toilet' to the rear of the 'new shops'. While the first of these provides us with one of Fisher's wonderfully low-key landscapes that are wholly adequate to their realistic presentation, the second brushes out all the detail to offer 'A plain ground as if white / stretching away nondescript' where everything is 'made of marking'—'Hedge-marks / Smoke-marks / roof-marks'. These markings are given as the poetic act, the transforming of detail into trace, an act of exchange which looks at the landscape to yield a superbly understated pun, looking 'Until it balanced / and tipped the flush / just as he reached for it'.[75] The topography of the landscape, specifically the exterior toilet among the 'dustbins' and behind the 'new shops' built over 'dumped ash' deposits, gives a broader context to the act of excretion. Where in 'Linear' the 'erosion that makes the world' has an egalitarian quality, here the occupant of the 'jakes' is himself positioned to suggest expulsion from the definable sites of order: his perceptions, like his dry turds, 'rattle' into the pan while their slight disruption presents no substantial threat to the factitious systems of material exchange occurring in the shops beyond. Here, the economic engine and its investment in avowedly 'solid' goods is placed in relation to that which is suppressed in the process—an insistently physical labour.

The landscape itself is shaped by the machinery of commerce, by the 'double road', 'railway' and 'farm' through which profit and goods are transported and transformed. The very solidity of that exchange, its precision and containability, marks a process which obscures any danger posed by the less ordered 'stinking and muddy' rawness of the field of kale. Strikingly, it is the sound of the launderette which makes the observer aware of his increasing chill—the sound of a service building dedicated to the removal of traces and evidences of collisions draws attention to the disorder and perpetual presence of 'what's behind us / leaning at our backs'.[76]

Excrement always returns to tip the balance ahead of the game, just prior to the moment of separation, disposal or temporary containment and definition. Roy Fisher, the fugitive, outlaw and spy, recognizes how, in the search for feelings of *and*, and *if* and *with*, for the conjunctive relations of his subjectivity, osmosis is prepared to adventure mutancy, enabling him, at the end of 'The Six Deliberate Acts' and remembering 'Without Location', to essay deliberation and 'arrive with himself' on a 'pulse'.

NOTES

1. Taped interview with Mary Ellison, 7 January 1992: transcribed by Meriel Lland.

2. Ellison interview. Fisher's sense of Creeley's poetry as 'a body of work so strenuously elliptical and under so much internal aesthetic pressure to shift its ground' could apply easily to his own (review of Cynthia Dubin Edelberg, *Robert Creeley's Poetry: A Critical Introduction* in *Journal of American Studies*, 14:2 (1980), p. 326).

3. *Poems 1955–1987* (Oxford: Oxford University Press, 1988), p. 185. 'The Lesson in Composition' has been suggested by Fisher as a good starting-place for an understanding of his poetics (conversation with Ian F. A. Bell, 20 September 1997).

4. Jed Rasula and Mike Erwin, 'An Interview with Roy Fisher', in Roy Fisher, *Nineteen Poems and an Interview* (Pensnett, Staffs: Grosseteste, 1975), p. 17.

5. *Ibid.*, p. 15. Fisher has observed of Rexroth that he 'never takes advantage of the releases from entailment offered by a fictional approach' (review of Kenneth Rexroth, *An Autobiographical Novel* in *Journal of American Studies*, 12:2 (1978), p. 255).

6. Rasula and Erwin, 'Interview', p. 16.

7. *Ibid.*, pp. 15, 12.

8. *P55–87*, p. 185.

9. *Ibid.*, p. 125. The poem is dedicated 'for M. E.'—a typographical play upon the title's other personal pronoun and which here registers a colleague at the University of Keele, the historian Mary Ellison. In her interview, Ellison asked of *The Ship's Orchestra* 'You're attempting to float over this as a kind of invisible and non-intrusive person presumably?' and Fisher replied 'Yes, but mind who you call you.'

10. These phrases are taken from the text Fisher refers to as his 'Autobiography,' published as 'Roy Fisher, 1930–', *Contemporary Authors (Autobiography Series)*, vol. 10, (Detroit, New York, Fort Lauderdale, London: Gale Research Inc., 1989), pp. 86, 91.

11. Rasula and Erwin, 'Interview', pp. 20–21.

12. William James, 'The Empirical Self or Me', in *William James: The Essential Writings*, ed. Bruce Wilshire (New York: Harper & Row, 1971), pp. 94–95.

13. Rasula and Erwin, 'Interview', p. 21. Fisher's commitment to what Jeremy Hooker has called 'the reality of human subjectivity' as the 'work of the mind upon the world of things' ('Roy Fisher, Magician of the Common Place,' *PN Review*, 22:3 (1996), p. 28) provides a useful pointer to James's reconstructions of subjectivity. For both, there is an emphasis on activity, on making, well-summarized on behalf of Fisher by John Matthias, drawing upon European modernist roots and providing an excellent gloss on Fisher's ambition to 'have floated real things into a fictive world' ('The Poetry of Roy Fisher', in *Contemporary British Poetry: Essays in Theory and Criticism*, ed. James Acheson and Romana Huk (Albany, NY: State University of New York Press, 1996), pp. 39–40). In a brilliant essay on the surplus and excess in Fisher's work, Andrew Crozier directs us to that relational feature which, as we shall see, is pivotal for Jamesian subjectivity ('Signs of Identity: Roy Fisher's *A Furnace*', *PN Review*, 18:3 (1992), pp. 27–28).

14. William James, 'The Stream of Thought', *Essential Writings*, p. 48.

15. *Ibid.*, pp. 54–55.

16. *Ibid.*, pp. 55–56.

17. *Ibid.*, pp. 57–58.

18. *Ibid.*, p. 58. Stuart Mills, in reviewing *The Ship's Orchestra*, has noted Fisher's resistance to writing 'about' something, while acknowledging the simultaneous urge to a 'common lingual currency' provided by the senses where 'Words are not used as vehicles for ideas but become malleable plastic bits, slotted together, pegged, grooved and jointed, perhaps painted or stained' (*Tarasque*, 5 (1967), pp. 29–31).

19. Rasula and Erwin, 'Interview', p. 16.

20. Ellison interview.

21. Rasula and Erwin, 'Interview', p. 37.

22. *Ibid.*, p. 16.

23. William James, 'The Stream of Thought', p. 60.

24. *P55–87*, p. 115. Ralph Waldo Emerson, 'Experience,' *Selected Writings of Emerson*, ed. Donald McQuade (New York Modern Library, 1981), p. 338.

25. William James, 'The Stream of Thought', pp. 61–62.

26. *Ibid.*, p. 62.

27. William James, 'A World of Pure Experience', *Writings, 1902–1910* (New York: Library of America, 1987), pp. 1160, 1163.

28. Rasula and Erwin, 'Interview', p. 16.

29. *P55–87*, p. 107.

30. *P55–87*, p. 111.

31. *P55–87*, p. 29.

32. In 'Is Radical Empiricism Solipsistic?' James offers his clearest account of the 'doctrine of the reality of conjunctive relations' in which these relations are 'parts constitutive of experience's living flow' and not 'as they appear in retrospect, each fixed as a determinate object of conception, static, therefore, and contained within itself.' It is against this 'rationalistic tendency to treat experience as chopped up into discontinuous static objects' that radical empiricism 'protests' (*Writings, 1902–1910*, p. 1204).

33. *Writings, 1902–1910*, p. 1204. Similarly, in 'A World of Pure Experience,' he had claimed: 'Life is in the transitions as much as in the terms connected; often, indeed, it seems to be there more emphatically, as if our spurts and sallies forward were the real firing-line of the battle, were like the thin line of flame advancing across the dry autumnal field which the farmer proceeds to burn' (*ibid.*, p. 1181).

34. Rasula and Erwin, 'Interview', p. 38.

35. William James, ' A World of Pure Experience', p. 1180.

36. See Fisher's jacket note for *Matrix* (London: Fulcrum Press, 1971), where he claims 'my poems are propositions or explorations . . . are to do with getting about in the mind, and I tackle that in any way I can. I have to get from one cluster of ideas to another without a scaffolding of logic or narrative'. Similarly, he writes of 'The Cut Pages' sequence: 'The aim in the improvisation was to give the words as much relief as possible from serving in planned situations; so the work was taken forward with no programme beyond the principle that it should not know where its next meal was coming from. It was unable to anticipate, but it could have on the spot whatever it could manage to ask for' ('Note', *The Cut Pages* (London: Fulcrum Press, 1971), pp. 6–7). The sturdy grit of the appetitive metaphor propels us firmly beyond any temptations towards associational free-play.

37. *A Furnace* (Oxford: Oxford University Press, 1986), pp. 41, 42.

38. *Birmingham River* (Oxford: Oxford University Press, 1994), p. 25.

39. Rasula and Erwin, 'Interview', p. 15.

40. *F*, p. 18.

41. Henry James, 'Alphonse Daudet', *Henry James: Literary Criticism. French*

Writers, other European Writers, the Prefaces to the New York Edition (New York: Library of America, 1984), pp. 239, 242.

42. Henry James, 'Preface' to *The American* in *Henry James: Literary Criticism*, p. 1064

43. *Ibid.*, pp. 1057–58.

44. Fisher is playful with such 'fun' on behalf of his own procedures in 'mutant' poems such as 'Irreversible' (*P55–87*, pp. 167–68) and he debates more formally the attendant issue of the substantive/transitive relation in 'The Open Poem and the Closed Poem' (*Ibid.*, pp. 166–67).

45. Henry James, 'Preface' to *Roderick Hudson* in *Henry James: Literary Criticism*, p. 1041.

46. *P55–87*, p. 90.

47. See Mikhail Bakhtin, *The Dialogic Imagination*, ed. Michael Holquist (Austin, TX: University of Texas Press, 1981).

48. This view of James is sustained in Ian F. A. Bell, *Henry James and the Past: Readings into Time* (London: Macmillan, 1991).

49. *P55–87*, p. 112. Ian Gregson has written well of Fisher's indeterminacy (*Contemporary Poetry and Postmodernism* (Basingstoke: Macmillan, 1996), pp. 173, 177), but tells only part of the story, stopping short of the radical possibilities opened up by the liminal and the osmotic and by Jamesian conjunctive relations.

50. 'Meaning is the first stage of becoming anaesthetized; unmeaning is consciousness of images of self and other without going the whole way to isolating abstraction' (Eric Mottram, 'Roy Fisher's Work', *Stand*, 11:1 (1969), p. 15).

51. 'Roy Fisher, 1930–', pp. 83–84, 96–97, 98, 99.

52. Rasula and Erwin, 'Interview', pp. 13, 38, 20–21.

53. Ellison interview; Rasula and Erwin, 'Interview', p. 37.

54. Ellison interview.

55. Rasula and Erwin, 'Interview', pp. 17–18, 37.

56. *Ibid.*, p. 13.

57. Roy Fisher 'On Ezra Pound' in *Sons of Ezra: British Poetry and Ezra Pound*, ed. Michael Alexander and James McGonigal (Amsterdam: Rodopi, 1995), p. 42.

58. *P55–87*, pp. 212–13.

59. Rasula and Erwin, 'Interview', p. 18.

60. *P55–87*, p. 212.

61. *Ibid.*, pp. 209–10.

62. *Ibid.*, pp. 211–12.

63. *Ibid.*, pp. 199, 202, 204, for example.

64. Elizabeth Grosz, *Volatile Bodies* (Bloomington and Indianapolis: Indiana University Press, 1994), pp. 192, 193–94.

65. *P55–87*, p. 217.

66. *Ibid.*, p. 202.

67. Ellison interview.

68. *P55–87*, p. 113.
69. *Ibid.*, p. 2.
70. William Carlos Williams, *Selected Poems*, ed. Charles Tomlinson (Harmondsworth: Penguin, 1976), pp. 48–50.
71. *P55–87*, pp. 144–46.
72. *Ibid.*, pp. 167–68; cf p. 145.
73. Rasula and Erwin, 'Interview', pp. 17–18.
74. The poem's fourth stanza delights in a lexical play on John Ashbery:

John Ashbery should watch out.
Hiding as John Ash in Haight-Ashbury
won't help in the clash
of Haight-Asch with John Ashbury;   (*P55–87*, p. 167).

75. *P55–87*, pp. 78–79, 80.
76. *Ibid.*, pp. 2, 78–9, 78, 77.

5

'Making Forms with Remarks': The Prose

ROBERT SHEPPARD

To write in prose grants a poet 'the freedom to construct a poetic entity capable of including what poetry has been told to exclude',[1] according to Stephen Fredman. His book *Poet's Prose* is an analysis of American writers who have felt the need to abandon lyric forms in favour of extended prose works that function a-generically and which defy the narrowness implied by the usual oxymoronic term for such work, the prose-poem. Fredman dismisses this term as the 'codification of a moment of generic dissolution'.[2]

'Poet's prose' seems a useful alternative for Fredman's purposes, which include the identification of a permanent crisis in American poetry, a post-colonial lack of confidence in lyric poetry as a vehicle of truth, and a concomitant turning to a 'prose of fact'. His acknowledgement of the anxiety of a poet who 'knowingly sacrifices a vast and recognisable prestige'[3] is useful, but it does not fit the position of British poets like Roy Fisher.

Fisher's partial renunciation of lyric from the mid-1950s onwards was a way of accommodating his own crisis of faith in the prestige forms of the empirical lyricism of the Movement orthodoxy, and a way of creatively avoiding its structures. Although it is beyond the scope of this essay, Fisher's detestation of the Movement's 'misanthropy, both social and artistic' led to a dual recognition that to de-Anglicize England meant in part to defamiliarize English poetry.[4]

Fisher's works in prose are generally hybrid forms; he has seldom turned to a formalized genre, such as prose fiction, nor to a fluid one, such as prose-poetry. They are nearly always the result of schemata or systems of writing developed solely for the purposes of generating themselves. The results of adopting these experimental processes and procedures are Fisher's most formally daring texts, which often withdraw from the topological and social concerns that are sometimes privileged in readings of his poetry.

The sixteen passages of prose in *City* (I am referring throughout to the text as it appears in *Collected Poems 1968* and in subsequent editions of poems) might be said to suggest such readings. Yet they were culled and then collaged from rather bleak novels and alienated diary-entries, and are best thought of as parts of an assemblage. They are not procedurally generated.

Passages which refer to the *angst*-ridden consciousness of the 'unwilling hero' or his analogues, are generally found in 'a sort of well-written yearning towards the end'.[5] This voyeur attempts an expression of community, to engage that which had remained invisible, or mute: 'I have often felt myself to be vicious, in living so much by the eye, yet among so many people', but he feels 'that I have inadvertently been looking through another's eyes and have seen what I cannot receive',[6] which is at least a partial description of Fisher's reaction to reading Movement poetry. 'I want to believe I live in a single world' (*P55–87*, p. 29) he immediately asserts, in the following section. The assemblage of *City* ironically works by counterpoint, to show multifaceted responses to a various landscape; it never appears as a 'single world' (*ibid.*).

Rather than analysing the recognisable prose passages, I want to concentrate on the one hybrid part of the 'well-written yearning' that points us towards his later prose practice. 'Starting to Make a Tree', which Jon Silkin has been forced uneasily to call 'a prose poem in what feels like stanzas rather than paragraphs',[7] has a title like the lyrics, but it is presented as blocked prose. The grammatical unit, at one point, does not coincide with the lineation of the 'paragraphs'. This unique text, by its assertive hybridity, draws attention to itself formally and to its thematic renegotiations of the whole of *City*'s impulse to discover a 'single world'.

'Starting to Make a Tree' is a textbook example of a defamiliarizing text, its aim being, to borrow Shklovsky's words, 'that one may recover the sensation of life; it exists to make one feel things'.[8] This is clear in its lengthy teasing description of a group of people constructing a 'natural' tree (which 'was to be very beautiful' (*P55–87*, p. 25)) from the 'cultural' detritus of an urban wasteland. How it got into this state is hinted at by two 'clues': the 'chemical blue' soil suggests toxic contamination and the 'flatness of the horizon' suggests the demolition described elsewhere, but behind both is the possibility of post-apocalyptic survivalism (*ibid.*).

Ian Gregson argues that this junk sculpting 'works self-referentially to show what Fisher was attempting in composing "City"'.[9] Certainly *City* is an assemblage: 'Like each material gathered . . . each bit of subject-matter that makes up "City" is a stubbornly diffuse and singular material derived originally from the local environment.'[10] This is only partly true, since Gregson ignores the aspect of community in these preparations for making. Using the first person plural, which is generally avoided elsewhere in *City*, the narrator is a calm, not at all 'anxious', meticulous observer, who is part of the population of this primitive-futuristic Birmingham; the tribe is preparing to radically transform its environment. The tree is to be made in the image of the human being: 'we . . . hindered the women at their cooking in our anxiety to know whose armpit and whose groin would help us most in the modelling of the bole, and the thrust of the boughs' (*P55–87*, p. 25), a making which, as Silkin has noted, is charged with 'sly sexuality'.[11] An erotico-aesthetic pleasure principle suggests that this monument might represent, however problematically, human beauty, to substitute the composite monstrosity of the city. The text ends as the hope is expressed—they never actually make the tree—but this fosters community as the tribe 'sat late, and discussed how we could best use' the parts to assemble their non-functional fetish (*ibid.*).

Although not a text produced by a generative schema, this hybrid form enables a freedom from both the constraints of British lyric poetry and from the overwhelming denotative realist use of documentary prose or of diaristic forms and confession found elsewhere in the prose of *City*. Its defamiliarized and de-Anglicized form and content proffers a theory of hybrid creativity, both for the poet as an assemblage-artist, as Gregson supposed, and for his community, as I have argued. It is the sole figuring of the image of that utopian 'single world' to haunt the work.

Interiors with Various Figures, composed in the early 1960s, is mostly lineated prose, with indented second and subsequent lines. At first sight the lines look like the long cadences of Whitman or Ginsberg but they are, in fact, 'antimetrical', according to Fisher.[12] Like 'Starting to Make a Tree', they project what Fisher usefully calls a 'head voice ... they are not articulated at all, although they are dramatic'.[13] Both of these examples contributed to the subsequent development of Fisher's verse, as metrical contours were loosened in response to the growing demands of this voice. Most surprisingly, the conceptual movement of the prose of *Interiors* is derived from 'reading the English translation and just getting the crack of' Wittgenstein's *Tractatus Logico-Philosophicus*.[14] Fisher adapted 'the idea of a proposition which is about to hold firm and to be expanded or qualified quite formally', in his reading of that work. 'I was just making forms with remarks'—Wittgenstein's own word for his later propositions[15]—'which, if written tightly, were my units'.[16]

Of all the rooms, this is a very small room.

I cannot tell if it was he who painted the doors this colour; himself
who lit the fire just before I arrived.   (*P55–87*, p. 40)

Given the concerns of the pieces—the relationship between various figures in various interiors, as here in 'The Small Room'—it seems that Fisher was simply deriving a form, but, as we shall see, he shares some concerns with the remarkable book that permitted the poem. Although he is not one of those featured in Marjorie Perloff's *Wittgenstein's Ladder*, he joins the large company of twentieth-century writers who have turned to that philosopher either for a poetics or for 'lyric paradigms', as Perloff puts it; Fisher also predates her identification of the 1980s and 1990s as the decades of those borrowings and it is interesting to compare Fisher's adaptation of propositional form with the parodic and poetic uses Rosmarie Waldrop makes of it in her 1987 book *The Reproduction of Profiles*.[17]

Although Fisher sees a strict logic and linearity in Wittgenstein's work, one which agrees with the philosopher's contention that his 'remarks' move 'in a natural order and without breaks', Wittgenstein warns the reader of occasions of 'sudden change, jumping from one topic to another'.[18] Privately his urge to order was more desperate, as he confided: 'Forcing my thoughts into an ordered sequence is a torment for me.'[19] Perloff's investigation of the famous numbering of the *Tractatus* (which *Interiors* does not emulate) shows that its progress is not as austerely logical, nor as 'firm', as Fisher supposed. She concludes that its inconsistencies operate as a *'clinamen*, a bend or swerve where logic gives way to mystery'.[20] Fisher's propositions, although not formally logical, have a similar temporary 'firmness', a provisionality, so that the 'expansion' is not always linear and we experience a Wittgensteinian 'jump' or a Perloffian 'swerve' into mystery and defamiliarisation. Indeed, Fisher has a practical but radical sense of his formalism: 'The only point of using any forms is to create freedom forms and not to do things about the imposition of order on chaos and this sort of rubbish.'[21] The necessity to escape deadening conformism suggests the attractions of a non-literary model.

The title, *Interiors with Various Figures*, stresses a painterly analogy, the emphasis upon the visual found here, and the procedures of painters. The 'figures'—usually pairs—are in relationships, and it is important to remember the 'various', for I am not convinced by Mottram's argument that the poems are 're-estimating married life',[22] nor as certain as Needham, in considering 'The Small Room', that 'one is invited to identify this woman trapped in a small room, with the woman in "Experimenting" who had wanted more walls.'[23] The identity of speakers is often indeterminate, though the sense of claustrophobia, or what Mottram calls 'the possible insanity of allowing hallucinatory vision of ordinary things and daily relationships to happen at all',[24] is pervasive.

The function of each interior is to effect a transformation of these 'various' persons. In 'The Small Room' the occupier has complete power over the room and thus over the person in it:

> He is allowed to buy the same sort of electricity as everybody else,
>   but his shirt, his milk bottle, his electricity resemble
>   one another more than they resemble others of
>   their kind. A transformation at his door, at his
>   voice, under his eye.   (*P55–87*, p. 41)

There is the suspicion that 'he' has willed the person there for the room's event; the poem defamiliarizes the experience of a hair-cut: 'Shave the hairs from my body. Which of us thought of this thing?' (p. 41). The room seems a closed system of correspondences, threatening the person's integrity. In the poem to which Needham compares this, 'Experimenting', the most dramatic of the texts, there is much play upon the role of the walls in protecting the stabilizing interior from the 'void' beyond. The woman, certainly nervous, but perhaps neurotic, claustrophobic, even agoraphobic,

> asks 'At least—why can't you have more walls?'
> Really scared. I see she means it.   (p. 39)

The narrator can offer small comfort ('there's one wall each, they can't outnumber us' (*P55–87*, p. 40)), can only remind her of the formlessness in the exterior: 'our situation's better than beyond the backyard, where indeed the earth seems to stop pretty abruptly and not restart' (*ibid.*). This is a terrifying vision of Wittgenstein's observation that 'A spatial object must be situated in infinite space.'[25] Yet there are interiors within interiors, claustrophobias within claustrophobias. In 'Experimenting', for example, the speech of the woman is an enclosed space, a trap:

> So I have to put my face into her voice, a shiny baize-lined
>   canister that says all round me, staring in:
> 'I've tried tonight. This place!'   (p. 39)

This relationship is conducted not so much by interpersonal reactions but through the objects of intersubjective space, 'Trying it on, though, going on about the milk bottle, tableleg, / The little things' (p. 39). But this affects the man's perceptions: 'Only a little twilight is left washing around outside, her unease interfering with it as I watch' (*ibid.*).

The motifs recur, repeated deliberately as part of the work's procedure, on the model of a painter using the same studio objects in several paintings. Each interior contains some of the oppressive elements, a fact that binds the texts together: alcoholic drinks, milk bottles, haircuts, as well as reappearing baize, and various cupboards, carpets, doors, walls and windows.

For example, the lampshade and the light switch—even electricity itself in 'The Small Room'—are aspects of one recurrence: the light bulb. In 'The Small Room', the narrator remarks, with contained paranoia: 'That bulb again. It has travelled even here' (*P55–87*, p. 40). Transferred between locations, it becomes a universal, not simply the usual permissable recurrences of simile and metaphor. The woman's fingers in 'Experimenting' are 'white like unlit electric bulbs' (*P55–87*, p. 39), and such repetition, painterly in procedure, also rehearses the ultimately threatening existential reality behind Wittgenstein's cool proposition: 'If I know an object I also know all its possible occurrences in space.'[26] But what is theorized as plenitude is experienced as a world of limited, conspiring elements or 'unscheduled things' as one poem puts it (p. 47). *Interiors* suggests finally that 'Objects are what is unalterable and subsistent; their configuration is what is changing and unstable',[27] something which disturbs the integrity of an observing self, which becomes the concern of Fisher's next work in prose.

The Ship's Orchestra (1966) is the nearest Fisher has approached to prose fiction, although the linearity of its discernible narrative, a supposed syntagmatic chain of events, is constantly disrupted by the formal method of returning motifs. As in *Interiors*, a paradigmatic recurrence unsettles and destabilizes the suspension of disbelief in its fictive 'reality'. For example, the text opens with a vision of the Ivory Corner, where the five musicians of the orchestra on the ocean liner hope to play.

> The Ivory Corner was only a wooden section of wall painted white, at the intersection of two passageways. To the left of it was the longer corridor; to the right at once there was the washroom door.   (*P55–87*, p. 199)

The recurrence of the Ivory Corner is increasingly infected with the fearful subjectivities of the musicians, particularly as it is clear that they are not going to be asked to play. The second paragraph is a subjective transformation, in terms of its interference with the self, both tactile and perceptual, of the first's objectivity:

> Ivory Corner for leaning against, the white pressing the forehead, the wood's vertical grain flickering beneath it up and down across the horizontals of the eyelids. (*Ibid.*)

The third paragraph, less readable as realist fiction, develops the vision of a dislocated body that haunts the work:

> Washroom door swings, has weight, has rubber silencers. Limbs overhanging it from the Ivory Corner get foggy, the elbow gone, winging; a hand spread on the panel beside it stays brown and dry and shiny. (*Ibid.*)

Much later the Ivory Corner menacingly becomes 'a tongue that licks me slowly as I approach' (*P55–87*, p. 208). The Ivory Corner comes to represent deeply irreconcilable desires for the two women musicians, Joyce, a seventeen-year-old drummer from Nottingham, and Amy, a dedicated black American trombone player, 'a musical shark' (p. 205); for the former the place is one of sentiment, for the latter, one of sadomasochistic fantasy:

> Ivory Corner for Joyce; on the white paintwork a big lipstick mouth to kiss her. Ivory Corner for Amy: padded hooks, to hold her up by the shoulder-straps. (p. 216)

Black Liverpudlian Dougal's Ivory Corner is less conventionally sadistic: 'Joyce, standing stark naked and freezing cold, with her eyes shut, at two in the morning' (p. 216). Merrett, the hard-drinking saxophonist, has more in common with the narrator's sense of the Ivory Corner as a haptic presence, a waiting place: 'with a heavy iron disc to press down on to the crown of his head when he stiffens upward' (*ibid.*).

The orchestra remains provisional; losing their professional roles, the musicians lose their reality and identity: 'We are accepted everywhere as what we have become' (p. 208), but what they have become is not clear, even when there appears an actor to play the narrator's 'part'. They begin to experience the shuddering ship, the 'interior' in which they are 'various figures', as a prison (in one paragraph it is imaginatively transformed into a penal railway), or as a fictive laboratory for testing their sensations, perceptions and the strength of the group identity: 'we are all lizards, or will be . . . And we shall not feel sorry for one another when the blunt scissors jag at us' (p. 202).

As in *Interiors*, objects negotiate relationship, in this case the unplayed instruments which could define the musicians: a trombone becomes an 'axe', a saxophone a 'Tusk', the piano 'one of the many kinds of box' (*P55–87*, p. 200). Yet as things fall apart, the possibility of a desperate unity haunts the text: 'If only we could all play on one single instrument!' (p. 216). This epiphany (the musicians' equivalent to making a tree) occurs just before the Ivory Corner becomes no more than a series of projections for their separate subjectivities, and it is lost as the realization strikes the narrator that such an instrument, by now, like the Ivory Corner, will be 'Not really a tangible thing' but 'an invisible sphincter in the sky somewhere, with a fivefold answer to our touches' (p. 217). The ship's cruise is its own deferral of function; there are no opportunities to manufacture trees, no *ex machina* deliverances.

The book ends 'at sea', where it began. The view of 'many black shoes, shuffling, swivelling' (*P55–87*, p. 223) at the end is too late to confer function upon the orchestra. It is fitting that the text—dramatizing the loss of self through loss of identity or role—should end with what David Punter has described as 'the primacy of the object over the merely human'[28] with a blinding, paradoxical vision of 'the bright fog of daylight' (p. 223) (yet even this fog is generated by the foggy limbs overhanging the Ivory Corner). Objects, such as this fog, the instruments, the Ivory Corner itself, oppress the characters.

The writing procedure is explained by Fisher; 'I had a starter', which was the Picasso painting *Three Musicians*, and the idea of possible music. 'I had certain revolving themes which I would feed in', as I have indicated in my analysis of the paradigmatic recurrences.[29] There was no revision of paragraphs, but 'complete linearity of composition'.[30] With additive procedure developing character and action, with a narrative that is not structural in the sense of being a plot, with a fictiveness that short-circuits the reader's usual sense of fiction, it is not surprising that its perceptual intensity 'has become in the act of writing an abstract problem, a subject for perceptual geometry' as David Punter puts it.[31] To concentrate as these lost characters do on one of the senses or upon a programmatic synaesthesia is to reach the edge of coherence, the edge of selfhood which is conventionally held together by consistent perceptions.

> Think of what all the people you see taste like and you'd go mad; all those leaping, billowing tastes through the world, like a cemetery turned suddenly into damp bedsheets with the wind under them ... there's an enormous stretch of meaninglessness in it ... it ought to mean; but how can anything mean *that*?
>
> (*P 55–87*, p. 201)

The characters seem to construct themselves in relation to recurring objects in their world; the foregrounded artifice of Fisher's characterization develops serially in the procedure. The challenge of the text is not to let us forget the latter, even whilst we are being convinced of the former.

The stated aim of the five 'Metamorphoses', in Fisher's accompanying note, was to change, 'in full view, one thing into another whose nature was quite unforeseen at the outset, the change to be worked by playing over the starting idea'.[32] This procedure, for the 1970 text, clearly develops from *The Ship's Orchestra*, particularly as I have outlined it in relation to its first three paragraphs.

In each text the 'starter' is an ordinary situation, a cat's face, the figure of a man in the street, a bowl of kidney beans, a man undressing, and—in the first—a woman sleeping. These changes are not embedded in narrative like *The Ship's Orchestra*. Each paragraph opening feels like a key change in music or a progressively focussed reoriented camera shot of a scene: a considered realignment within a perceptible continuity, but this is not at all like the propositional development of *Interiors*. Its repeating phrases introduce differing emphases:

> She sleeps, in the day, in the silence. Where there is light, but
> little else: the white covers, the pillow, her head with its
> ordinary hair, her forearm dark over the sheet.
>
> She sleeps and it is hardly a mark on the stillness; that she
> should have moved to be there, that she should be moving now
> across her sleep as the window where the light comes in passes
> across the day.   (*P55–87*, p. 82)

In the first the female's sleep is emphatically enveloped by time and
soundlessness. In the second, silence has becomes stillness; and it is
synaesthetically a background, a surface to be 'marked' (a characteristic Fisher lexis). In the first, the vision is of light illuminating
her and these surroundings, her lack of features ('ordinary hair')
and her contrasting dark arm. In the second paragraph, in a parallelism that matches those in the first sentence, 'she should' points
both back to her prehistory of arrival, and to the possibility of her
future movements, transformations, through the stillness of sleep.
The window itself seems to move as though the day (which she
was previously 'in') were passing (which in the colloquial sense
it is).

The third paragraph perceptually realigns towards considerations
of temperature, 'Her warmth is in the shadows of the bed', although,
as there are 'few shadows', there is little warmth (*P55–87*, p. 82). The
abstract 'day' transforms into the specifics of 'sky', in which the association of temperature allows a cloud to become, and be, 'smoke'
(*ibid.*). There are 'fish-trails high in the air'—clouds, punning verbally
and visually on fish tails and vapour trails (*ibid.*). Her sleep is now
mobile, no longer in, but on top of the other surface of the silence. It
is 'an open mouth travelling back on moving waves'—she is reduced
to a synecdoche of her own mouth; stillness reverses into motion
(*ibid.*).

From this point, a second metaphor, of 'fish' and 'waves', dissolves
the woman's presence further, associates her away, as it were, into her
constituent phenomenological elements. As they come free, she
'leaks' into the room itself, the opposite of the contained claustrophobia of *Interiors*.

Mouth open across the water, the knees loosened in sleep; dusks of the body shadowed around the room. (*P55–87*, p. 82)

By the time we reach the seventh and final paragraph, it is as though we are reading a description of a process where a painter has reduced a figurative portrait to abstraction and then re-figured it as a different set of objects: 'Water lights crossing and combining endlessly over the inward membrane of the roof, rising in a curve, almost a cone, to the round lantern with its dirty panes' (*ibid.*). The question of light, the content of a recognizable Fisher interior, and the liberated metaphor of water here have taken over entirely to reconfigure the world, where, to return to Wittgenstein, the objects *and* the configurations are 'changing and unstable'.[33]

The slowness of this overall method is seductive. It is not some cry of despair at the interchangeability of physical phenomena, the negation of value, but an act of faith in the mental processes of possibility and change, steady and controlled, exactly the 'slowed-down exploration of the kind of field in which ideas exist' of Fisher's slightly defensive 'Note'.[34]

This defensiveness may derive from what appears to be a wholly dedicated commitment to the phenomenology of radically changing perceptions. In *Interiors* and *The Ship's Orchestra* (both written before Fisher's long writing block of the late 1960s) there is a sense of menace in the ontological insecurity of the characters. Here there are virtually no characters, but a focus upon the 'field' of ideas, a more mobile, plural, sense of self as a deep inwardness, not of psychological reflection, but of perceptual fascination that characterizes the work following the block. As Fisher says, with a deliberate plural: 'I specialise in inner selves'. [35]

The Cut Pages was composed, as was *The Ship's Orchestra*, on a set number of sheets, and the work's title foregrounds this. The sheets were, in fact, sliced from a 'diary of demoralisation'[36] which contained personal matters and from which the author, now rejecting the stance of unwilling hero, wished to be free. It was, significantly, this work of 1970 which broke the four-year writer's block. The idea of 'cutting' also suggests both the procedure of the piece, the cutting loose of improvisation—Fisher writes of having 'no programme beyond the principle that it should not know where its next meal was coming from' (*Cut* (1986), p. 8)—and its thematic foci, ideas constellated around notions of patterning and transformation. The passages we are reading seem somehow excised, bracketed as the phenomenologists would say, in an ironical act of 'censoring in', rather than out, of materials.

Whereas the bleak diaries had been the composed record of actions that had already happened, an improvisation is the act of what happens, during composition. The programme of having 'no programme . . . produced very rapid changes of direction', as Fisher said (*Cut* (1986), p. 8). In contrast to the contemporaneous 'Metamorphoses', there is often discontinuity between paragraphs, and instead of the metaphor of key changes in music to describe a linear reading, the appropriate musical metaphor would be not the pre-war jazz favoured by Fisher himself as a musician, but the free improvised jazz practised by Evan Parker, Derek Bailey and others; as their music progresses there can occur complete changes of musical dynamic, the deliberate avoidance of pre-established patterns. When Fisher remarks, in what appears to be an embedded statement of intent, 'This discontinuity is my discontinuity' (*Cut* (1986), p. 30) he is not far from Parker, who is quoted in Bailey's book *Improvisation*, as saying, 'I change, the music changes'.[37] This is neither an admission of self-centredness, nor of formlessness. Another passage from the text reads: 'Laws for the empty. Patterns for the free' (p. 34). *The Cut Pages* necessitates the abandonment of concepts of form based upon fixed structures in favour of a fulfilling (the opposite of 'empty') pattern-making activity. Parker would agree: 'Improvisation makes its own form',[38] one coterminous with performance in music, coterminous with the print of the paragraph, or the space of the page.

Page-space is important in *The Cut Pages* as in no other work by Fisher (except the spatial *Cultures*).[39] Not only is the cut page the performance space, the paragraphs, varying in length from one word to several conventionally formed sentences, lack the solidity of the blocks of earlier works; if paragraphs are as emotional as Gertrude Stein claimed, then the emotion here is peculiarly tentative, the emotion generated is its own subject. The paragraphs end without full stops and seem to hang on the page. The apparent drop to the capital lettter of the subsequent paragraph often connects with re-directed energies. Implications for the visual presentation of the texts are not lost on Fisher, and this is the reason it has not been reprinted in collected editions, he says. 'It is out of scale to the rest of the writing ... it occupies an enormous amount of space for what is transacted in it ... I could see it better as a free-standing thing, pre-ferably artistically done and certainly not a small print text.'[40]

This question of the 'ratio of didactic event to space'[41] suggests that the fourteen 'pages', spread in the current edition over thirty-eight small-format pages, demonstrate a *lack* of rapid change, of something lightly textured. Fisher's unfulfilled desire for an 'artistically done'[42] large-print edition would realise the isolation of the paragraphs, make them available for bracketed contemplation, break the flow of the reading eye. When Fisher remarks, 'Occasionally artists take images out of it, I would like to have it so it would work for artists',[43] he seems to imply a process of freeze-framing and extraction, the opposite of the improvisation that produced it. This is possible with improvised writing since its reception can never be as durational as music. When Fisher states that he 'doesn't know the work very well', and that he could go 'back to it to see what is transacted' and 'use the energy' by rewriting it,[44] he is suggesting contemplation as improvisatory reading, as a spur towards further creativity. This is close to Fisher's recent description of his private notebook: 'It doesn't progress towards becoming a system ... I use it as a disorderly private oracle. I can move about in it, guided by its skeins of metaphors, elliptical jargon and obsessively-acquired images.'[45]

The Cut Pages, however, is not a notebook. It is an improvisation, complete, yet it can be reread (oracularly or not) across its formal dimensions, against duration. Whether following the 'page' or taking the isolated 'image', both ways of working amount to a radical abandonment of even the syntagmatic and paradigmatic possibilities found in *The Ship's Orchestra*. The reader is best guided by an un-attributed intentional statement communicated by John Matthias, one of the few critics before this volume to mention the work: 'Fisher says his readers should let the words come and see what sticks in their minds.'[46] Yet Matthias's reduction of this extraordinary text to 'personal need', a cure for writer's block, is a denial of this advice, and sits oddly with his own appreciation of the text's improvisation through a Heideggerean concept of 'listening': 'where nothing gets ... signified ... but things make their appearance in the sense of coming into their own'.[47] This is in accordance with J. D. Needham's characterization of *The Cut Pages* as 'an attack on those who would impose rigid structures upon their experience',[48] the emptiness of 'Law'.

Critics, such as Matthias, often quote the opening lines of the work because it offers itself as an exemplary passage, yet it is more obviously patterned than most: patterning is its thematic focus, structure its object of attack. Its parallel phrases offer verbal emphases lacking elsewhere, its visual arrangement the most unconventional of the book:

Coil   If you can see the coil hidden in this pattern, you're
            colour-blind

            Pale patterns, faded card, coral card, faded card,
            screen card, window fade

Whorl   If you can see this word and say it without hesitation
            you're deaf

            Then we can get on with frame

Frameless   Meat-rose, dog-defending, trail-ruffling
                                        (*Cut* (1986), p. 13)

The reader might recognise here a reference to the cards used for testing colour-blindness, as later in the section: 'If you can see the numeral 88 in the pattern' (*Cut* (1986), p. 14). It suggests the eighty-eight keys of a piano and a pattern in a wallpaper: 'The Old 88; the wallpaper piano' (*ibid.*). This is how the mind moves, when freed to follow its conceptualizations, not as a stream of consciousness, but as a conscious set of jumps, even as acts of language rather than of reference. As the text comments elsewhere: 'He will not refer, but will act (p. 22). The '88', a kind of quadruple coil, visually, operates by covert presence in a pattern; the eighty-eight keys of the piano are displayed linearly and indeed are only usable if they, and their patterning, are overtly recognized.

A series of such associative patterns or leaps, along with the sonic echoes of 'c's, 'f's, and 'd's, the 'patterns' and 'cards' of the second paragraph, for example, show not the results (whatever that could be) but the working of such thinking, ending with the filmic 'window fade' which seems to close visuality. 'Whorl', an almost synonym and almost rhyme for 'coil' (as well as 'word'), is foregrounded in its audial materiality; it is difficult to say with its 'h' sound.

Interestingly, the generative principle for such prose is not only improvisation, but repetition and parallelism, such as we see in the opening. There are frequent passages of lists with repeated nouns, as well as patterns of repetition which are similar to the incremental, intonational flow found in speech: 'On the march. March a path to march on' (*Cut* (1986), p. 15). Yet this text is not dramatic, and its apparent speech patterning, I think, rather reflects its improvisatory origin. Such marking, particularly noun repetition rather than the deployment of pronouns, exists in speech as a way of keeping the object of attention clear if the context is not. (Obversely, pronouns are used here without nouns, a feature of speech when the context is obvious, or shared.) The text evokes these structures of such self-evidence, although the discourse is far from clear. Additionally, there are words that repeat throughout the book, perhaps deliberately fed back into the improvisation, as in the generative processes of *The Ship's Orchestra*: there is in this lexis an understandable recurrence of words to do with patterning, and transformation, part of its metaphorical skein: cracks, growing, frame, breath, corrosive.

The remark 'Then we can get on with frame' teases at the edge of the idiomatic, but the lack of plural on frame, or the absence of an article for the noun, work against some skeletal plot possibility concerning an eye test for new glasses. 'If you can see' does suggest the voice of an optician, but on its second occurrence, it is transformed parodically, as often in Fisher's hybrid works, a common, and conscious, procedure, a weapon against rigidity. A frame will also fix (another repeated word), and the rejection of frame as concept introduces the reader to a series of alarming possibilities, even of perceptual and referential anarchy: 'frameless' and therefore unbound. The reader may sense the 'dog-rose' and the dog's tail in the word 'trail', in the last line above; the 'defending' suggests a guard dog, but this dog is more defended than defending, a characteristic reversal. Its significance here lies in the sense of its own process, the search for pattern. As Charles Bernstein puts it: 'Formal dynamics in a poem create content through the shapes, feelings, attitudes and structures that compose the poem.'[49] The entire project of *The Cut Pages* is to invite a reader to improvise, to see patterns where normally they are not; it issues a challenging 'if you can see' that remains conditional, that refuses the fixity of conclusion.

The Cut Pages is Fisher's most formally audacious work, which puts him firmly, if only temporarily, in the company of some of the American language poets with their poet's prose or new sentence work, such as Ron Silliman's *Tjanting* (1981), which is structured upon the Fibonacci number sequence, Rosmarie Waldrop's *The Reproduction of Profiles* (1987) and Jackson Mac Low's *Pieces o' Six* (1992), which are, like some of Fisher's works, improvisations on particular sized sheets. It can also be seen in the context of what Eric Mottram called 'The British Poetry Revival': from the hybrid prose in Gael Turnbull's *Trampoline* (1968), which may have suggested a model for many of Fisher's hybrid forms, to the improvisations of Tom Raworth, 'Stag Skull Mounted', composed within months of Fisher's 1970 pieces, in *Tottering State* (1988); from the defamiliarized prose of Barry MacSweeney's 'Just 22 and I Don't Mind Dying' (1971), in *Odes* (1978), to the minimal assemblage of Lee Harwood's 'Days and Nights: Accidental Sightings', in *Morning Light* (1998). *The Cut Pages* predates most of these experiments, and it is seldom acknowledged as an influence upon them. It is surprising that it is not more noted by both poets and critics. The text's elusive qualities make it oddly resistant to memory. Critics tend to select passages consonant with their general hypotheses about the rest of Fisher's work. If I have been as guilty of this, ignoring the text's own scepticism about the urge to fix unity, I hope I have given at least a sampling of its textures and procedures, without needing to argue for its cultural centrality.

> Centre. They brought a centre and set it up here, but it wouldn't take. It was rejected, and went off sideways. No sign of it now
> (*Cut* (1986), p. 42)

What is most surprising is the extent to which there has been little sign of prose in Roy Fisher's work since *The Cut Pages*. The exceptions are some of his finest short works of the 1970s.[50] The paragraphs of 'Rules and Ranges for Ian Tyson' do indeed read like instructions for a visual artist, or like a Dick Higgins text for a Fluxus event, yet they demand the impossible—'To walk along two adjacent sides of a building at once, as of right' (*P55–87*), p. 140—which recalls a similarly suggestive passage from *The Cut Pages*: 'A journey by car through many streets, seen through several windows, by more than one head' (*Cut* (1986), p. 32).

This desire for the multiple, amid perceptual disordering, akin to the interest in unique patterning in *The Cut Pages*, is found in one of the two paragraphs of 'rules' beginning 'Under the new'. Its conceptual content seems a development of the fragment already quoted, one of its 'rich variations':

> Under the new football rules the goals will be set, not facing each other … but at the centres of adjoining sides of a square pitch … Some minor changes in rules are bound to be necessary, but there will also be rich variations in styles of play.
> (*P55–87*, p. 140)

This manifesto for a deregulated action, for re-routed activity, now quite without a sense of menace, is found in another of these prose pieces, 'Releases', in which a jigsaw puzzle is re-functioned to show 'anarchy and nature to the child. It's not for solving, it's for the disordering of feeling' (p. 149). Yet alongside this familiar disposition in Fisher's work, and *because* it had become familiar, even amounting to a set of predictable remarks and demonstrations, there appears a fresh autobiographical voice, no longer leaving 'my own position /

empty for you in its frame' (p. 116). In two contiguous passages we find this narrative voice released in ironic self-reflection, followed by astonished self-commentary:

> The greater part of my life is past, and I seem to have done nothing. Yet I've achieved rather more than I've attempted, so that means I've kept my standards.
>
> It's amazing what you can say if you try.   (p. 149)

This prefigures the relaxed, experienced, anecdotal, dramatized voice found in some poems of the 1980s and 1990s, the voice of a quite willing, but ironically non-confessional, hero, which might be thought to be a prose voice: 'I'm old enough to want to be prosaic; / I shall have my way' (p. 186), ends one such text.[51] However, Fisher does have a more 'public' position in British poetry now, and the adoption of a prosaic public voice might seem suitable. Yet Fisher's prose has never been prosaic, as I hope I've shown. I believe he turned from prose to avoid repetitive structures of conceptualization that would defeat the point of his inventing 'freedom forms' in the first place. The hybrid and procedurally generated works I have examined here contain much, in their individual ways, that poetry has been told to exclude, thematically and stylistically, and use formal techniques that, in Britain at least, are still regarded with suspicion. These works cannot be written of (or even off) as minor or capricious productions. We cannot avoid the extent of such texts in the body of Roy Fisher's work, particularly given the fact that Fisher has mostly collected them in volumes with 'Poems' conspicuously in the title. However much these texts dissolve poetic conventions, they are to be judged as poetry, and only by extending the paradigm of what it is possible to call poetry; that is their greatest distinction and their greatest challenge.

NOTES

1. Stephen Fredman, *Poet's Prose: The Crisis in American Verse* (Cambridge: Cambridge University Press, 1983), p. 7.

2. *Ibid.*, p. 3.

3. *Ibid.*, p. 6.

4. Roy Fisher, BBC Radio 3: 'The Living Poet', broadcast 20 November 1981.

5. Eric Mottram, 'Conversation with Roy Fisher', *Saturday Morning*, 1 (1976), unpaginated [p. 16].

6. Roy Fisher, *Poems 1955–1987* (Oxford: Oxford University Press, 1988), pp. 28–29.

7. Jon Silkin, *The Life of Metrical and Free Verse in Twentieth-Century Poetry* (Basingstoke: Macmillan, 1997), p. 304.

8. Viktor Shklovsky, 'Art as Technique', in *Russian Formalist Criticism*, ed. L. T. Lemon and M. J. Reis (Lincoln NB and London: University of Nebraska Press, 1965), p. 12.

9. Ian Gregson, *Contemporary Poetry and Postmodernism: Dialogue and Estrangement* (Basingstoke: Macmillan, 1996), p. 176.

10. *Ibid.*, p. 176.

11. Silkin, *The Life of Metrical and Free Verse in Twentieth-Century Poetry*, p. 305.

12. Mottram, 'Conversation with Roy Fisher' [p. 14].

13. *Ibid.*, [p. 15].

14. Robert Sheppard, *Turning the Prism: An Interview with Roy Fisher* (Southwick: Ship of Fools, 1987), p. 7.

15. Ludwig Wittgenstein, *Philosophical Investigations* (Oxford: Basil Blackwell, 1968), p. vi.

16. Sheppard, *Turning the Prism*, p. 7.

17. Marjorie Perloff, *Wittgenstein's Ladder* (Chicago: University of Chicago Press, 1996), p. 200.

18. Wittgenstein, *Philosophical Investigations*, p. vi.

19. Perloff, *Wittgenstein's Ladder*, p. 8.

20. *Ibid.*, p. 42.

21. Mottram, 'Conversation with Roy Fisher' [p. 11].

22. Eric Mottram, 'Roy Fisher's Work', *Stand*, 11:1 (1969–70), p. 17.

23. J. D. Needham, 'Some Aspects of the Poetry of Roy Fisher', *Poetry Nation*, 5 (1975), p. 79.

24. Mottram, 'Roy Fisher's Work', p. 17.

25. Ludwig Wittgenstein, *Tractatus Logico-Philosophicus* (London: Routledge & Kegan Paul, 1961), p. 9.

26. *Ibid.*, p. 9.

27. *Ibid.*, p. 13.

28. David Punter, 'Metal on Stone', *Delta*, 62 (1981), p. 26.

29. Mottram, 'Conversation with Roy Fisher' [p. 13].

30. *Ibid.* [p. 13].

31. Punter, 'Metal on Stone', p. 26.

32. Roy Fisher, *The Cut Pages* (London: Fulcrum Press, 1971), p. 7.

33. Wittgestein, *Tractatus Logico-Philosophicus*, p. 13.

34. Roy Fisher, 'Note', *The Cut Pages* (1971), p. 7.

35. Sheppard, *Turning the Prism*, p. 5.

36. Roy Fisher, *The Cut Pages* (London: Oasis Shearsman, 1986). This is the second edition of the text (originally included in *The Cut Pages* (London: Fulcrum Press, 1971)), which will be referred to in the text as *Cut* (1986).

37. Derek Bailey, *Improvisation* (Derbyshire: Moorland Publishing, 1980), p. 151.

38. *Ibid.*, p. 133.

39. These texts were varieties of concrete poetry, with words arranged radially in a circle. They were published as *Cultures* (London: Tetrad, 1975). They are uncollected.

40. Sheppard, *Turning the Prism*, p. 8.

41. *Ibid.*

42. *Ibid.*

43. *Ibid.*

44. *Ibid.*, pp. 8–9.

45. Roy Fisher, 'Poet on Writing', in *Poets on Writing*, ed. Denise Riley (Basingstoke: Macmillan, 1992), p. 273.

46. John Matthias, 'The Poetry of Roy Fisher', in *Contemporary British Poetry: Essays in Theory and Criticism*, ed James Acheson and Romana Huk (New York: State University of New York Press, 1996), p. 53.

47. Gerald Bruns, quoted in Matthias, 'The Poetry of Roy Fisher', p. 47.

48. Needham, 'Some Aspects of the Poetry of Roy Fisher', p. 84.

49. Charles Bernstein, *A Poetics* (Cambridge MA and London: Harvard University Press, 1992), p. 8.

50. After a decade or more of no creative prose writing, it is a surprise to find the short passage of prose published in Roy Fisher, *The Dow Low Drop: New and Selected Poems* (Newcastle upon Tyne: Bloodaxe Books, 1996), which is part of the incomplete title poem, pp. 191–94. The topographical subject matter, rural rather than urban, and the imperative voice relate it to certain parts of *City*, but it is not clear whether this represents a significant development in, or even a return to, Fisher's use of prose.

51. 'The Lesson in Composition', *P55–87*, p. 186.

6

Cutting-Edge Poetics: Roy Fisher's 'Language Book'

MARJORIE PERLOFF

Surveying the items listed in Derek Slade's excellent bibliography of Roy Fisher, one cannot help speculating as to the curious turn in this poet's American reception. Why, to put it baldly, has Fisher's poetry, published and praised as it was in American avant-garde little magazines of the 1960s and 1970s, all but disappeared from their counterparts of the 1980s and 1990s? Does this disappearance mean that Fisher has become an Establishment figure or that his work is too insular for an American audience? Surely not, for as John Kerrigan observes in his review of Fisher's most recent collection, *The Dow Low Drop* (1996), 'His refusal to strike marketable postures ... has kept him relatively unknown' in England as well.[1] But if Fisher is, as Kerrigan suggests, an experimental, antithetical poetic figure, why hasn't his work caught on in such successors of *Kulchur* (which published 'Then Hallucinations' in 1962) or *Montemora* (which brought out 'Diversions', 1–20 in 1977), as *Sulfur* or *Temblor* or *Talisman*, or in the countless little magazines, both in the US and in Canada, associated with Language poetry?[2]

The American response would not be especially significant were it not that it *had been* so enthusiastic. Reviewing six Migrant pamphlets for *Kulchur* (Summer 1962), Denise Levertov declares that 'what English poetry desperately needed was a shot in the arm from American poetry.... Now at last something is happening' (pp. 4–5). And she singles out Fisher along with Michael Shayer as 'England's hope'. Fisher's *City* is compared to William Carlos Williams's *Paterson* and praised for its comparable 'nakedness', its 'directness of feeling' (p. 8). Again, in an interview of 1977, Jed Rasula compares *The Ship's Orchestra* to John Ashbery's *Three Poems*: 'Both books,' he remarks, '. . . have an extreme sort of concentration which is like wringing water out of a washcloth'. And the discussion moves on, as is typical of Fisher commentary in the 1970s, to the question of the poet's relationship to the American 'open form' poetics of William Carlos Williams, Charles Olson and Black Mountain.[3]

The link between Fisher (along with Tom Raworth, Gael Turnbull, Michael Shayer and a few others) and American counter-cultural poetics was first made by Donald Davie in *Thomas Hardy and British Poetry* (1972), although Davie subordinated that link to what he took to be a more powerful, if subconscious, similarity between Fisher and Philip Larkin and, *via* Larkin, to Hardy.[4] But the Williams–Olson–Creeley connection has since become a truism: as recently as 1993, Neil Corcoran, in his *English Poetry since 1940*, places Fisher, along with Christopher Middleton and J. H. Prynne, in a category called 'Varieties of Neo-Modernism', which is defined by

> three essential characteristics: a turning against what these poets read as a played-out native humanist or empiricist tradition; a deliberate indebtedness to the work (poetic, critical and aesthetic) of Ezra Pound and through him, of an American writing whose central figure is Charles Olson; and a readiness for an exploratory or experimental formal inventiveness not common in post-war British poetry.[5]

The reference here is to the much touted 'open form' of the 1960s, as proclaimed by Olson in his famous essay 'Projective Verse'. But the alignment of Corcoran's 'neo-Modernists' (along with others like Eric Mottram and Charles Tomlinson) to the Williams school has always been more apparent than real. In the 1960s, as Tom Raworth observes, these poets 'saw something fresh and useable in US work of the Williams/Zukofsky/Olson tradition . . . and, the British literary structure being so rigid, their use of these techniques was enough for them to be classed as "alternative" or "experimental" or whatever the label was then.'[6] And, one might add, their American counterparts were only too happy to admire those who were admiring them. In a 1989 interview with John Tranter, Fisher himself refers, somewhat ruefully, to the irony that his Fulcrum books found their audience, not at home, but in the US: 'When I went to America I met all the people who had bought my Fulcrum books. They hired me to do readings. That's where my Fulcrum books were, on American bookshelves, in houses on campuses. People who'd bought them in the late sixties.'[7]

What has changed in the intervening decades—and this is largely misunderstood in surveys of post-war poetry, both in the US and in Britain—is that the familiar tale of 1960s oppositionality, of the much touted 'breakthrough' of American 'open form' poetics, has itself come under fire. The fate of Olsonian 'projective verse' is a large topic to which I cannot do justice here. Suffice it to say that, at its best, as in the case of Robert Creeley's poetry, the phenomenology of 'open form', with its emphasis on authenticity, the simulation of the speaking voice, and the 'natural look', has evolved into a form of writing more consonant with the dislocations and simulacra of the mediated 1980s and 1990s.[8] Other poets in the Williams tradition—Levertov, Gary Snyder, David Ignatow—who have continued to mine the veins of Black Mountain, no longer have the standing they once had, and so Fisher's work may well have suffered a certain guilt by association.

What makes this neglect both unfortunate and ironic is that Fisher never had much in common with his American admirers like Levertov. Critics have been misled, I think, by Fisher's stated pre-dilection for a poetry of 'things'. Thus he tells Jed Rasula, with reference to *The Ship's Orchestra* (1966), that 'I work by perceptual attentions. For me the thing had to be grounded in sensations and in refinements of sensation, and indeed the book is written as an ela-boration of almost hallucinatory sensory effects—tactile, olfactory, visual of course, auditory.' And again, when asked to comment on the credo of Williams's *Paterson*: 'The trouble with "no ideas but in things" is that it has become an idea.' Whereas Williams's real strength is 'the wealth and diversity of sensations taken from ... a limited immediate perceptual field'.[9]

Following the poet's lead, critics have made much of the concreteness and 'perceptual attention' of his poems. Martin Dodman, reviewing *The Thing about Joe Sullivan* (1978), praises the 'graceful concision of a language pared-down to collocations of words that might have had their surfaces scraped away by contact with one another to reveal fresh significances and reverberate in new ways', and J. D. Needham talks of the 'startling immediacy' and 'vivid particularity' of the poems, citing as an example a passage, in the final poem of 'Matrix', where the poet looks down into a rock pool and 'finds it hard to distinguish between the water, the floor of the pool, the pool-life and reflections from the sky':

> long white and green
> ravels in the blue
> tensioned over the shimmering
> chalky surface; . . .[10]

In a similar vein, though more critically, John Kerrigan refers to the 'state of empirical overload', the 'exhausted encounter with the real', represented by such early poems as 'Seven Attempted Moves':

> A cast concrete basin
>   with a hole in the bottom
> Empty but for
>   a drift of black grit
> Some feathers some hair
>   some grey paper.
> Nothing else for the puzzled face to see.[11]

For a reader attuned to Williams's extraordinary precision, these assessments, whether pro or con, are puzzling, for the language cited is hardly that of concrete sensations. If, for example, the 'long white and green / ravels in the blue' (the noun 'ravels' is a rather fussy and obscure word for tangles, knotted threads), refers to the reflection of tall trees silhouetted against white cloud, the metaphor distances rather than concretizes the image. And the phrase 'tensioned over the shimmering / chalky surface' is not only abstract but confusing, for how can a chalky (and hence opaque) surface be 'shimmering'? How, moreover, does a chalky surface reflect those 'white and green ravels'?

The second example, a stanza from 'Seven Attempted Moves', is even less 'thingy'. Williams (and the Objectivists after him) would probably have omitted the opening article and preposition, to give us:

> cast concrete basin
> > hole in the bottom . . .

More important: Williams would have never used the bland adjective 'some', which tells us virtually nothing about 'feathers', 'hair' or 'grey paper'. And finally, the line 'Nothing else for the puzzled face to see' goes against all Imagist–Objectivist prescriptions: it is an example of telling rather than showing, of refusing to let the images do the work. 'Use no word,' said Ezra Pound, in what became a credo for Williams as well, 'that does not contribute to the presentation.'

All the same, Fisher was on to something when he insisted that for him 'the thing had to be grounded in sensations'. For 'ideas'—which Rasula takes to be the staple of Ashbery's *Three Poems*, as opposed to the 'things' in *The Ship's Orchestra*—are definitely *not* congenial to Fisher. 'That's partly,' he tells his interviewers, 'because I don't have any training in logic or any education in abstract thinking or any inclination towards it. I've got a great distrust of it', a remark that certainly separates Fisher from Louis Zukofsky and George Oppen. Rather, 'a poem has business to exist, really, if there's a reasonable chance that somebody may have his perceptions re-arranged by having read it or having used it . . . a poem is making some kind of potentially new dislocative effect in the minds of some readers'.[12]

This 'dislocated effect' has been related by Fisher's commentators to the Russian formalist doctrine of 'making it strange' or 'defamiliarization'.[13] But 'dislocated' from what and to what purpose? And is the 're-arranging' of the reader's 'perceptions' a sufficiently large ambition for poetry? Here Fisher's distrust of logic and abstract thinking is telling. He is a poet drawn to the 'perceptual field' of sensations, who doesn't in fact quite trust those sensations either—

hence the need to extrapolate, to explain, in the case of the 'feathers', 'hair' and 'grey paper' of daily life, that there is 'Nothing else for the puzzled face to see.' 'As a poet, I'm an image maker', Fisher insists,[14] deploring the tendency of many of his fellow poets to write a poetry of moral or political statement. But what happens when what Yeats called those 'images that yet / Fresh images beget' lose their power to charm and 'dislocate'? Even in *City*, as John Matthias has noted, Fisher's is not 'the imagination of a realist'.[15] Rather, the poet's great subject—and here his poetry has no school affinities, either in Britain or in the US—may well be the void confronted by a poet whose refusal to submit to the power of the Image is matched by his self-declared distrust of philosophy, of all 'education in abstract thinking'. The central text, in this regard, is one that has been, in John Kerrigan's recent words, 'left out in the cold'—namely, *The Cut Pages* of 1971.[16] In this, his most radical and misunderstood poetic sequence, Fisher's writing, I hope to suggest here, is closer to the minimalist prose of Beckett than to the precisionist lyric of Williams or the didactic projective verse of Olson. And, beyond Beckett, Fisher may be seen as the unwitting precursor of what Ron Silliman has called 'the new sentence' as well as of the visual poetics now practiced by such 'Language' poets as Rosmarie Waldrop and Joan Retallack.

'Different Shadows, Different Surfaces'

Fisher's introduction to the second (1986) edition of *The Cut Pages* is unusually candid and revelatory. Since this small-press book is not readily available and since, for reasons given in his introduction, Fisher has chosen not to include the sequence in *Poems 1955–1987* or in the 1996 collection *The Dow Low Drop*, I cite the introduction almost in its entirety:

> '*The Cut Pages* was written on sheets taken out of a notebook between whose covers I no longer wanted to work. The aim in the improvization was to give the words as much relief as possible from serving in planned situations; so the work was

taken forward with no programme beyond the principle that it should not know where its next meal was coming from . . .'

That phraseology gives the clue to what *The Cut Pages* really was: a document of release, a device for dissolving a prolonged stasis. Since writing the *Ceremonial Poems* early in 1966, I had been almost completely blocked for four years, and when, early in that period, I assembled my first collection (which was to appear in 1969 as *Collected Poems 1968*) I had no expectation that there would ever be anything to follow it. After a while I even gave up adding to the file of self-strangulated false starts, and let the phobia have its way.

But in 1968, at a little distance from the writing of texts which might one day be published, I resolved to tidy up my desultory habit of journal-and-notebook keeping and write a leisurely and expansive journal, with no day in the year passing without an entry. There was no intention of an imaginative performance on the lines of *Kora in Hell*; it was to be a quite ordinary conversation with myself. It was ironic that the starting of the journal coincided with the onset of a period of relentless stress and personal crisis which was to dominate my life on every day of that year and most days of the one that followed it. Each day I wrote in the journal, for the routine was something to hang on to; but I never wrote anything explicit about what was happening to me. The entries, in their hundreds, are oblique, coded, desperate and dispiriting.

Recovering from my troubles towards the end of 1969, I found—or so I came to interpret it later—that the ideas about myself which had gathered round me as inhibitors, eventually locking together to bar me from my writing, had been burnt away and would probably never bother me again. And as a memento of the experience I had a notebook, partly filled with a diary of demoralization but with many as-yet-unstained pages. These I cut free from their binding, and used for one of the run of writings, all concerned with the dissolution of oppressive forms, 'purposes' and personal identities, which suddenly presented themselves in the first weeks of 1970: the

Glenthorne Poems; *The Cut Pages*; *The Six Deliberate Acts*; *Metamorphoses*; the materials of the *Matrix* sequence.

Of the five, *The Cut Pages* is possibly the oddest. I think of it as being—simply from the point of view of the relation of length to density—out of scale with almost everything else I have published; and for this reason I have been unwilling to see it reprinted in the company of shorter works.

'[T]o give the words as much relief as possible from serving in planned situations': this seems to be the key to this 'oddest' of poetic texts, one that, as Fisher himself says, is 'out of scale with almost everything else' he has published. The 'planned situations' to be avoided here are, to begin with, the familiar alternatives advanced by Molière's Monsieur Jourdain: verse and prose. Everything Fisher had published heretofore was written in one or the other. Prose, as in *The Ship's Orchestra* and a large proportion of *City*, often seemed more congenial than verse, whether formal or free, but, as is evident in the shorter pieces included in the 1971 edition of *Cut Pages*, Fisher's highly wrought prose, its sound design built on a great deal of alliteration, assonance, and repetition, is syntactically quite normal:

> All the green fields are cold, the bright afternoon deserted. Faces look out of the cars that go by; that is what they do, those faces. There is a tower among the trees, a white drum on legs, and a road turns off beside it, sweeping down to a cinder patch by the river where the field-tracks join and cars can park. A path, much mauled and trodden, leads through the elders, and at one place, where it crosses a marshy dip, a sheet of corrugated iron has been wedged across, balanced on a springy root and half earthed over.[17]

The effects here are gained by metaphor (the water tower as 'white drum on legs') and metonymy ('the bright afternoon deserted'), the paragraph organized by the poet-observer's unfolding 'camera-eye' perception: first fields, then cars, then the road down to the river, then the path through the elders, and so on. The look of the text on the page doesn't especially matter; indeed, in *Poems 1955–87*, the typeface is smaller and what was a nine-line paragraph is reduced to eight.

In *The Cut Pages*, this paragraph unit (justified left and right margins) gives way to page design—a design, incidentally, maintained in the 1986 edition, the only distinction being that, in the original, each notebook section is introduced by a black square at the upper-left margin, a logo replaced in the second edition by an empty circle. Here is the opening text, as it appears one-third of the page down below the square or circle:

Coil   If you can see the coil hidden in this pattern, you're colour-blind

            Pale patterns, faded card, coral card, faded card, screen card, window fade

Whorl   If you can see this word and say it without hesitation you're deaf

            Then we can get on with frame

Frameless   Meat-rose, dog-defending, trail-ruffling

Dodge

The Redcliffe Hotel? Forget it

Coming in on the curve. Cross under the baffle. Dropped through, folded in the flags

Street work. Across purposes and down flights. Only male shades flit   (*Cut* (1986), p. 13)

In the Rasula and Erwin interview, Fisher insists that ' "The Ship's Orchestra" and "The Cut Pages" are composed works, they stand as they were composed, and if you'd seen them before they were finished you would have found them as they are', whereas ' "City" and some of the other prose pieces in "Cut Pages"—those are assemblages, they're albums'.[18] This explanation is somewhat misleading for 'composed' in Fisher's lexicon is by no means equivalent to improvisatory or random: the first thing to notice in the extract above is that the justified right margin in lines 1, 3, 5, 11 and 13 is obtained, as I discovered when I tried to reproduce the passage, only by artificial spacing, as in the extra spaces provided for 'Pale patterns, faded card, coral card, faded card' in line 3. And Fisher admits that his particular 'experiment' in *The Cut Pages* is 'methodical' in that 'I know what it's going to do as well as I would know if I were writing a Petrarchan sonnet'.[19] The analogy is by no means coincidental: even as the sonnet has fourteen lines, *The Cut Pages* has fourteen (unnumbered) sections.

The use of page as unit within the larger unit of the two- or three-page section, each section being a 'line' within the framework of the fourteen-line Petrarchan love sonnet, is a remarkable innovation—one that, as I have argued in my 'After Free Verse',[20] distinguishes recent cutting-edge poetry from the free verse that precedes it, a free verse designed to track the momentary temporal shifts of the speaking voice and the individual perception. The mode of *The Cut Pages* is, as Rasula noted about Fisher's poetry in general, 'space oriented rather than time oriented'.[21] We perceive the page as a whole as we do in the case of a painting or other visual construct, our eyes then moving up and down and sideways to take in the words themselves and make sense of their relationships.

Consider the relation of 'Coil' to 'Whorl' on Fisher's opening page, reproduced above. The two words, separated from the rest of the text, form a column; they are further related by consonance: '*coil*' | '*whorl*'. 'If you can see the coil hidden in this pattern, you're colourblind', reads the first sentence. The 'pattern'—and 'pattern' will become a key word in the composition—has no centre, no hidden spring ('coil') at its core. To imagine that there might be such a centre is to be 'colour-blind', which is to say, unable to discriminate difference. And that, in a nutshell, is at the heart of the poet's malaise—a malaise that, as he tells us in the introduction, had precipitated severe writer's block. The 'coil', like the chiming 'whorl' beneath it on the page, cannot be mastered: 'If you can see this word and say it without hesitation you're deaf'. This is literally so because one wants to say 'whirl' for the hard-to-pronounce 'whorl'. And this difficulty makes it all but impossible to perceive 'pattern', especially when the properties available are no more than a 'faded card, coral card, faded card, / screen card', the word 'fade' shifting from its normal verbal (or participial) position to that of noun, as in 'window fade' (with its play on 'window shade').

'Then', the poet remarks in line 7, 'we can get on with frame'. But when is 'then'? The next line, far from following up on the notion of getting on, negates it with the single word 'Frameless', set off from the words that follow. Disjunctive and fragmented as this notebook page may be, a form of 'patterning' is carefully established. For what this opening tells us is that 'pattern' has neither centre nor frame; the 'coil' or 'whorl' that motivates the poet's meditation (one thinks of Pound's 'VORTEX is energy!') is inscrutable. 'Where we have both dark and light', as Beckett put it, 'we have also the inexplicable.'[22] To escape one's predicament *via* such 'normal' activities as feeding one's pet ('Meat-rose, dog-defending, trail-ruffling') is only a 'Dodge', the monosyllable a nice anagram on 'dog', as well as a visual echo of the words 'Coil' and 'Whorl'. Thus, when we finally come to a specific image—'The Redcliffe Hotel?'—the poet quickly tells himself, 'Forget it'. Whether (rather like Prufrock) he actually goes out or just imagines going, his exodus is 'Across purposes [at cross purposes] and down flights' to a place (probably a pub) where 'Only male shades flit'. 'Dying to get out', we read on the following page, 'But is exposed to the open at all events' (*Cut* (1986), 14).

'I never', says Fisher in the introduction, 'wrote anything explicit about what was happening to me. The entries in their hundreds are oblique, coded, desperate and dispiriting.' To decode these entries, to allegorize Fisher's broken phrases and find a narrative thread in the notebook is certainly possible, but what would be gained? No doubt, at one level *The Cut Pages* constitute a coded account of Fisher's mid-life crisis: his divorce, guilt feelings, writer's block, search for meaning in life and the gradual forming of a new relationship. The man in the crowd, the claustrophobia of urban life, the inability to make contact with others: these are the sequence's 'themes'. But if this were all, the poem's momentum could hardly sustain itself for thirty-eight pages, and 'translating' the coded entries into something more recognizable would only obscure the real accomplishment of *The Cut Pages*.

The spatial structure of the sequence—a sequence that, as I shall

suggest later, also turns out to have a particular temporal trajectory—
is organized around three sets of verbal clusters: (1) references to
ordering, control, containment; (2) references to movement, change,
opening, journeying; and (3) images of vision and items that obscure
vision—shade, shadow, shutter. The intricate repetition and permu-
tation of these words and word groups provides precisely the 'relief
. . . from serving in planned situations' that Fisher talks about in the
introduction. For it is less a matter of concreteness and the 'perceptual field'—the 'thinginess' of Williams that is not, as I remarked
earlier, Fisher's forte—than of placing perfectly ordinary words in
contexts that force the reader to rethink their connotations. 'The
meaning of a word,' in Wittgenstein's words, 'is its *use* in the
language.' And although Fisher claims to have no interest in philosophical discourse, his poetry uncannily enacts the often disjunctive
aphorisms of Wittgenstein, the philosopher who himself rejected all
notions of a philosophical metalanguage.

Consider the references to pattern, form and structure subsumed
under what Wallace Stevens called 'ideas of order'. The word 'pattern',
introduced on the first page of the sequence—'If you can see the coil
hidden in this pattern'— comes up again on the very next page, after
a surreal description of 'Washes of screen. Men are fluttered. Houses
are being thrown away wholesale. Butchers are on air' (*Cut* (1986),
p. 14). The deflationary lines read:

> If you can see the numeral 88 in the pattern. The Old 88; the
> wallpaper piano

which repeats the 'If you can see' structure of the opening of *Cut Pages,*
as well as the notion of something unknown that animates pattern, a
figure in the carpet that could be deciphered but, judging from the
previous instance, should probably be left alone. The 'Old 88' is
probably a street address bearing memories of a former life of 'wallpaper piano' (which noun modifies which here?), but what those
memories are is finally less important than the longing for pattern
that activates them. Thus we find the poet 'Summoning all the
scratches into pattern' (p. 22), and searching for 'Patterns on the backs
of hands' (p. 45).

The heart of patterning, at once desired and feared, is the 'coil' of the opening sentence 'hidden' within it, the spring that animates motion. In *The Cut Pages*, it usually appears as a 'cluster'—one of the key words in the sequence. 'With that', we read in no. 7 (p. 28), 'everything has come to us in a cluster. Turn it inside out, and step out of it. Call for another'. Clusters, it would seem, act to keep us in line— 'Yes, forming into lines, little clusters of lines, little directional urgencies of line-clusters' (p. 18); they impede movement and freedom: 'A forked detail. A cluster. A generality' (p. 35).

'Pattern' and 'cluster' go hand in hand with a third item, 'frame'. At the beginning of no. 8, precisely at the *volta,* or turn, of this sonnet sequence, the poem reaches a crisis point, the sense of the 'un-differentiated' dialectically opposed to that of being 'Enclosed. At least by treaty or agreement. Framed, unmistakably' (p. 32). 'Frame' brings out the negative implications of 'pattern':

> In the angle of the frame over the gulf full of sunlit mist. The frame is modern, the ritual is modern. Every gulf will have its use. Plastic gold capitals swimming up, picked out by the sun
> (p. 44)

but in the course of *The Cut Pages*, it also allows the 'undifferentiated' to come into focus:

> Great square wings in which romantic visions of a softened city pass in coloured openings between black framings. Growing by pushing outwards into a stretched pallor; and sending itself away   (p. 46)

Those 'coloured openings between black framings' point to the second set of references, carefully placed in dialectic with the first in this ostensibly random composition. Images of opening, unfolding, changing are everywhere, the most pervasive one being that of the 'curve'. 'Coming in on the curve' (see the opening page reproduced above) sets the stage for the poet's obsession with 'Inhuman curva-tures' (p. 20), the need to 'Bend your back to the curvature' (p. 21), the descent of the steps 'Down around the outside of the curved wall' (p. 29) and the acceptance of 'nothing but the bare curve. Utterly without excrescence' (p. 37). 'The wrong side of a door' in no. 6 (p. 31) gives way to a 'revolving door' in no. 7 (p. 33). Curving, revolving, turning—these spell the gradual return to life recorded in the poem. Interestingly, the curve has a downward and diminishing trajectory rather than the upward spiral that one might expect here:

Dropped through, folded in the flags   (p. 13)

Dwindles to a cut   (p. 14)

Tumbled. Strewn. Built. Grown. Allowed   (p. 17)

It follows that *dropping* further—everybody takes counsel   (p. 22)

Into the *drop*-sheet, or past it   (p. 26)

Always *falling* to be away, never on the rise   (p. 28)

Always to be *going down*, arrested and spread   (p. 29)

There is a banner to be *dropped* from a beam   (p. 38)

some things have been *flowing backward*   (p. 47)

(my emphases)

And so on. The downward–inward–backward imagery points, of course, to an archetypal descent pattern, some sort of regression into the unconscious. But since the 'I' is dispersed, fragmented, a mere point of observation rather than controlling ego, the curvature is seen in abstract, generalizing terms—

> Tempestuous in the container, the simple brown sliding contents, having only one way of moving, one direction, the continuous slide   (p. 40)

—where the repetition of the prefix 'con-' at successive line endings is itself the container holding the continuous slide within its rhythmic limits. In the same way, the many references to change and motion, to climbing stairs and turning corners ('Corner. If you start from inside and travel out it's all corners' (p. 42)), or to taking 'a new direction' (e.g., p. 32), are cerebral rather than sensuous: an abstract—and often threatening—geometry of lines, curves, angles, and new directions.

The complicating factor is produced by the third set of references mentioned above—images of light and shade, of vision and blockage. Near the opening of the poem, we read:

> Stem of a spiral stair depending through glass light, in going down, in confined but neatly stacked office and reception space
>
> There is one flung out. On that one the light is sharp. There is no half-light; only the grace of diffusing what is full

(pp. 14–15)

Here light appears in the context of the change/framing tension already discussed: the 'spiral stair ... going down', 'confined' by the 'neatly stacked office and reception space'. 'Depending through glass light' is an oddly punning locution: we expect the stair to be 'descending,' not 'depending', the light to be 'gas' not 'glass'. But the puns make sense here, for how the 'stem of the spiral stair' is seen does in fact 'depend' on its reflection in the 'glass', and as we then learn, the spotlight is on the 'one' mysteriously 'flung out'—an external stair-case perhaps, or one of those 'ghastly grey underparts' (p. 14) that can be seen as one approaches the 'Works' on 'Leviathan Lane'. The lighting on this surreal shape is as equivocal as the nature of the object perceived. 'The light is sharp', we are told, and again, 'There is no half-light'; but the latter phrase is qualified by the disclaimer, 'only the grace of diffusing what is full'.

The discrimination of 'light' becomes, in any case, an obsession. Here are some variants.

> Decorated. This light falls through the dirtiest air in the world

(p. 22)

> The sunlight ran a rail and burst from the end (p. 24)

> Clothing rich but fusty, beaded with hard things. Kept in the bottom of a room, dusty velvet, dusty sun (p. 35)

> The sun is written on from the other side (p. 36)

> Cubes of light looking in on us at noon. Sunken floor, recessed. This is the moment when secession should stop. We're set down

(p. 39)

The light is given, on trust. The breath is given, on trust	(p. 40)

Red lights for peace. Peace tails	(p. 42)

Faith. The little red lights sailing over the precipice into the shadows	(p. 42)

Fisher's 'light' is an ironized version of Wordsworth's 'celestial light', but it isn't clear whether its source is natural (like the 'dusty sun') or artificial like the 'Red lights for peace' or 'Peace tails' ('tales'). Even the 'dusty sun', for that matter, is placed in apposition with 'dusty velvet', making it quite possibly no more than a painted sun on a tablecloth or bedspread. 'Cubes of light', in any case, are more often than not obscured by shades and blinds. 'Vestiges' reach us 'through the venetian blind' (p. 14); 'Slats and shades, heads and shoulders, afternoons look at afternoons' (p. 18). 'Enamel panels [are] passing, as if of use to the adjacent effort' (p. 21). 'The blind is lowering all the time and the world dives with it, answering with brilliance bursting from the glass' (p. 34).

The negotiation of light and shade is carried on by a series of mirrors. From the first, the poet sees himself as 'The Detective in the Driving Mirror' (p. 14). In the next section, Fishes writes punningly, 'The defective mirror plucks at a glove. It is passing, it is passing the mirror. The mirror's defect is to pluck what slips' (p. 17). And the following unit reads:

Tumbled. Strewn. Built. Grown. Allowed.

Five abrupt past participles as if to measure the havoc of reflection, 'Detective' having turned into 'defective'. When vision fails, the location of a given point cannot be made properly: 'Not located in ice, or mud, or flat plane. In air or glass. Counter-system that won't engage in a dialectic' (p. 28). And, in a surreal moment, 'Glass drops. They pile up in the bed' (p. 39).

In its emphasis on isolated nouns of light and motion—*shades*, *blinds*, *slat*, *panels*, *mirror*, *glass*, *spaces* (a noun used again and again, as in 'The spaces are alive' (p. 28); or 'Refer to the space beyond the reeds' (p. 44), *surfaces, vestiges, steps, curves, corners*—*The Cut Pages* recalls Beckett's *Unnamable* or *How It Is*. Like Beckett, Fisher dwells on the void:

> Nobody has to have a face. Nobody who has a face can keep it. They can never be recognized again. There are no voices asking to be remembered (p. 32)

And again on the same page:

> No one is found. The steps are empty in the sunlight. The place shouldn't be left empty: not all that plant

But Fisher's trajectory is ultimately more romantic than Beckett's. The lone word 'Soon' at the end of no. 9 (p. 36), following the contemplation of 'Miraculous urine, streaming among the ice', suggests that the sonnet's turn is finally coming. At the opening of no. 10, 'The streams ran through the garden round the house and in under the balconies. In some of the rooms there were channels of running water bridged by plank walks from which the plants trailed' (p. 37). 'The painted wheels hum in the early morning' and, in a Stevensian moment, 'Grey pigeons are lit from beneath' (p. 37). Most important for this world of shades and mirrors, 'Cracks appear everywhere, large and small, in all directions, on every surface. Wonderful', and the poet tells us hesitantly that 'There will be flakes' (p. 38). In the final poem, 'The palm leaves come as pads' (p. 49) and 'Sand hung in the sky, ready to start something'. The corner approached so apprehensively in the first few sections, now turns into a kind of soft sculpture:

> One corner was flattened into the mount, the other bent out and standing a few millimetres proud (p. 50)

The 'inhibitors', as Fisher refers to his morbid fantasies in his introduction, have been 'burnt away'.

From Cuts to Continuities

The best way to understand the achievement of *The Cut Pages* is to read it against the more conventional poems Fisher was writing at this time—for instance the 'Glenthorne Poems', first published, like *The Cut Pages*, in 1971. Here is 'Glenthorne', no. 5:

> At sunset over the water
> the nondescript cloud
> builds up and breaks
> in dirty dramas across the sky
>
> With colours from clinker beds
> brilliant in paradise rims
> or washed wide
>
> Sun dazzles along the waves
> and slaty shoals of low water
>
> Strikes up the cliff
> in under the dark of the bushes
> with tangles of burning wire
>
> To chance on a gold thrush[24]

Some of the vocabulary here echoes the phrasing of *The Cut Pages*: *rims, sun, water, dark, tangles*. But here the words and phrases are not left to create their own relationships by means of repetition, punning or sound play. Rather the poem opts for continuity, not only with respect to the syntax, which is perfectly straightforward, but in its assignment of value. The cloud is called 'nondescript' and it 'breaks / in dirty dramas across the sky'. Not much room for multiple interpretation here. And the metaphoric nature imagery is reassuringly tidy: the dazzling evening sun sends out its 'tangles of burning wire // To chance on a gold thrush'.

The poem does nice things with alliteration and assonance, as in '*S*un d*azz*les along the w*a*ve*s* / *a*nd *slat*y *shoals* of *low wat*er', but the mystery of *Cut Pages* is wholly missing. Consider this page from no. 3:

> Traces. So much isn't the railroad, so little is. We dot by traces
>
> Breathe again, we dot so small
>
> Stepping-stairs, leading round, leading to another platform with its rail from which we

Free our spread
How far through you will it come, sweet red,

           sweet stream of blue

River of artifice

Inhuman curvatures

Don't say. Engulf

Little character. Little distinction

Beating under the crossbeam   (p. 20)

'Traces' are what this poem delineates—the 'traces' we 'dot' and breathe in. No 'sun dazzles' here; rather, we find again the mysterious 'Stepping-stairs', stairs from and to we know not where, 'leading to another platform with its rail from which we ...' The sentence breaks off, possibly, but not necessarily, continuing in the next line, 'Free our spread'. This phrase, in turn, introduces echoes of pop song: 'How far through you will it come, sweet red / sweet stream of blue'. Here the rhyme—'we'/'free'; 'spread'/'red'; 'through'/'blue'—calls attention to the artifice of poetic composition, an artifice that comes to a head in the lines, 'River of artifice/ Inhuman curvatures'. Mimesis, Fisher seems to be saying, cannot occur: 'So much isn't the railroad, so little is', and one cannot tell whether that 'sweet stream of blue' and the 'River of artifice' are one and the same. Thus the words 'Don't say. Engulf' testify to the despair of one who perceives himself (or is he referring to someone else?) as one of 'Little character. Little distinction'. And the final line 'Beating under the crossbeam' is highly suggestive: one thinks of a bat, flying across the ceiling, leaving those 'Traces' mentioned in the opening line. The page is designed to descend from 'traces' to 'crossbeam', even as 'Breathe again' yields to 'Don't say. Engulf'.

The Cut Pages, says Fisher in his introduction, is 'out of scale with almost everything else I have published'. Readers have tended to agree: although the 1971 text of Fisher's 'diary of demoralization' was reprinted in 1986, the sequence has received almost no attention, even from the poet's admirers.[25] In the course of time, evidently, Fisher has himself come to regard *The Cut Pages* as something of an aberration; he has not, in any case, repeated the experiment. For British readers who have followed his career, Fisher has, on the contrary, turned into a more conventional lyric poet, as his 1988 and 1996 collections testify. As for his American readers, the Oxford and Bloodaxe volumes seem to have passed across the crowded poetry screen without much notice.

All the more reason, therefore, that Fisher's remarkable 'out of scale' experiment, a book that was, quite literally, ahead of its time, receive the attention it deserves. Consider the well-known Language poetry manifesto 'The New Sentence' (1987) by Ron Silliman. The essay outlines a 'new' form of poetic prose (not the same as the prose-poem) in which sentences that seemingly do not follow one another and do not connect are organized into paragraphs, the paragraph serving as 'unit of quantity, not logic or argument'. In the 'new sentence' paragraph, 'The limiting of syllogistic movement keeps the reader's attention at or very close to the level of language, that is, most often at the sentence level or below.' Accordingly, 'any attempt to explicate the work as a whole according to some "higher order" of meaning, such as narrative or character is doomed to sophistry, if not overt incoherence. The new sentence is a decidedly contextual object. Its effects occur as much between, as within, sentences.'[26]

An example from Silliman's own sequence 'Demo' (1992) goes like this:

> This is a test.
> The hammer of birds (rabbits) secure in the deficit garden, fog along the coast.
>
> Water, hammer, rock board—recurrence as key in phlegmatic analysis (fellaheen hurdling custard pie into the face of Bette Midler).
>
> Friends are perpetually 'going to get it together,' jobwise the coast is altered one quarter inch.

Just like that.

The window conceived as a form of torture, through which a century is expressed (blue hands, the chartreuse of a tennis ball): dobermans of delight crowd the sun.

Met against metaphor (I want white rooms): the cast is clear

Up against the woolite, desire for narrative condemns millions—French bread hard as a rock.[27]

Here is the phrasal structure with justified left and right 'prose' margins of *The Cut Pages*. Silliman's use of specific procedural (counting) devices to govern construction (devices I will not elaborate on here) accords with Fisher's parodic allusion to the fourteen-line sonnet. Both poets, moreover, take the page rather than the line or stanza as their lyric unit. Like Fisher, Silliman relies on metonymy and pun (e.g., 'the cast is clear') rather than metaphor; his sentences and syntactically ambiguous phrases don't 'follow', and their referents are often obscure, meaning arising from accretion and repetition ('The hammer of birds', 'Water hammer') rather than logic or temporal sequence. Again, as in the case of the 'Redcliffe Hotel', concrete references like 'Bette Midler' are introduced only to be rapidly deflected, permutated, and picked up later.

Silliman's discourse radius, with its up-to-date American colloquialisms and particularities is, of course, quite different from Fisher's. But what seems almost uncanny is that, quite inadvertently and within a thematic context quite different from Silliman's more jaunty meditation, Fisher's 'cutting' of the page, with its removal of words from their 'planned situations', anticipated a mode that became prominent in the US, not only in Silliman's poetry but in that of many other Language poets, at least a decade after Fisher had written the (evidently unknown to them) *Cut Pages*. Once this connection is understood, once the claim for a precisionist, projectivist aesthetic has been put to rest, Fisher's work, especially his 'prose' sequences, should find its audience among American poets and their readers as well as a new audience in Britain.

In the penultimate section of *The Cut Pages*, we read:

> There's no sign of anything. They're the sign. Maybe it's just
> that the time has come round. But some things have been flow-
> ing backward   (p. 47)

The time, we might extrapolate from this strophe, *has* come round,
and 'some things' that seem so new have in fact been 'flowing
backward'. That, it would seem is the 'sign' we must heed: its lesson
is that history, as that other American knew, has many curious
corridors.

NOTES

1. John Kerrigan, 'Rooting for Birmingham', *London Review of Books*, 2 January
1997, p. 30.

2. An exception to this neglect, but in scholarly book form rather than
periodical, is John Matthias's, 'The Poetry of Roy Fisher', in *Contemporary British
Poetry: Essays in Theory and Criticism*, ed. James Acheson and Romana Huk (Albany:
State University of New York Press, 1996), pp. 35–62. See also Keith Tuma's *Fishing
By Obstinate Isles: Modern and Postmodern British Poetry and American Readers* (Evanston:
Northwestern University Press, 1998), chapter 6.

3. Jed Rasula and Mike Erwin, 'An Interview with Roy Fisher', in Roy Fisher,
Nineteen Poems and an Interview (Penshett, Staffs.: Grosseteste, 1977), pp. 12–38.

4. See Donald Davie, 'Roy Fisher: An Appreciation', *Thomas Hardy and British
Poetry* (London: Routledge & Kegan Paul, 1973), pp. 152–79.

5. Neil Corcoran, *English Poetry since 1940* (London: Longman, 1993), p. 164. In a
discussion of *City*, Corcoran again makes the Black Mountain connection: 'The
punctiliousness of Fisher's exact and distinguished prose is the register of a desire
to get this "city" into his poem, to remake it in the place of writing; and, as elsewhere in the *oeuvre*, the form taken by this desire may be felt to owe something to
such comparable modern American efforts as those made by Carlos Williams,
Charles Olson, and Ed Dorn' (pp. 170–71).

6. Tom Raworth, e-mail to the author, 13 August 1997. Ellipses are Raworth's.

7. 'John Tranter Interviews Roy Fisher' (1989), *Jacket,* part 1, at http://www/ii-
net.net.au/-bryce/facp.html. The interview was also published in John Kinsella's
magazine *Salt*, 11 (1997).

8. For further discussion, see my *Radical Artifice: Writing Poetry in the Age of Media*
(Chicago: University of Chicago Press, 1992), and *Wittgenstein's Ladder: Poetic*

Language and the Strangeness of the Ordinary (Chicago: University of Chicago Press, 1996).

9. Rasula and Erwin, 'Interview', pp. 13, 20.

10. Martin Dodman, *Montemora* 7 (1980): 25; J. D. Needham, 'Some Aspects of the Poetry of Roy Fisher', *PN Review*, 5, (3:1) (1975), pp. 75, 82. 'Matrix' is the title poem of Roy Fisher, *Matrix* (London: Fulcrum Press, 1971); no. 10 appears on p. 25. The sequence is reprinted in *Poems 1955–1987* (Oxford: Oxford University Press, 1988), pp. 87–94, subsequently cited as *P55–87*. See also Glen Cavaliero, in a review of Fisher's *Poems 1955–1980* for *PN Review*, 20 (7:6) (1981), p. 62: 'Fisher has a rare ability to handle the prosaic as it should be handled in verse, with the natural precision of good prose. His world of tower blocks, by-passes, hoardings, cast-iron radiators, urinals and foundries is quite simply the known.'

11. 'Rooting for Birmingham', p. 30; 'Seven Attempted Moves', *P55–87*, pp. 50–55.

12. Rasula and Erwin, 'Interview', pp. 13, 23.

13. Specifically, Viktor Shklovsky's theory in 'Art as Device'. See, for example, Matthias, 'Poetry', p. 39; Corcoran, *English Poetry*, p. 172; Peter Barry, 'Language and the City in Roy Fisher's Poetry', *English Studies*, 3 (1986), pp. 234–49, esp. p. 239.

14. Rasula and Erwin, 'Interview', p.16.

15. Matthias, 'Poetry', p. 36.

16. 'Rooting for Birmingham', p. 31. The original edition of *The Cut Pages* (London Fulcrum Press, 1971) contains, aside from the title sequence, 'Metamorphoses', 'Stopped Frames and Set-Pieces', 'Hallucinations' and 'The Flight Orator'. The second edition (London: Oasis Shearsman, 1986) contains only the title poem, prefaced by a revealing introduction, of which more below. The epigraph from Blake's 'Gates of Paradise' ('Truly my Satan, thou art but a Dunce...') is eliminated, perhaps because its emphasis on the determination of identity seemed too emphatic for this 'diary' sequence. 'Metamorphoses' and 'Stopped Frames and Set-Pieces' are included in *P55–87*.

In what follows, I refer to the revised (1986) edition of *The Cut Pages*, subsequently cited as *Cut* (1986). References to the 1971 edition are cited as *Cut* (1971).

17. 'Metamorphoses' 2, in *Cut* (1971), p. 13; repr. in *P55–87*, p. 83.

18. Rasula and Erwin, 'Interview', p. 34.

19. *Ibid.*

20. Marjorie Perloff, 'After Free Verse: The New Non-Linear Poetries', in *Close Listening: Poetry and the Performed Word*, ed. Charles Bernstein (New York: Oxford University Press, 1998); repr. in *Poetry On and Off the Page: Essays for Emergent Occasions* (Evanston: Northwestern University Press, 1998).

21. Rasula and Erwin, 'Interview', p. 36.

22. Samuel Beckett, 'Interview with Tom Driver', *Columbia University Forum* (1961); repr. in *Samuel Beckett: The Critical Heritage*, ed. Lawrence Graver and Raymond Federman (London: Routledge & Kegan Paul, 1979), p. 220.

23. Subsequent references to *Cut* (1986) will give only page numbers.

24. Roy Fisher, 'Glenthorne Poems', *Matrix* p. 42; repr. in *P55–87*, see p. 74.

25. An exception is J. D. Needham's essay cited in note 10 above: see pp. 84–87. Needham speaks of the 'spirit of free play' in the poem and says 'it would clearly be pointless to seek too much pattern in *The Cut Pages*' (p. 85). But, as I have been suggesting, the poem is in fact highly patterned.

26. Ron Silliman, 'The New Sentence', *The New Sentence* (New York: Roof Books, 1987), pp. 91–92.

27. Ron Silliman, 'Demo', *Demo to ink* (Tucson: Chax Press, 1992), p. 9.

7

A Burning Monochrome: Fisher's Block

SIMON JARVIS

In an interview given in 1975 Roy Fisher described his relief at finding, in a memorial fountain, 'a landscape which didn't need to be rendered fictive since it WAS so'.[1] This was a relief for the reason that, he reported, 'I find it a bit of an irritation to have to make fictive things which look fictive in order to show that I am not a brute documentary writer who's only talking about a very simplistic level of immediate circumstances or issues or whatever.' Remarks like these initially appear to blurt out an unwelcome truth: as though artifice, or the fictive, were an extra component added on by the poet so as to persuade readers of the more than documentary character of his work. 'The fictive' runs the risk of turning into mere topping, no less inert than the data-set which it is supposedly to elevate into art. Without this fictive supplement, the remarks seem to say, the poet might as well be showing readers his snaps. Enthusiasts for Fisher's work sometimes appear to confirm such an impression. 'The ludic dimension of his (and all modernists') work is of little interest unless it is in constant tension with the realist impulse (as in Joyce's *Ulysses*), for the subversive text which undercuts and questions realism must also provide us with the material on which these subversive processes must operate.'[2] What are presented here as the preconditions for successful disturbance rather resemble those for the production of a commodity: the raw material of realism is worked over until it produces an object with value. Certainly, '[t]he tension between the fictive and the real is paralleled by the tension between his "hidebound" provincialism and his internationalism, between the traditions of English empiricism on the one hand and the perceptual experimentation and formalist artifice of European modernism.'[3] But whether this tension is not a nervous compromise, rather than an admirable collision, remains to be determined.

This essay explores the nature and consequences of blockage in Fisher's work. It concentrates upon the period immediately before and after the writer's block which Fisher experienced in the late 1960s. Starting with an examination of Fisher's attempt to dissolve the block, *The Cut Pages*, it then moves on to offer more extended readings of two poems written before it, one from *Interiors with Various Figures*, another from the seldom-reprinted *Ceremonial Poems*. This essay aims to bring into focus the vexed question of Fisher's relationship to the discursive, investigating Donald Davie's complaint that in the *Ceremonial Poems* Fisher 'seems to be on the brink of making definitive judgements (about metals and stone and urine-loosened brick as alternative media for human expression and association) which only a perverse allegiance to a non-discursive poetics prevents him from promulgating'.[4] It agrees that Fisher's poetry is at times incapacitated by its avoidance of concept, copula and cognition. Yet it also argues that such incapacitation is not Fisher's alone, but testifies to a real collective blockage of experience. The *block* in question here belongs not only to the writer's own history as a living subject or as a writer, but also to the partially blocked experience of every living subject under the cult of indifference. Fisher's best work, it is argued, faces this block without either denying its reality or promoting it into an absolute. Where his work is less impressive, it is suggested, this is often the result of a continual compensatory shuttling from object to subject, from data to artifice. What has sometimes been thought a solution, in other words, may instead be part of the problem.

I

The comparison between poet and camera has often appeared to worry Fisher. Elsewhere in the 1975 interview he talks of the need to stop his work 'turning into a collection of colour slides'.[5] Twenty-two years later he refers to the risk of finishing up with 'a colour photograph which looks as though it needs paraphrasing back into a black and white, but isn't a poem'.[6] One of Fisher's prose pieces seems to attempt an exorcism of this fear. The third of his 'Metamorphoses', the only sequence from *The Cut Pages* to be reprinted in *The Dow Low Drop*, introduces a scene in which someone is being watched: 'How does he come to be wearing that suit, clay-coloured, with a hang-off jacket and flapping trousers that make him seem to jerk? He's making for the ferry; no he's not. He stands a while and goes somewhere else.' The watcher appears to be invisible to the watched, scrutinizing his movements as though on film. This is confirmed in the final paragraph:

> No system describes the world. The figures moving in the background stop and wait in mid-step, the sound-track cuts out: the projector motor runs on, the beam doesn't waver. Among the whites and greys of the picture a golden shade is born, in the quiet, rippling slowly, knotting itself and suddenly swelling into a cauliflower head, amber and cream cumulus outlined in blistering magenta, erupting out of itself and filling the screen before shrivelling off upwards to leave a blank screen and a stink of fire.[7]

Here the reverse of the process feared in the later interview—a transcription of colour into black and white—is performed. The black and white film burns up into the gorgeous colours and textures which are elsewhere subject to strict sumptuary codes. Equally importantly, the figurative licence which Fisher often denies himself breaks out here into clouds and cauliflower heads.[8] The passage is reminiscent of a much earlier prose work by Fisher called 'The Doctor Died', written in 1954 but first published in *Three Early Pieces* in 1971.[9] There the diseased body of the doctor sprouts into a ghastly and highly coloured life. In the first case destruction, in the second decay, allow access to a colour and to a pleasure which are otherwise blocked.

A film appears to be the record of an experience, but is not. In this passage, the film is made an example of; it burns in token of all the monochrome quasi-experience it stands in for. Yet it is not only the projector which is not an experiencing self. Andrew Crozier has identified *alienation* as the diet of Fisher's earlier work: 'the alienation is radical, without redemptive possibility, and excludes pathos'.[10] In so far as the 'person' formally free to sell labour-power is not a self at all but a legal representation, a personification, its experience is disowned. The self may not really be an experiencing self either. The subject becomes a dummy subject.

Blockage is everywhere in the middle period of Fisher's oeuvre. In introducing the 1986 reprint of *The Cut Pages*, he sought to contextualize its earlier prefatory note. In 1971 Fisher had written of the method of the book as an attempt to 'give the words as much relief as possible from serving in planned situations; so the work was taken forward with no programme beyond the principle that it should not know where its next meal was coming from. It was unable to anticipate, but it could have on the spot whatever it managed to ask for.'[11] Fifteen years later, this rationale was abruptly psychologized: '[t]hat phraseology gives the clue to what *The Cut Pages* really was: a document of release, a device for dissolving a prolonged stasis. Since writing my *Ceremonial Poems* early in 1966 I had been almost completely blocked for four years, and when, early in that period, I assembled my first collection ... I had no expectation that there would be anything to follow it.'[12] The silence is broken only by projects which often do little more than point to the block: projects such as *Titles*, a collection of hand-printed title pages for unwritten books which rarely rise above sub-surrealism: 'The Rubber Cup of Tea'; 'Babies with Hairy Armpits'.[13]

Although the 1986 reprint seeks to place *The Cut Pages* within a personal history, the blockage which it seeks to break is not merely the one which results in a writer not writing. Fisher has discussed his blocked period in public on a number of occasions, but could hardly be further from imagining that it need be of any interest to anyone else: it is 'one of the most boring things in the world ... a very dull matter like anybody's neurosis'.[14] If a writer is blocked, this may be for good reasons, and it may not be a sign that the writer is doing anything wrong, any more than renewed activity need demonstrate literary good health. The blockage which the burst of work produced immediately after Fisher's four-year silence would get through, rather, is that which confines our collective experience. Fisher remarks of some of the work written shortly before his block—the 'Interiors with Various Figures', 'Seven Attempted Moves', *The Ship's Orchestra*—that

> [a]ll of these enact attempts, desperate or comic, to dissolve a sense of oppressive solidity, an impenetrable stasis, in all phenomena—not just bourgeois possessions or urban scenery. By 1965 or so, the stasis—brought on, as you might well say, by prolonged addiction to the study of appearances and end-products without the saving presence of some overriding or mobilising principle—was in full possession, and I endured a block which lasted four or five years.[15]

The volume Fisher mentions as having once thought of as his last contains these lines:

> Confinement,
> > shortness of breath.
> Only a state of mind.
> > And
> Statues of it built everywhere.

These lines at once indicate that the block which Fisher's work faces is more than personal depression.[16] For there to be experience there must be something, something which is not 'me', to be experienced. The point here is not that our built world does not reflect our human feelings, or, for example, that it is 'an environment that appears brutally unresponsive to human needs, and projects the grim fiction it has not been created by human labour at all'.[17] It is rather that this built world all too accurately reflects human feelings, indeed, that it reflects nothing else, offering statues of a 'state of mind'. Far from suggesting that 'social democracy on the British model' is sharply distinguished, in its dull but least-worst modesty, from its sublime but inhuman totalitarian competitors—as Davie's Cold-War reading would have it—these lines link the two.[18] 'There', certainly, a statue of the state cult-hero in every city square; but what if, 'here', the very squares themselves, or rather the built clumps which have replaced them, were also cult images? The totems, perhaps, of what, in the 1968 text of *City*, Fisher called 'a polytheism without gods'?[19] That expression sees how misleading is the sense of completed disenchantment presented by urban experience in a capitalist democracy. Fisher does not take the tower blocks at their word, as an expression of soberly functional imperatives. The cultic significance of these buildings, rather, is not less mystifying than that of any archaic temple, only less transparent in that it is referred to no transcendence, but belongs to a religion 'without gods'.

The 'shortness of breath' referred to in 'Seven Attempted Moves' is often heard in this middle period of Fisher's work. A line like 'And' is a strangulated printed gulp. Long lines elsewhere, though, imply no amplitude of spirit, but only that this blocked experience is hardly susceptible of being sung. It is in this context of confinement that the procedures of *The Cut Pages*, quite new within Fisher's work, need to be understood. In 1975 he spoke of his interest in 'hauling words towards concreteness'.[20] The prefatory note to *The Cut Pages* clearly envisages a particular way of trying to do this. Language is offered a certain kind of freedom, 'relief ... from serving in planned situations'. But the subsequent sentences set up a curious master–pet relationship between the poet and the work, which 'should not know where its next meal was coming from' but 'could have on the spot whatever it managed to ask for'. The work may be imagined as a living entity, but one which is constantly made to sit up and beg. Such anthropomorphic or animistic ways of talking about the work are frequent with Fisher, and testify to his sense of its autonomy from sheer subjective intention. Hence the way in which Fisher speaks of '*seeing* things as they are in the world and rendering them naturally without either becoming formalist or becoming stupifyingly realistic':[21] the twin dangers are of a language so entirely relieved from serving in planned situations that it can no longer refer to anything at all, and of a language whose obligations imprison it into absolute literalism.

Peter Robinson some time ago identified the drawbacks of any merely linguistic emancipation: 'the refusal of predication or the avoidance of syntactic obligations, rather than necessarily thwarting mere habituation, may render the work down into only inert bits, frustrated pieces.'[22] The idea of poetry as a special zone of freedom for language or syntax, which might proleptically stand in for a wider freedom of experiences, can leave us in practice, as Fisher is acutely aware, with its very reverse, the unfreedom of inert bits. Yet that the refusal of predication does not shape only Fisher's middle-period work can be seen in the last poem in *The Dow Low Drop*, 'The Slink', in which there are no propositions whatever, usually because of the absence of a copula or any main verb.[23] Fisher, as he has recently noted, 'slipped out of academic life before [he] had to use structuralist or post-structuralist analyses and techniques',[24] and although *The Cut Pages* sometimes read like L=A=N=G=U=A=G=E before the letter, they are more accurately connected with the half freedom of impro. They were 'rigorously improvised'. The echo of scientism in that 'rigorously' gives the clue to the other half of the romance: poetry as a research project in the field of human experience.[25] Work is in progress even when looking out of the window, and the dulled indifference felt by the poet at least reassures him that this really must be work, since it is hardly pleasurable enough to be play.

> A round red metal chicken used for holding lubricating oil.
> Surrender

Such a passage is typical in its double attempt to haul language towards concreteness.[26] The first line tries it by copiousness, as though really to get into words an object hitherto thought too banal, eccentric or irrelevant to be described would necessarily leave some of that object's own particularity embedded in the otherwise exhausted counters. The second line tries it by depriving language of its sense-specifying contexts: 'Surrender' may be a noun or it may be an imperative verb; it may be an inference from the sight of a round red metal chicken—see this and give up—or it may have no connection to it. The lines are recognizably neo-modernist or impro rather than L=A=N=G=U=A=G=E in that their artifice does not take signification to be endless. The fragments also set up weak hints of connection. The line 'Spread. Examine the spread and report back to spread-head' mimics the redundant vacuity of administrative imperatives, which remain self-identical whatever their supposed object: so that their syntax will still run on even if we place in front of them a void goal like 'spread-head'.[27] It is followed two pages later by:

> Free our spread
> How far through you will it come, sweet red,
>
> > sweet stream of blue
>
> River of artifice

The mock-managerial register is here matched by its opposite number, mock-libertarianism.[28] Just as the order 'Examine and report back' can be made to work with anything, so the slogan 'Free our . . .' can take any old object, a point bathetically made here by using just the same noun, 'spread'. But then a pathos (such as has often been thought excluded from Fisher's oeuvre) is implicitly heard, retrospectively, in the first line by reason of the pathetic address in the next two, which are empty of decisive indicators as to what the blue and red in question might be. Before we can imagine anything into 'stream' the possibility of reference is quickly removed, for this is a 'River of artifice' rather than of water.

The problem of pathos in Fisher's work is beginning to come into view. Absence of pathos is by itself no matter for celebration, not least because it is not possible. Any screening-out of the merely contingent would screen out—in vain—all life and experience, because in truth nothing is merely contingent. Such ordinances are literally self-denying: they deny the self. But they do not succeed in denying it, or in bracketing all pathos, because underlying such bracketing there is still and always one pathos left: the dogmatic despair—whether scientistically, politically or aesthetically figured—of the drive towards absolute indifference. Modern indifference rests on economism: on the illusory and in principle non-completable separation of the economic from the political, of private from public, of gift from exchange. Indifference is the 'state of mind' of which there are statues everywhere. Absolute indifference is a chimera; hence the need to put up 'statues' of it. But its cult is real enough; hence the justification for a reserve towards pathos: extravagant compensatory splatterings of feeling are the flip side of the cult of indifference, discounted in advance by what they would correct.[29] The danger for an oeuvre like Fisher's is exactly marked by the uncomfortable shuttlings between 'realism' and 'formalism', between 'object' and 'subject', between objectivity and pathos, between reference and artifice, which always appear bound into a compensatory circuit: as though too much foot on the realism-pedal could be counteracted by a swift lurch into the fictive. The point of convergence between inert facticity and empty spontaneity is reached in 'The Only Image'. The poem describes salts working their way to the outside of a plant pot and drying white. When it concludes with the assertion that

> The salts I can compare
> to anything there is.
> Anything.

it is impossible to gauge from the tone whether this is an emancipation or an imprisonment.[30] Where everything may be exchanged 'absolutely anything can be compared to absolutely anything else', but only because nothing has its own value: 'with this possibility a destructive, but just verdict is passed on the profane world: it is characterized as a world in which the detail is of no great importance'.[31] The abstract freedom to compare anything to anything else rests on indifferent nihilism, a nihilism in and against which this middle period of Fisher's work is struggling.

II

The Cut Pages, then, often appear incapacitated by a dispirited avoidance of concept, copula, cognition. Yet since the dejection is a shared one—objectively embodied in transportation hardware and interior design alike, rather than merely designating a private mood or feeling—Fisher's forms of attention to it are often worth greater consideration than those of superficially more animated verse. An especially notable case is offered by some of the *Interiors with Various Figures* which appeared in 1966. In these poems the gaze does not turn aside; the mouth eats up the whole godforsaken non-meal of seeming indifference.

THE FOYER

The foyer's revolving doors are fixed open to let the dull heat
          come and go;
This afternoon, old woman, the hotel extends a long way through
          the streets outside: further than you've just been,
          further than you can get.

Collapsed long-legged on a public armchair beside the doorway
          under the lamp whose straight petals of orange
          glass hide its bulbs,
You can't see the indoor buildings along the street;

You can see only me, roofed in with lassitude in the armchair
          opposite,
Against the brown panelling, under the criss-crossed baize letter
          board.

And not even that do you see, one hand spread like a handkerchief
          over the middle of your face—
My hand feels cautiously across my summer haircut; my suit's too
          big.

Your dress and cardigan, flowery and crisp, stand away from your
          brown collapse and resignation like a borrowed
          hospital bathrobe.

The heat flushes you in patches, the confinement takes your breath;

So many things are ochre and mahogany: the days, the flowers,
          an attempt to look a dog in the eye;

This seems to be the place where they wrap us in paper and tie
          us with string.

Though the windows are square and dingy here they're too big
            for you, the ceilings too high to think about,

The doorway too lofty.

To cut any sort of figure going out, you'd have to let me carry you
            through on my shoulders.

The piece is once more concerned with the 'confinement' of a built world and the resultant shortness of breath.[32] The lustreless prosody has stopped singing as though 'while there was time'; as though where breath is taken from us by confinement the poet himself can only be (or can only responsibly be?) too breathless for more than prose.[33] This confinement need not be taken so literally as the minibed, minibath, and minican of 'Seven Attempted Moves' would suggest. The doorway of the foyer is not too low but 'too lofty': 'confinement', not having enough space, results from the absence of any inhabitable scale in the world, the inability '[t]o cut any sort of figure'. The poet's suit is too big; the woman's clothing 'stands away' from her; the ceilings are 'too high' even 'to think about'. Just so the lengthier lines here, when contrasted with the later sequence, rarely imply any dilation of the spirit, since they are often a mutter of unstressed syllables.

As so often in Fisher's work, the technique of criss-crossing the concrete and the abstract provides the impression, not of an explosive clash of the incommensurable, but of a dispirited shuffling of the eternally self-same pack. The 'panelling' is brown, and so is the woman's 'collapse'; indeed 'So many things are ochre and mahogany: the days, the flowers, an attempt to look a dog in the eye'. The colours are at once dulled by their ubiquitous applicability. The difficulty of discriminating between the figural and the literal is experienced not as any kind of emancipation from sheer inert facticity, but rather as its absolutization. In the third line we at first think we have met a straightforward metaphor: the lamp owns 'straight petals of orange glass', and so is implicitly compared to a flower. But it is a lamp 'whose straight petals of orange glass hide its bulbs'. In theory what should have happened is that a dead metaphor has been brought back to life: to describe the glass filament cover as a 'bulb' was already a botanical metaphor, but one which has become so worn with use as to seem literal. Yet reading the line feels, not as though a lamp has been resurrected as a flower, but as though a flower has died into a lamp; as though the apparent metaphor of 'petals' has been deprived of its figurative force. In the next couplet, comparably, the poet is 'roofed in with lassitude'. At first readers might assume that this must be a metaphor, as though the poet's lassitude were a kind of roof over him, but they soon realise that the phrase applies more broadly: the poet, as well as the old woman, have accepted their literal roofing in, their confinement, with a lassitude which pervades the poem.

This lassitude is apparent in the way in which actions are blocked in the poem. Here its pronouns merit attention. The poem is notionally an address to the old woman of the second line. In fact it stands in for such an address; the poet says nothing to her, but borrows the fiction of a possible address to her as a way of foregrounding the failure of any of the figures in the poem to inhabit their supposed environments. The ablative absolute construction of the second couplet fixes the woman's inertia:

> Collapsed long-legged on a public armchair beside the doorway
>   under the lamp whose straight petals of orange
>   glass hide its bulbs,
> You can't see the indoor buildings along the street; . . .

The syntax prolongs the wait set up by 'Collapsed' through a series of prepositional clauses—'on . . . beside . . . under'—but when the subject arrives its verb is only negative: 'You can't see'. The notion that this space is a 'public' armchair marks what has become of public space, as the object-like embodiment of the ruling fiction that indifference is absolutizable. The possibility that the poem's 'you' might really be addressed only arises in its surprising final line, in which the poet suddenly imagines a single apparently spontaneous action which might at once allow the woman to 'cut a figure' in the inflated foyer, and the poet to bridge the gulf of inertia separating the human subjects in the poem: 'you'd have to let me carry you through on my shoulders.' But the gesture—as the poet surely knows, which is perhaps why the idea is presented hypothetically rather than as a real suggestion—is damaged by what it would compensate for. The woman is presented with a choice between different kinds of dependence, and the single moment of spontaneous freedom imagined by the poet is every bit as abstract as the facticity from which it would liberate the pair.

Who or what governs the action of this poem, then? The woman's 'actions' are largely passive or negative, the poet's tentative or imaginary. Although only mentioned once, the poem's centre of gravity falls on the 'they' of the fourth line from the end: 'This seems to be the place where they wrap us in paper and tie us with string.' That 'they' are never specified marks the critical difficulty with this poem: the difficulty of telling to what extent it dejectedly ratifies the condition it appears to diagnose. They are wrapping us up as though we were just parcels—how inhuman of them! But then *they* are precisely invoked in order to delegate the inhumanity of *our* own actions. 'It "was" always *they* who did it, and yet it can also be said that *no-one* did it.'[34] The notion that the idea of real or authentic experience is an 'ideology' is one way of misratifying a loss of experience as absolute, and another is to say that *they* have deprived *us* of it. 'The Foyer' confirms Fisher's stated distrust of the discursive in poetry.[35] The risk in this distrust is that writing may become powerless to do more than endorse the evacuated experience which it then sorts, not upbraids.[36]

III

I want to turn at this point to another current in Fisher's work of the mid-1960s, a current little discussed by Fisher's critics, and also one which Fisher himself now appears less interested in, if we are to judge by his decisions as to what to reprint: that represented by *The Ceremonial Poems*, first distributed in a typewritten format in 1966. These three poems are especially interesting here because they anticipate, as none of Fisher's other work written before the descent of his block does, some of the measures taken to escape from it in *The*

Cut Pages: in syntax, parataxis and the avoidance of copula; in lexicon, a breakdown of any means of mediating between the abstract and the concrete. Yet they also register at once the outbreak, and the silencing, of an expressionist Fisher largely absent from the later volume:

> Absolute
> Pity
> Advancing
>
> Out from the grove
> Of parsley elms
> On those that wait
> Staining
> Suit-knees
> With grass juice
>
> In the concrete rank, a panther cage.
> The panther hates, at morning and midday;
> Lies in the dust and stifles the sunbeams.
>
> —But turned inward,
> Studying one's very own:
> This curious corner—
>
> A urine-softened wall
> Meets an impervious hard one;
>
> Clay, cut like butter,
> Drags at the trowel,
> In cold sweat subsides;
>
> And golden drops
> Shake, and fling
> From the body, brightness
>
> Trembles the window,
> Dark strands
> Lick outward down the arms.

Fading
Short
And sudden when it comes,
White flash lost
In under the anvil cloud,

  Dark dust of shame
Raining down
Deep in the brickwork
Changes its face;

And falling
In the open,
Left out among the trees.

The opening of this poem is unlike anything in Fisher's work before or since.[37] It begins as though attempting to smash open the block in the most violent way possible: by naming an Absolute (something). Yet to this word we can attach no concept or intuition which would not appear inadequate, and it therefore has the effect of being an isolated intensifier pitching us at once into the most highly strung register that could be voiced. The next lines keep at this pitch, yet also perplex the purity of the opening. 'Absolute / Pity' is hardly easier to conceive than a floating 'Absolute' (how could pity be *absolute* without ceasing to be pity?), but when we hear of 'Absolute / Pity / Advancing' there is a strange combination of the archaic or flatly obsolete—as though the lost art of envisioning personifications might summon up the goddess 'Pity' and her train—with the menacingly expressive. (When speaking about this poem, Fisher himself referred disparagingly to 'a sort of crummy classical art which then gradually breaks and flows in all sorts of ways towards *my* sensibility which is where my things are'.)[38] Nowhere else does the 'shortness of breath' written of by Fisher so witness to an unequal and thus violent struggle not to be deprived of one's own experience. The lines are still lines, their initial majuscules insist, even should they be made up only of a single word. This produces an effect that is the reverse of any cool acquiescence in fragmentation, as of a struggle for an amplitude which is choked off. A comparable effect operates lexically. We may not be able to imagine Pity emerging from anything so particular as a 'grove / Of parsley elms', but the poem's pathos is just this tenacious insistence upon the reality of an experience which cannot but be quite stupidly idiosyncratic. 'Those that wait' clearly understand themselves to be in the presence of some powerful apparition; staining the knees of their suits on the grass makes them look at once silly and singular. The refusal to mediate universal and particular, its potentially bathetic collision of the two, in truth witnesses to the possibility that *singular* experience is not arbitrary, is not merely private, waste matter which must be excised from the poem if it is to address its readership. As John Wilkinson has written, 'our nature is my greatest privacy, and this is the sustaining and silly paradox, that the most idiosyncratic and inadmissible is the most deeply shared'.[39]

Then as suddenly this tenacity is lost. The poem's nerve appears to slip, and a setting is described: 'In the concrete rank, a panther cage.' The falling-off is made still more evident in the version printed in the 1968 *Collected Poems*, where a full stop cordons off the first two groups of lines from the rest of the poem.[40] It is telling that for Fisher this appears to be just the moment where impugnable abstraction is broken into the particular sensibility where he takes 'his things' to be situated. Yet although we have been given a situation, the poem remains unusually obscure. It is clearly interested both in the textures of objects —'A urine-softened wall / Meets an impervious hard one'—and in the unfamiliar beauty and affective resonance of the most quotidian acts: we need the context of the 'urine-softened wall' to take the exultant lines 'And golden drops / Shake, and fling / From the body, brightness' as a description of urination. An event of some kind appears to be presented as central, but remains as impossible to focus on as lightning: 'Fading / Short / And sudden when it comes, / White flash lost / In under the anvil cloud'. Despite the apparent centrality of this breaking storm, the poem's pathos remains that of 'the feel of not to feel it', and all its lines, from the word 'grass-juice' onwards, have the sense of a muted postlude: the ceremonial event does not appear to have taken place, and the passionate attempt to hammer the block open has been thwarted.

Fisher's declared lack of interest in 'very discursive poetry' reads as a direct counter to Davie's complaint that he perversely avoids it.[41] The allegiance to a non-discursive poetics is of course so little *perverse* that it has been incipient ever since 'poetry' began to be distinguished from 'philosophy' or any other kind of science.[42] It is equally clear, of course, that this long separation of poetry from cognition has been accompanied by a wide variety of counter-movements, insisting in different ways on poetry's capacity to bear a philosophical truth-content, one of which is covered, but ill described, by the term Romanticism. The slogan 'No ideas but in things', a slogan which appears only to become the more important the more individual poets disclaim its relevance to their own work, needs to be understood as standing inside this *longue durée* of the real withdrawal of cognition from poetry, and the various compensatory counter-movements to that withdrawal. Part of what objectivism has sometimes stood for is that aspect of modernism which has turned against modernism's (in fact ineliminable) connection with Romanticism. Fisher has described himself as having 'started as a Romantic', 'reading, oh, leftover Romantics like Vernon Watkins ... Americans if I could get them, Russians if I could get them ... I met Gael Turnbull and I was exposed on one day to Olson, Creeley, Bunting, Zukofsky, Duncan, Ginsberg, Corso, Ferlinghetti, Ray Souster and, most of all, William Carlos Williams'.[43] The encounter with Williams, Olson, Zukofsky and others appears to have been, in differing ways, both enabling and incapacitating, allowing modes of attention unusual in English poetry of the 1960s to be attempted, yet also perhaps initiating that 'prolonged addiction to the study of appearances and end-products without the saving presence of some over-riding or mobilising principle'[44] later diagnosed by the poet. 'No ideas but in things', like many slogans, has dropped the main verb; and, as with many slogans, the main verb's absence is in fact the crucial point, since it allows the mood of the assertion to remain ambiguously either indicative or imperative. It is unclear whether we are being told that there *are* no ideas but in things, or whether there *ought* not to be (in particular, that there ought not to be in poems). So the slogan recruits the force of both possible meanings, both an objectivist ontology and an objectivist poetics, into its blurred imprecision.[45]

The movement of Fisher's poetry has often appeared to be an initial deletion of the subject along these lines, followed by a compensatory attempt to put the subject, which is imagined to have been all too successfully deleted, on the evidence of the blocked addiction to appearance, ~~back~~—by adding some component of artifice, fictiveness or figurativeness. Fisher's mixed feelings about the slogan in interview look symptomatic:

> The trouble with 'no ideas but in things' is that it has become an idea . . . The doctrine of ideas in things is the nearest to a slogan of any poetic slogan that I'd want to carry around, that I WOULD want to carry around, but I wouldn't want to carry it around all that much, because it can just turn into a thing to hit myself over the head with.[46]

Is 'no ideas but in things' an idea or a thing? Formulations arrived at in interview are often understandably approximate, but the movement of these thoughts is telling. The trouble with the slogan is initially that it 'has become an idea', but then Fisher fears that 'it can just turn into a thing'. In truth, however, the trouble with 'no ideas but in things' is that it is not *even* an idea, just because of its avoidance of the copula or other main verb which might specify its mood and meaning. The slogan might be the name of Fisher's block—yet not only of Fisher's, but of that which really governs what he has acutely named our polytheism without gods. A poetry which is to do more than ratify this polytheism could do worse than learn, not only from Fisher's willingness to allow its emptiness into the texture of his verse, but also from the trajectory of damage which the work of his critical middle period traces.

NOTES

1. Jed Rasula and Mike Erwin, 'An Interview with Roy Fisher', in *Roy Fisher, Nineteen Poems and an Interview* (Pensnett, Staffs.: Grosseteste, 1975), p. 32.

2. The view of Peter Barry in a generally valuable article, 'Language and the City in Roy Fisher's Poetry', *English Studies*, 67:3 (June 1986), pp. 234–49, at p. 248.

3. John Ash, 'A Classic Post-Modernist', *The Atlantic Review*, new ser., 2 (1979), pp. 39–50.

4. Donald Davie, 'Roy Fisher: An Appreciation', *Thomas Hardy and British Poetry* (London: Routledge & Kegan Paul, 1973), pp. 152–72, at p. 167.

5. Rasula and Erwin; 'Interview', p. 21.

6. 'People Who Can't Float: Roy Fisher interviewed by Ra Page', *Prop*, 2 (1997), pp. 28–30, at p. 28.

7. Roy Fisher, *The Cut Pages* (London: Fulcrum Press, 1971), p. 14. The text reprinted in *The Dow Low Drop: New and Selected Poems* (Newcastle upon Tyne: Bloodaxe Books, 1996), pp. 89–90, at p. 90, reads 'fixures' for 'figures'. There is also a fifth prose piece not reprinted in the later volume.

8. Andrew Crozier describes the 'amalgamation of propositional and figurative modes' in Fisher's work in his 'Signs of Identity: Roy Fisher's *A Furnace*', *PN Review*, 18:3 (January–February 1992), pp. 25–32, at p. 28.

9. Roy Fisher, *Three Early Pieces* (London: Transgravity Advertiser, 1971).

10. Crozier, 'Signs of Identity', p. 26.

11. *The Cut Pages* (1971), p. 6.

12. Fisher, *The Cut Pages* (London: Oasis Shearsman, 1986), n.p.

13. Fisher, *Titles* (Tarasque Press, 1969), n.p.

14. Michael Peter Ryan, 'Career Patterns among Contemporary British Poets', unpublished Ph.D. dissertation, University of London, 1980, p. 238.

15. Paul Lester and Roy Fisher, *A Birmingham Dialogue* (Birmingham: Protean Pubs, 1986), p. 27.

16. 'Seven Attempted Moves', *Collected Poems 1968: The Ghost of a Paper Bag* (London: Fulcrum Press, 1969), pp. 60–61, at p. 61.

17. Paul Lester's view in *A Birmingham Dialogue*, p. 12.

18. Davie, *Thomas Hardy and British Poetry*, pp. 171–72.

19. *CP68*, p. 38.

20. Rasula and Erwin, 'Interview', p. 20.

21. *Ibid.*, p. 21.

22. Peter Robinson, 'Liberties in Context', *Grosseteste Review*, 13 (1980–81), pp. 83–92, at p. 84.

23. *DLD*, pp. 203–04.

24. 'People Who Can't Float', p. 28.

25. See Rasula and Erwin, 'Interview' p. 31.

26. *The Cut Pages* (1986), p. 22.

27. *Ibid.*, p. 18.

28. *Ibid.*, p. 20.

29. These are not claims about the content of Fisher's work, but about lived experience in economistic societies. It is claimed, however, that aspects of the truth of Fisher's poetry can be assessed in relation to these theses. They are drawn from work in progress towards a reformulation of the theory of donation and exchange, and a reconsideration of the nature of works of art in modern societies in the light of this reformulation; they cannot be made good in full here. For some preliminary sketches of aspects of this work, see my 'Soteriology and Reciprocity', *Parataxis: Modernism and Modern Writing*, 5 (1993), pp. 30–39; and 'Prosody as Cognition', *Critical Quarterly*, 40:4 (Winter 1998), pp. 3–15.

30. Fisher, *Nineteen Poems and an Interview*, p. 5.

31. Walter Benjamin, *The Origin of German Tragic Drama*, tr. John Osborne (London: Verso, 1985), p. 75. For a trenchant discussion of the limits to such abstract freedom, see again Robinson, 'Liberties in Context', pp. 88–89.

32. *CP68*, p. 49.

33. See 'Why They Stopped Singing', *CP68*, p. 12.

34. Martin Heidegger, *Sein und Zeit*, 16th edn (Tübingen: Max Niemeyer, 1986), p. 127.

35. Rasula and Erwin, 'Interview', p. 20.

36. In Marvell's double sense: *The Complete Poems*, ed. E. S. Donno (Harmondsworth: Penguin, 1972), p. 100.

37. It is quoted here from the 1966 text: Roy Fisher, *The Ceremonial Poems* (n.p., 1966). The version printed in *Collected Poems 1968* shows minor but significant variants in lineation and punctuation.

38. Rasula and Erwin, 'Interview', p. 20.

39. See John Wilkinson, 'Cadence', *Reality Studios*, 9 (1987), pp. 81–85, at p. 82.

40. *CP68*, p. 77.

41. Rasula and Erwin, 'Interview', p. 24.

42. Marcel Detienne, *Masters of Truth in Archaic Greece* (Chicago: Zone Books, 1990); Bruno Gentili, *Poetry and its Public in Ancient Greece* (Princeton, N. J: Princeton University Press, 1996).

43. Michael Peter Ryan, 'Career Patterns among Contemporary British Poets', p. 86.

44. *A Birmingham Dialogue*, p. 27.

45. No judgement is made here about Williams's own relation to any objectivist moment. The slogan itself exemplifies objectivism in the sense in which this essay uses the term.

46. Rasula and Erwin, 'Interview', p. 20.

8

'The Secret Laugh of the World'

IAN SANSOM

Roy Fisher is not amused: 'I know that if I hadn't got a handful of burlesques and a rather smaller handful of topographical poems with beginnings, middles and ends—discrete entities—I wouldn't have any profile at all. In my sort of gang I'm the odd one who's been published by capitalist publishers.'[1] Fisher's words here are both touching and rather touchy, from the one pathetic 'handful' that even as he speaks slips though his fingers into the other 'rather smaller handful', through the hand-washing separation of 'discrete entities', to the gratuitous gesture towards the publishers, the word 'capitalist' wielded as a term of abuse rather than as description. The sentences amount to the self-mocking 'odd one' in weary affirmation, both modest and belligerent, of group loyalty, of 'my sort of gang'; a hard-boiled phrase with a curiously soft centre, 'sort of' deliciously imprecise, classifying yet failing to define, a phrase somehow—sort of—appropriate to Fisher's own uncertain procedures.

Not that all this hand-wringing has deterred Fisher's 'capitalist' publishers (the charitable-status Oxford University Press and the avowedly counter-cultural Bloodaxe Books). His 1996 Bloodaxe collection of new and selected poems, *The Dow Low Drop*, according to the book's jacket blurb, 'celebrates forty years of Roy Fisher's wonderfully witty and anarchic poetry . . . The reputation he gained in the 60s and 70s as a difficult poet is wrong: this book shows that he is one of the funniest, most open and liberating writers of his generation.'[2] The intriguing suggestion here—the pitch—is far from the usual rallying cry that Fisher's work has been neglected, but rather that Fisher has been taken too seriously; the implication being, of course, that his poetry needs to be, to borrow a phrase from Philip Larkin, 'rescued from among our duties and restored to our pleasures'.[3] Despite the presumably dubious—'capitalist'—motives behind this attempt at remodelling, or repackaging, some restoration work on Fisher's reputation is clearly necessary.

Fisher's poetry, when it has not merely been valued negatively for what it does not do and what it is not, has often been seen as purveying a content susceptible to summary and paraphrase, even by those critics who are committed to resisting totalizing systems of explanation.[4] Solemnity seems often to have been required when dealing with his work, and an aspect of grave regard is common among descriptions of the poems: thus, for example, Michael Shayer in his preface to the first edition of *City* (1961), announcing portentously that 'What follows seems to me a ruined work of art' and then going on swiftly and inappropriately to invoke the Holocaust and to draw comparisons between *City* and *The Waste Land*, *Ulysses*, and the *Cantos*.[5] In Fisher's poetry, it is generally agreed, readers are faced with an instance of the difficult, or at least the highly unusual: he is, according to Robert Sheppard, 'a very *un*Orthodox writer', who possesses an 'antagonistic relation to the dominant modes of British poetry'; his 'position', according to John Ash, 'is not an easy one' (he is, adds Ash parenthetically, 'the least facile of poets'); Anne Cluysenaar regrets that 'I never feel I "have" him altogether'; and Laurence Lerner simply gives up trying to 'have' Fisher altogether and complains that the poems 'seem simply to have put up "No Entry" signs' (responses that recall searching words from John Ashbery's poem about poems, 'Paradoxes and Oxymorons': 'You have it but you don't have it. / You miss it, it misses you. You miss each other').[6]

There is then no denying that Fisher is a poet whose readers take him seriously. And yet, as Fisher himself seems aware, the complexities of his work are as much imagined as they are real—'it has always been my practice', he claims, 'to write as simply and starkly as possible'[7]—and its gravity has often been over-estimated. In a poem written for Eric Mottram, the long-time ringmaster of the British alternative poetry scene, Fisher writes:

> And how well you've
> misunderstood us at those
> moments when a good
> misunderstanding's what we've
> most been needing!⁸

At the risk and in the expectation of adding further to the misunderstanding, I want to take a lighter look at some of Fisher's work.

Fisher's purely—consolidated—comic poems are rare pleasures. The *Consolidated Comedies* contains just ten poems, eight of which failed the round-up into the collected *Poems 1955–1987* (the exceptions being 'Pete Brown's Old Eggs Still Hatch' and 'Irreversible').⁹ The eight that got away are elusive in more ways than one. George Orwell, in his long definition of the English character in his short book *The Lion and the Unicorn: Socialism and the English Genius* (1941), remarked that in England, 'Literature, especially poetry, and lyric poetry most of all, is a kind of family joke, with little or no value outside its own language-group', and the poems in *Consolidated Comedies* bear out, for better or for worse, the truth of Orwell's observation.¹⁰ *Consolidated Comedies* consists of two jokey dramatic monologues ('Forward the Light Brigade' and 'The Dream'); a playful mock will ('Uncle Jim's Will'); a wry reminiscence of teaching ('One World'); a light-hearted meditation on mutability and the meaning of names ('Irreversible'); a snort at critics ('Just Where to Draw the Line'); a whimsical observation ('Pete Brown's Old Eggs Still Hatch'); a wistful comment on ageing ('Jim Burns Entering the Seventies'); a surreal list (' "Other Titles by Roy Fisher" '); and a revel-song for the in-crowd ('North Wind Harrying the North'). For all their differences, these poems—casual, self-referential, one notch above nonsense and way below the sublime—are fine examples of the Eng. Lit. in-joke.

The poem ' "Other Titles by Roy Fisher" ', for example, lists the titles of books that Fisher has not written, including 'THE RUBBER CUP OF TEA', 'BABIES WITH HAIRY ARMPITS' and 'WITH A SMILE ON

THE SIDE OF MY HEAD'.[11] The titles are funny because they send up Fisher's own surrealist pretensions. To the uninitiated, however, this sort of self-tickling list might seem merely frivolous, or might even mistakenly be taken at face-value (a television advertisement during the late 1980s for the *Yellow Pages* featuring an elderly author called J. R. Hartley searching for a copy of his long out-of-print book, *Fly Fishing*, proved so popular with viewers, the author's quest so poignant, that the imaginary book was summoned into being; a triumph of literalism, if not of literature).[12] A number of other poems in *Consolidated Comedies* present rather more troubling problems of comic interpretation.

The poem 'One World', for example, relies for its comedy on a principle of exclusion and division.[13] The poem describes an illiterate 'them', 'born on a council estate / halfway to the next town, / sold into the lowest stream / at five or so', whom the poem's narrator is employed to teach. Years later, looking back, the teacher-narrator reflects:

> By now, some are dead. I read of one
> suicide and one broken skull.
> The rest will be going on thirty. About them
> I know I can generalize without offence.
> But to name names: if John Snook,
> Ann Pouney or Brian Davidson,
> Pat Aston or Royston Williams,
> should, of their own accord and unprompted,
> read over this and remember me—well,
> if they're offended, they can tell me about it:
> it would be good to know
> we all look at the same magazines.

In a poetry like Fisher's, of considerable reticence and moral delicacy, the naming of names here is both unusual and disconcerting. What is disconcerting is that, despite the scrupulous handling of the named individuals which clearly raises them above the stereotypical 'them' established at the beginning of the poem, and despite the poem's generous invitation for these chosen individuals to come forward

and shame the speaker ('they can tell me about it'), the poem's compassion is undermined by its final twist, or punchline.

The lines 'it would be good to know / we all look at the same
magazines' are like the flash of a smile, transforming an otherwise
unremarkable poem into something both funny and sad. The
poignancy of the lines derives from the fact that we *do not* all read the
same magazines, that it is in fact highly unlikely that the likes of 'John
Snook', 'Ann Pouney', 'Brian Davidson', 'Pat Aston' or 'Royston
Williams' will be reading, say, *Steaua* (the Romanian magazine where,
apparently, 'One World', translated into Romanian by the improbably
named Dimitri Coicoi-Pop, first appeared).[14] The world of 'One
World' is therefore divided—its title is ironic. 'I want to believe I live
in a single world', Fisher writes in *City*, expressing hope, but he
confesses that separation inevitably occurs: 'The light keeps on separating the world like a table knife: it sweeps across what I see and
suggests what I do not ... Each thought is at once translucent and
icily capricious.'[15] Like many of Fisher's comic poems, 'One World' is
a piece of caprice which hovers uncertainly between rueful self-pity
and compassion: 'I was', regrets the narrator, 'no help'.

Fisher raises another desperate laugh in a poem not included in
Consolidated Comedies, 'Paraphrases', perhaps the most famous and
celebrated of what he calls his 'burlesques'.[16] (The *Oxford English
Dictionary* defines 'burlesque' as 'That species of composition which
excites laughter by caricature of serious works, or by ludicrous
treatment of their subjects ... To turn into ridicule by grotesque
parody.') Michael Hulse, the poet and critic, in a review of Fisher's
Poems 1955–1980 in 1981 claimed that the poem was evidence of
Fisher's 'hilarious wit'; eight years later, in a longer article, Hulse calls
it 'hilarious' again.[17] It is certainly boisterous. In 'Paraphrases' Fisher
paraphrases, or parodies, letters to a poet from readers, and holds
them up to ridicule. Thus, we are invited to laugh at the thesis-
writing correspondent for pompously referring to 'articles by Davie,
D., / and Mottram, E.'; this is funny, 'hilarious' even, because the
poem's narrator, and any reader of Fisher's poem, might be expected
to refer to Davie, D. more familiarly as Donald Davie and Mottram,
E. as Eric Mottram (Mottram, E., incidentally, is the only critic to

have detected the note of malice in some of Fisher's humour, comparing him with misanthrope Tony Hancock, who Mottram suggests shared 'something of Fisher's sad affectionate contempt and fascination for the end-of-the-pier or local hop or rotary club musicians').[18] Hilarious too is the audacity of the punningly named schoolteacher Avis Tree who presumes to suggest to the 'Roy Fisher' of the poem that he might wish to meet up with her and discuss his work, in particular his poem 'Starting to Make a Tree' (hence the teacher's name: 'avis' being both the Latin for 'bird' and also an obsolete form of the word 'advice' or 'advise'; Avis Tree, thus, perhaps, '*re* the tree', an example of the unwritten trochee hovering at the end of several of Fisher's comic poems—'Get it?'). The unfortunate Ms Tree's impertinence is thoroughly ridiculed:

> —Dear Ms Tree,
> It's true I'm in Rugby quite often, but the train
> goes through without stopping. Could you fancy standing
> outside the UP Refreshment Room a few times so that
> I could learn to recognize *you*? If you could
> just get hold of my four books, and wave them,
> then I'd know it was you. As for my own appearance
> I suppose it inclines more to the
> Philip Larkin side of Ted Hughes's looks . . .
> See if you think so as I go by . . .

Despite the self-deprecating joke about his looks, the 'Roy Fisher' of 'Paraphrases' clearly takes himself pretty seriously: how dare this silly woman ask to meet him! The poem is a dramatization of—is itself— an act of self-preservation, which requires both wit and a ruthless self-determination.

'Paraphrases', then, is no joke, but it is funny, and although Fisher could hardly be described, in Gavin Ewart's benchmark terms, as a 'laughter-smith', who regularly has 'his audience rolling about in stitches at the mead-bench' there are, none the less, numbers of his poems that are serio-comic, or half-humorous, or playful, or which deploy the structural features of the joke—delay, substitution, sudden reversal.[19] The margin of the comic in his work is in fact extremely wide, extending from the modest doodling of the misleadingly titled 'Epic' ('Men call me Roy / Fisher. Women call me / remote') to the annotating whimsy of 'The Poetry of Place', a poem about the sale of William Carlos Williams's original red wheelbarrow, and the fond footling poems about Basil Bunting, 'The Ticket-of-Leave Man' and 'News for the Ear', to the pointed satire of 'Artists, Providers, Places to Go', and 'The Nation', a poem about a national day, when the 'national sport was / vigorously played all day / and the national drink drunk', and whose last line turns a leer into a grimace:

> And from midday till late in the evening
> there arose continually from the rear
> of the national prison the sounds of the national
> method of execution, dealing out rapid
> justice to those who had given way
> —on this day of all days—
> to the national vice.[20]

'The Nation' successfully subverts the idea of national pride and nationhood; Wendy Cope's 'All-Purpose Poem for State Occasions' performs the same trick, but plays it strictly for laughs:

> In Dundee and Penzance and Ealing
> We're imbued with appropriate feeling:
> We're British and loyal
> And love every royal
> And tonight we shall drink till we're reeling.[21]

Cope's poem is light verse; 'The Nation' is a serious joke.

Fisher explained his method for writing comic verse in an interview in 1996:

> The comic ones are cartoons . . . I'll polish the story in my mind and probably have it finished before I write it down. Just as if you're going to tell a joke to the best advantage. You will ignore truth and almost everything apart from timing.[22]

This explanation, or confession, of his privileging of timing at the expense of truth might explain why Fisher's comic and semi-comic poems tend to be among the more contrived and less successful examples of his work, and may also help explain Julian Symons's insight, in a review of the *Collected Poems 1968*, that 'what Fisher has to say is not always as interesting as his way of saying it'.[23] Parts of *The Ship's Orchestra* (1966) for example, might usefully be read as 'cartoons', humorous sketches, more entertaining than they are enlightening—the captain's hat that 'revolves, returns, revolves, returns, never completing a revolution', for example, like the hat routine from the *commedia dell'arte*—or the ghoulish meditation on taste which begins, 'Think of what all the people you see taste like and you'd go mad.'[24] Fisher clearly intends these sorts of scenes to have some kind of unsettling, dislocative effect—a poem, he writes, should be 'making some kind of potentially new dislocative effect in the minds of some readers'[25]—but in fact dislocation is often felt as a form of satisfaction by readers; a shock can be as much a pleasure as it is a pain. There is a great deal of pleasure to be had, for example, in coming across the sudden let-down of 'Mœurs Contemporaines', from Ezra Pound's 'Soirée':

> Upon learning that the mother wrote verses,
> And that the father wrote verses,
> And that the youngest son was in a publisher's office,
> And that the friend of the second daughter was under-going a
>   novel,
> The young American pilgrim
> Exclaimed:
>   'This is a darn'd clever bunch!'[26]

And there is a similar pleasure to be had at the end of Fisher's 'The Intruder', where the reader is led to expect some comforting musing, and instead suffers a sharp, low jab to the sublime:

> The wisest thing
>
> seems to be, by way of the road with the little river
>   and the deep shining yellow
> to retire discreetly, and leave the sulky bitch to it.[27]

Immanuel Kant, *Critique of Judgement*: 'Laughter is an affection arising from the sudden transformation of a strained expectation into nothing.'[28]

In his comic poems, therefore, Fisher is at his most unsubtle—chuckling and sniggering, naming names, nudging, pointing, catching out, tripping up. But there are strains of another kind of light-heartedness in his work, sometimes hidden, and not always to be found where one might expect ('What is lighthearted in art is, if you like,' writes Theodor Adorno, who does like, 'the opposite of what one might easily assume it to be: not its content but its demeanor, the abstract fact that it is art at all, that it opens out over the reality to whose violence it bears witness at the same time').[29] In the third of his talks on Radio 3 broadcast in the late 1970s Fisher discussed the meaning of individuality in language-use:

> In reality, of course, the idiosyncratic elements in anybody's speech or writing constitute only a minute perception of it, but it acts like a drop of concentrated flavouring, dispersing itself through the whole.[30]

Fisher's principle of perception here might usefully be applied to the humour in his own poetry. Humour is, after all, etymologically, a kind of flavour—'Any fluid or juice of an animal or plant, either natural or morbid' (*Oxford English Dictionary*)—and Hazlitt famously adjudged the correct proportion of flavouring to food in his lecture 'On Wit and Humour': 'Wit', he warned, 'is the salt of conversation, not the food.'[31] The congealed mass of the *Consolidated Comedies*, the comic poems and the burlesques, are perhaps not best representative of Fisher's humour: they are, one might say, a little over-egged, or too salty.

Fisher's early poem 'Toyland' is flavoured with just a pinch, or a hint, of wit, which is just enough to make it poignant. Observing people coming out of church on a Sunday, in what Donald Davie describes as 'the most important of Fisher's early poems', the speaker of 'Toyland' remarks:

> The secret laugh of the world picks them up and shakes them
>   like peas boiling;
> They behave as if nothing happened; maybe they no longer
>   notice.

> I notice. I laugh with the laugh, cultivate it, make much of it,
> But I still don't know what the joke is, to tell them.[32]

Davie is only interested in 'Toyland' insofar as it relates to Fisher's development and dissatisfaction with open form. He determinedly reads the closing lines as an 'honest confession of some dissatisfaction with the inconclusiveness which that sort of open form brings with it'.[33] The content of the poem—and in particular the concluding statement about the observer being party to some great cosmic joke, even though he does not know what it is and cannot tell anybody else about it—doesn't interest Davie in the least. And yet Fisher's statement, which reverses the common wisdom of Ella Wheeler Wilcox's 'Solitude' ('Laugh and the world laughs with you; / Weep, and you weep alone') is a part of what makes 'Toyland', as Davie rightly intuits, 'important'.

The poem's 'secret laugh' perhaps requires some explaining. Laughter is a bodily phenomenon, 'a physiological trick carried down from our monkey days', and for it to be secret requires either an act of suppression or some kind of withdrawal.[34] A laugh may be suppressed for a number of reasons: the suppression may, for example, be psychological in origin, a consequence of repression. 'Remaining serious', notes Sandor Ferenczi, typically po-faced, 'is successful repression'; Freud, quoting someone called Fischer—Kuno Fischer, and his *Über den Witz* (2nd edn, Heidelberg, 1889)—in his work on 'Jokes and their Relation to the Unconscious', famously stresses the aspect of revelation and concealment in the functioning of the comic.[35] A 'secret laugh' might therefore conceivably be interpreted as a sign of the imminent return of the repressed, signalled in a poem perhaps by furtive puns, rhymes or concealed meanings. But there are no furtive puns, rhymes or concealed meanings in Roy Fisher's poem, and no need for depth psychology: 'the secret laugh' in 'Toyland' is an open secret, available to all; it's just that 'maybe they no longer notice'.

Exactly what and why 'they' no longer notice is never made clear: it may be that the laugh is a secret because it is in some way embarrassing, shameful or socially unacceptable. (In a famous letter to his son

warning him against the dangers of laughter, Lord Chesterfield
boasted that 'I am sure that, since I have had the full use of my reason,
nobody has ever heard me laugh', but then Lord Chesterfield, we now
know, had good reason to keep his laughter a secret: according to
Lord Hervey, in his *Memoirs*, Chesterfield was not merely 'a person as
disagreeable as it was possible for a human figure to be without being
deformed', being 'clumsily made', 'short, disproportioned, thick' and
with 'a broad rough-featured ugly face', but he also had unsightly
black teeth; the portrait of Chesterfield painted by Gainsborough in
1768 shows him thin-lipped and toothless.)[36] The public's neglect of
the 'secret laugh' in 'Toyland', though, does not appear to be the result
of social, physiological (or dental) defects or pressures; on the
contrary, the 'secret laugh' signals a significant act of withdrawal on
the part of the poem's narrator, a withdrawal not dissimilar to that
which might be found in poems by Philip Larkin. In Larkin, the
withdrawal often takes the form of retreating to high places: in 'Un-
finished Poem', for example, the narrator, a fretful young man who has
'squeezed up the last stair to the room in the roof' stands, as 'The dew
came down', 'looking over the farbelow street / Of tramways and
bells'.[37] The drawing apart from the crowds in Fisher's 'Toyland' is
implicit, rather than explicit, as it is in Larkin, but the privileged
hawk's eye perspective is none the less quickly established in the
poem's opening lines—'Today the sunlight is the paint on lead
soldiers / Only they are people scattering out of the cool church'. The
withdrawal up and away from the people is clearly a necessary act, in
the same way it was necessary for Larkin, and for the mood-lofty
Stevie Smith, who explained her own reasons for retreating from the
world in a self-interrogating article in *Vogue* magazine in 1969:

> Why are so many of my poems about death, if I am having such
> an enjoyable time all the time? Partly because I am haunted by
> the fear of what might have happened if I had not been able to
> draw back in time from the husband-wives-children and pet
> animals situation in which I surely should have failed.[38]

As Smith draws back from 'the husband-wives-children and pet
animals situation' through fear of failure, and Larkin does so in the

interests of contemplation, so Fisher's cultivation of separation in 'Toyland' is initially justified as a means of heightened aesthetic appreciation: 'For the people I've seen, this seems the operation of life: / I need the paint of stillness and sunshine to see it that way.' But the drawing apart clearly assumes a standing above; the narrator's knowledge of the little people's lives ('we know what they will do when they have opened the doors of their houses and walked in') implies a God-like omnipresence; 'unto whom', in the words of the Collect of Holy Communion, 'all hearts be open, all desires known, and from whom no secrets are hid'. Christopher Ricks is cunning in his judgement of Stevie Smith, that 'She cultivated the art of sinking'; what he doesn't say is that she was also practised in the art of rising above (and rising again: 'She went to bed / To doze, / And rose / To find that she was dead / How, no one knows').[39] Tom Paulin, meanwhile, in an essay on Larkin, argues that the various 'attics, flats and single rooms' in Larkin's poetry are symbols of his 'sacred privacy', and he compares the symbol of the single room in Larkin to the symbol of the tower in Yeats and Shelley, interpreting Larkin's high rooms as a sign of his 'secret idea of the poet' as seer and visionary.[40] Larkin shares this little secret with Fisher.

The narrator's silent and puzzled appreciation of the 'secret laugh' in 'Toyland' is similar in kind to the strange vision described by T. S. Eliot in his 'A Note of Introduction' to David Jones's *In Parenthesis*:

> mystical illumination is a vision which may be accompanied by the realization that you will never be able to communicate it to anyone else, or even by the realization that when it is past you will not be able to recall it yourself.[41]

Indeed, the immediate source for Fisher's 'secret laughter' in 'Toyland' may be Eliot's own hidden laughter in 'Burnt Norton':

> Go, said the bird, for the leaves were full of children,
> Hidden excitedly, containing laughter.
> Go, go, go, said the bird: human kind
> Cannot bear very much reality.[42]

The 'children in the foliage', 'Quick now, here, now, always' appear again in the closing lines of 'Burnt Norton', and again in the apple-tree at the end of 'Little Gidding': 'Not known, because not looked for / But heard, half-heard, in the stillness / Between two waves of the sea.'[43] In 'Toyland' Fisher translates Eliot's garden-setting into the suburban and does a comic turn on Eliot's high-flown theologizing, swapping a bird's eye view for a Bird's Eye view ('The secret laugh of the world picks them up and shakes them like peas boiling'), rendering the sublime trivial (he does it again in *The Ship's Orchestra*, when 'Throwing up in the washroom the other day I had a vision of a dark pink, double-tailed mermaid' perhaps recalls the mermaids in 'The Love Song of J. Alfred Prufrock').[44] But there is none the less a residue of Eliot's metaphysical speculation in Fisher's material; his 'secret laugh' suggests that the mundane world is alive—somewhere, somehow—with other meanings. Fisher's famous statement in his poem 'It is Writing'—'I mistrust the poem in its hour of success, / a thing capable of being / tempted by ethics into the wonderful'[45]— does not preclude the possibility of a poem's succeeding into the wonderful, but it does resist it: the struggle that takes place in 'Toyland' is not merely with Eliot, but with finding the words to articulate a sense of the mystery of life without resorting to mere twinkliness, prose or blurted sentimentality.

The 'secret laugh of the world', then, is the sound of this struggle; the attempt to come to terms with the everyday 'operation of life', which the narrator of 'Toyland' observes from a distance, through a 'paint of stillness and sunshine'. This last gloss is in fact vitally important to Fisher's poetic technique, which he has described as a method of 'epiphanic revelation'.[46] Not only are there several points of light in 'Toyland' ('sunlight' at the beginning, 'sunshine' at the end, a policeman with 'the sun glinting on his helmet-crest', 'The lights darting on in different rooms as night comes in'), but there are dots of light throughout his work, suggesting a fascination with the scintillant world: the way the streets 'still shine under the irregularly-set gaslamps' in *City*; the 'silver / envelopes of afternoon'; the 'glitter on the roadways' and 'Silvered rails'; the 'lopsided ochre panel of lit pavement'; the 'Far towers, daubed with swollen light'; the 'luminous

// haze underneath the sun' in *A Furnace* (1986); the 'gleams without form' in the recent 'It Follows That'.[47] In 'The Hill behind the Town', from *City*, there is even a hint of a white eschatology:

> The day's on end; a loop of wire
> Kicked from the dust's bleak daylight leaves
> A blind white world,
> Blind white world.[48]

To trace and connect these points in Fisher's work might reveal another important sense, at least thematically, on the level of the image-complex, in which he writes 'light' verse; and no joke.

NOTES

1. Interview with Ra Page, 'People Who Can't Float', *Prop*, 2 (Winter 1996), p. 30.

2. *The Dow Low Drop: New and Selected Poems* (Newcastle upon Tyne: Bloodaxe Books, 1996).

3. Philip Larkin, 'The Pleasure Principle' (1957), in *Required Writing: Miscellaneous Pieces, 1955–1982* (London: Faber & Faber, 1983), p. 82.

4. See, for example, J. D. Needham, 'Some Aspects of the Poetry of Roy Fisher', *Poetry Nation,* 5 (1975), pp. 74–87; Neil Corcoran, *English Poetry since 1940* (London: Longman, 1993), chapter 12; 'Varieties of Neo-Modernism: Christopher Middleton, Roy Fisher, J. H. Prynne'; John Matthias, 'The Poetry of Roy Fisher', *Contemporary British Poetry: Essays in Theory and Criticism*, ed. James Acheson and Romana Huk (New York: SUNY Press, 1996), pp. 35–62.

5. *City* (Worcester: Migrant Press, 1961), pp. 3–4.

6. Robert Sheppard, 'De-Anglicising the Midlands: the European Context of Roy Fisher's *City*', *English*, 41 (1992), p. 49; John Ash, 'A Classic Post-Modernist', *The Atlantic Review*, new series 2 (Autumn 1979), p. 46; Anne Cluysenaar, *Stand*, 20:3 (1979), p. 71; Laurence Lerner, 'Wrestling with the Difficult', *Encounter*, 57:3 (September 1981), p. 63; John Ashbery, 'Paradoxes and Oxymorons', *Shadow Train* (New York : Viking Press, 1981), p. 3.

7. 'People Who Can't Float', p. 30.

8. *Alive in Parts of this Century: Eric Mottram at 70*, ed. Peterjon Skelt and Yasmin Skelt (Twickenham: North and South, 1994) p. 141.

9. *Consolidated Comedies* (Durham: Pig Press, 1981); 'Pete Brown's Old Eggs Still

Hatch' and 'Irreversible' in *Poems 1955–1987* (Oxford: Oxford University Press, 1988), pp. 165 and 167–68.

10. 'The Lion and the Unicorn', in *My Country Right or Left, 1940–1943*, vol. 2 of *The Collected Essays, Journalism and Letters of George Orwell*, ed. Sonia Orwell and Ian Angus (London: Secker & Warburg, 1969), p. 66.

11. *Consolidated Comedies*, p. 13.

12. J. R. Hartley, *Fly Fishing* (London: Stanley Paul, 1991).

13. *Consolidated Comedies*, p. 8.

14. See Derek Slade's 'Roy Fisher: A Bibliography', below, p. 333.

15. *P55–87*, p. 29.

16. *Ibid.*, pp. 130–31.

17. Michael Hulse, 'Dirty Dramas', *London Magazine*, 21:1–2 (April/May 1981), p. 113; Michael Hulse, 'Roy Fisher and the Weight of Attribution', *Poetry Durham*, 22 (1989), p. 26.

18. Eric Mottram, 'Roy Fisher's Work', *Stand*, 2:1, (1969–70), p. 14.

19. Gavin Ewart, 'Introduction' to *The Penguin Book of Light Verse*, ed. Gavin Ewart (London: Penguin, 1980), p. 27.

20. 'Epic', *DLD*, p. 195; 'The Poetry of Place' and 'The Ticket of-Leave Man', *Birmingham River* (Oxford: Oxford University Press, 1994), pp. 24 and 35; 'News for the Ear', 'Artists, Providers, Places to Go' and 'The Nation', *P55–87*, pp. 189, 98, and 190.

21. Cope, *Making Cocoa for Kingsley Amis* (London: Faber & Faber, 1986), p. 14.

22. 'People Who Can't Float', p. 28.

23. Julian Symons, 'Sensational Journalism', *London Magazine*, new series 9:7 (October 1969), p. 93.

24. *P55–87*, pp. 211 and 201.

25. Jed Rasula and Mike Erwin, 'An Interview with Roy Fisher', in Roy Fisher, *Nineteen Poems and an Interview* (Pensnett, Staffs.: Grosseteste, 1977), p. 23.

26. Ezra Pound, *Collected Shorter Poems* (London: Faber & Faber, 1968), p. 197.

27. *P55–87*, p. 4.

28. Immanuel Kant, *Critique of Judgement*, trans. J. H. Bernard (London: Macmillan & Co., 1892), p. 223.

29. Theodor Adorno, 'Is Art Lighthearted?' (1967), in *Notes to Literature*, ed. Rolf Tiedemann, trans. Shierry Weber Nicholsen, vol. 2 (New York : Columbia University Press, 1992), p. 248.

30. *Talks for Words* (Cardiff: Blackweir Press, 1980), p. 14.

31. William Hazlitt, 'Lectures on the English Comic Writers', in *Collected Works of William Hazlitt*, ed. A. R. Waller and Arnold Glover, vol. 8 (London: J. M. Dent & Co., 1903) p. 27.

32. Donald Davie, *Thomas Hardy and British Poetry* (London: Routledge & Kegan Paul, 1973), p. 155; 'Toyland', *P55–87*, p. 3.

33. Davie, *Thomas Hardy and British Poetry*, p. 156.

34. 'Physiological trick', Stephen Leacock, *Humour and Humanity* (London: Thornton Butterworth, 1937), p. 21.

35. Sandor Ferenczi, posthumous paper 'Laughter' (*c.* 1913), in *Final Contributions to the Problems and Methods of Psycho-Analysis*, ed. Michael Balint, trans. Eric Mosbacher (London: Hogarth Press, 1955), p. 180; Sigmund Freud, 'Jokes and their Relation to the Unconscious' (1905), *The Standard Edition of the Complete Psychological Works of Sigmund Freud*, trans. James Strachey, vol. VIII (Hogarth Press: London, 1964), pp. 13–14: 'We have already learnt from the connection of jokes with caricature that they "must bring forward something that is / concealed or hidden" (Fischer, [*Über den Witz*] 1889, 51). I lay stress on this determinant once more, because it too has more to do with the nature of jokes than with their being part of the comic.'

36. *The Letters of Philip Dormer Stanhope, Earl of Chesterfield*, ed. Lord Mahon, vol. I (London: J. B. Lippincott & Co., 1892), p. 126; John, Lord Hervey, *Some Materials Towards Memoirs of the Reign of King George II*, ed. Romney Sedgwick, vol. I (London: Eyre & Spottiswoode, 1931), p. 72; see also William Connely, *The True Chesterfield* (London: Cassell, 1939), p. 444, and Samuel Shellabarger, *Lord Chesterfield* (London, Macmillan, 1939), frontispiece and p. 189.

37. Philip Larkin, *Collected Poems*, ed. Anthony Thwaite (London: Faber & Faber, rev. edn, 1990), p. 60.

38. Stevie Smith, 'What Poems are Made Of', in *Me Again: Uncollected Writings of Stevie Smith*, ed. Jack Barbera and William McBrien (London: Virago, 1981), p. 128.

39. Christopher Ricks, *The Force of Poetry* (Oxford: Clarendon Press, 1984), p. 253; Stevie Smith, 'Siesta', *The Collected Poems of Stevie Smith* (London: Allen Lane, 1975), p. 113; see also Stevie Smith, 'If I lie down', p. 176; 'The Hound of Ulster', p. 15; 'Up and Down', p. 31; 'Suburb', pp. 81–82.

40. Tom Paulin, 'She Did Not Change: Philip Larkin', *Minotaur: Poetry and the Nation State* (Faber & Faber: London, 1992), pp. 233–51.

41. T. S. Eliot, 'A Note of Introduction' in David Jones, *In Parenthesis* (London: Faber & Faber, 1961), p. viii.

42. T. S. Eliot, *Four Quartets* (London: Faber & Faber, 1944), p. 8.

43. *Ibid.*, pp. 13 and 44.

44. Roy Fisher, *P55–87*, p. 205; T. S. Eliot, 'I have heard the mermaids singing', from 'The Love Song of J. Alfred Prufrock', in *Collected Poems, 1909–1962* (London: Faber & Faber, 1963), p. 17; Eliot's source is Donne's 'Song', 'Goe and catche a falling starre', in *The Poems of John Donne*, ed. Herbert J. Grierson, vol. I (Oxford: Clarendon Press, 1912), p. 8.

45. *P55–87*, p. 111.

46. Fisher, 'Roy Fisher reviews Roy Fisher', *The Rialto*, 35 (1996), p. 31.

47. *P55–87*, pp. 14, 5, 26, 22, 27; *A Furnace* and 'It Follows That', in *DLD*, pp. 150, 201.

48. 'The Hill behind the Town', *City*, *P55–87*, p. 24.

9

'Exhibiting Unpreparedness': Self, World, and Poetry

MICHAEL O'NEILL

I

'The plastic flowers // get more approximate: they're not even symbols anymore, only a drained colour'.[1] In this extract from his 'Prose for Roy Fisher' John Ash recalls the resistance to 'symbols' flaunted by poets convinced, as Eric Mottram puts it, 'that nothing can really *stand* for another thing'.[2] Such a conviction issues in writing that admirers respect for its 're-assuringly inductive and empiricist' credentials; the more sceptical may sometimes detect a selling-short of poetry's possibilities.[3] Teasingly Ash suggests that empiricism may imprison as much as reassure. Fidelity to perception, he hints, involves acceptance of the fact that things 'get more approximate'. In so doing he contributes a characteristically sly insight to a rumbling and sometimes heated poetic debate.

A sign of Roy Fisher's importance is that he turns out to be a poet hard to enlist in poetic camps. His 'Staffordshire Red', dedicated to Geoffrey Hill, reads, in part, as a good-humoured riposte to Hill's way with landscape and history. In place of Hill's tensed formalism, a medium for intimating ironic conflict between ideas and realities, transcendence and the sublunary, Fisher substitutes a conversational, short-lined free verse. Yet Fisher also shows that his style is capable of rhetorical daring as it stretches itself to suggest journeys between different realms: 'clefts cut in the earth / to receive us living' may, the poem half-speculates, be the more authentically there for being casually ambushed by the sidling imagination: 'I had not been looking for the passage, / only for the way' (*P55–87*, p. 141). The Eliot of *Four Quartets* is audible behind those last-quoted lines, and in the ensuing movement away from discovery into 'vacancy'; the poem plays with a deadpan refusal to commit itself to meaning—'It was as it had been'—that is a signature of Fisher. Where Fisher differs from others writing in an 'empiricist' manner is his awareness of that style's potential limitations.

Marjorie Perloff, who likes to assign poets their place on a critical map, takes Pound and Stevens as contrasting types of modern poet: the latter (honoured by Harold Bloom and Helen Vendler) deriving his beliefs and stance from romanticism, and offering 'a vision of Reality'; the former seeing modernism as a break with romanticism and concerned to make 'its processes imitate the processes of the external world as we have come to know it'.[4] One problem with Perloff's antithesis is that it slices too cleanly. Poets in the so-called Stevens tradition often mirror through their verbal 'processes', 'the processes of the external world'; poets in the so-called Pound tradition do not entirely shun the prospect of 'a vision of Reality'. Another problem is that her 'we' in 'as we have come to know it' presumes the existence of common knowledge. This presumption underplays the efforts of a poet like Fisher to communicate his sense that knowledge of shared reality is likely to be individual and private. At the heart of his work is the unignorable fact of his own subjectivity.

Illustrating the 'empiricist' mode in Fisher's work, Peter Barry quotes the assertion from 'Introit', the preliminary section of *A Furnace*, that 'This light … binds in / this alone and suggests / no other.'[5] Yet, as Barry points out, *A Furnace* goes on to challenge the authority of the ' "low mimetic realist" ' mode, a style associated, for Barry, with ' "modernist" aspects of Fisher's work' and fraught with complications throughout his career.[6] Intent on disclaiming certain forms of poetic authority, it substitutes its own. For instance, in the lines just quoted, the reliance on the referential force of language is almost touchingly disingenuous: 'This light', Fisher writes, pressing the reader to imagine a particularized 'light', without troubling to particularize it, except to say that it is 'low and strong'.

In fact, the poetry undermines its particularizing assertions straightaway when 'This light' gives way to 'this alone'. The second 'this' floats free of description and shivers before us, denuded of referential content, merely a linguistic counter. More positively, 'this alone' might suggest the poem itself. This is not to assert that the poem, for all its fascination with the 'animist, polytheist, metaphoric', embraces the notion of art as self-referringly autonomous. In fact, it is in its hoverings between styles, its awareness of style as possible distortion, that the distinction of *A Furnace* resides. Paradoxically the poem conveys a vivid impression of an individual voice into which such hoverings and awareness are built. Barry, analysing section III ('Authorities'), points to the presence of 'a "baring-of-the-device" in the Formalist manner'. He reads this presence as a postmodernist critique of the claims of modernist realism, a critique that admits complicity with what it undermines.[7] This reading is valuable in that it suggests the importance of being alert to Fisher's recoil, or stealthy withdrawal, from any single perspective. If there are moments in section III when, in Barry's words, 'authorial magic is abjured', there are also occasions in the section (as the same critic suggests) when the writing outwits its conscientious rejection of art's claims to represent experience.[8] Even as Fisher half-derides the idea that 'this morning street' could be 'robustly done' (*F*, p. 24) in the style of Courbet, he allows a subordinate clause to take him into a vennel of suggestion: that, having 'no need / to be lifted by art out of / the nondescript general case', there might be a chance of 'detectable / identities' 'coming through unimpeded' (*F*, p. 25). The passage sways to and fro, its twitches and hesitations mimed by the movement of the lines. The reader takes from it not so much a meaning as a sense of having been positioned in the midst of a swirl of possible significances. Such a piece of writing begins to seem less the product of a theorized or coherent poetic and more the expression of a poet's aversion from stopping to say what he means (to borrow Fisher's phrasing from 'Barnadine's Reply' (*P55–87*, p. 127)).[9]

Preoccupied in *A Furnace* by the relationship between 'Mind / and language', Fisher insists that language will fail 'Unless // thrown', as he puts it in an aggressive enjambment. 'Thrown' resists even as it takes on Heideggerean colouring. The word may briefly evoke the notion of *Dasein* as ' "thrown" ', in Terry Eagleton's words, 'into reality in the first place as houseless and unprotected, and summoned beyond this dismal facticity into an authentic encounter with its own lonely finitude and death'.[10] But, for Heidegger, this condition of 'thrownness' describes how things are. For Fisher 'thrown' implies— unexpectedly given his usual circumspection—a wrestler's strength; it is as if, for a vibrant instant, he fantasizes about the overthrow of class-ridden 'antinomies'. The very difficulty of the passage—as often in Fisher extraction of paraphrasable meaning is impossible—bears witness to a struggle with the barely formulable.

The use of 'thrown' implies that 'language' must attempt 'an authentic encounter' with modes of thinking and social forces that distort, repress and de-humanize. What is admirable about *A Furnace* is not only the speed with which Fisher can move between different styles but also the poem's recognition of what is at stake in the deployment of types of language. Fisher's Preface alerts us to the fact that, with altering degrees of intensity, the poem will address and incorporate opposites, tensions and superimpositions: the poem 'is an engine devised, like a cauldron, or a still, or a blast-furnace, to invoke and assist natural processes of change; to persuade obstinate substances to alter their condition' (*F*, p. vii). Fisher proceeds to write that 'the sequence of its movements is based on a form which enacts, for me, the equivocal nature of the ways in which time can be thought about'. The poem wishes, therefore, to 'assist' in helping along 'natural processes of change', yet it proposes to do this by enacting and laying bare something 'equivocal'. It is at once descriptive and meditative, anti-authoritarian to a point that grows polemical in places and concerned as well to convey the experience of living in 'working- / class streets where work and wages / hid' (*F*, p. 21). Mythic and animist, it is also historical and wary of the poet's ability to defeat 'obstinate substances' through the medium of language. Passage by passage, the poem mediates deftly, and yet with awareness of recalcitrance, between these oppositions and possibilities.

However, finally, it prefers the twist of the spiral that ascends towards the imagining of change. The claims of 'realism' give way in the final section of *A Furnace* to a Rilkean attendance on being shaping itself through various becomings:

> They have no choice but to appear.
>
> We knew they existed, but not what they'd be like;
> this visitation is the form that whatever
> has been expected but not imaged takes
> for the minutes it occupies now. (*F*, p. 45)

Towards the close of the ninth of the *Duino Elegies* Rilke links 'Things, / which live by perishing' to our 'praising': 'They want us to change them, utterly, in our invisible heart, / within—oh endlessly—within us! Whoever we may be at last'.[11] Rilke is jubilant in the face of 'change'; Fisher is expectant in the face of appearance; but both poets find that through time time is conquered—if only for the duration of a poetic intuition. 'Apocalypse', as the section from *A Furnace* will assert, 'lies within time', and the time within which it lies is that of the poem whose 'form' makes possible the 'visitation' of the 'They', presences the more strongly felt for remaining unnamed, though identifiable with the 'gods'—forces both chthonic and quotidian, numinous and weirdly commonplace. A word that resonates throughout this quirky, upbeat section is 'choice': for the poet, it is implied, 'There's a choice of how to see it' and the only fatedness resides with the 'they' who 'have it / laid on them to materialize in the cold / upper air of the planet' (*F*, p. 46). If realism encourages determinism, Fisher's quasi-religious, sci-fi imaginings delight in the minute-by-minute materializations taking place in the poem; yet even as realism is being ousted by the poem's own 'Mythos', the real returns in the last lines of the poem as the last twist of the poem settles on the rising spirals of 'The snails of Ampurias' (*F*, p. 47). Simultaneously epiphanic image and unsymbolizing particulars, the snails bring together 'art and art': the art of observation and the art of imagining.

Yet *A Furnace* does not as a whole climb free of the difficulties that vitalize Fisher's dealings with 'realism'. In the earlier 'For

Realism' the poet seems committed to what he represents as elusive: a representation of experience that 'tries to record, before they're gone, / what silver filth these drains have run' (*P55–87*, p. 55). That poem ends on the ghost of a rhyme as if to confess the desire to clinch meaning. The meaning concerns the poet's view that it is his job to render life as it is—a factory shift finishing, 'foodshops open late', a man 'straddling to keep his shoes dry'—in a way that defies the decrees of 'A conscience' associated with a bureaucratic programme of rebuilding (and consequent rehousing and uprooting). But the poem's opening strikes a self-conscious note at odds with surrender to life as it is, the poet announcing, 'For "realism" ' (p. 54). Part of the jostling ambivalence of 'silver filth' comes from the clash between the recording and the transforming impulses of the poet, and that clash becomes an almost hopeless quarrel in those scenes in *A Furnace* that focus on quandaries of representation. Section III, in particular, is 'stalled and stricken' (*F*, p. 24), and yet quickened, by the recognition that art may at once beguile and falsify.

II

A Furnace handles with force and subtlety perplexities that haunt Fisher's work, often fruitfully, and it is with the success of this poem in mind that a survey of his other poems will be offered. Elsewhere in his work, Fisher is unsure whether he wishes to be a poet of protest. In *City* he asserts that 'In this city the governing authority is limited and mean' and that 'Most of it [the city] has never been seen' (*P55–87*, pp. 22, 23), and this vein of hostility to state authority runs through the work. *A City* shares with *A Furnace* a kind of local piety, alluding to 'A polytheism without gods'. But it is more entangled by doubts about the poet's 'living so much by the eye' than the later poem, and much of its value lies in its disquieting inability either to 'live in a single world' or wholly to trust that 'The imaginary' is as valuable as 'The real' (pp. 29, 28, 29). In commenting on his political attitudes, Fisher's stance is close to self-advertizing reticence. He has expressed dislike of anything too moralistic or programmatic: 'as a poet I'm an imagemaker', he says in an interview, 'and I wouldn't sloganize a mass of really quite scattered or branching or complicated reactions to social matters.' And he goes on: 'If your image is capable of being moralized, in this country particularly, it will be. The moral will be screwed out of it. I deplore this; it's a simplifying tendency.' Perhaps sensing that his anti-moralizing can itself 'simplify', Fisher adds, 'For my taste I moralize too much already.'[12]

It is evident, though, that Fisher's work is more bothered by the impulse to moralize than he is prepared fully to admit. He says of himself that he is 'an anarchist who simply has no time whatever for hierarchical systems, monotheisms or state authority'.[13] Fisher is playing Narcissus on Narcissus here; to publish a review of one's own work, however mock-plangent the tone, is to display a vulnerable degree of self-preoccupation. In the interview just quoted he describes his poems as 'sceptical formulations of life ... an anarchic response to ... the whole rubble, the whole mass of tiny interlaced circumstances that carry you along, make the present in which you exist.'[14] To be sure, a Fisher poem can be accurately described as 'tiny interlaced circumstances that carry you along'. But Fisher comes close, in these assertions, to having his cake and munching it steadily. He is not a moralist, and he deplores simplifications; but he is an anarchist sceptical of authority. So the self-idealization runs. The main body of this essay will contend that Fisher is often a darker, more self-subverting poet, a poet who, as *A City* shows overtly, thrives on emotional obliquities and near-voyeuristic separateness.

Much of his work invents ways of retreating from the sort of confessional revelations made in *City*: 'I come quite often now upon a sort of ecstasy, a rag of light blowing among the things I know, making me feel I am not the one for whom it was intended, that I have inadvertently been looking through another's eyes and have seen what I cannot receive' (*P55–87*, p. 29). The Rilke of *The Notebooks of Malte Laurids Brigge* ('I have never been aware before how many faces there are') criss-crosses here with an Eliotic gaze into 'the heart of light, the silence'.[15] That this meshing works less than satisfactorily—in an otherwise appreciative piece John Kerrigan points out that '*City* sometimes reads as more literary than lived in'—shows in the ersatz mysticism of 'a sort of ecstasy' and that moth-eaten 'rag of light'.[16]

But the moment fascinates; it is proof that Fisher, no less than any other contemporary poet, whether neo-modernist or post-Movement in manner, is vexed by '*self*, that burr that will stick to one', in Shelley's phrase.[17] Fisher has a variety of strategies to represent the self. One is to work by analogy, to praise, say, Joe Sullivan in terms that are so resolutely other-centred they grow reflexive. Fisher's couplets mime the pianist's 'mannerism of intensity' with such mimetic verve, 'such / quickness of intellect', that among the 'shapes' that 'flaw and fuse' are those of the poem's subject and its authorizing consciousness. Sullivan, the poem tells us, will 'strut', 'amble, and stride over / gulfs of his own leaving, perilously // toppling octaves down to where / the chords grow fat again' (*P55–87*, pp. 53, 52), and the performance is captured with a gusto that indicates Fisher has desired at least one man's art and scope. Elsewhere, Fisher sets going a *dédoublement* that allows him to create and watch himself create. In 'The Memorial Fountain' he at once stages 'the scene' and gives himself a walk-on part at the close:

> And the scene?
> a thirty-five-year-old man,
> poet,
>   by temper, realist,
> watching a fountain
> and the figures round it
> in garish twilight,
>   working
> to distinguish an event
> from an opinion;
>   this man,
> intent and comfortable—

Romantic notion.   (*P55–87*, p. 61)

For Ian Gregson, Donald Davie was wrong to 'suggest profound affinities between Larkin and Fisher', since they do not share the same attitude to 'realism': Larkin assumes 'realism' is true whereas Fisher questions 'realism', especially the notion of 'a unitary self'.[18] But 'The Memorial Fountain' suggests the difficulty of escaping the 'self' (scarcely more unitary in Larkin than it is in Fisher: one thinks of the elongating perspectives that open up in poems such as 'Dockery and Son', threatening the self's sense of meaning and stability). Fisher's poem is a beautifully controlled illustration of the impossibility of distinguishing 'event' from 'opinion', if one sees those loaded terms as corresponding (roughly) to such binaries as 'objectivity' and 'subjectivity', 'description' and 'interpretation', 'fact' and 'metaphor'. The semi-humorous phrase, 'by temper, realist', implies that 'realism' is a 'construction' (to borrow Fisher's own proleptic word from the poem's opening). Yet to say one is 'by temper' a 'realist' may concede that 'realism' involves subjective preference, but it does not free one from the dilemma that poetic knowledge will negotiate between 'event' and 'opinion'. The poem can expose, but not escape, its dependence on the need for such negotiations. Language will not permit the self to be banished; words will only allow the self to be seen in an estranged way. There is a flicker of projected self-criticism in 'intent and *comfortable*' (emphasis added). The adjectives reveal Fisher's awareness that his poem's nimble self-monitoring is hardly putting the author under much duress. 'Romantic notion' attaches itself with calculated imprecision to the preceding passage to which it is connected by the suspended dash after 'comfortable': calculated, because, throughout the passage, Fisher is alert to the contribution made by his 'temper' to the construction of the 'scene', and he wishes to leave open the possibility not only that 'Objectivity is a Romantic notion because events tend to blur together', but also that awareness of such a possibility is itself 'Romantic'.[19] The poem displays an eloquent guardedness about the rewards of the self-scrutiny to which it is impelled.

Another, at times less impressive, strategy for depicting the self is to mock the idea of poetic personality. What is finally unsatisfactory about such 'reading circuit' poems as 'Paraphrases', in which Fisher caricatures the voice of an ill-informed acolyte 'writing / a thesis on your work' (*P55–87*, p. 130), is their element of self-regard. To enjoy this poem the reader needs to feel that Fisher has earned the right to take on the mood of wearied, if amused, master. Alexander Pope shutting the door against the importunities of Grub Street in the 'Epistle to Dr Arbuthnot' is one thing; Roy Fisher, drawing attention to articles on his work, and linking himself (in however comic a spirit) to Hughes and Larkin, is another. The flip side of this self-satisfied comedy is a tendency in Fisher to deplore the excesses of confessional contemporaries, as in the strikingly un-Ianist piece 'Occasional Poem 7.1.72' ('Ianists are the most implicit / of all known people', 'On the Neglect of Figure Composition: Prelude' (*P55–87*, p. 193)). This response (one assumes) to the suicide of John Berryman, who jumped to his death on 7 January 1972 in Minneapolis, consists of explicit if not very coherent rant: 'The poets are dying because they are told to die' (*P55–87*, p. 99) it begins, as if taking issue with a culture which tells poets that their true subject is death and, more precisely, self-destruction. At the end, though, the fault is with poets who 'testify' where they should not. Fisher does not quite get his ironies under control in the poem, partly mocking and partly supporting the view that it is 'tasteless to talk about' death, then attacking the very notion of 'taste' as an irresponsible aestheticizing: 'Taste is what death has for the talented? Then / the civilization is filth, its taste / the scum on filth' (p. 99). Fisher's own 'tasteful' refusal to bare his soul sounds self-concerned. The reader is (or ought to be) startled by Fisher's indifference to the achievement of the poet whose death has sparked off his poem. Fisher does not even begin to acknowledge Berryman's hilarious agonizings, explosive changes of register and persona, and unflinching intelligence. 'Occasional Poem' depends on an ill-defined ethics of non-revelation.

In contrast, Fisher impresses when his language does justice to the situatedness of the self in the culture and to the fictiveness that may well colour any representation of such situatedness. 'Item' begins with its iconic object, 'A bookend', then immediately ironizes (without rejecting) the process of poetic 'consideration' to which the bookend lends itself: 'Consider it well / if that's the way your mind / runs'.[20] The opening mocks and obeys the poetic (and scriptural) formula, 'Consider', since it is clear that the way Fisher's mind 'runs' is to track the bookend back to its origins and forward to its possible end. In a possible gesture of respect towards William Carlos Williams, afflicted in later life by a stroke that was, at least partly, responsible for his preference for the 'three-ply' line, Fisher writes in three-line stanzas. A subordinate clause takes him into a personal register that the quirky line-breaks keep from self-pity ('One-handed // this year at least, and lame'), before conceding the challenge posed by the bookend to certain frail post-objectivist tenets: 'even I', he writes, placing a not untypically assertive stress on the first pronoun, 'even I / get driven to consider it, // putting myself at risk of unaccustomed / irony, metaphor, moral'. That assertiveness bespeaks Fisher's amused inability to escape the coil of self-consciousness.

In 'Item' the poem's vigilance is acute and, in its own way, funny. Like a chess-player, Fisher seems aware of various possible moves he can make in relation to his poem's subject; at the same time each line is a further choice and, therefore, a closing down even as it is an opening up. At times, too, Fisher glimpses a potential way forward, then turns away quietly from the prospect. Such a virtual perspective suggests itself when, after a detailed depiction of the bookend as a material object, Fisher makes a connection between the object's ultimate fate and his own mortality: 'When my life's props come to suffer dispersal / this piece gets dumped, if I've not / done it myself first.' Given that 'this piece' might describe the poem as well as the bookend, the lines show Fisher occupying familiar lyric territory; Marvell hearing his song cease to echo in a marble vault is not so very far away. But 'Item' shifts away from preoccupation with the writer's mortality to the humorous yet increasingly serious investigation of the bookend's 'unshakeable provenance' ('provenance' picking up on the 'Antiques Roadshow' suggestions of 'piece'). Again, the issue of choice comes in as Fisher declares his decision not to 'suppress' the bookend's 'provenance', a moment which is—once more—mockingly wise to a charge commonly brought against poems and poets (that they engage in 'suppression' of historical circumstances).

The bulk of the poem thereafter is taken up with consideration of the bookend's place of origins, how it was made 'at the enormous works of the Birmingham / Railway Carriage and Wagon Company', a company which in the war made 'Churchill tanks', then 'troop-carrier gliders'. Just as the historical takes centre stage, Fisher alludes to a possible casting 'when this poem's filmed', as if to remind us that the poem is a constructed shaping of experience and language. The bookend-making emerges as a mildly illegal project that excites Fisher's sympathy, as though, he implies, creativity has its roots in outlawed activity: when he writes that 'it was forbidden // ever to reveal the sources of one's secret bookends', the prohibition glances at the 'Romantic notion' that creativity itself is a 'secret'. Creativity as an outlawed venture enters the poem more sadly in the account of the foreman's daughter's abortion: 'Another little knot of illegalities', writes Fisher, whose view of the daughter—'Well-provided: plenty of body'—may seem disquietingly unempathetic. Yet the poem's turn back to its subject—'As to this bookend'—audibly welcomes respite from suffering. Fisher ends his self-aware and wide-ranging poem with a joke: the notion that the bookend's first 'load' was 'a crimson-backed set of miniature / home encyclopaedias, forced into the house // in the newspaper wars of the Thirties by the agents / of Beaverbrook, later Minister of Aircraft Production'. Such a notion, Fisher concludes, 'would be artistic, ironic, and, just possibly, untrue', pointing up at the close how a poem's artistic ironies might—'just possibly'—involve 'untruth'.

III

Among Fisher's strategies for representing the self is to treat it as strands of tobacco to be rolled up in the Rizla paper of poetic self-reflexivity. Whether the ensuing smoke satisfies varies from poem to poem—and reader to reader. In such poems the 'I' may be the creation of the poem's winks and nods. The pronoun may try to unburden itself of foresuffering and endurance through time, refusing to commit itself to stable identity. And yet it is as sovereign an ego as any to be found in contemporary poetry. Discovering postmodernist 'anxieties about the reality of the observing "author"' in the poetry, Bert Almon takes the view that Fisher is to be praised, in terms borrowed from Andrew Crozier, for not taking for granted 'an empirical self', and selects as an illustrative text 'Of the Empirical

Self and for Me'. One may find the dedication ('for M. E.') less 'witty' than smart-alecky. But Almon also points out that 'the self is the source of Fisher's poem and must work to render perceptions accurately'.[21] Given that the poem knows this, it starts into contradictory life. Its opening expects to be contested:

> In my poems there's seldom
> any *I* or *you*—
>
> > you know me, Mary;
> > you wouldn't expect it of me—   (*P 55–87*, p. 125)

Self-absorption sounds through the opening phrase—'In my poems'—and mocks itself in the hackneyed appeal, 'you know me, Mary'. Fisher asks to be taken seriously, but cannot be read straight. So, 'you' may be an invented 'alter ego'.[22] The very word is like a bell to toll us back to a sense that the sole self that counts is the subject as writer. But the poem is caught between affirming and denying the reality of what it calls in its title 'the Empirical Self'. After all, it goes on to spin a mini-plot of misconception and perceptual error. A passer-by mistakes for '*a cup of | coffee*' the 'glasses of white milk' that the poem's 'I' and 'you' are drinking. The passer-by is said to be 'A tall man', walking 'what looks like a black dog': as Almon points out, 'The dog may be a black dog, if it is a dog at all', and even the detail of the man being 'tall' is subtly disquieting. The two sitting on the seemingly substantial 'bench under the window' are 'invisible ghosts'. No sooner does the man cease speaking than he 'vanishes' across an expressive line-ending. Yet the notion of error brings into play the possibility of truth; the poem both 'dramatizes perceptual uncertainty' and depends for doing so on the notion of perceptual certainty.[23] If the man is wrong about the milk being coffee, that is because the speaker is right about the coffee being milk. The poem finds itself needing to believe in, even as it questions, the self and the world. However ironically, the idea of an absolute self shows in the title's distinction between 'the Empirical Self' and 'Me', where 'Me' may briefly put one in mind of 'the Me myself' in Whitman's *Song of Myself*, section 4. There is an intriguing affinity, too, between Fisher's phrasing and the Whitman who, in 'As I Ebb'd with the Ocean of

Life' asserts that 'before all my arrogant poems the real Me stands yet untouch'd, untold, altogether unreach'd, / Withdrawn far, mocking me with mock-congratulatory signs and bows, / With peals of distant ironical laughter at every word I have written'.[24]

Fisher's turns on the self are as low-key as Whitman's are operatic, and in the suspended 'So—' that follows, the poem hits a pause. The moment gathers to itself the to-and-fro implications of what has gone before. 'So' may imply that the self and the world are unreliable, given to vanishing. It may imply the need to stand back from that conclusion, even to contest it—or at least to allow the possibility of a different mode of interpreting. In the ensuing question 'What kind of a world?' Fisher confirms yet resists the poem's push towards in-determinacy. The question suggests that the world cannot be defined and that the poet does, and yet does not, wish to define it. Elliptically Fisher asserts, 'Even / love's not often a poem': the reader of his poetry learns to expect this kind of effect where the diction is simple but the impact is obscure. To the degree that they demand the reader's involvement, such effects energize the process of response. But, at times, they risk mannerism. Here Fisher means, one presumes, that there is a gap between feeling and art, that even if the 'you' were a real other loved by the poet, there would be no assurance that a 'poem' would ensue. The following assertion is also suspended across a line-break, though this time less precariously: 'The night / has to move quickly.' 'The night' emerges as a distinct if ephemeral fact; in having 'to move quickly' it is subject to the same imperative as the poem in pursuit of its meaning and the reader in the wake of the poem. 'Sudden rain' followed by 'Thunder bursts across the mountain' recalls the symbolic plot of 'What the Thunder Said' in *The Waste Land*. Yet, like Eliot, Fisher proposes a symbolic meaning without committing himself to it. Still, the less agitated lineation is the strongest clue to a new trust in language:

> Thunder bursts across the mountain;
> the village goes dark with blown fuses,
> and lightning-strokes repeatedly
> bang out their own reality-prints

of the same white houses
staring an instant out of the dark.

As the 'lightning-strokes repeatedly / bang out their own reality-prints', they serve as images of Fisher's own verbal activity, his words 'banging out' (on a typewriter, perhaps) 'their own reality-prints'. In fact, so snug is the fit between word and referent that the passage verges on a traditional metaphoric identification and plays with the capacity of language to persuade one of such an identification. As in Williams's work, the poem's denial of metaphor is not, in practice, complete. The 'houses / staring an instant out of the dark' suggest reality's impingement, through language, on consciousness. Yet 'reality-prints' may imply, too, in the best empirical manner, that the world is known only through possibly unreliable sense-impressions. But this is only one of several implications, and when Ian Gregson writes of these lines that 'the transformation of reality into "prints" suggests the distortions of representation' he is too quick to allow 'transformation' to slide into 'distortions'.[25] There is a further self-reflexive twist in the use of 'prints': the word draws attention to the representation of 'reality' on the printed page looking up at the reader, challenging him or her to decide whether 'transformation' is 'distortion'.

For all its resolute indeterminacy, then, the poem displays a fascination with the very things—self and reality—that it seeks to present as elusive. In 'If I Didn't' indeterminacy and scepticism prove to be riven with paradox. If one has decided in advance that reality is indeterminate, one has made a determinate interpretation; if one is committed to scepticism, scepticism turns into a kind of faith in the rightness of scepticism. At their best Fisher's poems string along and outmanoeuvre these self-cancellings, as 'If I Didn't' shows. The poem begins with a characteristic assertion of diffidence, Fisher shaping a tangled scenario in which he is forward about his backwardness in being forward: 'If I didn't dislike / mentioning works of art' (*P55–87*, p. 128). These opening two lines separate themselves from the main clause by means of an emphatic gap. The effect, as often in Fisher, is of uneasy parody. Part of the opening registers a genuine 'dislike' of artistic chat; part recognizes that the poet, by writing about writing, is forever 'mentioning works of art'. Here this contradiction gives impetus to the self-reflexive journey on which, almost with a guilty rush, the poem embarks:

> I could say
> the poem has always
> already started, the parapet
> snaking away, its grey line guarding
> the football field and the sea

'I could say' places the lines after it in a conditional mood. But the line also suggests—especially after 'always'—that were the poet to 'say' what, in fact, he goes on to say, he would only be saying what a poem always, in some sense, does say. Ian Gregson points out that 'the words "poem" and "parapet" are connected to each other through an ambiguity achieved by parataxis—a parataxis character-istic of later Fisher in the way it deliberately questions boundaries'.[26] Gregson's own prose seems inadvertently to join in the self-reflexive dance. It is hard not to feel that 'parataxis' has been provoked by alliteration and echo; the boundary between poem and critical dis-course is blurred with worrying ease and 'parataxis' emerges too conveniently as a label to justify Fisher's elliptical transitions. What saves the poem is its 'snaking' away from the banal observation that the poem is a poem and has been written 'already'.

In the following lines 'always already' repeats itself— '—the parapet / has always already started / snaking away'—but this time the phrase has no need for the surprise-inducing line-break. It may be that the repeated phrase conveys, in Almon's words, 'a sense of the continuous present both in the poem ... and the world'.[27] But to communicate this is to make 'the world' a place of continual, in-exhaustible activity. The poem enlarges its scope through this hardly intended hint of celebration; 'under whatever progression', as it goes on to say, it 'takes things forward'(*P55–87*, p. 129).

The couplet from which these phrases are quoted is isolated, as though the poet were rescuing from the surrounding flux the poem's principle of being, a commitment to taking 'things forward'. Fisher is self-aware yet freed from self-reflexive paralysis because word and world have begun to mesh in his lines. As is often the case when his poems work, the poem's 'movements' from now on are sure and surprising; commitment to forward movement gives way (as the poem moves forward) to a sense of 'looking down / between the moving frames', a looking down that takes the poet back into the past, or at least into a dimension 'close to recall'. Here the poem does not play games merely; it opens up new territory as it develops. The poet leads himself and yet is led, with a bemused tentativeness, into the domain of memory; of 'those other movements' Fisher writes, reluctantly owning up to ownership, 'All of them must be mine, / the way I move on', and then moves on into the past:

> and there I am,
> half my lifetime back,
> on Goodrington sands
> one winter Saturday,
>
> troubled in mind: troubled
> only by Goodrington beach
> under the gloom, the look of it
> against its hinterland
>
> and to be walking
> acres of sandy wrack,
> sodden and unstable
> from one end to the other.

Again, one is struck by the way concern with subjectivity comes to the fore. Fisher makes strange his presence ('and there I am') by placing himself in a 'there' that turns out (after the line-ending) to be 'half my lifetime back'. He plays up and plays down a 'troubled' element; he was, we assume in the past ('one winter Saturday') 'troubled in mind', but this confessional gesture is immediately cancelled by the next, seemingly appositional phrase, 'troubled / only by Goodrington beach...' And yet that second instance of being 'troubled' will not stay attached wholly to the first and might refer less to the past time than to a present feeling of being 'troubled' by a past memory. Lending support to this reading is the untethered syntax of 'and to be walking', as though the 'walking' were less remembered than current. It is as if the past memory has turned, by virtue of being conjured up in the poem, into a present image for the poet's 'movement' into the past. In Neil Corcoran's words (describing a general condition of Fisher's work), 'landscape' undergoes 'displacement into mindscape'.[28] Hauntingly, the self discovers itself 'walking / acres of sandy wrack', momentarily recalling the Wordsworth who sees in his mind's eye the Leech-gatherer wandering continually. The terrain of poem and self may be 'sodden and unstable', but the poem traces it 'from one end to the other'.

This terrain seems post-Romantic rather than postmodernist. With its emphasis on 'movement', 'If I Didn't' brings to mind Perloff's description of the Poundian 'rule . . . that anything goes as long as the poet knows, in Charles Olson's words, how to "keep it moving"'.[29] But Fisher's design is far less restlessly open than Olson's dictum suggests, and it comes to a rest on a keenly plangent sense of experiential and poetic self-discovery. Admittedly, Fisher's poetic 'movements' can seem 'driven' (to use his own telling word) by an innate wariness, a reluctance to submit to the demands of emotional revelation. Yet the display of this reluctance is ostentatious, as 'A Poem to be Watched' half-confesses. In this brief, self-mirroring piece Fisher redescribes and mimics the complications of his poetic. His poetry is 'driven to exhibit / over and over again / unpreparedness' (*P55–87*, p. 182). That it does so 'over and over again' implies an ethos of authenticity (every start is a new beginning) and an aesthetic of knowingness: continually 'to exhibit . . . unpreparedness' suggests a preparedness to display one's unprepared state. The difficulty for Fisher, and the challenge for his reader, is bound up in the relationship his poems seek to create between authenticity and knowingness.

This relationship is the foundation of his most persuasive work. Even when Fisher allows poetic self-reflexiveness to take a back seat, as in 'The Running Changes', evocativeness of description—to adapt the end of 'A Poem to be Watched'—will never permit itself to 'be caught / born'. 'The Running Changes' (*P55–87*, p. 183) may appear to be like 'If I Didn't' with the metapoetic dimension omitted. But this dimension is the more potent for being inexplicit. Again, there are allusions to past emotional difficulties, as Fisher begins with melo-dramatic bravura, driving away from 'a panic and ruin of life'. As with 'troubled in mind' in 'If I Didn't', the phrase seems deliberately to jar on the ear. It is as if Fisher smuggles back a language he has outlawed, as if he assumes the voice of one who, having denied himself the language of subjective feeling, has recourse to it *in extremis*—sounding, in so doing, awkward, half-way between embarrassment and mockery. He is certainly not on even terms with the rhetoric of disaster in the way that John Berryman is in, say, *Dream Songs*, 45, which opens, 'He stared at ruin. Ruin stared straight back. / He thought they was old friends'.[30] Here the poetry strips 'ruin' of its terrors and yet implies that Henry has good cause to speak of 'ruin' in such comradely tones. After all, he has lost papers 'rich with pals' secrets', and crossed paths with ruin in jail and 'in an Asian city / di-rectionless & lurchy'. Berryman's poem depends on switches of mood, from a down-in-the-mouth wryness to—at the poem's end—an unexpected deepening and darkening: 'He did not know this one. / This one was a stranger, come to make amends / for all the im-posters, and to make it stick. / Henry nodded, un-.' 'To make amends' there is wolfishly gleeful as it ushers in its sinister phrasal *alter ego*, 'to make it stick'. The poetry's particularity lies in its dramatic vividness; it sounds as though it is catching the inflections of this 'stranger' which (or who) is strangely kin to 'Ruin', so that when 'Henry nodded, un-' he responds to a voice: his truncated prefix might herald a scary 'unnerved' or a jittery 'unconvinced'.

Fisher is uncomfortable in the territory of 'Ruin' and mental 'trouble', settling for an altogether more English account of weather and landscape. Indeed, it is as 'panic and ruin' resume their status as discarded props that the poem breaks through to its own special emotion: the sense of relieved escape from a 'trouble' that still ghosts the poem. What brings about this relief is the way that landscape takes on a quality of inner weather as 'the look of the road up to Kirkby, / the plainness and dark of it, settled / my stomach'. Here Fisher's nerves are 'settled', unsettlingly, by a road marked by 'plain-ness and dark', and at moments such as this he again brings to mind certain Wordsworthian effects. The poem escapes 'trouble' by entering into a fluid, not quite articulable, relationship between inner and outer. Yet it would be wrong simply to see Fisher as eluding subjective troubles by embracing the 'world', as the poem half-encourages one to do; with Berryman's hyper-neurotic but witty confrontation with 'ruin' in one's mind, one can see that Fisher tactfully concedes that there are times in poetry when the 'world' is a refuge from the mind's troubles. Partly admitting this, partly, in his inward way, exulting in his break-out from 'panic and ruin', Fisher describes how the plainness and dark and blackness of 'Brough / Keep', looming effectively across the line, 'made me for that day / my own man, out over cold stripped Stainmore'. This assertion begins as a low-key, slangy rewriting of egotistical sublimity (the Lake District will have beckoned, just out of sight, to Fisher on his journey). But it ends with a fine blending of the human and the landscape in that phrase, 'out over cold stripped Stainmore'.

The poem, in fact, is constructed as a diptych, setting against the first drive northwards a southward drive, 'coming down in peace out of Durham'. The writing from here on takes on a new assurance and buoyant urgency, as the poet celebrates a fugitive but sustained vision lit by 'sunlight from no sure source'. After the poem's initial sense of 'trouble', this vision seems like an unexpected grace. Fisher's account of his drive through 'a late snowstorm' is suffused with an energy that reconciles and transforms. So the lorries are seen 'thrashing their way up over Stainmore / in spray-wave of rose-tinged slush', the phrasing mingling the metaphoric and the quotidian. Though 'rose-tinged', the 'slush' is not seen through sentimentalizing spectacles, even as the springing, clustering stresses keep any incipient irony at bay. And yet, as the poem reaches forward to observe 'the vanishing up' of the sunset 'into the grey', and to conclude with 'Brough Castle / marking the turn southward, / and being dark', Fisher brings the running changes of his lyric to an affecting and sombre close. That 'dark', rhyming with the 'marking' performed by the Castle (no longer a Keep), retains its own secrets, refusing to confirm Fisher in his sense of himself, to make him his own man; he is confronted, at the end, by a 'dark' that has its own 'being' and cannot be seen as a 'source'. Still, it is through such explorations of the wariest of subjectivities as it engages in the practice of writing that Fisher earns his high place among contemporary poets. Like Osip Mandelstam's Dante in being 'terrified of the direct answer', Fisher is also, in the Russian author's words, one of those rare poets 'who shakes up meaning'.[31]

NOTES

1. Quoted from John Ash, *Selected Poems* (Manchester: Carcanet, 1996), p. 17. For the same author's perceptive reading of Fisher as a poet of 'exemplary honesty', see John Ash, 'A Classic Post-Modernist', *Atlantic Review*, new series, 2 (1979), pp. 39–50; the quoted words are from p. 39.

2. Eric Mottram, 'The British Poetry Revival, 1960–75', in *New British Poetries*, ed. Robert Hampson and Peter Barry (Manchester: Manchester University Press, 1993), p. 24.

3. The phrase is Peter Barry's in his ' "Fugitive from All Exegesis": Reading Roy Fisher's *A Furnace*', *Dutch Quarterly Review of Anglo-American Letters*, 18:1 (1988), p. 5.

4. Marjorie Perloff, *The Dance of the Intellect: Studies in the Poetry of the Pound Tradition* (Evanston, IL: Northwestern University Press, 1996; first published by Cambridge University Press, 1985), p. 22.

5. *F*, p. 1; Barry, ' "Fugitive from all Exegesis" ', p. 5.

6. *Ibid.*, p. 3.

7. *Ibid.*, p. 9.

8. *Ibid.*, p. 12; see also p. 15, 'Yet these people are to some extent, and in spite of earlier denials that this would be done, immediately rendered into "art".'

9. The poem includes an image of 'images without words / where armed men, shadows in pewter, / ride out of the air and vanish, / and never once stop to say what they mean'; see the comments in A. Kingsley Weatherhead's chapter on Fisher in *The British Dissonance: Essays on Ten Contemporary Poets* (Columbia: University of Missouri Press, 1983), p. 55.

10. Terry Eagleton, *The Ideology of the Aesthetic* (Oxford: Blackwell, 1990), p. 295.

11. *The Selected Poetry of Rainer Maria Rilke*, ed. and trans. Stephen Mitchell, intro. Robert Hass (London: Picador, 1987), p. 201.

12. Jed Rasula and Mike Erwin, 'An Interview with Roy Fisher', in Roy Fisher, *Nineteen Poems and an Interview* (Pensnett, Staffs: Grosseteste, 1977), p. 16.

13. Roy Fisher, 'The Thing about Roy Fisher', in *Bloodaxe Books: The Catalogue* (Newcastle upon Tyne: Bloodaxe, 1997), p. 35. (This review first appeared as 'Roy Fisher Reviews Roy Fisher' in *The Rialto*, 35 (1996).)

14. Rasula and Erwin, 'Interview', p. 17.

15. Rainer Maria Rilke, *The Notebooks of Malte Laurids Brigge*, trans. M. D. Herter Norton (New York: Norton, 1964; reissue in paperback of 1949 edn), p. 15; T. S. Eliot's words come from 'The Burial of the Dead' in *The Waste Land*.

16. John Kerrigan, 'Rooting for Birmingham', *London Review of Books*, 19:2 (1997), p. 30. Kerrigan argues that 'Fisher rewrote *City* not least because he came to feel that the alienations of its narrator owed too much to his own sense of being oppressed by local detail', p. 30.

17. *The Letters of Percy Bysshe Shelley*, ed. Frederick L. Jones, 2 vols (Oxford: Clarendon Press, 1964), vol. 2, p. 109.

18. Ian Gregson, 'Music of the Generous Eye: The Poetry of Roy Fisher', *Contemporary Poetry and Postmodernism: Dialogue and Estrangement* (Basingstoke: Macmillan, 1996), p. 191. Gregson makes the apposite point that 'Fisher is as respectful of realism as he is sceptical of it', commenting that the 'poems contain a nostalgia for the "real" and inscribe in their structures a significant sense of its bewildering loss', p. 191.

19. Bert Almon, ' "If I Didn't Dislike Mentioning Works of Art": Roy Fisher's Poems on Poems', *Ariel*, 22:3 (1991), p. 12.

20. 'Item' is quoted from *New Writing 6*, ed. A. S. Byatt and Peter Porter (London: Vintage in association with the British Council, 1997), pp. 302–5.

21. Almon, ' "If I Didn't Dislike" ', pp. 8, 12, 13.

22. *Ibid.*, p. 13.

23. *Ibid.*

24. Quoted from Walt Whitman, *The Complete Poems*, ed. Francis Murphy (Harmondsworth: Penguin, 1975).

25. Gregson, 'Music of the Generous Eye', p. 190.

26. *Ibid.*, pp. 182–83.

27. Bert Almon, ' "If I Didn't Dislike" ', p. 16.

28. Neil Corcoran, *English Poetry since 1940* (London: Longman, 1993), p. 172.

29. Marjorie Perloff, *Dance of the Intellect*, p. 22.

30. Quoted from John Berryman, *The Dream Songs* (London: Faber & Faber, 1990).

31. Osip Mandelstam, 'Conversation about Dante', in *The Collected Critical Prose and Letters*, ed. Jane Gary Harris, trans. Jane Gary Harris and Constance Link (London: Collins Harvill, 1991), p. 416.

10

'Coming into their Own': Roy Fisher and John Cowper Powys

RALPH PITE

Roy Fisher dedicated *A Furnace*:

> To the memory of John Cowper Powys
> 1872–1963

It is an unexpected choice. Powys's longwinded and agitated novels seem quite foreign to the compactness and downbeat understatement that often characterize Fisher's work. Where Fisher is reticent and oblique, Powys is insistent or oratorical. Fisher follows through on his dedication, however, by citing Powys as a source for key-ideas in the poem:

> I am indebted to his [Powys's] writings for such understanding as I have of the idea that the making of all kinds of identities is a primary impulse which the cosmos itself has; and that those identities and that impulse can be acknowledged only by some form or other of poetic imagination.[1]

This is a good summary of what Powys believes. In his novels, animals and plants, even stones and minerals, are not only all alive, but each kind of living thing possesses its own quality of consciousness and seeks to become as completely itself as possible. Moreover, in an age obsessed with a scientific account of truth, something akin to 'poetic imagination' is needed in order to recognize the real nature of the universe. As I hope to show, this aspect of Powys's work and belief-system underlies and informs Fisher's work, *A Furnace* in particular.

Powys's conviction that the universe is animated in all its parts drives his lifelong and passionate hostility to vivisection. It is also expressed with extraordinary directness in everything he writes:

> Silent and alone too the now-darkened conservatory listened to the placid sub-human breathings of heliotrope and lemon verbena, the latter with a faint catch in its drowsy susurration, where one of its twigs was bleeding a little from the impact of the fingers of the indignant Mr Didlington.[2]

This is from near the beginning of *A Glastonbury Romance* (1933) in which Mr Didlington figures as a minor villain. His officious cruelty makes an 'impact' greater than he realizes. His non-recognition of his own impact is the source of his cruelty, in fact—a form of cruelty analogous in Powys's mind to the evil of vivisection. Because Didlington treats plants as if they were just material objects, he prunes them without a second thought and leaves them 'bleeding'. He would not recognize that the twig was literally bleeding and neither does he hear the 'sub-human breathings' of these living things, the murmurous half-speech that reveals their consciousness.

For Powys as for Blake, 'everything that lives is holy'; indeed, everything lives and because it lives, it is holy. Nothing can be excluded. He emphasizes this by focussing on the conventionally insignificant or unattractive, on what one feels justified in using for one's own purposes, such as a decorative houseplant, or in dismissing, such as a fly. In the first of Powys's 'Wessex novels', *Wolf Solent* (1929), Wolf Solent begins the novel travelling by train to Dorset. When he arrives:

> He rose from his seat and took down his things from the rack, causing, as he did so, so much agitation to his only travelling companion, the bluebottle fly, that it escaped with an indignant humming through the window into the unfamiliar air-fields of Dorsetshire.[3]

The anthropomorphism of this sounds whimsical (especially by comparison with the passage from *A Glastonbury Romance*). It is a manner, however, that Powys grew increasingly fond of, especially after the Second World War. In *Atlantis* (1954), for instance, extended philosophical discussions take place between a moth, a fly and a wooden club.

Though Fisher refers to *Atlantis* in his preface and though the novel is extremely important to *A Furnace*, Powys's *Weymouth Sands* (1935)[4] shows more clearly the impulse towards making identities which Fisher refers to and the importance of 'some form or other of poetic imagination' to recognizing that impulse. *Weymouth Sands* is the novel by Powys most concentrated on a single place and Powys sees the objects that make up the town of Weymouth as forming a community, comparable to the animate and the human communities which inhabit it:

> it might be easily conceived that between St Alban's Head, the White Nose, the Nothe, Chesil Beach, the Breakwater, the Town Bridge, the White Horse, Hardy's Monument, King George's Statue, St John's Spire, the Jubilee Clock, and this perpetual crying of sea-gulls and advancing and retreating of sea-tides, there might have arisen, in their long confederacy, a brooding patience, resembling that of an organic Being; a patience that approached, if it could never quite attain, the faint, dim embryonic half-consciousness that brooded in the sea-weeds, the sea-shells, the sea-anemones, the star-fish and jelly-fish, that lay submerged along those beaches and among those rock-pools. (*WS*, p. 190)

It 'might be easily conceived' yet the character in the novel who conceives it most is an eccentric and outcast, Sylvanus Cobbold, who is accused of interfering with young girls and is finally incarcerated in a mental institution. None the less, it is Sylvanus who sees the animatedness of nature and within it the source of animation that lies beyond:

> It was an Absolute that saturated with itself certain concrete objects more than others; and the girls began to divine that they could find it in the smallest 'minute particulars' of their own lives. (*WS*, p. 323)

Sylvanus is speaking to the girls as they make this discovery and what the girls 'divine', almost without realizing, Powys returns to several times, as if it is a perception repeatedly attained and never quite understood even by Sylvanus.

As is often the case with Powys's novels, the narrative line of *Weymouth Sands* is hard to make out. Powys gives the novel the appearance of a thriller—one of the characters is plotting throughout to murder another—and of a romance—Perdita Wane, the heroine, is found and lost and found again. These plots become secondary, however, to a less linear and progressive element in the novel: the different characters' separate moments of insight, similar to Sylvanus's. Powys's understanding of community is based upon the awareness that all insight is distinctively personal and unique, while also being linked by common qualities and features to the perceptions that other people have. These common features are not so much those of the Freudian unconscious; rather, each person's insight approaches 'the mysterious Beyond-life' which forms out of that multitude of perceptions a consciousness that resembles a single 'organic Being'. The book's structure suggests that an underlying unity is continually forming itself out of individuated, often lonely, people and is able to take up only the most distinctive qualities of every person. When, therefore, people in the novel follow the impulse to make an identity, they are drawn into a closer relation with the 'primary impulse which the cosmos itself has', which is to make an identity for itself. That implies a closer link to other people but a link which relies upon the separate identity of each being realized as much as possible. There are political implications to this idea though Powys does not bring them out in *Weymouth Sands*. That absence is consistent rather than evasive because Powys is a kind of anarchist, I think, for whom 'the political' implies the normative and oppressive.

What Sylvanus sees when he looks at Portland Bill is a moment of rising and separation in which the particular object becomes most completely itself, unencumbered by its surroundings and unsubmissive to external pressures. That individuation does not create an atomized universe of separate 'minute particulars'; instead, each particular when most individual is most saturated by the

Absolute. 'To make ourselves better understand,' Powys wrote in *Suspended Judgements*, 'we have to emphasize our differences, and to touch the universe of our friend we have to travel away from him, on a curve of free sky.'[5] Powys's own distinctiveness lies in his sense that being separate produces rejection. His most individuated characters are hounded by society's men of power, hounded towards conformity. Similarly, the novels frequently express anxiety about the relation between individuation and (in particular, male) sexuality. Though the novels celebrate sensuality, they tend to recoil from penetration, seeing it as a form of violation. That recoil, though, may turn into a rejection of the other's impulse towards self-fulfillment and, hence, towards making an identity. The apparently generous desire not to possess the woman can become a means of oppressing her most natural impulses. Dud No-Man in *Maiden Castle* is the most detailed study of this contradiction and of its roots in a fear of sexual inadequacy. Dud is contrasted with his father, Enoch Quirm (who has renamed himself Uryen Quirm).[6] Quirm's sexual desire neither possesses women nor rejects them; he enables the women he loves to fulfill their own impulses, even when these are lesbian (as is the case with Thuella Wye).

Quirm is heroic because he wants to allow everyone to achieve their own truest nature and to encourage them in that even when it means opposing society's conventional restraints. Powys's elaborate style arises out of the same impulse: everything is given ample room to present itself and the voice of the prose is comically undiscriminating and consistent. The self-love of a minor character or of a jellyfish or even a stone is credited by the novels. Accordingly, everything is described with equal weight and with exuberant overstatement—an overstatement designed to challenge the reader's inherited and conventional sense of hierarchy. For the same reasons, Powys disappoints narrative conventions. Superficially, people are interlinked within a social hierarchy and jostle for dominance; more profoundly, they are entirely separate and entirely equal. He uses and distorts conventional narrative patterns in order to present that profound truth and its relation to superficial appearances.[7] Powys's prose style (with its baroque complication and self-conscious absurdity) can be irritating; none the less, its purpose is intimate with Powys's sense that the universe has nothing in it which is not trying to *be* and nothing which does not deserve to be given its chance to achieve itself. He fears that his style of writing replicates the elaborate sexual caution of characters such as Dud No-Man while feeling, at the same time, that this is preferable to the manipulative and dominant descriptive methods which would be typical of his capitalist villains. In his Wessex novels, Powys's writing repeatedly moves towards the unspeakable insights which form the consciousness of his heroic, visionary characters (such as Uryen Quirm or Sylvanus Cobbold). In his post-war work, whimsicality and apparent childishness try to capture (and simultaneously show as lying beyond words) the extraordinary reality of animated things.

Fisher's language could not seem more different, perhaps, yet it is often driven by a similar impulse: to allow things to be themselves despite the domineering tendency of his own words. 'I mistrust the poem in its hour of success,' Fisher remarks in 'It is Writing' and 'mistrust' dominates his accounts of how language treats materials.[8] In 'New Diversions' (roughly contemporary with *A Furnace* and included in the 'Poems 1979–1987' section of *Poems 1955–1987*), Fisher dreams about 'a suppressed / novel by John Cowper Powys' and discusses it in the dream with 'a divine / worldly and humorous, the prime / scholar'.

> we spoke easily
> of the round grey nondescript mere
> the author had left undisturbed
> right through the action
> in a dull meadow off to one side. 'It's
> the only true *Pool*
> in the whole of our literature!'
> cried the scholar. Both claim and pool
> seemed still to be
> there to be agreed with.   (*P55–87*, p. 179)

Because it was 'left undisturbed', the pool is still there, present and capable of being addressed. Fisher's scholar cannot face the apocalypse that Powys describes in the imaginary novel: 'it was something / deeper and more frightful than an embarrassment' (*P55–87*, p. 179). Instead, he claims and acclaims the untouched object which prompts attention because it has been left alone. '[O]ld Powys with his one / visionary eye' (*P55–87*, p. 179) reaches an apocalyptic insight which the scholar evades and replaces with a celebration of the ordinary, the marginal and dull. Though the scholar is frantic and overpitched, what he celebrates and the claim he makes for it both possess an apocalyptic quality, albeit a more muted one. Fisher's writing senses the comedy of the scholar's contradictions. The irony of celebrating passivity is that by doing so you make a claim. And, with equal irony, that claim may be appropriate. The nondescript may be a vision of 'the only true'. This claim gains in importance when seen in the context of the rest of Fisher's work; moreover, the clash between scholar and visionary is repeated in the structure of *A Furnace*.

The dream of Powys in 'New Diversions', partly because it is a dream, strikes a more buoyant note than do many of the other poems in the sequence:

> A burnt year. Trick riders blunder about the concrete,
> aimless, with no idea.
> Open season for old wounds, odd jobs,
> travelling from the one door to the other
> over and over,
> hamming it up, on the booze.   (*P55–87*, p. 177)

I assume that the 'Trick riders' are kids on BMX bikes, popular in the mid-eighties, or on skateboards. Their clatter in precincts sounds shapeless and relentless, yet Fisher at once admits it is no worse than his own 'odd jobs' and reopening of old wounds. Then, characteristically, in the last line, both the moan and the comparison seem factitious: 'hamming it up', Fisher says, as if complaining about either the disturbance or the aimlessness were another piece of pointless interference. The self-mistrust in this section makes the scholar's claim the more poignant or haunting later on—his claim that something can remain undisturbed while being rendered fully and truly present.

It is a problem for Fisher, then, that one is continually troubling the world in order to make it visible:

> A plain ground as if white
> stretching away nondescript
> set out with tracks
> and heaps of things
> all made of marking
>
> The more he looked
> the more he saw   ('The Six Deliberate Acts', *P55–87,* p. 80)

The neatness of the last two lines, like an epigram turned into a jingle, makes close attention into fantasy. This featureless ground is 'set out' with opportunities for looking and interpreting. It is made of 'marking' in the sense of traces, signs of occupation and of what one notices ('Mark that, sirrah!'). The opening of 'A Poem Not a Picture' is similar:

> On a ground remarkable for lack of character, sweeps of direction form.
>
> It's not possible to determine whether they rise from the ground's qualities or are marked on to it.   (*P55–87,* p. 112)

And more bleakly in *The Cut Pages*, Fisher makes this problem in perceiving a problem in being:

> There's no choice. There's everything, but no way of choosing. Nothing comes away. *You* come away, pulling things with you. No choice for you, no choice for them[9]

In some poems, none the less, things do come away, separate and independent, usually by chance. '[T]here is blankness / and there is grace' he writes in 'Some Loss' (*P55–87,* p. 116) and in '3rd November 1976' a 'sculptor innocent of bureaucracy / raises his fine head to speak out'. At that moment, he 'is made clear' (*P55–87,* p. 144). Speaking about 'Handsworth Liberties', moreover, Fisher suggests that writing may make possible a similar kind of freedom, as it were releasing things back into themselves:

In writing the poems I detached the locations from their
musics. That was their liberty, in return for their having to
work for me in a new way and earn a little of their keep for a
while.[10]

The key-word, perhaps, in all this side of Fisher's work is 'nondescript': 'the round grey nondescript mere' of 'New Diversions'; 'a
plain ground . . . stretching away nondescript' in 'The Six Deliberate
Acts'; and this from 'Handsworth Liberties' itself:

> Riding out of the built-up
> valley without a view
> on to the built-up crest
> where a nondescript murky evening
> comes into its own
> while everybody gets home
> and in under the roofs.
>
> A place for the boys,
> for the cyclists,
> the strong.   *(P55–87,* pp. 120–21)

The speaker seems not to be one of the boys and neither is he like
everybody else, getting 'home / and in under the roofs'. Is he 'Riding'
a bicycle or a bus? (Fisher often places himself on buses or trams,
notably in the 'Introit' to *A Furnace.*) Because we are not sure about
this, we are uncertain which group he is closest to, if either. Is he
retreating, like 'everybody', or is he self-involved and heroic, like 'the
cyclists', 'the strong'? The evening seems to 'come into its own' when
people ignore it, either going indoors or playing their own games,
using the hill as a test of strength. The speaker, doing neither of these
things, seems less willing to allow the hill simply to be. It is as if it
'comes into its own' despite his intruding, unnecessary presence; as if
he would be more human and more admirable if he let it alone.

In this context, 'nondescript' reflects the writer's wish not to
intrude and by not intruding to allow the evening to reassert itself. It
means 'featureless, indeterminate . . . undistinguished' in modern
English; earlier it meant unknown: 'Of a species: not hitherto

described.'[11] By ignoring it, you let it remain itself, unmarked by the features you would discover. By finding it featureless, you restore its uniqueness. Within the ubiquitous lies the genuine, travestied by all description, by any effort to make distinctive. Fisher is not, as I say, always as hard on himself as this. In 'Staffordshire Red', a poem dedicated to Geoffrey Hill, he goes through 'a nondescript cleft in the trees', a cutting for a road 'through / sandstone at Offley'. 'Nondescript' here reflects his own casual speed, which loses sight of the place as soon as it's behind him. When he goes back, it is no different:

> It was as it had been.
> The savage cut in the red ridge . . . .
>   How hard
> is understanding? Some things
> are lying in wait in the world,
> walking about in the world,
> happening when touched, as they must.   (*P55–87,* pp. 141–42)

These lines close the poem and they resemble Philip Larkin's lyrically colloquial endings, particularly the last lines of 'To the Sea' from *High Windows*: 'teach their children by a sort / Of clowning; helping the old, too, as they ought'. Larkin's pathos clashes with his pointed, tacitly censorious use of 'as they ought'; Fisher's 'as they must' seems fatalistic by comparison and yet the certainty of these necessary events comes across as a positive pleasure. It is a relief to Fisher, a burden lifted from him, to find that things happen without his asking and without any interference from him. Even his unconcern can be accidental, it seems; it need not be made as stringently absolute as it was in 'Handsworth Liberties'.[12]

Fisher, then, is connected to John Cowper Powys by a shared concern with allowing places and objects to 'come into their own' at particular moments and, following from that, by the desire to write in such a way as to give places back 'their liberty'.[13] Frequently, Fisher casts himself as a type similar to Dud No-Man—as someone who is anxiously unpossessive of objects and is struggling with the contradictions involved in attempting to be unpossessive, as someone who

is neither 'everybody' nor 'the strong', rejected by both and not
convinced that this rejection gives him the status of a prophet. *A
Furnace* is perhaps the exception to that rule. It is Fisher's longest
work after *City* and, reviewing himself in *The Rialto*, Fisher calls it:
'for all its unconscious or unashamed solipsism, one of the most
ambitious recent English poems'.[14] In the same article, Fisher comes
across as more confident and more angular than one might expect,
describing himself as:

> an anarchist who simply has no time whatever for hierarchical
> systems, monotheisms or state authority; or for capitalism,
> along with the absorbent, malleable selves it breeds and with
> which it populates its democracies and its literatures.[15]

This abrupt, bare-knuckle rejection of 'malleable selves' also comes
through when Fisher is being interviewed. Despite being 'notor-
iously emollient', he is trenchantly self-possessed. When asked, for
instance, about Gael Turnbull's possible importance to his work,
Fisher replies: 'Gael and I: very different people, but I suspect we
influence each other in funny ways as the years go by.' The reply is
cool and liberating. The two writers are paired and, at the same time,
simply 'very different', neither ferociously independent of each other
nor Freudian rivals. Similarly, though more crossly, Fisher dismisses
Donald Davie's account of him (in his 1973 book, *Thomas Hardy and
British Poetry*) as simply irrelevant: 'I wasn't aware that he'd exactly
written about *my* work in that book!' He is not to be fashioned or
marshalled by a market-maker like Davie; his work (which is *his*
work) remains defiantly separate from the uses critics put it to.[16]

The self-certainty of these remarks surfaces again in *A Furnace*. The
poem appears to have an epic scope and 'might equally appear to be
written in the prophetic mode', as Andrew Crozier says. These may be
(in the end) misleading terms, but they are ones the poem deliberately
invokes. Similarly, the poem's concerns are undeniably grand:

> What is imagined—the timeless identities entering nature—
> might yet give even well-disposed readers pause. And I think
> we should at least pause to ask if *A Furnace* does not arrive,

finally, at a heterodox mysticism. Is its aim to annul the natural fact of death? To offer a prospect of transcendence?

Crozier answers these questions in the negative, rejecting transcendence on principle, I think, and seeing in the poem, instead, a concern 'with human complexity and the negation of identity by structures of authority'.[17] This judgement underplays, in my view, the 'heterodox mysticism' of the poem, misconstruing its relation to Powys and its extraordinary structure. It is as if Crozier cannot believe that Fisher could do such a thing.

Fisher quotes in *A Furnace* from Powys's *Maiden Castle*. 'Whatever breaks / from stasis', he says, 'fetches the timeless flux / that cannot help but practise / materialization' and fetches too 'timeless identities / riding in the flux'. These identities were once living and are now in the flux because 'cast out of the bodies / that once they were'. Though fluid and 'with no / determined form' these identities remain:

> trapped into water-drops,
> windows they glanced through
> or had their images
> detained by and reflected
> or into whose molten glass the coloured oxides
> burned their qualities;
>
> *like dark-finned fish embedded in ice*
> *they have life in them that can be revived.*   (*F*, pp. 11–12)

The last two lines are from the novel, where they are spoken by Enoch Quirm during a discussion of a 'votive image' that has recently been excavated from Maiden Castle:

> those horns and that tail, carrying those three half-men, seem to me—Well! It's not classical symbolism anyway, it goes back further; and when you talk of science you must remember that these things are like dark-finned fish embedded in ice. *They have life in them that can be revived.* And I must say this to you, Mr. Cask: it is *not* science that can revive them. But go on with your excavations... But you must remember when you're dealing with *that* place you're vivisecting something different from a

dog! . . . What you and your kind call Evolution I call Creation: and it would do no harm to just remind you that those who create can also destroy![18]

Quirm warns against the presumptions of science: excavated objects possess life still, a life that may revive and come back to haunt Mr Cask, the rational archaeologist and tomb-robber, like the curse of Tutankhamun. The forces trapped in objects are less menacing in Fisher, and Quirm's grim warning is made into something full of possibility. Fisher echoes prophecy in a less forbidding key, less troubled by the violations and ignorance of a scientific, materialist culture, more evenly convinced for the moment that that 'doesn't matter'.

The passage from *A Furnace* opens the second section of the poem, 'The Return', and with the 'molten glass' and 'coloured oxides', it is a reminder of the beginning of the first, 'Calling': 'Ancient / face-fragments of holy saints / in fused glass, blood-red and blue' (*F*, p. 5). The opening section repeatedly has fixities ambiguously breaking out of their entrapment, as pieces of stained glass 'pierce the church wall / with acids', as people are subject to 'Sudden and grotesque / callings' (*F*, pp. 5, 8). The second section reverses that: when something breaks out for a moment, it immediately fixes again: 'suddenly / over' it brings the timeless 'into sense, / to the guesswork of the senses' (*F*, p. 11). The quotation from Powys appears to promise that this refixing can again be reversed: that revival is always possible, that what is trapped can be freed again to become in turn the prompt for a further materialization of timeless identities. That materialization is asserted without qualification. Fisher's writing in 'The Return' has not only control and deftness; it is firmly definitive. As Quirm opposes scientific self-confidence with his pulpit oratory and stance of a prophet, Fisher resists the weak 'drive to be in, / close to the radio, / the school, the government's wars' and does so through the 'dream or intention: of encoding / something perennial / and entering Nature thereby.'

> But still through that place
> to enter Nature; it was possible,
> it was imperative.
>
> (*F*, pp. 14, 12, 14)

'But still' is characteristic of Fisher in this section: 'but still . . . the other dream or intention: of encoding'. It is consciously exceptional and conscious of being ignored, acting despite the pressure to conform and making itself 'still' in order not to become malleable. The 'drive to be in' recalls 'Handsworth Liberties' where 'everybody gets home / and in under the roofs'. The speaker of both finds himself estranged from social conformity; *A Furnace*, however, sees no conflict between the place 'coming into its own' and the observer doing the same:

> Bladelike and eternal, clear,
> the entry into Nature
> is depicted by
> the vanishing of a gentleman . . .
>   he having lately walked
> through a door in the air
> among the tall
> buildings of the Northern Aluminium Company
> and become inseparable
> from all other things, no longer
> capable of being imagined
> apart from them, nor yet of being
> forgotten in his identity.   (*F*, pp. 12–13)

These authoritative paradoxes ('no longer . . . apart . . . nor yet . . . forgotten') resolve the tension of 'nondescript' in the earlier poem— the gentleman entering Nature does not impose upon its blank features his own meanings. He is inseparable and transparent, yet (like the nondescript object) also entirely himself. It is an extra-ordinary thing to say.

A Furnace, then, has bold, visionary forcefulness, based upon ideas similar to those of John Cowper Powys and voiced with the self-certainty *in extremis* of Powys's prophet figures. Allowing places their liberty involves 'vanishing' still, but a vanishing into them, so that you become inseparable from them and 'no longer / capable of being imagined / apart'. There is a double movement in 'Calling' and 'The Return', a movement in one direction of submission to what is given, however strange and grotesque, and, in the other direction, of domination over it and of invasive 'encoding'. This double movement repeats the ambivalence of 'nondescript'. It also achieves true liberty, by contrast with 'war service, wage-labour, taxes, / custodial schooling, a stitched-up / franchise' (*F*, p. 17) and:

> Joe
> Chamberlain's sense of the corporate
> signalling to itself with millions of disposable
> identity-cells, summary and tagged.   (*F*, p. 26)

Fisher is often a comic poet, drolly mocking bureaucracy and scholarship. He is more rarely as indignant and excoriating as he is in *A Furnace*. Without the private and unrewarded work of entering Nature, through the equally energetic movements in opposite directions of acceptance and command, the self goes soft and malleable, identities become disposable and are disposed of at the whim of a bigger, no more coherent identity-cell, 'the big city / [which] believed it had a brain' (*F*, p. 26).

The double movement is crucial to the poem, in feeling and in structure. It appears again in Fisher's use of a second quotation from Powys. Fisher refers to *Atlantis* as his source for the idea of a poem 'which gains its effects by the superimposition of landscape upon landscape rather than rhythm upon rhythm' ('Preface', *F*, p. vii). The words are Powys's, quoted again in section VI, 'The Many':

> *Landscape superimposed*
> *upon landscape.* The method
> of the message lost
> in the poetry of Atlantis
> at its subsiding to where all
> landscapes must needs be
> superimpositions on it.   (*F*, p. 41)

In Powys's novel, a 'long poem about the beginning and the end of everything, a poem which still remains the greatest oracle of man's destiny existing upon the earth' sank with Atlantis, having been read by only a few privileged people, and of these

> only the Seven Wise Men of Italy have so much as begun to penetrate its contents; and these have only revealed the fact that it is landscape superimposed upon landscape rather than rhythm upon rhythm that is the method of its message.[19]

Not 'the method in its madness' nor 'the medium is the message'; instead, a cross between the two: 'the method of its message' or, in Fisher's reworking, 'The method / of the message'. Fisher's lineation and his definite article bring out, for a moment, a hint of secret codes and Cold War thrillers, where the crucial signal is intercepted but cannot be cracked. In Powys, the message is lost and the method remains, perhaps to be imitated and tried out as a way of rediscovering the lost message. In Fisher, both method and message seem to be lost and yet, at the line's end, they are seen as 'lost / in' something else, the poetry of Atlantis. 'All landscapes', Fisher goes on, 'solid, and having transparency' (*F*, p. 41), like photographic negatives or pieces of film. The method of superimposition involves becoming lost in things. Similarly, the order of priority is continually open to question: Fisher's quotation from Powys first suggests a landscape superimposing itself on another beneath and then reverses the order, so that sunk Atlantis is superimposed on by landscapes from above. The authority of 'impose' within 'superimpose' is dissipated because in superimposition you can never tell which is on top; that is the meaning of transparency. Likewise, Fisher's quaintly archaic phrase 'must needs be' combines the control of 'must' with the dependency of 'needs' as if, again, the method of superimposition prevents hierarchy.

Fisher designs *A Furnace* in the shape of a double spiral: 'whose line turns back on itself at the centre and leads out again, against its own incoming curve ... the seven movements proceed as if by a section taken through the core of such a spiral' (*F*, pp. vii–viii). It is an 'ancient figure' as he says, but one, perhaps, suggested by Powys's ideas of superimposition. It may be indebted as well to Powys's presentation of fire:

> The element of fire, though taking up only so small a space compared with the terrific mass of water that surrounded it,

drew into itself and flung out of itself, as it whirled its bloody circles round and round, an essence of existence that was at once absolute and unique.   (*Atlantis*, p. 370)[20]

This fire, lit on the boat in which Odysseus and his companions are travelling westwards, draws into itself and flings out of itself an essence of existence. Powys contrasts that vitality with the drowned city of Atlantis, which is a spiral moving in one direction only:

the two of them progressed onwards in what they both divined would probably turn out to be intricate curves returning by degrees to the region of the city from which they had set forth
(*Atlantis*, p. 428)

The monster of the science who founded this city of the dead 'made with outstretched and inwardly curved fingers a series of gestures, of a dangerously magnetic nature, compelling him to approach her' (*Atlantis*, p. 437). The pull inwards, into 'circumambient greyness' (p. 431), into a city of the drowned where no bodies can be found (pp. 438–39), ends in a centre of tyranny and imprisonment:

'From now on, to the end of your lives,' the voice from the Entity . . . grimly grated like a wheel . . . 'you three migrants to my kingdom . . . will go about the world proclaiming my kingdom's laws. . . . This law will be absolutely and entirely scientific. . . . It will care nothing about the happiness of people, or the comfort of people, or the education of people, still less, if that be possible, about the virtue or the righteousness or the compassion or the pity or the sympathy of people.

'It will use people—that is to say men, women, and children as it uses animals.'   (*Atlantis*, pp. 451–52)

Atlantis, a sublime, impressive and literally vacant city, empty with its own claim to power, echoes Blake's London. It resembles too the city of *A Furnace*, the 'glassy metaphysical void' which 'Something will be supposed / to inhabit' with 'spastic entrepreneurial voyages twitched out / from wherever its shores may lie' (*F*, p. 35). Thatcherite economics, which celebrated the 'entrepreneurial' spirit, assume it will progress towards a glorious future. For Fisher, the project is doomed because it has no established point of departure. The 'shores' of the city 'lie' everywhere so that one can appear always to be starting afresh and can never, actually, begin. Equally, the void at the centre is void because it is centreless. The terms of this hostility are repeated elsewhere in Fisher's work. Consider 'Centre. They brought a centre and set it up here, but it wouldn't take. It was rejected, and went off sideways. No sign of it now' from *The Cut Pages* (*Cut* (1986), p. 42) or 'there is a world. / It has been made / out of the tracks of waves / broken against the rim / and coming back awry' in 'Handsworth Liberties' (*P55–87,* p. 117). However, in *A Furnace*, the endless, shapeless forward movement is placed in opposition to the forward and back motion, the acceptance and resistance of the double spiral.

Nothing in Fisher's work is comparable to the structuring of *A Furnace*. His poems are often in sequences and these are usually given titles in the plural: 'Handsworth Liberties', 'Metamorphoses', 'The Six Deliberate Acts', 'Diversions', 'Releases' and so on. *A Furnace* implies greater unity, even singularity, as if the poem's various materials do make up a single thing and its constituent elements are being fused. The poetic imagination seems to be the fire that powers the melting and fusing that the poem performs and it claims to reveal, in the process, a primordial reality. In that respect, Fisher gives an entirely (and exceptionally) prophetic account of the poetic imagination. Resolving the difficulty of his own intrusiveness leads to and depends on the poem's 'heterodox mysticism'. The structure also repeats the terms on which that initial difficulty is resolved. It produces a continual movement between submission and imposition in order to create, at once, identity and transparency. Without that movement, the poem would risk becoming transcendental (as Crozier notices); more importantly, it might become megalomaniac. Michael Hulse is perceptively worried about this: 'The anti-democratic power-worshipper ... broods over much of Fisher ... In Roy Fisher a wary and not always tenable balance is struck between sympathy for Creation and fascination with the Will.'[21] Powys's in-and-out movement differs from Fisher's double spiral but shows, none the less, how necessary it is if Fisher is to avoid either of these dangers.

In *Atlantis*, characters escape the grasp of the tyrant-monster by cunning, obstinacy and violence, and sail further west to make landfall in a Manhattan peopled by Red Indians. The travellers, escapees, are untwitchy and non-malleable and, as in Fisher, they are so because they are 'as self-centred as a diamond' (*Atlantis*, p. 114) and because, at the same time, they are indistinguishable from the world. Odysseus's nearest kindred spirit is a Dryad whose 'slowly dying oak . . . was in a sense her house, and in a sense herself.'

> It was especially the curious hieroglyphs and mysterious patterns which are the written messages from all the unnoticed things that die to make the dust out of which other things are born that fascinated the aged Dryad as she moved day by day about her wild garden. (*Atlantis*, pp. 50, 44)

The paradox is the same as that in other Powys novels and in Fisher: self-centredness and sensitivity go together; the impulse to make an identity brings one closer to 'unnoticed things' which, unnoticed and unacknowledged, possess the same impulse.

For Powys, the paradox is a certainty, voiced at its most extreme because the fuller the identity of the self, the larger the scale of the world with which it is joined. His visionary characters move 'up and out' as they become more separate in their identities:

> as the land narrowed to the Bill he [Sylvanus] felt as if the whole promontory were lifted up, up and out and away, from all the rest of the earth and was propelled by some unknown force to sail alone through empty space. . . . It gave him a feeling as if Nature were returning to God, as if the Relative were returning to the Absolute, as if Life were returning to some mysterious Beyond-life. (*WS*, p. 388)

The idea of moving 'up and out and away' recurs in Powys. *Up and Out* (1957) is his next to last book, a pair of science-fiction short stories. 'Out', though, is 'into' a widening cosmos and not away from the cosmos into a transcendent realm. The returning quality of 'out' is reflected in Powys's narrative structures. His novels often place their moments of greatest vision at some roughly central point which is followed by the resumption of normal affairs. For instance in *Maiden Castle* Enoch Quirm tells Dud No-Man that he is his long-lost father and, in the same scene, that he believes himself to be the same as the person Uryen, from the ancient past, whose name he has adopted. These revelations (of personal identity and of an identity beyond the personal) occur on pages 241–47 in a novel of 496 pages. *Weymouth Sands* has several points of narrative climax: arguably, for Jobber Skald and Perdita, the moment comes when they walk to the end of Portland Bill and gaze down into a chasm in the 'sea-jutting platform of solid rock' (*WS*, p. 348). This incident occurs roughly two-thirds of the way through the book and nothing that follows for Jobber or Perdita is as revelatory. Normal life might seem a comedown afterwards and, for Dud No-Man, the future at the novel's end appears mundane: 'He must go on as best he could in his own way ... He could *not* live, as this dead man [Enoch] had done, in a wild search for the life behind life' (*MC*, p. 496). *Weymouth Sands* is in some ways similarly stoical and resigned; most importantly, however, Powys introduces a stranger, Dr Mabon, into Weymouth, who has some of the bewitching power of Sylvanus and none of the bombast. He can charm children by attention to 'minute particulars', their own and those of a sea-shell:

> Dr Mabon seemed to have a special look for everyone, with its own humorous commentary upon the world, but a *different* commentary for each separate person in any group. He became very grave, however, when he had examined this particular shell and looked at Caddie.
>
> 'It's a Pholas,' he murmured, and his voice was as caressing and tender as if he had been the god who had just created this fragile entity.   (*WS*, p. 495)

The novels conclude by hanging, with the pathos of romance, between the possibility that visionary ambition is in vain and the hope that when the dream is over, the world is seen afresh. Continuing the movement 'up and out' is possible, if at all, through the movement back and in—towards the material and sensational, into the particulars saturated by the absolute.

Fisher's *A Furnace* departs from Powys in this because he sees the movement forward and out as coexisting with the movement back and in. You can hardly tell which is which, even though he explains carefully in the preface that:

> the odd-numbered [sections are] thematically touched by one
> direction of the spiral's progress, and the even-numbered so
> touched by its other, returning, aspect ...   (*F*, p. viii)

This is what happens but the alternatives are not discrete: going into things (in section I) is seen as creating resistant materializations (in section II); those 'timeless identities', however, suggest 'another world / not past, but primordial, / everything in it simultaneous, and moving / every way but forward' (*F*, p. 14). The break from stasis of 'Callings' itself seems to possess a kind of fixity, an insistent forward trajectory, by comparison with the timelessness it enters. In this jostling forward and back, Dr Mabon's serene tenderness is never to be attained. Instead, Fisher hears 'Birmingham voices in the entryways / lay the law down' and, hearing them, his 'surprise / stares into the walls' (*F*, p. 19). The epiphanic object is aggressive and it makes Fisher observe the naivety of his own surprise. It comes at him and, overwhelming him, shows him the invasiveness of his own attention. Fisher is not balked or baffled, neither can he be saintly and calm. Rather, one motion balances the other: the fixity of the law comes forward and the probing gaze is, momentarily, arrested. 'Calling' and 'The Return' interact because they are superimposed upon one another.

Accordingly, in the final section of *A Furnace*, the movement 'up and out' is seen as a materialization. Fisher writes of snails as a kind of angel:

> The snails ascend
>   the thin clear light,
>   taking their spirals higher;
>   in the dusk
>   luminous white, clustered
>   like seed-pods of some other plant;

> quietly
> rasping their way round
> together, and upward;
>
> tight and seraphic.   (*F*, p. 48)

In the lyricism of these closing lines, the snails seem, for a moment, serene as they ascend, as if they have gone beyond the clashing energies in which the cosmos expresses its impulse to make identities. They seem to be moving up and out, into the ideal community of the angelic hosts. Fisher entitles section v 'Colossus' and section vi 'The Many'. 'Seraphic' implies a heavenly solution to the problem of the one and the many, a glimpse of the new Jerusalem. Even so, Fisher continues to stress the unlyrical: snails make for unlikely angels, they 'infest / the wild fennel' (p. 48), reminding us of the ghosts that 'infest the brickwork' earlier on (p. 18). Similarly, although quiet, they are 'quietly / rasping', ambitiously climbing and voraciously eating as they go. The move from one line to the next is like a moment during a nature film when the microphone is turned up high, allowing you to hear the hideous grinding of invisible teeth. (Snails, like other molluscs, possess minute teeth sometimes referred to as 'rasps'; hence, perhaps, Fisher's use of 'rasping'. See *Oxford English Dictionary*, definition 2b: 'The radula of a mollusk, or one of the teeth on this'.) Similarly, as well as being seraphic, the snails are 'tight'—tightly coiled, strongly attached, parsimonious, focussed. They are 'self-centred as a diamond', as Powys put it, even while they are moving gently about this wild garden. *

It follows that Fisher's poem needs to be both closely and energetically read—with attention to local detail and to the wider context of the poem as a whole. Nothing stands apart yet nothing follows programmatically from anything else. The best guide to the special demands the poem makes and to the sources of its language's resonant equilibrium is given by another Fisher sequence, entitled *Cultures* and published in 1975.[22] These poems are printed on five circular discs, contained in a gate-fold sleeve. On each disc are phrases ('the loose stones / rattle and / then are still', 'settle into / anything / that gives / hope', for example) which are arranged in five concentric circles, six phrases in each circle. Phrases in the outer circle are lined up with those in the third and fifth, phrases in the second with those in the fourth. The reader looks for phrases to follow on from one another, the eye moving either round a circle, or vertically into the centre, or both round and down to the nearest phrase in an adjoining ring. For instance: 'settle into / anything / that gives / hope' seems linkable to 'straight / into a / tangle' (vertically down) or to 'order has / chaos for / a foundation' (next one along in the same ring) or to 'walking on / walking on / air' (up and along). The reader is also drawn sometimes to discover sequences spiralling out of or into the centre, as on one disc this sequence: 'confusing / the blue / wires', 'fingers / fingers', 'if the / skin / should never / die', 'a million / changes / in a single / sleep', 'or less / than a / single / change'. Fisher also uses italics to hint at connections between the disks, even the trace of an order.

The discs are like ten-inch records, suggesting the 78s Fisher listened to with the 'elephantine pickup of my hand-cranked gramophone' ('Handsworth Compulsions', p. 25). They are also like the X-ray diffraction images used to reveal the structure of molecules. Spiral and crystal compete for dominance as you try to structure a reading. That competition implies the conflict between escape and stability, calling and return, identity and flux. The sequence demands to be read in a way which reperforms that clash and such a demand is very similar to the one made by *A Furnace*. However, the jostling coexistence of fixity and movement intimates something about 'cultures' as well because, historically, all cultures are members of a sequence while each is also entirely unique; in the same way, jazz tunes are generic *and* 'this particular three minutes of music, improvised pretty casually one day in 1933' ('Handsworth Compulsions', p. 24). The structures of time and history organize and cannot regiment improvisation—the unforeseen, the unplanned. 'Cultures' also suggests bacterial cultures, as if the discs were large petri dishes and the phrases dots of growth or mould. A symmetrical arrangement contains and distorts into a convenient pattern the unpredictable outbursts of organic life. Finally, these mock-records suggest a further source for the structure of *A Furnace*. Seventy-eights in particular are numbered in a spiral-like sequence: in a four-record set, for example, side one is backed by side eight, side two by side seven, side three by side six, side four by side five. You place the records on top of each other and turn over all four when the machine reaches the end of side four. The playing-arm on a multi-player goes in, then up and out, before beginning again. You turn the records over at the dead centre of the sequence and play them in reverse order, as the 'line turns back on itself . . . and leads out again, against its own incoming curve' (*F*, pp. vii–viii).

NOTES

1. Roy Fisher, *A Furnace* (Oxford: Oxford University Press, 1986), pp. v, vii. Powys is similar to one type of 'isolate' in the poem: 'priests' / sons with dishevelled wits, teachers / with passed-on clothes and a little Homer' (*F*, p. 23). Powys's father was ordained; Powys himself taught at private schools as a young man and published a book on Homer: *Homer and the Aether* (London: Macdonald & Co., 1959). He feared going mad and had sadistic sexual fantasies, similar to the 'Sadist-voyeur' in *F*, p. 24. For Fisher's comments on Powys's fetishes and their importance to *A Furnace*, see ' "They Are All Gone Into the World": Roy Fisher in Conversation with Peter Robinson', in Tony Frazer, ed., *Roy Fisher: Interviews Through Time, and Selected Prose* (Kentisbeare, Devon: Shearsman, 2000)

2. John Cowper Powys, *A Glastonbury Romance* (London: John Lane, The Bodley Head Limited, 1933), p. 47.

3. John Cowper Powys, *Wolf Solent* (1929; Harmondsworth: Penguin, 1964), p. 21.

4. *Weymouth Sands* was first published in 1935, with the title *Jobber Skald*. Powys changed the title and obscured the novel's precise localities to avoid the accusations of libel (which had beset *A Glastonbury Romance*). The novel first appeared in its original form in 1963. Quotations are from John Cowper Powys, *Weymouth Sands* (London: Picador, 1973), cited as *WS*.

5. John Cowper Powys, *Suspended Judgements: Essays on Books and Sensations* (1916; New York: America Library Service, 1923), p. 3.

6. There is a similar contrast between Magnus Muir and Sylvanus Cobbold in *Weymouth Sands*.

7. Glen Cavaliero is right, I think, to highlight this aspect of Powys's achievement in *Weymouth Sands*: 'at its best, as in the "Punch and Judy" chapter, the book

achieves a narrative method peculiarly Powys's own' (Glen Cavaliero, *John Cowper Powys: Novelist* (Oxford: Clarendon Press, 1973), p. 92).

8. Roy Fisher, *Poems 1955–1987* (Oxford: Oxford University Press, 1988), p. 111.

9. Roy Fisher, *The Cut Pages* (1971; London: Oasis Books / Shearsman Books, 1986), p. 40.

10. Roy Fisher, 'Handsworth Compulsions', *Numbers*, 2:1 (Spring 1987), pp. 24–9, at p. 28.

11. *Chambers: Combined Dictionary Thesaurus*, ed. Martin Manser and Megan Thompson (Edinburgh: Chambers, 1995) and *Oxford English Dictionary*, nondescript, *adj.*, definition 1. The *OED* does not give the modern sense. Fisher comments that the word 'nondescript' may recur so frequently in his poems because it is 'a low-level conceptual fetish, a thought-counter' forming part of 'a specialized micro-language' (' "They Are All Gone Into the World": Roy Fisher in Conversation with Peter Robinson', p. 119).

12. Philip Larkin, *High Windows* (London: Faber & Faber, 1974), p. 10. The relaxed quality of the poem and its feeling that, after all, understanding may not be as hard as we imagine, both suggest a rebuke to Geoffrey Hill whose work is certainly difficult. '[H]appening when touched, as they must' also recalls phrases from *A Furnace*: 'through a single / glance of another force touching it' and 'makes, where it collides, cultures' (*F*, pp. 11, 47).

13. Compare Andrew Crozier, 'Signs of Identity: Roy Fisher's *A Furnace*', *PN Review*, 83 (January / February 1992), pp. 25–32, at p. 28: 'this is defamiliarization not by making strange but by making other . . . . there is . . . a surplus of reference that allows what was observed to stand free of its description.' 'Handsworth Liberties' is connected to *A Furnace* in other ways, particularly to 'Introit'. 'On the way to anywhere / stop off at the old furnace— / maybe for good' (*P55–87*, p. 122) foreshadows: 'I'm being swung out / into an unknown crosswise / route' which ends at 'the biggest of all the apparitions, / the great iron / thing, the ironworks' (*F*, pp. 1, 4).

14. 'Roy Fisher Reviews Roy Fisher', *The Rialto*, 35 (Autumn 1996), pp. 30–32, at p. 31. Part of its ambition lies in its complex symmetries (which I discuss below); part comes from the number of different points of literary reference—not only Powys but notably Heraclitus as well—and from the 'superimposition' of different landscapes and historical periods. The poem's subtle allusiveness is indicated by Fisher's mentioning 'the road / from Bilston to Ettingshall' (*F*, p. 2)—the last blast furnace in the Black Country (closed down on 12 April 1979) was in Bilston. See Gordon E. Cherry, *Birmingham: A Study in Geography, History and Planning* (Chichester, New York, Brisbane, Toronto, Singapore: John Wiley & Sons, 1994), p. 203.

15. 'Roy Fisher Reviews Roy Fisher', p. 32.

16. *Ibid.*, p. 30; Jed Rasula and Mike Erwin, 'An Interview with Roy Fisher', in Roy Fisher, *Nineteen Poems and an Interview* (Pesnett, Staffs.: Grosseteste, 1975), p. 18; Robert Sheppard, *Turning the Prism: An Interview with Roy Fisher* (London: Toads

Damp Press, 1986), quoted in Crozier, 'Signs of Identity', p. 25. Turnbull's 'Residues: Thronging the Heart' is very close to *A Furnace*: 'to sublime, to heat / to transformation // by dint / of each particular' (Gael Turnbull, *A Gathering of Poems, 1950–1980* (London: Anvil Press Poetry, 1983), p. 149). See also David Miller, 'Heart of Saying: the poetry of Gael Turnbull', *New British Poetries: The Scope of the Possible*, ed. Robert Hampson and Peter Barry (Manchester and New York, NY: Manchester University Press, 1993), pp. 183–97.

17. Crozier, 'Signs of Identity', pp. 26, 31–32.

18. John Cowper Powys, *Maiden Castle* (1937; London: Macdonald & Co., 1966), p. 167; hereafter cited as *MC*. The section Fisher uses is quoted in Richard Perceval Graves, *The Brothers Powys* (1983; Oxford: Oxford University Press, 1984), p. 274. Graves's quotation may have reminded Fisher.

19. John Cowper Powys, *Atlantis* (London: Macdonald & Co., 1954), p. 336. Cited as *Atlantis*.

20. Fisher directs his readers to Heraclitus (*A Furnace*'s 'fire is Heraclitean, and will not give off much Gothic smoke' (*F*, p. vii)). Gerard Manley Hopkins's sonnet, 'That Nature is a Heraclitean Fire and of the comfort of the Resurrection' may also have been in his mind. Compare Hopkins: 'in pool and rutpeel parches / Squandering ooze to squeezed dough, crust, dust' (*Gerard Manley Hopkins: The Oxford Authors*, ed. Catherine Phillips (Oxford and New York, NY: Oxford University Press 1986), p. 181) with 'striking for a while / fire meadows out of red-brown softrush, / the dark base, the hollows, the rim swiftly / blackening and crusting over' (*F*, p. 10).

21. Michael Hulse, 'Roy Fisher and the Weight of Attribution', *Poetry Durham*, 22 (1989), pp. 24–27, at pp. 25 and 26.

22. Roy Fisher, *Cultures* (London: Tetrad Press, 1975). See also *The Cut Pages*: 'Once the hiding place had also swallowed up the last of the pursuers into its winding and blind ends, the pursued ones started dismantling it around the pursuers, who were thus driven in deeper and deeper, like hares in the corn' (p. 46).

11

A Furnace and the Life of the Dead

CLAIR WILLS

'[T]here's a reference system like the blood or the lymph,
that passes through the poem, which is various ways of
treating death. There's an ongoing discussion of death . . .
and the burial of the dead.'[1]

At the risk of sounding capricious I want to begin this discussion of
'the burial of the dead' in Roy Fisher's *A Furnace* by referring to an
ostensibly very different writer—the contemporary American poet
Susan Howe. Howe opens her 1990 collection *The Europe of Trusts*
with an autobiographical prose piece designed to orient the reader in
her work, but which offers a fix on a much wider body of contemporary writing. The piece is entitled 'THERE ARE NOT LEAVES
ENOUGH TO CROWN TO COVER TO CROWN TO COVER'. Ostensibly,
the title mourns the awful fact of bodies left unburied, uncovered; it
expresses the desire to raise them up to hero status, to crown them
with laurel leaves.[2] Such anxiety or ambivalence as the title suggests
seems to spring from an equivocation between the need to bury the
dead, to lay them finally to rest, and the impulse to lift them up, to
bestow recognition. As the line starts to repeat itself, however, other
cracks begin to show. Is there relief that they remain uncovered, that
there are traces left behind so that something remains almost visible?
And have the dead escaped a fateful heroization? Put more strongly,
is not crowning itself the ultimate covering?—for nothing robs the
dead of their lives more effectively than absorption into a triumphal
narrative. This is also a question about poetry, of course—the leaves
are also the leaves of a book. There are not enough pages to do justice

to the dead, to celebrate their heroism; there are not enough words to mourn them, to put them to rest. But again, to crown them with words would be to absorb them into the poet's own project, while to mourn would be to believe the dead can be buried and done with. Howe has expressed the wish to 'tenderly lift from the dark side of history, voices that are anonymous, slighted—inarticulate'. Yet she also states, 'North Americans have tended to confuse human fate with their own salvation. In this I am North American.' [3] The difficulty is how to acknowledge the dead, to give them space, without placing them in a narrative of redemption. How can the poet reveal presence by pointing to absence?

This moral and aesthetic conundrum, I want to argue, is also central to Fisher's *A Furnace*. Fisher has suggested on several occasions that one of the central themes of his long, ambitious poem *A Furnace* is—as he puts it in section III of the poem—'the life of the dead' (*F*, p. 17). The poem is animated by a sense of the responsibility to keep things unburied—to articulate their presence without denying their absence. And again, the problem is intensified by the fact that offical forms of recognition and registration are the antitheses of such an ambivalent holding. What kind of record can weigh against the 'public records' which hide—keep secret—the lives they ostensibly chronicle? And conversely, how can we respect the secrets of the dead, yet tell of their existence? Furthermore, recognition by the state is not the only form of preservation Fisher must combat. Clearly, what he means by 'the life of the dead' is something very different from Christian notions of an afterlife; given the pervasive lingering of such notions, even in a post-Christian culture, Fisher's struggle to define the life of the dead cannot help but bring him into conflict with religious narratives.

Fisher's concerns in *A Furnace* might seem, at first sight, to carry him onto the terrain of elegy. Of course, the poem is not a lyrical exploration of subjectivity, of feelings of loss and grief—but what we might term 'postmodern' elegy has stretched the idea of the genre to such an extent that personal lament and recovery through form are no longer central. Much contemporary elegy (a prominent example would be Paul Muldoon's 'Yarrow', an elegy for his mother) is reluctant to offer consolation and often eschews lyrical form altogether. Fisher's work is certainly closer to this than to the notion of elegy as a way of seeking redress or consolation, in the absence of other (religious) systems for doing so. He is not seeking a relation between aesthetic form and the healing of hurt and trauma, either personal or historical, and he is sceptical of the Freudian notion that, by returning to the past, we can exorcize ghosts. Yet it might be objected that the notion of elegy, even in its postmodern guise, is inappropriate to the discussion of Fisher's poem. After all, no particular deaths are mourned in *A Furnace*, there is no direct expression of bereavement and grief. The sequence maintains a dialogue on the question of poetic consolation, perhaps even a kind of poetic 'redemption', a dialogue which has its roots in Fisher's own romanticism ('I think he's a Romantic, gutted and kippered by two centuries' hard knocks').[4] But the concern of the poem is with the temporal relations—the over-lapping and occlusion—of landscapes, cities and cultures, rather than with anything in the domain of personal experience.

In this sense *A Furnace* belongs to the modernist tradition of med-itation on the state of a civilization and social world which begins with T. S. Eliot's *The Waste Land*. We find in both Eliot and Fisher the same impersonal treatment of cultural cycles, the same 'masculine' avoid-ance of sentimentalism. If there are elegaic elements in *The Waste Land*, if the poem is in part a response to personal loss and to the carnage of the Great War, these elements are nevertheless subsumed in a general sense of cultural disorientation and decay. The difference between the ways the two poets operate in this genre lies in the contrast between Eliot's cultural pessimism, which was eventually to lead him to Christianity, and Fisher's more defiant targeting of social and political shibboleths. Whereas in Eliot—despite the poet's underlying sympathy with his characters—the working-class voices are expres-sions of the same nihilism and depair that typifies modern urban society as a whole, Fisher's aim is to restore a sense of the dignity of buried, occluded, everyday lives that swarm around us, yet are over-shadowed by the immense material presence of the city itself.

To put this in another way: one of the most striking aspects of Fisher's poem—given his materialist bent—is its gothic aura;

throughout the sequence an almost mystical phenomenology vies with a dark but precise realism. I use the term 'gothic' knowingly, despite Fisher's disclaimer in the Preface to *A Furnace,* where he describes the poem as 'an engine devised, like a cauldron, or a still, or a blast-furnace, to invoke and assist natural processes of change; to persuade obstinate substances to alter their condition and show relativities which would otherwise remain hidden by their concreteness; its fire is Heraclitean, and will not give off much Gothic smoke.'[5] Fisher may abjure superstition and the supernatural, but in fact all is not dissolved in his poem into an immanent, natural flux. He preserves an indeterminacy, a suspension between a robust naturalism and what he calls 'the other dream or intention: of encoding / something perennial' (*F*, p. 12), which is reminiscent of gothic ambivalence towards supernatural forces. *A Furnace* is marked by the impossibility of telling signs from coincidences, portents from accidents; it achieves an unlikely marriage of secular doubt and a sense of trans-human powers, which keeps me returning to the poem, and which I want to explore.

Fisher's early poetry was concerned with the precise rendition of an urban landscape, of the apparently mundane detail of his physical surroundings. He reflects, for example, on the way urban redevelopment threatens to eradicate the experience of people whose lives are cleared along with their homes. Yet there's none of the nostalgia we might associate with poems about lost or hidden lives, perhaps because for Fisher such lives are only hidden, not gone. He has a powerful sense that the material remains of the past are the most vivid testimony to the lives of earlier generations. As he says of *City*:

> In many cases the cultural ideas, the economic ideas, had disappeared into the graveyards of the people who had the ideas. But the byproducts in things like street layouts, domestic architecture, where the schools were, how anything happened—all these things were left over the place as a sort of script, an indecipherable script with no key.[6]

Such statements have most often been interpreted as suggesting that the poet's task is to renew our tired and predictable perceptions, to find a way of rendering the city's script meaningful once more. Yet surely what Fisher is really talking about here are ghosts. The feeling of an obscure secret which determines life in the present (and indeed the future), the feeling of being haunted by a buried past which is only imperfectly articulated, is what I am calling the 'gothic' element in Fisher. The gothic hinges on an ambivalence concerning the relation between Enlightenment and the supernatural. The mystery or horror at the centre of the gothic tale *may* be susceptible to a naturalistic explanation, but this reassuring elimination of the supernatural is never fully achieved. The same could be said of the Freudian 'uncanny': the inexplicable residue derives its power of disturbance precisely from its emergence within a predominantly rationalized world. This moment of resistance in the gothic articulates, in a different register, the problem of acknowledging the dead with which I began.

We find the same privileging of perception in the later sequence, the same focus on our ability to be 'called' by our physical surroundings—indeed Fisher seems to look on a passive receptivity to the world as a type of duty, an obligation which in turn may bring us wonders. But undoubtedly *A Furnace* pursues these themes in a more apocalyptic, Blakean register. Description and testimony were always interwoven in Fisher's work, but now the sense of the past in the present has become much more insistent, even obsessive. *A Furnace* deals with the past in the form of 'obstinate substances'; Fisher describes the poem as concerned with the presentation of fetishes, objects which have some numinous power, or at the very least a power around which meanings and identities crystallize. The poem revolves around what remains, despite the passage of time: 'A good deal of what I'm on about is the lives of the dead, their lost histories ...*A Furnace* is in large part a piece of frustrated ancestor-worship, a running of a familiar type of tribal model over whatever recent history shows up on the ground.'[7]

Fisher's use of the term 'fetishes' in this context announces a view of the formation of identity which is at once close to and far removed from the psychoanalytic model which it evokes. Fetishes stabilize our identity, but in Freud the fetish is a substitute, a covering over of the trauma of the discovery of sexual—and other fundamental—differences. By contrast, for Fisher the emergence of nodes of meaning seems to be a spontaneous, almost organic, process: in the Preface to the poem he describes 'the making of all kinds of identities' as 'a primary impulse the cosmos itself has' (*F*, p. vii). Correspondingly, the obstinate remnants of the past in Fisher are something very different from the traumatic kernel of neurosis in Freud, which needs to be confronted and dissolved. So while Freud famously describes the unconscious as 'timeless', and *A Furnace* invokes 'timeless identities', in Fisher's case the atemporal dimension is not populated by repressed elements which might disruptively return. At first sight, this might seem to contradict what I said earlier about Fisher's battle with official, 'repressive' forms of memorialization, whose effect is 'to have the rest, / the unwritten, / even more easily scrapped' (*F*, p. 16). But the point is that, for Fisher, the dead are pervasive presences which never really went away. They are 'uncovered', if you like, and the poet needs to find a way of disclosing this uncoveredness without implying that poetic acknowledgement is already tantamount to redemption.

   One upshot of this sense of the presence of invisible lives is that *A Furnace* is a far more populous poem than Fisher's earlier city works. The poem is haunted by ghosts, by the successive generations of urban dwellers, and indeed the people of the rural world which the city covered over in its inexorable expansion. Take, for example, those fantastic, surreal sequences in section II of the poem, 'The Return'. Here Fisher focusses—in part—on the area of Handsworth where he was born. In the early part of this century this was still a new development; in an exuberant image Fisher represents it as painted or rollered on top of the rural residue of fields and pastures:

> then suddenly printed across with
> this century, new, a single
> passage of the roller
> dealing out streets of terraces
> that map like ratchet-strips, their gables

gazing in ranks above the gardens
at a factory sportsground,
a water-tower for steam-cranes, more
worksheds, and,

> hulking along a bank
for a sunset peristyle, the long dark
tunnel-top roof of a football stadium.   (*F*, p. 13)

As soon as it is laid out, the dead crowd across the centuries into this new urban development. Fisher describes the division between worlds as a 'trench' or a 'pit', and one might think first of the slaughter and devastation of the First World War. But behind such images there surely also lies a shadowy evocation of Odysseus' journey to the brink of the underworld in book XI of the *Odyssey*. Odysseus digs a deep pit which he fills with the blood of slaughtered sheep in order to attract the dead from Hades. Through this ritual sacrifice he is able to converse with the dead, learning of his family and his own fate from his mother and from Tiresias. In contrast Fisher laments our inability to perceive, let alone learn from, the life of the dead around us. His Blakean blasts against the destructive alliance between church and state education are a protest against the corruption of our senses by a system which requires us not to see: 'wherein the brain / submits to be / cloven, up, / sideways and down / in all of its pathways' (*F*, p. 16). While we search for evidence of our ancestors in public record offices, they are present in the fabric of our environment:

> They come anyway
> to the trench,
> the dead in their surprise,
> taking whatever form they can
> to push across. They've no news.
> They infest the brickwork. Kentish Road
> almost as soon as it's run up
> out in the field, gets propelled
> to the trench, the soot still fresh on it,

> and the first few dozen faces
> take the impress, promiscuously
> with door and window arches; . . .   (*F*, pp. 18–19)

In an earlier section of the poem Fisher describes the sense of being 'called' by these presences through the physical fabric, the contours of the familiar, everyday environment: streets, houses and rooms are marked, clung to, sometimes almost engulfed by an elusive, semi-hallucinatory kind of life. The 'unstable overgrown philadelphus' which covers the end wall of the house opposite in section I, 'Calling', seems to flicker with darting animation in the light of the street lamp. It is eventually 'sawn back / for harbouring insurrection and ghosts'. Likewise, within the house

> a stain in the plaster that so
> resembles—and that body of air
> caught between the ceiling
> and the cupboard-top, that's like
> nothing that ever was.   (*F*, pp. 6–7)

It is worth noting the domestic nature of this haunting—Fisher's concern is with the intimacies of human continuity, the succeeding generations of families, local allegiances. This is one of the points at which he diverges from the 'masculine' models of modernism, despite the bluffness of his own rhetoric.

A sense of haunting by the past, of ghosts appearing in the most unexpected places, an awareness of another world of supernatural beings, is familiar in contemporary poetry in the Irish tradition. But by and large it has been excised from the more empirical English strain of recent poetry, with Larkin's 'Aubade' perhaps the most forceful articulation of death's physical finality. There is an undertow of stoicism here, an attempt at an unflinching confrontation with the prospect of extinction, which shuns romantic pantheism and the Victorian toying with spiritualism. At first glance, then, Fisher might seem to represent a lapse from the austerity of his twentieth-century compatriots. After all, the central section of *A Furnace* does strive to capture what might be regarded as a mystical experience ('Inside a total stillness / as if inside the world but nowhere / continuous with it' (*F*, p. 29))—although one in which it is almost impossible to distinguish rapture from the encounter with death. Despite his 'sceptical materialism', we could be tempted to read Fisher as clinging to a residual notion of teleology, a sense of meanings conferred rather than constructed. Indeed, it is precisely this ambivalence or doubt which draws the reader in. Fisher is neither offering Larkinian extinction of hope (which in fact contains its own curious consolation), nor is he seduced by intimations of transcendent meaning. Instead, he tries to offer a real alternative to the post-Christian dilemma of implausible faith or facile nihilism.

Further comparison with the Irish ghostly tradition may be instructive here. This tradition has pre-Christian, folkloric roots—it is based on the sense of another world that lies alongside the natural world, the perceivable world. Certain poets have invested this parallel world with religious, liberatory meanings—there is a sense that it is from there that the messengers come, that we can be enlightened, as in Heaney's *Station Island*. But just as often, work drawing on this tradition conveys a sense of being held captive by the burdens of the past—a feeling that it is impossible to move on. In the nineteenth-century Irish Gothic tradition, for example, this feeling takes the form of a haunting—within the house, within the family, there is a secret which cannot be spoken but which throws the shadows of history onto the present. Perhaps the paradigmatic twentieth-century text in this regard is Joyce's 'The Dead': Gabriel Conroy's cultural (and sexual) confidence is thrown out of kilter by his sudden awareness of a past whose meanings he cannot control. The 'dead' of the title are revealed to be buried all over Ireland in the final passages of the story, yet they maintain their power in the present.

The dilemma explored in the Irish Gothic tradition is of course a particular example of the equivocation of the gothic which I mentioned earlier. The ghostly undertow of the narrative of 'The Dead' questions its own realistic premise—a realism most often associated with the heyday of nineteenth-century British industrial and imperial power, confident of cultural and economic progress. As several critics have commented, gothic fiction and its contemporary legacy, the ghost story, seem particularly suited to express the situation of a society with a colonial history, a culture haunted by a violent past which it cannot simply leave behind. Toni Morrison's *Beloved* famously uses the metaphor of haunting to explore the lineaments of a culture trapped by an horrific, unarticulated past. And in contemporary Irish literature, too, the obsession with ghosts continues—a sign that the demons of the past have not been laid to rest. In Seamus Deane's recent novel *Reading in the Dark*, for example, a community's secrets become destructive hauntings—the ghosts are those of a violent history, living on just out of sight. The child at the centre of the novel wants to uncover the secret which he sees as causing damage but, delicately and insistently, the book suggests that the growing boy's eagerness to 'spell out' the secret, to find the literal truth behind the constrained and damaged lives of those around him is no less violent than the original violence it seeks to uncover. Similarly, throughout Paul Muldoon's work, the stories he tells are underpinned by the ghosts of a violent past. The ghosts intrude, push the narrative sideways, disrupting simple notions of progress and teleology. In both these cases there is a resistance to the therapeutic, Freudian account of the disturbing impact of the past, and its resolution.[8] Here telling will not help; it is not possible to appease, only to acknowledge an obscure burden. Indeed, the more we learn and tell, the worse things seem to get in some respects.

Fisher too is interested in uncovering the underside of a realism associated with a confident nineteenth-century belief in progress. Yet he traces the presence of ghosts not in the periphery of the metropolitan culture, its colonial margins, but in the centre of industrial Britain, in a city once flushed with the pride of imperial power. So the relationship between that which is secret or hidden and that which is manifest cannot be mapped onto any simple geographical opposition. Rather, the concealed and the manifest are interwoven, in privileged moments of experience, in the fabric of the city itself. Despite their association with insurrection, Fisher's ghosts are not revenants from a violent history: there is little sense of rupture from the past, or of a need to escape or release its unbearable pressure. As I have already suggested in drawing a contrast with Freud, one of the most striking aspects of Fisher's poem is the *lack* of trauma. Fisher's ghosts, his 'material spirits' do not intervene from another world, they are not privileged messengers (and not even disruptive anti-messengers of the Muldoonian kind). Accordingly, they do not discourage or encourage, terrify or console, partly because 'They've no news'. They've not been anywhere anyway to gather news, they know no more than we do. The power to disturb which they undoubtedly possess derives not from their intrusive force, but from a kind of obstinate resistance, an imperviousness to narratives of development and progress, epitomized by the industrial city. Past and present are coexistent: there is no triumphal advance from one to the other.

Perhaps we could say that it is the very inconspicuousness of the ghosts, their lack of difference from us, which is source both of disturbance and (possible) consolation. If there is a politics in *A Furnace*, it does not arise from some history of conquest and exploitation which leaves deep psychological wounds; it is the hiddenness not of the violent exception, but of the everyday—and in particular the hiddenness of working-class lives—which constitutes the central injustice. If there is a continuous passage between life and death, this is not just because the dead continue to live, but also because those alive are only living a half-life. Fisher reserves his anger for the fact that such lives can not even be articulated to each other, because of some obscure sense of shame.

>   —Don't
> ask your little friend
> what his father does;
> don't let on we've found out
> his mother goes to work;
> don't tell anyone at all
> what your father's job is.
> If the teacher asks you
> say you don't know.   (*F*, p. 21)

Fisher's sense of loss is not for the myriad lives of the dead as such, since he does not see death as final; it arises from their obliteration from the record, their marginalization even within the lives they themselves lived. The gothic 'haunting' in Fisher's poem is not that of a traumatic event which has to be excluded from memory, but of lives which have not even entered into memory, which were 'forgotten' from the beginning.

What kind of accounting and recognition can be given in this situatation? Certainly not a strenuous memorialization, for the reasons I outlined at the beginning. Such a strategy would be complicit with Freudian (and Christian) narratives of progress or salvation, and would celebrate the powers of poetry rather than respect the lives of the dead. Fisher's answer is that it is the obstinate, unobtrusive presence of the dead, the repeated spiralling movement between life and death, which offers the only 'consolation', if this word can be applied to such an ambiguous movement. Fisher's poem is suffused with a sense that those who are lost are not also gone. It emphasizes continuity and suspension, refusing to neatly separate the dead from the living (as also in the beautiful passage in 'They Come Home' where Fisher's parents-in-law are 'won back' (*BR*, p. 51) by allowing their ashes to experience everyday life, including a visit to the car-exhaust workshop). There is a sense that things which seem lost for good can return. Even the immense hulks of sunken battle-ships can be retrieved, raised from the bottom of Scapa Flow; meanwhile factories, towering buildings can be erected and just as easily—after a few years—demolished. There is a continuum of creation and destruction, and his poetry is a process of sensitizing us to this continuum, rather than of coming to terms with trauma.

Other poets have written movingly of the continuance of the dead, the way that they live on—and one might instance here Muldoon's elegiac volume for his father, *Meeting the British*, where the dead remain part of life in an almost physical sense, in the objects which surround us, and which we recycle. But *A Furnace* goes further in refusing to recognize death as an end in a more fundamental sense. Fisher declines to draw a clear line between the living and the dead, exploring the state of suspension between life and death—a state evoked in the central section 'Core', around which the spiralling movement of *A Furnace* revolves. Indeed, suspension is a central figure of the poem,

recurring in the allusion to the 'selfless / demonstration' (*F*, p. 17) of
Poe's character M. Valdemar, who agrees to be hypnotized at the point
of death, and undergoes a profoundly disturbing prolongation of his
existence. Such allusions highlight once again the poem's 'gothic'
ambivalence—for Valdemar is subjected to an experiment in the new
'science' of mesmerism, and his posthumous continuation, despite the
paradoxical moment at which he announces himself to be dead,
cannot be assigned unequivocally to the natural or the supernatural.
Several other references in Fisher's poem emphasize the connections
between mysticism and natural science—such as the appearance (and
disappearance) of the alchemist Doctor John Dee.

As I have suggested, we can read this pessimistically—being
suspended means not only that the dead are living, but that the living
are not really alive. Think, for example, of the next-door neighbours
who terrified Fisher in his childhood, living the death of miserable,
unacknowledged lives, witnessed only by their 'dung-coloured' dog
('barren couple, the man desperate, / irascible, the woman / nameless,
sick, tottering' (*F*, p. 25)). But the message could also be one of a
kind of immortality. Take the old woman described in section II of
A Furnace:

> Massive in the sunlight, the old woman
> dressed almost all in black, sitting out
> on a low backyard wall,
> rough hands splayed on her sacking apron
> with a purseful of change in the pocket,
> black headscarf tight across the brow, black
> cardigan and rough skirt, thick stockings,
> black shoes worn down;
>   this peasant
> is English, city born; it's the last
> quarter of the twentieth century
> up an entryway
> in Perry Barr, Birmingham, and there's
> mint sprouting in an old
> chimneypot. No imaginable

<blockquote>
beginning to her epoch, and she's
ignored its end.   (F, p. 15)
</blockquote>

This woman comes from an immemorial past, and is living beyond the end of her epoch. She is in a state of suspension which refuses to acknowledge the end of life. Here timeless identity is in one sense biographical—it is the endurance of this particular woman. But it is also something more abstract and symbolic. The furnace effects a transformation, burns away the slack; it reveals the essence, the unmoving core, 'something perennial' in peoples and cultures, and in landscape superimposed on landscape. The city itself is an organism with a life of its own which overlays the life of nature, just as, in the final image of the poem, an ancient Roman settlement in Catalonia succumbs to nature's snail-like colonization.

This kind of 'immortality', if such it is, clearly has little to do with the Christian model, which Fisher satirizes elsewhere in the poem as 'Sale and Lease-back' (*F*, p. 17)—a cynical system predicated on fear and ignorance. Fisher has described the double spiral (which appears on the cover of the Oxford University Press edition) as primarily an aid to composition[9]. But clearly it is also a more fundamental figure for the constant winding passage back and forth between life and death, between death-within-life and life-within-death, with which the poem is concerned:

<blockquote>
Under that thunderous
humbug they've been persistently
coming and going, by way of
the pass-and-return valve between the worlds,
not strenuous; ghosts
innocent of time, none the worse
for their adventure, nor any better;

that you are dead
turns in the dark of your spiral,
comes close in the first hours after birth,
recedes and recurs often. Nobody
need sell you a death.   (F, p. 18)
</blockquote>

Just as Fisher's 'alternative' to Christianity questions the boundary between the living and the dead, so he questions the boundary between the artificial urban environment and nature—nature is perhaps the most potent embodiment of the notion that what preceded the urban still surrounds it. Indeed, the city does not cut us off irremediably from the natural world, as many nostalgic critics of urbanism have suggested: 'still through that place / to enter Nature; it was possible, / it was imperative.' For Fisher, there is always a fluid boundary between 'in' and 'out'—and it is hard indeed to tell by his syntax whether even to be alive is to be in or out:

> Something always
> coming out, back against the flow,
> against the drive to be in,
>
> >   close to the radio,
> the school, the government's wars;
>
> the sunlight, old and still,
> heavy on dry garden soil,
>
> and nameless mouths,
> events without histories, voices,
> animist, polytheist, metaphoric,
> coming through;
>
> the sense of another world
> not past, but primordial,
> everything in it
> simultaneous, and moving
> every way but forward.   (*F*, p. 14)

On one reading, Fisher seems to be suggesting here that poetry can now do what animism could do. Metaphor enables us to perceive the inanimate, material world as imbued with spirits or spiritual powers. Does this suggest that poetry takes over from religion and does the same kind of things? Does it offer a way of consoling us, of giving meaning to randomness?

This fluidity between life and death could be called a kind of immortality, and the poem does indeed seem committed to a notion of the timeless. At one point Fisher suggests that 'Clarity / of the unmoving core / comes implacably out / through all that's material' (*F*, p. 34). But the fact that an apparent residual belief in nature as a source of eternal, transcendent meaning is counterbalanced by a stress on materiality is important here. Fisher is haunted by the possibility of hidden meanings, and he suggests that the poet is defined by a certain capacity to be 'called' by the perceived world, by an ability to respond to and render the flashes of meaning in the contingent and material. The experience of such fragile illumination is literally imaged in the 'festive little bulbs' (*F*, p. 7) bobbing in the dark which he passes in his car one night, and which he receives as a sign which 'rides over intention, something / let through in error.' Such 'Sudden and grotesque / callings' (*F*, p. 8) seem to be successors to the romantic notion of revelation, glimpses of the numinous suddenly available in the everyday.

But, for all this apparent openness to the notion of meanings conveyed to us through our experience of the material world, Fisher retains his scepticism: 'The idea of revelation is, of course, a projection of the condition of the perceiving self—it's not that I believe there to be a troupe of Beings behind a curtain, poking meaningful things through'.[10] Are the meanings which are 'pushed through' from the other side just a matter of our subjective orientation or are there really meanings out there? 'From time to time I'm impelled to small sceptical perambulations—which I don't, incidentally, see as acts of commitment to postmodernism: there's still such a thing as *honest* doubt.'[11]

Towards the end of the poem, Fisher speaks of a

> Cargo-cult
> reversed. There have always been
> saucers put out for us
> by the gods. We're called
> for what we carry.   (*F*, p. 46)

At first sight this might look like caustic satire on the notion of transcendent sources of meaning ('saucers put out for us / by the gods'). But Fisher's stance in fact suggests a dilemma, rather than simply endorsing the notion of an advance towards stoic enlightenment. For he goes on to say that 'In barbarous times / all such callings / come through as rank parodies' (*F*, p. 46), suggesting that it is some deep deficiency of our context, rather than the 'true' nature of reality which has occluded the sense of transcendent meanings.

This ambivalence of Fisher's stance—what he refers to as his 'honest doubt', as opposed to the facile scepticism of postmodernism—gives us, I think, a clue to the function of the religious framework for the poem, which begins with an 'Introit' and ends with the ascension of the seraphic snails. If the poem is indeed in the form of a parodic prayer, then it is a kind of counter-parody—a parody of a belief in meaning which, on Fisher's account, has already become parodic for us. Like the saints' faces in the broken stained glass window—'freed' (*F*, p. 5) by a boot or a stone to be randomly gathered together in reconstituted art work—the shattering of religious tradition—or its jumbled, 'parodic' preservation—now seems to contain the numinous in a way which the tradition itself no longer can. Apocalypse, Fisher states, 'lies within time' (*F*, p. 45): it is happening now, and always. There is no last judgement, no final summation, no revelation beyond the momentary callings of the perceiving self, whether these callings are wished for or not.

A Furnace straddles the dividing line between world as a place of mystery (the domain of fetishes, folklore and religion) and world as a set of processes to be explained (the domain of realism, enlightenment and natural science). To stay only within the first vision would be a failure to acknowledge the lostness of the dead. To remain only within the second would be a denial of their continuing presence. Fisher's poem seeks a new way of talking, one which will neither cover the dead nor leave them lying forgotten and neglected. It opens a space for histories which remain mute and unarticulated, delicately avoiding their absorption into some narrative of poetic salvation.

NOTES

1. 'John Tranter Interviews Roy Fisher', *Jacket* (http://www.jacket.zip.com.au./jacket01/fisheriv.html).

2. I am indebted to Isabelle Parkinson for this reading.

3. Susan Howe, *The Europe of Trusts* (Los Angeles: Sun and Moon Press, 1990), p. 14.

4. 'Roy Fisher Reviews Roy Fisher', *The Rialto*, 35 (1996), pp. 30–32, at p. 31.

5. Fisher, *A Furnace* (Oxford: Oxford University Press, 1986), p. vii.

6. Jed Rasula and Mike Erwin, 'An Interview with Roy Fisher', in Roy Fisher, *Nineteen Poems and an Interview* (Pensett, Staffs: Grosseteste Press, 1975), p. 18.

7. ' "They Are All Gone Into the World": Roy Fisher in Conversation with Peter Robinson', in Roy Fisher, *Interviews Through Time, and Selected Prose*, ed. Tony Frazer (Kentisbeare, Devon: Shearsman, 2000), p. 111.

8. I refer here to a certain strand of psychoanalytic thinking which focuses on the 'working through' of trauma towards eventual resolution. Other views of psychoanalysis, which can equally claim the legacy of Freud, stress some version of the idea that at the core of the self there is a mystery which has to be borne rather than resolved.

9. 'They Are All Gone Into the World', p. 116.

10. *Ibid.*, p. 106.

11. *Ibid.*, p. 104.

12

Last Things

PETER ROBINSON

I

Opening Roy Fisher's first hardback book of poetry, published in 1969, I found on the half-title page: *'the ghost of a paper bag'*. Leafing over a couple of pages, there it was again, this time looking like an epigraph to the collection, a volume called by its dust jacket *Collected Poems*, but by its title page and spine, give or take a pair of capitals: *collected poems 1968*. When I first stumbled upon this slim, eighty-page book, I had never heard of Roy Fisher or read anything by him; but then, at nineteen, this was a common experience with volumes of collected poems. Yet his was so short, and, since the dust jacket informed me that the author had been four in May 1935, I deduced that he had published his collected poems at the age of about thirty-eight. Nothing on the jacket blurbs suggested that he was dead, so what had happened? No sooner had Roy Fisher opened up shop, than he was pulling down the shutters. In fact, many one-book poets debut with their last things, but the difference here was that this writer, who, I noted, had anyway published a prose book called *The Ship's Orchestra*, also appeared to know it at the time.

Reading on, I came across that enigmatic phrase once more, this time as part of 'The Billiard Table'. The last poem in a section entitled *Interiors with Various Figures*, it describes a scene (partly prompted by a canvas of Braque's)[1] in which an 'I' and a 'you' confront an unnamed thing that seems to have slept the night on the billiard table. There is a 'mess of sheets on the green baize' which 'Suggests a surgery without blood', but, while the poem's 'you' keeps glancing at it, 'the tangle looks like abandoned grave-clothes.' Then comes the sentence including that half-title phrase:

> And watching it from where I sit
> I see it's the actual corpse, the patient dead under the
>   anaesthetic,
> A third party playing gooseberry, a pure stooge, the ghost of a
>   paper bag;
>
> Something that stopped in the night.   (*P55–87*, pp. 46–47)

Placing first-person subject, verbs and definite article ('I see it's the') in a commanding position at the beginning of the line starts an expectation that the correcting account will follow, but any security that 'I' knows better than 'you' what this mysterious thing might be is quickly dissipated in the sequence of predicates which grow more abstract and far-fetched as the list continues. The poem then changes both style and tack: the line shortens, the 'I' asks an unguarded question of the 'you' which hints that they may be married ('Have you ever felt / We've just been issued with each other / Like regulation lockers / And left to get on with it?')—the elusive object becoming not the 'patient etherised upon a table' of T. S. Eliot's '... Prufrock', or a 'corpse', an empty tomb, or returning 'ghost' of literary and religious associations, but a new-born baby. The protagonists are described as 'Making unscheduled things like what's on the table'—not a planned pregnancy. The poem concludes with two lines like alternative endings: the former of these, 'No longer part of us, it's still ours', catches the moment a couple find themselves with 'A third party playing gooseberry', their first child; the latter, with tacit reflexivity, unifies the over-identified target of the poem's imaginative trajectory with the implication that this is an as-yet-unnamed infant: 'Bring the milk jug, and let's christen it.'

Calling your first-born 'the ghost of a paper bag' would be cruel, but it's by no means a hopeless name for a book of verse, as Fisher explains:

I had first of all titled the collection 'The Ghost of a Paper Bag' as being the expressive title. Over the time it took to assemble and publish it, which was, I suppose, about three years, I wasn't writing at all and didn't imagine that I was going to write again. The exigencies of publishing brought up a possibility of calling it *Collected Poems*, and since I thought it probably was my total work, I let it be called *Collected Poems*. Typographically, I wanted the title 'The Ghost of a Paper Bag', which was still how I thought of the book, ghosted in in grey inside the book, but it got ghosted in black on a page of its own, and it is still sort of drifting around there in the book. It looks like a motto but in actual fact it was the original title. It's always been reviewed as 'Collected Poems'.[2]

So this was 'the expressive title', but expressive of what? 'Something that stopped in the night', perhaps, or at any rate, something that stopped: 'I . . . didn't imagine I was going to write again.' The work gathered in this collection is the revenant of an everyday object, one which has died in the unfamiliar way that paper bags do die, then come back to haunt us. Though *Collected Poems 1968* is a largely paper container with a bundle of texts placed in it for safe-keeping, the volume resembles more a carefully organized book than a round-up collection, an impression strengthened by comparing it with *Poems 1955–1980*—a publication which prints the texts in almost chronological order.

'Aside to a Children's Tale', a poem in rhyming quatrains about a funeral cortège passing through a city street, opens both volumes with an invocation of a last thing written when the poet was twenty-five. He had already composed floridly on this, my essay's theme, in 'The Doctor Died' from the year before, and deaths had touched other early pieces like 'The Military Graveyard in France' and 'The Lemon Bride', but with 'This dead march is thin / in our spacious street', the poet hits his stride, only to stop after four short verses:

> and four men like pigs
> bear high as they can

>   the unguarded image
>   of a private man;
>
>   while broken music
>   lamely goes by
>   in the drummed earth,
>   the brassy sky.   (*P55–87*, p. 1)

Fisher's 'Aside to a Children's Tale' introduces a number of recurrent motifs and concerns, uppermost being the place of social and artistic formality in the cultural management of death. Though the final verse refers to a 'broken music', the two-stress metre and rhymes move to a mended theme. This not-so-broken music appears to be taken up and commented on by the next poem, 'Why They Stopped Singing'—a glance at the chronology of his writings indicating that, during the fifteen months separating their compositions, Fisher wrote only three uncollected pieces. The title's seemingly programmatic resistance to musicality, a musicality that has been long associated with consolation and transcendence, may also acknowledge an involuntary stopping. In the book's second poem, lyric composition is detached from the rhythmic movement of music and, equally, the time-resisting stasis of visual art objects:

>   They stopped singing because
>   They remembered why they had started
>
>   Stopped because
>   They were singing too well   (*P55–87*, p. 1)

The poem does not rhyme and is in no regular metre. The two-line stanza is little more than an ordering device for its spoken prose syntax. By stopping their production of requiem-like lullabies, they, the poets, might have been learning to talk.

Turning to the close of *Collected Poems 1968*, a similarly careful ordering has been performed. The penultimate work, 'Three Ceremonial Poems', is a charm against entrapment. Fisher referred to the second of these as 'a sort of crummy classical art which then gradually breaks and flows',[3] but the 'crummy classical art' does appear to have been established by the end of the first. The evocation of 'Laurel bars, enamelled / with laurels, the bronze / on matted hair, blades / designed on guns' (*P55–87*, p. 66) near its opening is capped with the closing image of a 'live mask plated over // Warrior, the stopped man' (p. 67). Fisher has commented on his attraction to images that are, or have, stopped:

> I'm fascinated by the element of arrest and the stopping of life in the picture, the photograph. Frozen movement interests me, partly because it seems to imply life. You look at something which is still, and you have to say: Alright, what is it still compared with?[4]

This comment was made after the publication of *Matrix* in 1971, when Fisher had come through his much-mentioned block of the later 1960s. Yet it would be more accurate to say that the poet has written at intervals from the edge of a permanent state of resistance: 'so I tend to have a skeleton at the feast,' he has insisted, 'but to me it is a positive fact of writing, that one writes on the edge of a block, or under whatever the block is, the shadow of something.'[5] This shadow might be signalled by the poet's attraction towards the static and choked off (like a skein that needs to be broken so that language can break and flow), as in the second of 'Three Ceremonial Poems' where the 'live mask plated over' is contrastively transformed to a 'Dark dust of shame // Raining down / Deep in the brickwork' which 'Changes its face' (*P55–87*, p. 68). As if to keep commentators away from his ulterior motives, Fisher has tended to insist on the poem 'as art', a work which turns 'pity into an artistic composition'. This is merely true; yet, at a level which the poem does not articulate conceptually, 'Three Ceremonial Poems' shapes a transformative variation on satirical modernist militarism ('Stone, bronze, stone, steel, stone, oakleaves, horses' heels / Over the paving')[6] with 'Absolute / Pity / Advancing' (p. 67) and 'shame // Raining down'. The 'stopped man' may well be dead, but pity and shame, with their present participles, have been set in motion. Thus, 'as art' the poem embeds an assumed ethics with political ramifications.

Collected Poems 1968 closes with 'After Working', making the poem figure as a postscript to the collection of work I had been reading. This point of organization is underlined by the poem's having figured as the opening piece in the Northern House pamphlet *The Memorial Fountain* (1966), whose contents are in this and other ways not replicated by the section of the book with that title.[7] 'After Working' is, unsurprisingly, a poem about being released from constraint. It describes how, looking up, 'The thoughts I'm used to meeting / at head-height when I walk or drive' (which being at 'head-height' have a social and communal familiarity) 'get lost here in the petrol haze / that calms the elm-tops'. Having managed a deflection away from what the poet is 'used to meeting', the poem then moves inward to the pictured 'half light of a night garage / without a floor', and on down to conclude in a darkness that is either the landscape of its starting point after sunset, or, freed from constraint, the territory of imagination: down past the 'shores of what might be other / scummed waters / to oil-marked asphalt / and, in the darkness, to a sort of grass' (*P55–87*, p. 49). Once there, though, Fisher's poem and his *Collected Poems 1968* abruptly stop.

Nevertheless, finding a copy of *Matrix* made it evident that 'After Working' was not, in the chronologies of composition or publication, anything like Fisher's last thing. The not absolutely total writing block of the years in which he put together *Collected Poems 1968* proved to be one more of many stoppings to start again that has characterized the poet's creative life. Talking in 1977, Fisher admitted that 'I know my breath is short',[8] as if echoing the close of 'Seven Attempted Moves' with its 'Confinement, / shortness of breath. / Only a state of mind' (*P55–87*, p. 52). A person with short breath more frequently inspires and as frequently expires. These are also little deaths and reprieves experienced daily. That this 'shortness of breath' is a 'state of mind' with 'Statues of it built everywhere' underlines the difficulty and necessity of the title's 'Attempted Moves'. Escaping from tight corners into which it may have painted itself, or scaling the walls of creative cul-de-sacs, are situations that Fisher's sensibility characteristically finds itself needing to perform. The uncollected 'Kingsbury Mill' opens by wishfully thinking that 'If only, when I travelled, / I could always really move, / not take the apparatus'.[9] A comment on his style from some twelve years later implies that this wish has become the deed:

> I'm not a spontaneous singer. I make sure when doing work of this kind that isn't discursive, by travelling light, that I have a medium which I have a feel for. *The Ship's Orchestra*, which is a bit dense for what I do now, was written in writing units—and you can see the length of them, two words, four or five lines of prose, occasionally a paragraph. It's quite simply beginning and then having the feel of the line, just as if you were drawing a line, until it ceased to be genuine, became fraudulent and just kept going by being inflated. I learnt to be honest with myself about the time I wrote *The Ship's Orchestra* and the 'Interiors with Various Figures', and drop the line when it felt fraudulent.[10]

Even 'Continuity', written as Fisher was emerging from that block, figures images of stoppage: 'The fish-trap gives the waters form, / Minimal form, drawn on the current unattended, / The lure and the check.' The poet's forms, here, structure his lines upon those essential aspects of language use, the tiny stops and starts that give words significant shape and the further poetic stops and starts of caesura, line-ending, enjambment, and stanza break. Yet no communication occurs if through these little deaths and resuscitations there is no flow—not, that is, for the trapped individual fish, but for the sustaining medium: 'So much free water.' The conundrums in this creative condition are contrastively related to the poet's recurrent material in the close of 'Continuity', where 'The towns are endless as the waters are' (*P55–87*, p. 71), and at the close of 'The Sky, the Sea':

> and beyond what has to be done
> there is nothing; the dusk
> free to come down,
> filled with cities of division.   (*P55–87*, p. 96)

All of Fisher's longer works are shaped by versions of his stop–start aesthetics: the collaged poems and prose fragments of *City*; the separately composed phrases, sentences, and paragraphs of *The Ship's Orchestra*; those emblematically extreme fragmentary words, phrases, and passages of 'The Cut Pages'; the various sequences of lightly built lyrics; the thematically associated verse-units of varying length that make up 'Wonders of Obligation' and the book-length *A Furnace*, which is composed by sequencing, with asterisk-marked pauses, passages of verse that vary in length from three to one hundred and one lines. Thus, at the heart and lungs of his poetics is a cadence that might be called the temporary close—a close that rounds off its passage, allowing breath to be drawn, preparatory, perhaps, to starting up again—as in 'Keats's death-mask / a face built out from a corner'; but then there's a stanza break, and these last words: 'If you're living / any decor / can make a wraith of you' (*P55–87*, p. 110).

II

'Death is not an event of life':[11] these seven words begin by seeming to challenge a common assumption, but, once qualified ('Death is not lived through'), take on the air of a truism. So when Ludwig Wittgenstein was on active service with Austrian forces in the Great War, what he came to understand by 'Der Tod' was: an individual's own death. There is no need to fear death; it cannot be experienced. Yet, equally truistic: dying is an event of life, as are other people's deaths. These, you *can* fear. And, while we're at it, you can fear the effect of your own death on others, such as those whom you love and who, you believe, love you: your death is an event of other people's lives. During the early 1960s, Fisher 'decided that Wittgenstein's *Tractatus* was a very splendid sort of stylistic influence for one to adopt, and I paid far more attention to the *Tractatus* as a mode of lineation, say, than to any poet.'[12] Robert Sheppard noticed this remark and asked for clarification. His interviewee enthusiastically obliged:

> You know how he writes it: the idea of a proposition which is about to hold firm and then to be expanded on or qualified quite formally ... That's what I'm talking about: lineation possibly in a conceptual, rather than a metrical, sense ... It's an utterly pragmatic, not theoretical, acknowledgment that I made

to Wittgenstein. I was just reading the English translation and just enjoying the crack of it.[13]

This is no doubt true as far as it goes, which is to brush off any hint of a claim to having developed a 'philosophy' or 'philosophy of composition' from Wittgenstein's picture theory of elementary propositions. However, numerous passages in Fisher's work indicate that he also paid at least some attention to what the more aphoristic remarks in the latter part of the *Tractatus* might mean, imply or prompt—remarks such as 'Death is not an event of life. Death is not lived through.'

'As He Came Near Death', the poem by Fisher that D. J. Enright picked for *The Oxford Book of Death*, re-envisages spatial relations between first a dying, then dead man and his relatives. 'As he came near death things grew shallower for us', the poem begins, making dying an event of his life, and his death an event of ours:

> So that he lay and was worked out on to the skin of his life and
> left there,
> And we had to reach only a little way into the warm bed to scoop
> him up. (*P 55–87*, p. 47)

Death is a creator of simultaneous intimacy and distance; Fisher conveys this by at once drawing the participants close together ('things grew shallower for us') and effecting a withdrawal into numbed isolation. The intimate distance is further sharpened by details from the funeral:

> Then the hole: this was a slot punched in a square of plastic grass
> rug, a slot lined with white polythene, floored with
> dyed green gravel.
> The box lay in it; we rode in the black cars round a corner, got out
> into our coloured cars and dispersed in easy stages.
>
> After a time the grave got up and went away. (*P 55–87*, p. 47)

If the last line parodies the Christian promise in the resurrection of the dead, it also figures a fading away of care in the dispersal of the living and the disappearance of the dead relative's grave. This final detachment is prepared for by a superficially uncomprehending distance in the narrating voice which recounts the events with a cultural inwardness that has, as it were, come out on the other side of the conventions—failing to take for granted the communal naturalization it nevertheless understands. Fisher's approach does not so much make routine and ritual strange, but rather draws out the strangeness in these cultural practices; one consequence is the poem's reducing to invisibility, at least partially or temporarily, the ties between people and things which make events of life conventionally intelligible: 'de-socializing art' (*P55–87*, p. 186), as the poet himself puts it in his much later 'The Lesson in Composition'.

In an early, relatively socialized poem (incorporated into the collage of *City*) relative clauses shape the distances in a family disclosed through bereavement after a bombing raid. Fisher has disparaged this early work of 1957 for its unchallenging familiarity:

> what happens to me is that I do get people, more people as it were, reading me with more energy because I have written about an industrial city, because I have written at least one simple narrative poem about some of my relatives getting killed in an air raid. It's the thing most untypical of anything I believe about poetry that I ever wrote.[14]

This exaggeration was formulated to counter the version of his work being propagated at that time by Davie's pioneering critical study. 'The Entertainment of War'—whose memory-stimulating title was found in 'a newspaper editorial or a correspondent's report which I've lost'[15]—does, nevertheless, use a child's-eye-view to turn away from any implied anger or bitterness at the wartime deaths it narrates. Unlike Dylan Thomas's poem of the Blitz, 'A Refusal to Mourn, the Death by Fire, of a Child in London', Fisher's stanzas need not refuse to mourn: they barely register that cultural requirement and are not tempted, directly at least, to fulfil it. The child's perspective sustained for the first nine of twelve verses is integral to the events described, the bombing and its aftermath, so that, despite the poem's conventional narrative mode, the family's existence is given perceptual density:

When I saw it, the house was blown clean by blast and care:
Relations had already torn out the new fireplaces;
My cousin's pencils lasted me several years.   (*P55–87*, p. 18)

The corpse of the house is picked to the bone by relations, and the
poet as a boy is closely involved in the sharing out of the distant relatives' property. Like so much of Fisher's work, 'The Entertainment
of War' also intertwines mortality and style. The ambivalences caused
by loss, grieved over or not, are formalized into patterns of proximity
and distance, of being here, seeming to go away there, and of
appearing then to come back, while having perhaps been here, or
shifting back and forth between the terms, all the while.

The poem's observation that 'Never have people seemed so absent
from their own deaths' (p. 19) touches Wittgenstein's remark—in this
sudden death of an entire family where no experiences of dying or
grieving involve their end with those who have survived. This,
though, is how it felt to the poem's narrator remembering boyhood,
not how it felt to an older relative:

But my grandfather went home from the mortuary
And for five years tried to share the noises in his skull,
Then he walked out and lay under a furze-bush to die.   (p. 19)

The circumstances of this grandfather's death are narrated with more
detail in Fisher's autobiographical essay: 'there were perpetual
ringing noises in his head. His trouble was probably tinnitus, but the
general opinion—which he may have shared—was that he was losing
his wits as he approached eighty.' The poet's relative either drifts off
altogether or decides to make an end of it: .

One January day, he disappeared, and the dog with him. Late
the next day, and a dozen miles away in Sutton Park, the dog led
a passerby to where he lay dying of exposure after a freezing
night. I think everybody considered it a good death for him.[16]

There is no need to fear death: 'Death is not lived through'? But the
threat or vicinity of death can be feared, as can its effects on others
who survive. During the war, Fisher's brother and brother-in-
law 'spent years in danger' and the poet-to-be 'would engage in

elaborate daily muttered rituals, which grew longer and longer, in order to ensure their safety, which I believed depended only on me.' Here, the springs of art in childhood omnipotence fantasies, recognized as such, are succinctly outlined. Just as for so many who lived through those years, 'there was', Fisher adds, 'with the prolongation of stoicism, a deadening of areas of feeling.'[17] The boy narrator in 'The Entertainment of War' outlives the war death of his relations' family, then uses their total disappearance as a means for holding off fear:

> But had my belief in the fiction not been thus buoyed up
> I might, in the sigh and strike of the next night's bombs
> Have realized a little what they meant, and for the first time
> been afraid.   (p. 19)

Wittgenstein's remark in the *Tractatus* could be understood as a charm against the fear of extinction. Though habitual accounts of Russian formalist techniques in Fisher's oeuvre suppose that they are used to make experience more vitally perceived, 'The Entertainment of War' and 'As He Came Near Dear' can be seen controlling, by giving an oblique perspective to, the emotions that are usually associated with the deaths of family members. In each case, this is achieved by the adoption of a strategy which involves a calculated and partial non-understanding—in a context where the common appreciation of what has happened is assumed. 'As He Came Near Death' fuses details from the poet's father's death in 1959 and his first wife's grandmother's in 1964, but it gives to them a paradoxical alien familiarity, as if being studied by an anthropologist not fully inside the forms of the culture being studied; 'The Entertainment of War', prompted by the *donnée* of its title, exploits the faux-naive potential in a boy's-eye view of sudden, violently public, yet also domestic and remotely familial death.

Two further sources of Fisher's sustained preoccupation with last things are suggested by the poet's autobiographical essay. The first of these is a bout of pneumonia survived at the age of twelve. 'That illness', which Fisher describes as 'a couple of months away from the world after passing through mortal danger' was 'a rite of passage':

it was as if I'd been somewhere unknown, and had come back altered. Wherever it was, it's the location of my imagination; it's still the place I have to find in order to write, and it's essential qualities never alter. It combines a sense of lyrical remoteness with an apprehension of something turbulent, bulky, and dark. There, I don't have to bother to grow older.[18]

There are many such objects or events and scenes in Fisher's work. One encounter predates by nine years the bout of pneumonia. In 'Rudiments' from 1979 the poet's father shows him first '*The Barge*', 'a dead black V in the murk, / gapped, with its bad face upturned.' The 'three- / year-old illiterate' and his dad are surrounded by 'turbulent, bulky, and dark' forms: 'Behind us, the biggest thing I'd ever seen, / the dark gas-holder / filled up the sky.' Finally, there is '*The Canal*' itself:

> A black
> rippled solid, made of something
> unknown, and having the terrible property
> of seeming about to move,
> far under our feet. I'd never
> seen so much water before.   (*P55–87*, p. 165)

This childhood thing which seems to be 'solid', but is also 'moving' and 'dark', provides an emblematic instance of shapes and forms, points of arrival and departure, in much of Fisher's work: through, for example, the night scenes of *City*, at the close of 'After Working', or in 'the sight of Brough / Keep, black as could be' that returns at the close of 'The Running Changes': 'there, once again, was Brough Castle / marking the turn southward, / and being dark' (*P55–87*, p. 183).

The confinements of childhood illness and its requiring the sufferer to pass periods of time alone have helped prompt many a creative imagination, but a second source for Fisher's last things theme is distinctly more unusual. He describes how in early 1946 he decided that he was suffering from a form of undetectable tuberculosis and had no more than three years to live:

> At all events, I now held the biggest of all my secrets. I was
> dead. No one must know. The shock would kill my parents,
> naturally; so delay their knowledge about it as long as possible.
> As the possessor of a deadly disease, I had the power of life and
> death over everybody I met.

The benefit of this 'hysteria', as Fisher calls it, was that it allowed him
radically to 'revalue the currency of my dealings with my life: I re-
negotiated my contract.' In practical terms, this appears to have
involved establishing a private self-importance ('the power of life and
death over everybody') on the margins of his own existence: 'I'd had
almost enough of life: I didn't want in, but I didn't want out strongly
enough to commit suicide.' It is likely that many adolescents who are
going to achieve things in the arts need to develop just such a secret
self-importance that places them at a fluid distance from their surroundings. What is unusual about Fisher's way of achieving this is
that he did it by imagining himself dead. This delusion lasted
through the transition from grammar school to university:

> When I left school my remote and disaffected manner earned
> me a beta-plus for Personality in place of the customary straight
> A awarded to Head Prefects. It was an unprecedented snub. I
> thought it no bad score, for a corpse.

At nineteen the university medical check and required visits to the
local doctor made it quite plain that Fisher was, in fact, in reasonably
good health: 'My game was up and I had to recognize it.' He describes
how he then promptly forgot the delusion for two years: 'It was only
then that I understood how mad I'd been, and it was the forgetting I
found more frightening than the delusion itself.'[19]

'And there was another thing which was again merely personal',
the poet observed in a discussion of inspiration for the composition
of texts that went into *City*:

> my father was dying, and he was very closely associated with the
> city, with these areas over a period of forty years. Seeing this life
> ending, and the inevitable process of turning up old photo-
> graphs, old apprenticeship papers, extended time that made

you realize more than usually how much the place was dependent upon very evanescent, temporal, subjective renderings of it, which might never BE rendered. And at that point my own lifetime was extended through his.[20]

Fisher's unpublished novel-fragment, 'The Citizen', contains an account of his father's last weeks, from which the 'Brick-dust in sunlight' (*P55–87*, p. 20) passage of *City* was culled. At no point does the collage appear as an elegy for the poet's father, but there are moments when this 'merely personal' process of bereavement does touch the prose in that group of paragraphs: 'I look for things here that make old men and dead men seem young. Things which have escaped, the landscapes of many childhoods' (*ibid.*). Within the same sequence, the work's 'Byronic'[21] narrating subject fends off a mock-gothic, or for that matter Hardyesque, sense that the dead can appear to us as revenants: 'I can see no ghosts of men and women, only the gigantic ghost of stone' (*P55–87*, p. 21). Later in the collage, Fisher's narrator-character attempts to distance himself from a further animating concern of nineteenth-century art, namely the life and death cycle implied by organicist metaphors for cultures and societies:

> Once I wanted to prove the world was sick. Now I want to prove it healthy. The detection of sickness means that death has established itself as an element of the timetable; it has come within the range of the measurable. Where there is no time there is no sickness.
>
> (p. 27)

As Wittgenstein puts it in that same proposition 6.4311: 'If by eternity is understood not endless temporal duration but timelessness, then he lives eternally who lives in the present.'[22] The teenage Roy Fisher had used the idea of his own death to keep the world at a distance by a fanciful management of time. The *City* passage hints at the need to rid itself of such temptations to a false omnipotence. Yet it contains a puzzling contradiction, for the detection of health—a concept which must lack meaning without the complementary concept of sickness—would also signify that 'death has established itself as an element of the timetable'. Just as the poet's imaginative hinterland, like the lyrical flights of poets who would 'so live ever',[23] is a place where he does not have to 'bother to grow older', this passage, conundrum and all, contains a desire to get beyond being in sickness and in health, 'out past' death, as a later poem puts it, revealing Fisher as by no means the first and surely not the last poet who has needed to announce that 'death shall be no more; Death thou shalt die'.[24]

III

J.-K. Huysman's *A Rebours* contains a section in which the aesthete protagonist, des Esseintes, as if attempting to outdo the pet lobster of Gerard de Nerval, has a tortoise studded with precious jewels; heavily underlining the narrative's message, the poor overwrought creature gives up the ghost. Discussing synaesthesia and the crudeness of olfactory imagery with Fisher in 1977, I was reminded of this same character's liqueur harmonica and mentioned the book. 'I haven't read it,'[25] the poet replied. The son of a man who had been apprenticed to a paternalist jewellery firm in 1903, and who had been put to the craft as a boy because 'Jewellery of some sort had been the family trade for at least three generations',[26] Fisher will doubtless have noticed the interplay between luxurious artifice and mortality in the aesthetics of Symbolism. In his much-claimed foreshadowing of 'The Death of the Author', Mallarmé described 'la disparition élocutoire du poète' as a ceding of the initiative to words, words which 's'allument de reflets réciproques comme une virtuelle traînée de feux sur des pierreries'.[27] Fisher is, after all, a writer only a short distance from the 'two or three / generations of Symbolist poets' (*F*, p. 24). alluded to in *A Furnace*, one of those 'Grotesquely called' (*F*, p. 23) and 'compelled / by parody to insist / that what image the unnatural / law had been stamping / was moving into Nature' (*F*, p. 24). Just as the 'Three Ceremonial Poems' evoked a 'live mask plated over', so *A Furnace* pictures an old couple close to death and their dog being 'beaten pewter'; it describes how the surviving husband's widowhood 'was modern and quiet, his death / art'. What kind of art? That, for example, of the jewellery trade's elecroplating: 'He was silvered. It was done' (*F*, p. 26). 'Not that he actually enjoyed making jewellery', Fisher writes of his father, and his son's poetry too shows many signs of resistance to western art's habitual buying of timelessness with precious obduracy.

There has been a slowly retrospective filling out to Fisher's 'death as art' studies: publication of *Matrix* collected the 'Five Morning Poems from a Picture by Manet', written twelve years earlier, while 'In Memory of Wyndham Lewis', written in the same August of 1959, had to wait until *Poems 1955–1980*. Both sequences reveal that a thematic interest in the aesthetic rendering of mortal stoppage and how to sidestep it—though not the most congenial style for its articulation—were in place seven years before the 'Three Ceremonial Poems':

> Death music sounds for a boy by a stream,
> urgent as waves, as polished shoes,
> though amber screens of light shade him from time.
>
> (*P55–87*, p. 10)

The last line sees in a visual image defence against dances to the music of time and inevitable death. Details in the previous two lines imply qualms about such a transformation. 'Death music' indicates a doubt about the reward of eternal art conferred on, for instance, Yeats's golden bird. There is a dramatic act in the Irish poet's wish to be 'out of nature', a death-defying posture. The 'boy by the stream' and the 'polished shoes' in Fisher's poem figure an interest in the specificity of lived circumstances, over which the music plays, giving an urgency to life in time, while threatening those circumstances with the death that will obliterate them: 'As in death, too, the world does not change, but ceases',[28] in the words of Wittgenstein's *Tractatus*.

'Once out of nature I shall never take / My bodily form from any natural thing,'[29] Yeats writes in 'Sailing to Byzantium'. The sea journey in progress is a one-way traffic: from life into art. The artifice, the golden bird, commands a music of unchanging forms. The Emperor and attendants can make the bird sing, but can not themselves command the forms. 'Five Morning Poems from a Picture by Manet' examines the effect on life of such song. It feeds back on to the

life which is supposed to enjoy such artifice the message of its un-
sensual music. These are also 'mourning poems'. Fisher has described
his discomfort with the insistently heightened style of the sequence's
fourth section:

> for a long time I didn't publish that poem or think much about
> it. Because in terms of its style at that particular point it had a
> savage and black turn which didn't catch the tone of the way I
> usually think ... in that poem, in fact, I talk about ordinary
> people who die and their death is given ceremony on an almost
> Yeatsian level. But they're certainly portrayed as dead who have
> been tricked and bamboozled by the world itself.[30]

Into the picture of an inhabited urban landscape, comes the first
person pronoun, deployed in this part as nowhere else in the 'Five
Morning Poems':

> Looking for life, I lost my mind:
> only the dead
> spoke through their yellow teeth
> into the marble tombs they lay beneath,
> splinters of fact stuck in the earth's fat rind.   (*P55–87*, p. 10)

The stanza begins by indicating that the mind is dispossessed by
pressing home such understanding as only the dead may own. The
gravestones are 'splinters of fact'—material objects which also serve
to symbolize the only sure fact of life, its end. Living, according to
the poem, seems closed to the understanding of the living. Similarly,
as death completes a life, ending it, so it becomes a fact which, limited
in time, can be understood. Because such understanding is useless to
those still alive, 'I lost my mind' when 'looking for life'; the knowledge of the world that the dead have access to will not aid in living:

> Muttering, they told me how their lives
> from burial
> spiked back at the world like knives
> striking the past for legacies of wrong—
> the fiction of understanding worst of all.   (p. 10)

In 'Blood and the Moon', Yeats had asserted that 'wisdom is the property of the dead, / A something incompatible with life'.[31] In rewriting 'wisdom' as a more Stevens-like 'fiction of understanding', Fisher demurs at the 'Yeatsian level'. If his poem alludes to the lines by Yeats, it does so in order to contradict them—not only by saying that the dead do communicate, but by stating that they are not wise after the fact and that if the dead do possess knowledge it may only be about how they have been 'bamboozled by the world itself.'

Fisher may slightly misremember his early poem here; the people who have died do not seem bamboozled by the world itself. Rather, according to the syntactically unstable final line of the third stanza, it seems to be the 'legacies of wrong' which do the bamboozling. Thus, it was the 'fiction of understanding' the world that misled them about the world. This fiction, identified with the dead, can also be associated with the aesthete's hope, that time can be transcended by means of an artwork's atemporal artifice. 'The fiction of understanding' may then be one of the knives that strike back at the world, at the reader of the poem and even its writer—*via* the stylistic and conceptual hand-me-down of an earlier period's poetry. Not only is Yeats echoed here, but Eliotic 'Thunder' too in 'Then I heard what the corpses said' (p. 10). Almost three decades later, stripped of their rhythmic and lexical melodrama, these same figures 'come away / to the trench, / the dead in their surprise, / taking whatever form they can / to push across' and as Fisher adds, unlike those earlier embittered and bamboozled ones, 'They've no news' (*F*, p. 18).

Interviewers have turned more than once to the artistic sources for Fisher's mysterious 'Matrix' sequence of 1970. The poet had assumed that everyone knew one such source, but elsewhere he was inclined to offer a lead: 'The cypresses, and the hooded figure, and the boat, and the place of the dead are out of a painting by a chap called Boechlin called *The Isle of the Dead* which is a popular late nineteenth century piece of terrible painting.'[32] Fisher's adjectives 'popular' and 'terrible' roughly graph a mood in the third part of 'Matrix':

> This is where the dead
> are still supposed to make
> their disappearance:
>
> but always the same dead
> seem to be walking.
>
> Spectres of respect.   (*P55–87*, p. 88)

Catching at the symbiotic relationship by which the dead thwart the living through the conventions of gothic art, that sardonic last phrase looks to have been found in the fact that 'spectre' and 'respect' are anagrams. As in the 'Five Morning Poems', Fisher's work imaginatively inhabits Böcklin's painting, setting what had been the still paint of an evocative scene in motion:

> separate plots of twilight
> running the same destiny:
> the boat, with muffled oars,
> the hooded figure, B.D.,
> its hand upraised . . .   (p. 89)

'B.D.' is not the initials of a name, but a qualification; the hooded figure is a priestly person who has received a Bachelor of Divinity, someone initiated in the theology that Fisher has elsewhere called a 'hoax area'.[33] The track of the poem takes in the architectural style of this hoax: 'a small classical temple / of the Lutheran cast', turning the teleology of absent last things into the aesthetic power of structures present in the world. The dark of the place where the dead are 'supposed to make / their disappearance', adding instant mystery with its twist on the expected words 'their appearance', is reorientated at the section's close:

> The mountains of the cypresses
> are the real dark of the path,
> humping their way higher;
>
> always a dark like that,
> set off by some artifice,
>
> growing.   (p. 89)

These closing lines redirect the reader towards a 'real dark': one produced by art's rendering of natural phenomena, as opposed, perhaps, to the unreal dark of an afterlife to which the dead go, or from which ghosts come. While Fisher's poem glancingly mocks a romantic cult of death by treating its conceptual markers as questions of style, it feeds on what it evokes. The quiet voicing of this passage does not over-dramatize—as phrases like 'O sepia-blooded soldiers' (*P55–87*, p. 12) or the 'ordure of decay' (p. 13) from 'In Memory of Wyndham Lewis' do—but its pared-back artifice is sustained by the spaciously gloomy mysteriousness of its source. If *A Furnace*, written over a decade after *Matrix*, 'will not give off much Gothic smoke' (*F*, p. vii), it is because the long poem has found a strategy for the critical treatment of such material with far less of mockery's parasitic relationship to what it disparages.

A good deal of authority in human culture's history has rested, in the last resort, upon power over life and death. While earlier works of Fisher's had touched on complexes of assumption in our management of death, *A Furnace* confronts some of the cultural ideas that structure these powers—the ways, for example, that the clergy may have contributed to a willing, and seemingly needed, dispossession of the dead and of our own deaths:

> Accept
> that the dead have gone away to God through
> portals sculpted in brass to deter,
> horrific. The signs of it, passably
> offensive in a cat or a herring,
> in a man are made out
> unthinkably appalling: *vide*
> M. Valdemar's selfless
> demonstration; drawn back and forth,
> triumphantly racked in a passage without
> extent, province of the agent,
> between antithesis and thesis.   (*F*, pp. 16–17)

M. Valdemar's demonstration is 'selfless' because 'It was his custom, indeed, to speak calmly of his approaching dissolution, as a matter neither to be avoided nor regretted.' The story's narrator, offering 'the *facts*' (as he tells us) of his experiment with mesmerism, puts his subject into a trance and has him speak from both sides of the edge of death: 'Yes;—no;—I *have been* sleeping—and now—now—I *am dead*.' His suspension somewhere, 'in a passage without / extent', between life and death is a literalized, pseudo-scientific enactment of the nineteenth-century's morbidified wish for immortality through art: 'It was evident that, so far, death (or what is usually termed death) had been arrested by the mesmeric process.' The story's ghastly allure, drawing the reader on towards a glimpse of the Beyond which ends in Valdemar's horrific dissolution into 'detestable putridity',[34] is a version of Fisher's aversion to the placing of a fixed, dualistic barrier between life and death, turning a natural process between imprecisely delimited states into an iron curtain of separation and denial. *A Furnace* takes the binary terms, subjects them to a sceptical blurring, and transforms them back into natural processes. His materials are, at times, gothic or, perhaps better, mock-gothic, but his burner efficiently transforms them into a smokeless fuel.

Andrew Crozier has proposed that 'we should at least pause to ask if *A Furnace* does not arrive, finally, at a heterodox mysticism. Is its aim to annul the natural fact of death?' The critic would 'argue against such readings' because the poem contains no 'self-adequate symbolism'.[35] Perhaps so; but I would add that the 'aim to annul the natural fact of death' would qualify as another instance of infantile omnipotence in the absence of such symbols, and would be wishful even with them. After all, Donne's 'Death thou shalt die' evokes the Christian promise of eternal life, which can only be had, if at all, by first dying. John Matthias alluded to Crozier's pausing to ask—citing only as far as 'heterodox mysticism'—so as to offer the counter-claim: 'It seems to me that it does.'[36] Are these views wholly incompatible? Fisher's later death studies need not aim to annul the natural fact of death, which might be just pie in the sky anyway, so as to qualify for the term 'heterodox mysticism'. The work that *A Furnace* does with the life–death binarism requires a basic, and 'by temper, realist' (*P 55–87*, p. 61), acceptance of death. Coolly acknowledging the necessary interrelation of the binary terms, their natural overlap, and the numerous ways (e.g., the 'involuntary memory' of genetics, dialect, environment, cultural and family traditions) that the dead of many centuries are actively present within and around us, Fisher's poem discovers a mysticism in the patternings by which all our lives-and-deaths are part of the process. In this too, his work extends a shadow cast by the early Wittgenstein: 'Not *how* the world is, is the mystical, but that it is.'[37]

Yet while the poet was working to identify cultural patterns in the various cults of death, others have played its literary junctures quite differently. His recent poem, 'At the Grave of Asa Benveniste', begins by noting a 'Churchyard woman coming quickly from under the wall: | *You're looking for Plath*. No question-mark.'[38] Fisher had earlier lashed out at the exploitation of poets' suicides. On 22 January 1973 in conversation with Eric Mottram, he remarked that 'I think I've never written anything that I've kept, that was a straight reaction to an event, any thing in the world'.[39] However, on a prolific Friday just over a year before, he seems to have composed 'Occasional Poem 7.1.72'. John Berryman threw himself off a bridge at about 9 a.m. in Minneapolis on that day, and it is difficult not to think that Fisher's poem is a response to the news, as also to literary journalism about poetry and suicide: 'The poets are dying because they are told to die. | What kind of dirt is that?' Poets die just as everyone else does, those pupils in 'One World', for example: 'By now, some are dead. I read of one | suicide and one broken skull.'[40] Fisher's angry occasional poem proposes that as a civilization which 'is filth' gets its hands on the controlling categories of 'taste', 'talent' and 'death', so the poets

> are going to be moving on out past talent,
> out past taste. If taste
> gets its gift wrappers on death—well—
> out past that, too. There are courts
> where nobody ought to testify.   (*P55–87*, p. 99)

As when overtaking a parked car, 'to be moving on out past' something, you must first acknowledge its presence there. Just how Fisher was to move 'out past' death in his poetry would take the composition of *A Furnace* to make clear.

IV

'Inscriptions for Bluebeard's Castle', like its probable source in Béla Balán's libretto for Bartók's opera, evokes, without ever directly stating, the central fact of Bluebeard and his murdered wives; in 'The Lake of Tears', for example, 'Day has turned to a silver mirror / whose dead extent the weeping / eyes could never see', or in 'The Treasure House' where 'What / the sun touches / shines on forever dead / the dead images of the sun / wonderful'—an idea echoed in 'The Last Door' with its 'Moonlight the dead image of the day' (*P55–87*, pp. 101–02). The word 'dead' in these brief passages, taken in the context of the poem's title, cannot help but evoke the dynamics of a moral tale about curiosity and fate which will be the death of Judith. Though human languages are indelibly suffused with the complexly conflictual ethics and morals of the cultures in which they are spoken, Fisher has seen a benefit in tactically 'de-moralizing' as well as 'de-socializing' literary art:

> In this country people take a little bit of poetry, a little bit of literature, and if there's a moral in it, however crude, it will be taken, it will be coarsened still further ... For my taste I moralize too much already.[41]

A good deal has been made of the poet's deploring this supposed simplifying tendency of readers and critics to take the moral, or equally of some poets to 'sloganize' their images. Crozier notes that 'his findings are kept provisional'.[42] Ian Gregson says his poems are 'indeterminate in their form and meaning' and present themselves as 'provisional statements leading to other provisional statements.'[43] Sean O'Brien cites Gregson and sums up the situation: 'Fisher is a markedly anti-foundationalist poet: we might say that his *modus operandi* depends on rejecting the idea of ends and purposes.' However, the critic, an admirer of Fisher's writings, if not of some of the company they have tended to keep, adds that 'his work also reveals the mind's hankering after teleology'.[44]

Praise for the provisional, for the 'anti-foundationalist'—from these different critical perspectives—is bought at the cost of tacitly shoring up the very foundations which Fisher is said to be against, foundations represented by some demonized monger of definitive findings (often a travestied, ghostly Davie). As O'Brien's second thought demonstrates, the provisional is conveniently given its street value by being contrasted with systems of uttered verities about ends, purposes and various last things. But what if, as so much of Fisher's poetry affirms, such systems are at best dubious illusions, nothing more than a 'hoax area'? Though the hankering that O'Brien detects may perhaps be construed out of *City* and other work from the 1960s, later writings, such as *A Furnace*, are less amenable to this view of Fisher as an experimentalist with recidivist backslidings towards 'ends and purposes'. There is, after all, Fisher's tendency, despite comments in interviews, to issue (however uncomfortably) definitive-sounding statements in poems: 'I want / to remark formally, indeed // stiffly, though not complaining, / that the place where I was raised / had no longer deference for water' (*P55–87*, p. 161). In a world without foundations, such moments in Fisher's work constitute neither the uttering of gilt-edged securities nor the provisional 'takes' of an anti-foundationalist loosening a stiff world propped up on doubted—yet, by that token, needed—foundations; they are readings which neither ask for, nor require, future revision, nor come offered as a tentative choice among Art's marvellous 'selection of skies' (*P55–87*, p. 106).

Gregson concedes to Davie the assumption that Hardy, Larkin and Fisher 'are all sceptics'.[45] Yet while Hardy and Larkin have poems such as 'The Oxen' or 'Church-Going' which insinuate the 'hankering' that O'Brien notes (suggesting that they are reluctant, nostalgic or frightened poets wishing, but unable, to believe in such purposes and ends), Fisher seems a different brand of sceptic—more thorough, more like the 'honest doubt' of David Hume, with his arguments about causality, his distinction between fact and value, or his holding firm to atheism in the jaws of death and despite Boswell's obstinate questionings. Nor could it be said of Hume that his lack of belief in teleological foundations prevented him from making definitive statements. Indeed, in the fully credited Heraclitean world of *A Furnace* where all is flux and, as 'Handsworth Liberties' had earlier stated, 'in the crowd of exchanges' we not only 'can change' (*P55–87*, p. 118) but can not avoid doing so, definitive statements are in any case provisional (since nothing is not), so the provisional ones may as well be framed in as definitive a style as they need to be.

In his interview with John Tranter, Fisher notes of *A Furnace* that

> There's an ongoing discussion of death, whether the reader likes it or not. I'm talking about death quite a lot, and I'm like this evangelist who's at your elbow, saying 'Talking about death . . . we just had this bit about sex and drink or whatever and birth, I was thinking about death while we were doing this, let's think about death again a bit, and the burial of the dead.' I go back to it because that's the thing I'm riding through the poem.[46]

Though Crozier rightly noted that the poem is not 'exclusively about last things', he also observed that 'a main topic of *A Furnace*' is 'the connection of the living to the dead, one's own life and death.'[47] Matthias remarked that 'The Return', a section which 'no one to my knowledge, has traced back to Ezra Pound's early poem of the same title or to Yeats's use of it in *A Vision*, is uncanny in its dealings with the dead.'[48] Something of this uncanniness can be evoked by noting that Fisher's poem is not so much, and not only, concerned with 'the connection of the living to the dead', but of the dead to the living. After all, the former can be subsumed under the familiar sources and resources of poetic inspiration: active remembering. The latter takes seriously 'the life of the dead' (*F*, p. 17) as not merely a substitute vitality that the living attribute to them, but a range of energies which impress them upon the living. The 'Who / shall own death?' section of *A Furnace* explores some of the belief structures, or lack of them, that had driven the poet's earlier stylistic approaches to the role of death in culture:

> and Lazarus the test case. Only Almighty
> God could have worked that trick. Accept
> that the dead have gone away to God through
> portals sculpted in brass to deter,
> horrific. (*F*, pp. 16–17)

Those 'portals sculpted in brass' are the shading in of his older theme, as, later, are the description of those local deaths: 'Had the three of them been art, it would all have / been beaten pewter' (*F*, p. 26). 'Death is not an event of life', Wittgenstein asserted, but Fisher now contradicts that with some of the knowledge familiar to poetry:

> that you are dead
> turns in the dark of your spiral,
> comes close in the first hours after birth,
> recedes and recurs often. Nobody
> need sell you a death.
>
> (*F*, p. 18)

'Frozen movement', Fisher had said, 'interests me, partly because it seems to imply life.'[49] This passage works at loosening the hold of the life–death binarism by registering the interdependence of the concepts, the sense that through a human span they will recede and recur, that no one need sell you a death, because being alive your death is already implied and necessary. Even so, it may not be an event of your life, but it is the one event not of your life to which you are inescapably connected. It is also true that in the English language 'Nobody / need sell you a death' because the word 'death', if it is not to function abstractly, tends to take an identifying genitive form: your death, the death of me. Shakespeare's Feeble encourages himself with the thought that 'we owe God a death', which is true enough if glossed as 'a man can die but once',[50] though it is not true (as *A Furnace* would prefer) if it implies that death is on loan from some higher power. The supposed ownership of death by a transcendent force is described as a conceptual strategy by which civic authority can assert its cultural control over the citizenry: 'as if it were a military installation', they will 'specialize and classify and hide / the life of the dead' (*F*, p. 17).

Fisher's remark in the Tranter interview 'I'm like this evangelist' suggests a subject with more of a palpable design—'whether the reader likes it or not'[51]—than is usually supposed by criticism of his work devoted to the exposition of compositional strategies. Not that Fisher's writings had previously been devoid of such designs; there is, for example, the section in 'Wonders of Obligation' where 'I saw /

the mass graves' prepared for those 'the air-raids were going to kill'.
Having sidled into the passage with that vulnerable two-syllable line,
'I saw', Fisher gives it reiterative impetus in mid-flow:

> some will have looked down
> into their own graves on Sundays
>
> provided
> for the poor of Birmingham
> the people of Birmingham,
> the working people of Birmingham,
> the allotment holders and Mother, of Birmingham.
> The poor.   (*P55–87*, p. 155)

If you take an adjective and put a definite article in front of it, you'll
probably have a prejudice: 'The poor.' Fisher's sequence 'poor',
'people', 'working people', 'allotment holders and Mother' subjects
the pigeon-holing noun phrase to a mutedly angry scrutiny. Silkin
could respond to this aspect of Fisher's work without difficulty,
finding a 'sober dismay at the treatment individuals receive at the
unkind hands of authority'.[52] There is a metaphor setting up the
passage's main theme: 'mass graves dug / the size of workhouse
wards'. The wartime surplus of death is found to be one of the routes
by which a civic authority can impose itself on lives, using the
methods of Poor Law social control:

> Once the bombs got you
> you were a pauper:
> clay, faeces, no teeth; on a level
> with gas mains,
> even more at a loss than before,
> down in the terraces between the targets,
> between the wagon works
> and the moonlight on the canal.   (p. 156)

In the news documentary section of 'Stopped Frames and Set Pieces',
the circumstantial detail of deaths appears to propel the composing
attention into an aesthetic response: 'From the dead there were
long runs of blood, right down into the gutters. Its brightness was

astonishing, the gaiety of the colour' (*P55–87*, p. 35). In the later poem, 'the moonlight on the canal' has an initially similar brightness, yet here the announced reluctance to 'sloganize . . . an image'[53] homes in on a glanced at political-cultural point ('even more at a loss than before') through a change of perspective ('between the targets . . . moonlight on the canal'). Fisher's turned colloquialism 'even more at a loss' finds a continuity between the puzzlement of the local people and their greater confusion when dead; his deft use of paired prepositions ('down in') puts the reader into the cockpit of a Dornier 217 or Heinkel 111 following the lit canal's map reference point so as to hit the wagon works—though as likely beginning the process of demolition and rehousing in this working-class district of Birmingham that had provided the source material for 'The Entertainment of War'.

It is hard not to feel that, if Fisher has been able to move 'out past' death in *A Furnace*, he has done so by getting beyond the debilitating reluctance of 'It is Writing'—which properly mistrusts a poem's wanting 'to glorify suffering' because 'it could do it well', yet in which, making definitive statements once more: 'I mistrust the poem in its hour of success, / a thing capable of being / tempted by ethics into the wonderful' (*P55–87*, p. 111). This counter-ethic has the limitations of any negative injunction. Invoking what it rejects, its little moral-aesthetic would commit the poet to avoidance tactics—tactics such as those of the murderer in 'Barnardine's Reply':

> Barnardine, given his life back,
> is silent.
>
> With such conditions
> what can he say?
>
> The talk
> is all about mad arrangements, the owners
> counting on their fingers,
> calling it discourse, cheating . . .   (*P55–87*, p. 126)

This character, 'a dissolute condemned prisoner' in *Measure for Measure*, makes an emblematic figure to take as the victim of experience sentenced to him by higher suspect powers. Not inclined to 'Be absolute for death',[54] as the Duke in a monk's disguise urges Claudio, but dissolute for survival, Barnardine—'whose sole insight into time / is that the right day for being hanged on / doesn't exist' (*P55–87*, p. 126)—may not influence his or others' fates by talking, as variously the play's main characters can and do; rather, he defers the day of his execution by remaining drunk, in which condition a priest cannot give him the last rites. Reprieved as part of a puzzling plot wind-up in the final act, he exits without a line. 'Barnardine's Reply' represents this silence as the only suitable response to the play's 'talk', called 'discourse', which is 'all about mad arrangements'. It is as if the power of the authorities to arrange Barnardine's reprieve in *Measure for Measure* is so detached from the lives being arranged, that anyone who experiences these is wholly unable to describe or comment on what happens: 'seeing / what was never to be said', as a phrase from 'In the Wall' has it, because 'lacking, in any case, / discourse' (*P55–87*, p. 109). Barnardine is a curious representative of those many urban figures in Fisher's work who must try to avoid 'a bare-buttocked, incontinent, / sunken-cheeked ending' (p. 98) within living conditions and an environment that have been given as 'a free sample from the patentholders' (p. 126). But *A Furnace* is by no means 'silent' on such issues of ownership and power; its achievement is to reinhabit the territory of the poet's earlier work, flushing into the open values and beliefs, implied or assumed, that had already inclined him to forms, methods and subjects over many years. His long poem thus deploys, and frequently states, an evolved outlook, an ethics of attention to the world—one which is most tested, as an ethics tends to be, in its relations with death and the dead.

The later volume *Birmingham River* contains 'They Come Home', an episode originally part of the 'Core' section of *A Furnace*—which seems, naturally enough, to inhabit the spiritual climate of the long poem. Fisher has described this work as a 'straight autobiographical piece … about my wife Joyce's parents who had died within a fortnight of each other in 1980'.[55] Its relation to his 'engine devised, like a cauldron, or a still, or a blast-furnace, to invoke and assist natural processes of change' (*F*, p. vii) appears in the double burning of the loved-ones' remains. First their ashes are brought home from the crematorium, releasing them from the grip of the civil authorities' version of how the dead are to be disposed. The unflustered polemic of the poem evokes what may be done with the ashes as a project to keep our losses with us: 'by no means separate the dead / from anything' (*BR*, p. 51). This proposal takes on its own Heraclitean dimensions when—matter being neither created nor destroyed—some of the ashes are re-cremated with kitchen rubbish in a municipal refuse disposal kiln:

> They're going again in a day or two:
>
> to be in part twice-burned
> in city flames; eight hundred
> degrees of the lance-burner
> under the oven's
> brick arch, and then whatever
> blast of the municipality
> lifts the remainder haze clear of Sheffield
> and over the North Sea.
>
> (*BR*, p. 52)

The dead parents, far from being 'out of nature' (as Yeats had hoped to be), come home to their daughter's domestic garden, where 'your / fingers and mine' are 'mixing your dead / in a layer across the topsoil' (*BR*, p. 51); *via* a thematically apt exhaust-pipe refit shop. Inside the car, they are jacked up with the vehicle, then come home not just into the ordinary life of their survivors, but home to nature, to the continuum of matter and energy of which we form a part, finally dispersed into the air we breathe: 'By no means separate / from anything at all' (*BR*, p. 52).

A section from Fisher's recent 'The Dow Low Drop' puns on the drop of being hanged, by presenting in outline one of the poet's contemporaries at school who had perhaps miscalculated in an erotic game and died, self-hanged, wearing his mother's underwear. The poem imagines this person's future life:

> He's quieter. A good
> career in a science behind him
> following a narrow squeak in youth.

The Thing about Roy Fisher: Critical Studies

> I could greet him, dull idea,
> if I didn't believe my knowledge.   (*DLD*, p. 193)

This 'dull idea' evokes so as to fend off a dialogic encounter with the dead, the kind of poetic occasion that has been revived with recourse to European epic traditions, and in particular Dante's *Divine Comedy*, on innumerable occasions over the past century, among the most recent being Seamus Heaney's 'Station Island' sequence. Fisher's lines eschew the tactical mock-surprise in T. S. Eliot's adaptation of *Inferno* xv: 'What! are *you* here?'[56] The boy's death at fifteen is reported to his classmates:

> The censors of the day
> comforted the boys with *suicide*,
> *impatience*, *despair*, *tragedy*. Said
> nothing about the underwear.

The fear of this supposed perversion implied in the censors' economy with the truth is dispelled by the poem's even-pitched, unemphatic candour. Knowledge of a teleology which would have required those last things of judgement and punishment to structure its afterlife is implied, but fended off—not evoked for furnishing a literary occasion. The poem is aware of this much-worked theme, but takes it to be 'dull', perhaps from over use; for this poem, the presence of the dead in the world of the living does not require an afterlife, merely a life, one in which this presence is felt without need of either doubt or surprise. The poet might have to greet 'My schoolmate, D., / forty-seven years hanged' only if 'I didn't believe my knowledge' (*DLD*, p. 193). This is a winning turn because knowledge—and that is what the line asserts it to be—does not usually require belief anyway.

In the work of *A Furnace* and after, the poet has been quietly re-negotiating for a secular culture what are nevertheless humanly necessary relations between the living and the dead. Yet while 'They Come Home' significantly revises the anthropology of 'As He Came Near Death', the short poem 'Going'—also from *Birmingham River*—was written from one of Fisher's more casually socialized perspectives:

When the dead in your generation are still few,
as they go, they reach back; for a while
they fill the whole place with themselves,
rummaging about, inquisitive,
turning everybody on; bringing
their eyes behind yours to make you see things for them.

Now there are more, more every year,
sometimes a month packed full with them
passing through, first dulled, preoccupied, and then
taken quickly to silence. And they're gone, that's all.

(*BR*, p. 10)

Not inclined to see this conclusion as contradicting the presentation
of death and the returns of the dead in *A Furnace* or 'They Come
Home', Fisher has described this poem as one in which 'Death, the
Sniper, was taking all the initiatives.'[57] Its composition and publication after the longer works nevertheless point to a poet not inclined
to depend on the insights of his own previous work as the parameters
of future perception. 'Going' remains alive to further ways in which
death, for the living, is an event of life. Fisher's later poetry has not
aimed to annul the natural fact of extinction, but by taking on 'Death,
the Sniper', it has perhaps partially disarmed him.

Among Fisher's most recent writings are pieces that belong to the
end game of an oeuvre. In 'Item', the poet describes in passing the
bodily effects of his stroke: 'One-handed / this year at least, and
lame';[58] in the first of 'Four Songs from the Camel's Coffin', he states
that 'I've come apart.'[59] Like 'The Collection of Things' with its
'cracked gold / high-heeled slipper' (*BR*, p. 1), 'At the Grave of Asa
Benveniste' evokes the residual power of objects to carry meaning
beyond the lives of their owners: 'Asa, / your hat's in the bathroom.'[60]
What will survive of us is things, and these last things, like so much
of his work, are things that will surely last. And to end with, there is
now a piece by Fisher called 'Last Poems':

Thinning of the light
and the language meagre;
an impatient shift under the lines

> maybe to catch the way
> the lens, cold
> unstable tear, flattens and tilts
> to show codes of what may be flaring
> at the edge and beyond.
>
> Absence of self-pity suggests
> absorption in something or other
> new, never to be defined.
>
> But in all those years before
> what *was* his subject?[61]

While the opening lines sketch conditions of lack which might imply 'self-pity', its announced absence evokes the still vital possibility of 'absorption in something or other / new'. Fisher's way of approaching the new requires him to be wary of preventing its appearance by knowing what it might be. It is 'never to be defined' because to do so would prevent it from coming into literary being—as happens with the compositional demise outlined in the fifth of the 'Diversions': 'I saw what there was to write and I wrote it. / When it felt what I was doing, it lay down and died under me' (*P55–87*, p. 133). So then, 'what *was* his subject?' Nothing that you could know beforehand, but a thing at last made manifest by the works in which it is embedded.

Two of the great perennial subjects for poets have been love and death. In 'Of the Empirical Self and for Me', he writes that 'Even / love's not often a poem' (*P55–87*, p. 125). From first to last, though, for Roy Fisher death often is.

NOTES

1. 'Interview: Roy Fisher by Helen Dennis', University of Warwick Audio-Visual Centre, typescript, 9 May 1984, p. 130.

2. 'Conversation with Roy Fisher: Eric Mottram', *Saturday Morning*, 1, (Spring 1976) unpaginated [p. 1].

3. Jed Rasula and Mike Erwin, 'An Interview with Roy Fisher', *Roy Fisher, Nineteen Poems and an Interview* (Pensnett, Staffs.: Grosseteste, 1975), p. 20.

4. 'A Tuning Phenomenon: An Interview with Roy Fisher', *Sad Traffic*, 5, (Barnsley, 1971), p. 33.

5. *Saturday Morning* [p. 2].

6. T. S. Eliot, 'Coriolan', *Collected Poems, 1909–1962* (London: Faber & Faber, 1963), p. 139.

7. *The Memorial Fountain* (Newcastle upon Tyne: Northern House, 1966), pp. 3–4.

8. 'Roy Fisher Talks to Peter Robinson', *Granta*, 76 (Cambridge: June 1977), p. 17.

9. 'Kingsbury Mill', *The Memorial Fountain*, p. 13.

10. 'Roy Fisher Talks to Peter Robinson', p. 17, but citing the corrected text in Roy Fisher, *Interviews Through Time, and Selected Prose*, ed. T. Frazer (Kentisbeare, Devon: Shearsman, 2000), p. 74.

11. Ludwig Wittgenstein, *Tractatus Logico-Philosophicus*, tr. C. K. Ogden (1922; London: Routledge & Kegan Paul, 1995), p. 185.

12. *Saturday Morning* [p. 12].

13. Robert Sheppard, *Turning the Prism: An Interview with Roy Fisher* (London: Toads Damp Press, 1986), pp. 17–18.

14. Rasula and Erwin, 'Interview', pp. 24–29.

15. 'Interview: Roy Fisher by Helen Dennis', p. 129.

16. 'Roy Fisher 1930–', *Contemporary Authors (Autobiography Series)*, vol. 10 (Detroit, New York, Fort Lauderdale, London: Gale Research Inc., 1989), p. 81.

17. *Ibid.*, p. 90.

18. *Ibid.*, p. 91.

19. *Ibid.*, pp. 92–93 (three citations).

20. Rasula and Erwin, 'Interview', p. 19.

21. *Ibid.*, p. 36.

22. Wittgenstein, *Tractatus*, p. 185.

23. *John Keats: The Complete Poems*, Penguin English Poets, ed. J. Barnard (Harmondsworth: Penguin, 1988), p. 452.

24. *John Donne: The Complete English Poems*, Penguin English Poets, ed. A. J. Smith (Harmondsworth: Penguin, 1971), p. 313.

25. 'Roy Fisher Talks to Peter Robinson', p. 18.

26. 'Roy Fisher 1930–', p. 79.

27. Stéphane Mallarmé, 'Cris de vers', *Mallarmé*, ed. A. Hartley (Harmondsworth: Penguin, 1965), p. 171; for an analysis of Roland Barthes' use of Mallarmé, see Seán Burke, *The Death and Return of the Author: Criticism and Subjectivity in Barthes, Foucault and Derrida* (1992; Edinburgh: Edinburgh University Press, 2nd edn 1998), pp. 8–10.

28. Wittgenstein, *Tractatus*, p. 185.

29. W. B. Yeats, 'Sailing to Byzantium', *The Collected Poems*, ed. R. J. Finneran (London: Macmillan, 1991), p. 194.

30. Rasula and Erwin, 'Interview', pp. 22–23.

31. W. B. Yeats, 'Blood and the Moon', *The Collected Poems*, p. 239.

32. 'A Tuning Phenomenon', p. 32.

33. Rasula and Erwin, 'Interview', p. 20; in his autobiographical essay, Fisher describes 'an act which seems to me far more bizarre than my imaginary illness, but of which I'm more ashamed, since it was real, I joined a Christian church, on an intellectual whim' ('Roy Fisher 1930–', p. 95).

34. Edgar Allen Poe, 'The Facts in the Case of M. Valdemar', *The Fall of the House of Usher and Other Writings*, ed. D. Galloway (Harmondsworth: Penguin, 1986), pp. 351, 350, 357, 358, 359.

35. Andrew Crozier, 'Signs of Identity: Roy Fisher's *A Furnace*', *PN Review*, 83 (18:3), (January–February 1992), p. 32.

36. John Matthias, 'The Poetry of Roy Fisher', *Contemporary British Poetry: Essays in Theory and Criticism*, ed. J. Acheson and R. Huk (New York: State University of New York Press, 1996), p. 56.

37. Wittgenstein, *Tractatus*, p. 187.

38. *Poetry Review*, 86:3 (Autumn 1996), p. 28.

39. *Saturday Morning*, [pp. 2–3].

40. *Consolidated Comedies* (Durham: Pig Press, 1981), p. 8.

41. Rasula and Erwin, 'Interview', p. 16.

42. Crozier, 'Signs of Identity', p. 26.

43. Ian Gregson, *Contemporary Poets and Post-Modernism: Dialogue and Estrangement* (London: Macmillan, 1996), p. 172.

44. Sean O'Brien, *The Deregulated Muse: Essays on Contemporary British and Irish Poetry* (Newcastle upon Tyne: Bloodaxe, 1998), p. 112.

45. Gregson, *Contemporary Poets*, p. 171.

46. 'John Tranter Interviews Roy Fisher', *Jacket*, 1 (1987) part 2 (http://www.jacket.zip.com.au./jacket01/fisheriv.html)

47. Crozier, 'Signs of Identity', pp. 26, 27.

48. Matthias, 'Poetry of Roy Fisher', p. 56.

49. 'A Tuning Phenomenon', p. 33.

50. William Shakespeare, *2 Henry IV*, iii.ii.228–29.

51. 'John Tranter Interviews Roy Fisher'.

52. Jon Silkin, *The Life of Metrical and Free Verse in Twentieth-Century Poetry* (London: Macmillan, 1997), p. 305.

53. Rasula and Erwin, 'Interview', p. 16.

54. William Shakespeare, *Measure for Measure*, *dramatis personæ* and iii.i.5.

55. '"They Are All Gone Into the World": Roy Fisher in Conversation with Peter Robinson', in Roy Fisher, *Interviews Through Time, and Selected Prose*, p. 111.

56. T. S. Eliot, 'Little Gidding', *Collected Poems 1909–1962*, p. 217.

57. '"They Are All Gone Into the World": Roy Fisher in Conversation with Peter Robinson', p. 112.

58. 'Item', in *New Writing*, 6, ed. A. S. Byatt and P. Porter (London: Vintage, 1997), pp. 302–05.

59. *A Gallery for Gael Turnbull*, ed. Peter McCarey (Glasgow: Au Quai, 1998), p. 9.

60. *Poetry Review*, 86:3 (Autumn 1996), p. 29.

61. *CCCP 8*, Programme and Anthology of the Eighth Cambridge Conference of Contemporary Poetry, 24–26 April 1998, p. 26.

Roy Fisher: A Bibliography

DEREK SLADE

Contents

Acknowledgements

In compiling this bibliography I have benefited greatly from the assistance of others, many of whom helped with the 1987 version upon which this is based. First and foremost, I must thank Roy Fisher, not only for his unfailing patience and good humour in answering innumerable questions but also for providing the invaluable composition chronology that is the backbone of section C. I am greatly indebted to John Kerrigan and Peter Robinson for their sound editorial advice. I must also thank John Barker, Peter Barry, Professor Ian Bell, Richard Boston, Jim Burns, Richard Caddel, James Codd of the BBC Written Archives Centre, Andrew Crozier, Ian Gregson, Alan Halsey, David Hart of West Midlands Arts, James Keery, Ronald King, Tim Longville, the late Eric Mottram, John Osborne, Peter Riley, Neil Roberts, Robert Sheppard, Geoffrey Soar, and Jonathan Vickers of the National Sound Archive. Finally, I should like to thank my wife, Mary, for her support and encouragement throughout.

A. Books and Pamphlets by Roy Fisher

City, Worcester, Migrant Press; date of publication given as May 1961
   actually appeared June 1961. This version of *City* contains prose-
   paragraphs and three poems—'The Judgement', 'Do Not Remain
   Too Much Alone' and 'Toyland'—omitted from the revised *City*
   printed in the Fulcrum Press *Collected Poems 1968*. Neither 'The
   Judgement' nor 'Do Not Remain Too Much Alone' has been
   printed elsewhere. 'Toyland' appeared as a separate poem in *Collected
   Poems 1968, Poems 1955–1980, Poems 1955–1987* and *The Dow Low Drop*
   (*see below*). An edition of approximately 300 copies.

Then Hallucinations, Worcester, Migrant Press, 1962. An edition of
   approximately 200 copies.

The Ceremonial Poems, privately printed by Gael Turnbull, 1966. A run of
   76 roneod copies, not commercially circulated.

Interiors: Ten Interiors with Various Figures, Nottingham, Tarasque Press,
   1966. An edition of 250 copies.

The Ship's Orchestra, London, Fulcrum Press: date of publication given as
   1966, actually appeared March 1967. Cover from a wood engraving
   by David Jones. Ordinary edition unknown; a numbered signed
   edition of 50 copies. A few copies were published with green dust-
   wrappers; those of the rest are cream. [In 1964 a small number of
   photocopies of the original typescript were made by Fred Hunter
   for the author's use; these were not commercially circulated.]

The Memorial Fountain, Newcastle upon Tyne, Northern House: date of
   publication given as 1966, actually appeared September 1967.
   Edition unknown.

Collected Poems 1968: The Ghost of a Paper Bag, London, Fulcrum Press, May
   1969. Ordinary edition unknown, 100 copies with an extra poem,
   'The Flight Orator' (later published in *The Cut Pages* (1971), Fulcrum
   edition), specially bound and numbered and signed. (Hereafter
   CP68.)

Titles, Nottingham, Tarasque Press, 1969. An edition of 50 copies, 25 of
   which were numbered and signed.

The Cut Pages, London, Fulcrum Press, July 1971. Ordinary edition
   unknown. 75 copies separately printed and specially bound,
   numbered and signed.

Matrix, London, Fulcrum Press, July 1971. Cover and title page by Tom

Phillips. Ordinary edition unknown. 75 copies separately printed and specially bound; numbered and signed. (Hereafter *M*.)

Three Early Pieces, London, Transgravity Press, 1971. An edition of 300, plus a limited signed edition of 20 copies.

Nineteen Poems and an Interview, Pensnett, Staffs., Grosseteste Press, June 1975. Cover by Tony Wild. An edition of 300 numbered copies, of which the first 30 were signed. 2nd edition, with different cover by Tony Wild, published in 1977; edition unknown.

Four Poems, Newcastle upon Tyne, Pig Press (Hasty Editions), 1976. An edition of approximately 75 copies.

Barnardine's Reply, Knotting, Beds., Sceptre Press, 1977. An edition of 100 unsigned copies and 50 numbered and signed copies.

The Thing about Joe Sullivan: Poems 1971–1977, Manchester, Carcanet New Press, November 1978. An edition of 2000 copies. (Hereafter *JS*.)

Comedies, Newcastle upon Tyne, Pig Press (Misty Editions), 1979. An edition of 200 copies, 10 of which were numbered and signed.

Wonders of Obligation, Bretenoux, France, Braad Editions, date of publication given as 1979, actually appeared July 1980. Drawings by John Furnival. A numbered edition of 450; numbers 1–26 signed.

Poems 1955–1980, Oxford, Oxford University Press, November 1980. An edition of 1750 copies. (Hereafter *P55–80*.)

Talks for Words, Cardiff, Blackweir Press, 1980. Edition unknown.

From Diversions 2nd Series, Leamington, Bath Community Arts Press, April 1981. An edition of 100 numbered copies.

Consolidated Comedies, Durham, Pig Press (Crusty Editions), December 1981. Edition unknown; 26 copies lettered and signed.

Running Changes, Colchester, Ampersand Press, Essex, 1983. An edition of 200 copies.

A Furnace, Oxford, Oxford University Press, March 1986. A first edition of 2000 copies; a further 500 copies were printed in November 1986. (Hereafter *F*.)

The Cut Pages (2nd edition), London, Oasis Books/Shearsman Books, December 1986. Cover and title page by Ray Seaford. An edition of approximately 500 copies.

Poems 1955–1987, Oxford, Oxford University Press, September 1988. An edition of 2000 copies. (Hereafter *P55–87*.)

Near Garmsley Camp, Madley, Five Seasons Press, Hereford, 1988. Cover and drawing by Caroline Hands. An edition of 275 signed copies.

Birmingham River, Oxford, Oxford University Press, 1994. An edition of 1500 copies. (Hereafter *BR*.)

It Follows That, Durham, Pig Press, 1994. An edition of approximately 300 copies.

The Dow Low Drop: New and Selected Poems, Newcastle upon Tyne, Bloodaxe Books, 1996. An edition of 2000 copies. (Hereafter *DLD*.)

B. Collaborations with Artists

Correspondence, London, Tetrad Press, 1970. Text by RF, print by Tom Phillips. An edition of 500 copies.

Metamorphoses, London, Tetrad Press, 1970. Text by RF, print by Tom Phillips. See Tom Phillips's 'treated Victorian novel' *A Humument*, 1st edn, London, Thames & Hudson, 1980, p. 158, for an image reminiscent of this print and an apparent verbal reference to RF and *Metamorphoses*. An edition of 100 copies.

Also, London, Tetrad Press, 1972. Text by RF, seven prints by Derrick Greaves. Edition unknown.

Bluebeard's Castle, Guildford, Surrey, Circle Press, 1973. Text by RF, nine 3-dimensional pop-up designs by Ronald King. An edition of 125 copies.

Cultures, London, Tetrad Press, 1975. Designed by Ian Tyson: five radial texts by RF. An edition of 250 copies.

Neighbours—We'll Not Part Tonight! Guildford, Surrey, Circle Press, 1976. Text by RF, seven serigraphs by Ronald King. An edition of 30 copies.

On the Open Side, West Midlands Arts' Poster Poem, edn 1, no. 4, 1977. Text by RF, artist David Prentice. Edition unknown.

Scenes from the Alphabet, Guildford, Surrey, Circle Press, 1978. Text by RF, cut-out alphabet design by Ronald King. An edition of 115 signed copies; 2nd unsigned edition of 200 copies, 1984. A miniaturized version of 'Scenes from the Alphabet' can be found on unnumbered pages at the centre of *The Looking Book* (*see below*).

Dark on Dark, privately printed, undated (probably late 1970s). Text by RF, embroidered canvas by Matthew Tyson. Edition unknown.

The Half-Year Letters, Guildford, Surrey, Circle Press, 1983. Text by RF, alphabet book design by Ronald King. An edition of 300 copies.

The Left-Handed Punch, Guildford, Surrey, Circle Press, 1987. Text by RF, book design by Ronald King. An edition of 80 numbered books signed by RF and Ronald King.

Top Down Bottom Up, London, Circle Press, 1990. Text by RF, six deeply embossed wire-prints by Ronald King. An edition of 120 copies.

Anansi Company, London, Circle Press, 1992. Text by RF, rod-puppets by Ronald King. An edition of 120 copies.

Cathy Courtney, *The Looking Book: a Pocket History of Circle Press*, London, Circle Press, 1996. This contains photographs of, and commentary on, all collaborations between Roy Fisher and Ronald King: 'Bluebeard's Castle' (pp. 110–16), 'Neighbours—We'll Not Part Tonight!' (pp. 126–9); 'The Alphabet Series' (including 'Scenes from the Alphabet') (pp. 140–1), 'The Left-Handed Punch' (pp. 146–9); 'London Series', including 'Top Down Bottom Up' (pp. 160–2); 'Anansi Company' (pp. 164–7). Roy Fisher discusses his contributions.

Roller, London, Circle Press, 1999. Text by RF. Design by Ian Tyson, execution by Karen Bleitt. A folded graphic work in 13 folds. An edition of 250 copies.

C. Composition Chronology and details of publication

(Note: where a publication is referred to more than once, full details of publication are given only at the first reference.)

1950

'Old Man in a Shower of Rain' (October 1950)
    Mermaid, 17:3, June 1951, ed. R. A. Foakes, University of Birmingham.
    Uncollected

1951

'A Vision of Four Musicians' (23 August 1951)
    Mermaid, 18:1, October 1951, ed. Roy Fisher, University of Birmingham.
    Uncollected

'A Conceit for the Empress' (December 1951)
    Mermaid, 19:1, January 1953, ed. James Heron, University of Birmingham.
    Uncollected

1952

'Hough! Hough!' (1 February 1952)
  Mermaid, 19:1
  Broadcast on 13 July 1955 as 'The Moral' (*see* section F).
  Uncollected

1953

'The Military Graveyard in France' (8 February 1953)
  Origin, 20, Winter 1957, ed. Cid Corman.
  Uncollected
'Piano' (November 1953)
  Three Early Pieces (*see* section A)
  Uncollected
'La Magdalena' (November 1953)
  Broadcast on 'Signature', Western Region Service, 13 July 1955.
  Uncollected

1954

'The Lemon Bride' (March 1954)
  The Window, 9, n.d. (*c*. 1955), ed. John Sankey, London.
  Uncollected
'Pharaoh's Dream' (*c*. May 1954)
  Three Early Pieces
  Uncollected
'The Doctor Died' (*c*. May 1954)
  Three Early Pieces
  Uncollected

1955

'A Gift of Cream' (January 1955)
  Origin, 20
  Uncollected
'Aside to a Children's Tale' (5 May 1955)
  The Poet, 14, 1956, ed. William Price Turner, Glasgow.

Origin, 20
Collected: *CP68, P55–80, P55–87, DLD*
'Double Morning' (September 1955)
    Delta, 10, August 1956, ed. Christopher Levenson
    Uncollected

1957

'Midlanders' (12 January 1957)
    Mica, 4, Fall 1961, ed. Helmut Bonheim, Santa Barbara, CA.
    Uncollected
'Neighbours—We'll Not Part Tonight!' (15 January 1957)
    Neighbours—We'll Not Part Tonight! (*see* section B)
    Presences of Nature: Words and Images of the Lake District, ed. Neil Hanson.
      Carlisle, Carlisle Museum and Art Gallery, 1982.
    Uncollected
'Why They Stopped Singing' (16 January 1957)
    The Poet, 15, 1957, ed. William Price Turner, Glasgow.
    Clare Market Review, Spring 1963
    Children of Albion: Poetry of the 'Underground' in Britain, ed. Michael
      Horovitz. London, Penguin Books, 1969.
    Looking Glass: an Anthology of Contemporary Poetry, ed. Eric Williams.
      London, Edward Arnold, 1973.
    Giovani Poeti Inglesi, Italy, Einaudi, 1976 (English text, and translation
      into Italian by Renato Oliva).
    Windows, 2, February 1977
    Contemporary British Poetry: Patterns from the 1950s to the Present Day,
      Francesco Dragosei, Milano, 1989.
    Collected: *CP68, P55–80, P55–87, DLD*
'The Lover' (20 January 1957)
    Migrant, 5, March 1960, ed. Gael Turnbull, Worcester.
    Uncollected
'Unravelling' (28 January 1957)
    Curtains, 1, 1971, ed. Paul Buck, Maidstone, Kent.
    Uncollected
'Linear' (29 January 1957)
    Combustion, 4, October–December 1957, ed. Raymond Souster, Toronto.
    Collected: *CP68, P55–80, P55–87*

'Silence' (30 January 1957)

    Combustion, 4

    Uncollected

'Toyland' (10 February 1957)

    City (Migrant Press edition only—*see* section A)

    Combustion, 4

    Children of Albion

    Looking Glass

    Widening Circles: Five Black Country Poets, ed. Edward Lowbury. Stafford, West Midland Arts, 1976.

    Englische Lyrik der Gegenwart: Gedichte ab 1945, ed. Michael Butler and Ilsabe Arnold-Dielewicz. Munich, C. H. Beck, 1981 (English text and translation into German by the editors).

    Contemporary British Poetry: Patterns from the 1950s to the Present Day

    The Hutchinson Book of Post-War British Poetry, ed. Dannie Abse. London, Hutchinson, 1989.

    The Harvill Book of Twentieth Century Poetry in English, ed. Michael Schmidt. London, Harvill Press, 1999.

    Collected: *CP68, P55–80, P55–87, DLD*

'Grotesque' (12 February 1957)

    Extra Verse, 7, Summer 1962, ed. Peter Williams, Birmingham (second half of poem only)

    Uncollected

'When the Time Comes' (12 February 1957)

    Extra Verse 7

    Uncollected

'Three Moments' (February 1957)

    Samphire, 12, May 1971, ed. Kemble Williams and Michael Butler.

    Uncollected

'Variations' (March 1957)

    Beat Dreams and Plymouth Sounds: an Anthology, ed. Alexis Lykiard. Devon, Plymouth Arts Centre, 1987.

    Uncollected

'Faces of Time' (April 1957)

    Combustion, 1959 ed. Raymond Souster, Toronto (second half of poem only).

    Uncollected

'The Intruder' (5 May 1957)

    Broadcast on 'Poetry Now', Third Programme, 23 August 1959.

New Orleans Review, 22:2, 1996, New Orleans, Loyola University.
 Collected: *CP68, P55–80, P55–87*
'A Debt for Tomorrow' (2 December 1957)
 Migrant, 5
 Collected: *P55–80, P55–87*

1958

'Sonnet' (28 August 1958)
 Migrant, 8, September 1960, ed. Gael Turnbull, Worcester (entitled
  'While the Young Hero . . .').
 Uncollected
'As the White Chalk Cliff' (9 September 1958)
 Combustion, August 1959, ed. Raymond Souster, Toronto.
 Uncollected
'The Estuary' (9 September 1958)
 Samphire, 12
 Uncollected

1959

'Then Hallucinations' (1959)
 Then Hallucinations (*see* section A)
 Kulchur, 2:6, Summer 1962, ed. Lita Hornick, New York (entitled 'Then
  Hallucinations (City II)').
 Collected: *The Cut Pages* (1971, Fulcrum Press edition only)
'Leaving July' (12 January 1959)
 Phoenix, 7, Spring 1962, ed. Harry Chambers, Liverpool.
 Collected: *P55–80, P55–87*
'Necessaries' (May 1959)
 Phoenix, 7
 Collected: *CP68, P55–80, P55–87*
'The Hospital in Winter' (7–8 June 1959)
 Migrant, 8, September 1960, ed. Gael Turnbull, Worcester.
 Yorkshire Post, 25 November 1961.
 The Bed Post: A Miscellany of the Yorkshire Post, ed. Kenneth Young.
  London, Macdonald, 1962.
 Children of Albion

British Poetry since 1945, ed. Edward Lucie-Smith. London, Penguin Books, 1970.

Looking Glass

Widening Circles

Poems of Warwickshire, ed. Roger Pringle. Kineton, Roundwood Press, 1980.

Contemporary British Poetry: Patterns from the 1950s to the Present Day

Palgrave's Golden Treasury: New Edition, ed. F.T. Palgrave, new section ed. John Press. Oxford, Oxford University Press, 1994.

Settling the Score: Twenty East Midlands Writers, ed. Ross Bradshaw, Loughborough, East Midlands Arts, 1999.

The Memorial Fountain (see section A)

Collected: *CP68, P55–80, P55–87, DLD*

'Anecdote' (8 July 1959)

Yorkshire Post, 10 February 1962.

Uncollected

'Five Morning Poems from a Picture by Manet' (9–27 August 1959)

Extra Verse, 8, Autumn 1962, ed. Peter Williams, Birmingham (poems II and IV only).

Stand, 11:1, 1969–70, ed. Jon Silkin, Newcastle upon Tyne.

Poetry of the Committed Individual: A Stand *Anthology of Poetry*, ed. Jon Silkin. London, Penguin Books, 1973.

Widening Circles (poems I, III and V only)

Raster, 4, 1977, Amsterdam, De Bezige Bij (translation into Dutch of poem I).

Collected: *M, P55–80, P55–87*

'Four Poems to the Memory of Wyndham Lewis' (31 August–3 September 1959)

Mica, 2, February 1961, ed. Helmut Bonheim, Santa Barbara, CA (poems II and IV only).

Collected: *P55–80, P55–87*

'The Check' (30 October 1959)

Migrant, 8

Uncollected

1960

'Night Walkers' (3 August 1960)

Living Arts, 1, 1963, ed. Theo Crosby and John Bodley (as part of *City*, though this poem was not included either in the Migrant *City* or the subsequent revised version).

Uncollected

'Script City' (20 August 1960)

Poetry and Audience, 9:7, 1961–62, ed. Norman Talbot, University of Leeds.

Uncollected

'The Judgement' (24 August 1960)

Collected: *City* (Migrant edition only—*see* section A)

'Something Unmade' (24 August 1960)

Poetry and Audience, 9:7

The Outsider, 1:3, Spring 1963, ed. John Edgar Webb, New Orleans.

Uncollected

'After Midnight' (26 August 1960)

Sixty-One, February 1962, ed. David Kerrison, Leeds.

Uncollected

'Morning Bus' (1 September 1960)

Mica, 2

Uncollected

'Complaint' (6 September 1960)

Mica, 2

Uncollected

'The Tidings' (7 September 1960)

Mica, 2

Extra Verse, 9, Winter 1963, ed. Peter Williams, Birmingham.

Uncollected

'The Bachelors Stripped Bare By Their Bride' (28 December 1960)

Curtains, 1

Uncollected

'Lost, Now' (31 December 1960)

Poetry and Audience, *c.* 1961, ed. Norman Talbot, University of Leeds.

Uncollected

City

Prose sections mainly 1959

'Lullaby and Exhortation for the Unwilling Hero' (3–13 August 1960)

Britische Lyrik der Gegenwart: Eine Zwei Sprachige Anthologie, ed. Iain Galbraith. Mainz, Joachim Hempel, 1984. English text and translation into German by Martha Peach.

'The Entertainment of War' (23 January 1957)

Ikon, 1:4, March 1966
Children of Albion
Echinox, 1973, Romania, Clug (translated into Romanian by Dimitri Coicoi-Pop).
The Faber Book of Modern Verse (4th ed.), ed. Michael Roberts, rev. Peter Porter. London, Faber & Faber, 1982.
The Penguin Book of Poetry from Britain and Ireland since 1945, ed. Simon Armitage and Robert Crawford. Harmondsworth, Penguin, 1998.
'North Area' (19 August 1960)
Widening Circles
'By the Pond' (2 June 1957)
The Firebox: Poetry from Britain and Ireland after 1945, ed. Sean O'Brien. London, Picador, 1998.
'The Sun Hacks' (1 September 1960)
Extra Verse, 8 (entitled 'The Valley Hacks')
Steaua, 1973, Romania, Clug (translated into Romanian by Dimitri Coicoi-Pop).
Poems of Warwickshire
'The Hill Behind the Town' (8 June 1959)
'The Poplars' (5 February 1957)
Combustion, 4
Migrant, 5
'Starting to Make a Tree' (28 December 1960)
Jazz Poems, ed. Anselm Hollo. Vista Books, 1963.
Poetmeat, 8, n.d. (*c.* 1965), ed. Dave Cunliffe and Tina Morris, Blackburn, Lancs.
Poetmeat, 13, Spring 1967, ed. Dave Cunliffe and Tina Morris, Blackburn, Lancs.
Children of Albion
Steaua, 1973 (translated into Romanian by Dimitri Coicoi-Pop).
Giovani Poeti Inglesi (English text and translation into Italian by Renato Oliva)
The Orchard Book of Poems, ed. Adrian Mitchell. London, Orchard Books, 1993.
'The Wind at Night' (10 January 1961)
Outposts, 49, Summer 1961, ed. Howard Sergeant, Dulwich Village.
Jazz Poems
Alembic, 4, Winter 1975–76, ed. Robert Hampson, London.
Widening Circles

Windows, 2 February 1977.
'The Park' (21 February 1961)
> *Widening Circles*
>
> *City* was printed in its entirety in *Living Arts* 1, with the variations noted above, and in *Twenty-Three Modern British Poets*, ed. John Matthias. Chicago, Swallow Press, 1971.
>
> Collected: *CP68, P55–80, P55–87, DLD*

1961

'Do Not Remain Too Much Alone' (1 January 1961)
> Collected: *City* (Migrant edition only—*see* section A)

'Division of Labour' (11 February 1961)
> Uncollected

'Chirico' (22 November 1961)
> *The Outsider*, 1:3
>
> Collected: *CP68, P55–80, P55–87*

1962

'Uncle Jim's Will' (6 October 1962)
> *Curtains* 1
>
> *Comedies* (*see* section A)
>
> *Consolidated Comedies* (*see* section A)
>
> Uncollected

The Ship's Orchestra (23 November 1962–1 October 1963)
> A section from *The Ship's Orchestra*, translated into French, was published in *Matieres d'Angleterre: Anthologie bilingue de la Nouvelle Poesie Anglaise*, ed. Paul Joris and Paul Buck, France, Les Trois Cailloux, 1984.
>
> Collected: in addition to the Fulcrum Press publication (*see* section A), *The Ship's Orchestra* is collected in *P55–80, P55–87, DLD*

'Interiors with Various Figures'
> 1   'Experimenting' (26 August 1962)
>
> *Living Arts*, 3, April 1964, ed. Theo Crosby and John Bodley.
>
> *Poetmeat*, 8
>
> *Children of Albion*
>
> *British Poetry since 1945*
>
> *Englische Lyrik der Gegenwart* (translated into German by the editors).

2   'The Small Room' (August 1963)

Living Arts, 3

3   'The Lampshade' (6–8 November 1963)

Borderlines: Contemporary Poems in English. Toronto, 1995.

4   'The Steam Crane' (25–27 November 1963)

Alembic, 4

Giovani Poeti Inglesi (English text, and translation into Italian by Renato Oliva).

5   'The Wrestler' (14 July 1964)

6   'The Foyer' (18 July 1964)

New Measure, 2, Winter 1966, ed. Peter Jay, Oxford.

The North, 22, 1998, ed. Peter Sansom and Janet Fisher, Huddersfield.

7   'The Wrong Time' (20 July 1964)

New Measure, 2

(Not included in *CP68*; published in *M* as 'Interior')

8   'Truants' (12 August 1965)

Arts in Society, October 1966, ed. Morgan Gibson.

Giovani Poeti Inglesi (English text, and translation into Italian by Renato Oliva).

9   'The Arrival' (13 October 1964)

Giovani Poeti Inglesi (English text, and translation into Italian by Renato Oliva).

10   'The Billiard Table' (24–25 October 1964)

Stand, 7:3, n.d. (*c*. 1965), ed. Jon Silkin, Newcastle upon Tyne.

Arts in Society

Widening Circles

Borderlines: Contemporary Poems in English

Interiors: Ten Interiors with Various Figures (*see* section A)

Collected: *CP68* (with the omission of no.7, 'The Wrong Time'), *P55–80, P55–87, DLD*

1964

'The Flight Orator' (February 1964)

Collected: *CP68* (limited edition only), *The Cut Pages* (1971, Fulcrum edition).

'As He Came Near Death' (5 July 1964)

Extra Verse, 24, Winter 1964–5, ed. D. M. Black, Edinburgh.

Young Commonwealth Poets' 65, ed. P. L. Brent. London, Heinemann, 1965.

The Faber Book of Modern Verse, 4th edn.

The Oxford Book of Death, ed. D. J. Enright. Oxford, Oxford University Press, 1983.

The Long Pale Corridor, eds. Judi Benson and Agneta Falk. Newcastle upon Tyne, Bloodaxe Books, 1996.

The North, 22

The Memorial Fountain (*see* section A)

The Harvill Book of Twentieth Century Poetry in English

Collected: *CP68, P55–80, P55–87, DLD*

'Big Girl' (15 July 1964)

Move, 1, December 1964, ed. Jim Burns, Preston, Lancs.

Uncollected

'Colour Supplement Pages' (21 July 1964)

Collected: *CP68, P55–80, P55–87*

'After Working' (22 July 1964)

Stand, 7:3

A Various Art, ed. Andrew Crozier and Tim Longville. Manchester, Carcanet Press, 1987.

Settling the Score: Twenty East Midlands Writers

The Memorial Fountain (*see* section A)

Collected: *CP68, P55–80, P55–87, DLD*

'How Heavily She Lies' (24 July 1964)

Move, 1 (entitled 'Interior 10', though not included in the sequence 'Interiors').

Uncollected

'Stopped Frames and Set Pieces' (July–August 1964)

Contemporary British Poetry: Patterns from the 1950s to the Present Day (contains a section from this work)

Collected: *The Cut Pages* (1971, Fulcrum Press), *P55–80, P55–87*

'Seven Attempted Moves' (21–22 November 1964)

Sum, 5, April 1965, guest editor Andrew Crozier, Buffalo, New York.

Cambridge Opinion, 41, October 1965.

Stand, 7:3

Poetry of the Committed Individual

Conference Booklet: Modern British Poetry Conference May–June 1974, ed. Christopher Brookeman, Polytechnic of Central London.

The Memorial Fountain (*see* section A)

Collected: *CP68, P55–80, P55–87, DLD*

1965

'The Thing about Joe Sullivan' (28–30 July 1965)
  Samphire, 13, September 1971, ed. Kemble Williams and Michael Butler.
  New Poems 1971–72: A PEN Anthology of Contemporary Poetry, ed. Peter
    Porter. London, Hutchinson, 1972.
  Antaeus, 12, Winter 1973, ed. Douglas Dunn.
  Imprint, 1, 1980, eds. Terry Boyce, Helene Li, Tony Frazer; Hong Kong.
  The Harvill Book of Twentieth Century Poetry
  Collected: *JS, P55–80, P55–87, DLD*
'For Realism' (21 June –1 August 1965)
  Stand, 8:1, 1966, ed. Jon Silkin, Newcastle upon Tyne.
  Poetry of the Committed Individual
  A Various Art
  Borderlines: Contemporary Poems in English
  The Memorial Fountain (*see* section A)
  The Firebox: Poetry from Britain and Ireland after 1945
  Collected: *CP68, P55–80, P55–87, DLD*
'Kingsbury Mill' (25 July 1965)
  Other Rooms, ed. Tamar Hodes. Keele, Keele University Press, 1994.
  The Memorial Fountain (*see* section A)
  Uncollected
'At No Distance' (2–3 August 1965)
  Collected: *CP68, P55–80, P55–87*
'The Memorial Fountain' (9–11 August 1965)
  Resuscitator, 6, February 1966, ed. John James and Nick Wayte, Bristol.
  Alembic, 4
  The Memorial Fountain (*see* section A)
  Collected: *CP68, P55–80, P55–87, DLD*
'Report on August' (12–13 August 1965)
  Resuscitator, 6
  Children of Albion
  Looking Glass
  Giovani Poeti Inglesi (English text, and translation into Italian by Renato
    Oliva).
  Artis, 9, December 1983, Athens, Greece (translation into Greek by
    John Stathatos).
  The Penguin Book of Poetry from Britain and Ireland since 1945
  Collected: *CP68, P55–80, P55–87*

'From an English Sensibility' (13–24 August 1965)
   Resuscitator, 6
   A Various Art
   Collected: *CP68, P55–80, P55–87, DLD*
'In Touch' (15 August 1965)
   Tlaloc, 9, series 2:3, 1965, ed. Cavan McCarthy, Leeds.
   Collected: *M, P55–80, P55–87, DLD*
'Studies'
  1 'Convalescent' (7 September 1965)
  2 'Civic Water' (7–8 September 1965)
   Resuscitator, 6
   Arts in Society ('Convalescent' only)
   Collected: *CP68* ('Convalescent' only), *M* ('Civic Water' only), *P55–80, P55–87*
'Quarry Hills' (22 September–1 October 1965)
   Resuscitator, 6 (entitled 'Rowley Hills')
   Collected: *M, P55–80, P55–87*

1966

'White Cloud, White Blossom' (16–23 January 1966)
   Collected: *M, P55–80, P55–87*
'Three Ceremonial Poems'
  1. (31 December 1965–16 January 1966)
  2. (21 April–11 August 1966)
  3. (8 September 1966)
   The Ceremonial Poems (*see* section A)
   Henry Dumolo's Needless Alley Rag, 1, 1969, ed. Andrew Tuffin and Stephanie Smolinsky, Birmingham (poem 1 only).
   Conference Booklet: Modern British Poetry Conference (poems 1 and 2 only)
   Collected: *CP68, P55–80, P55–87*
'Abraham Darby's Bridge' (August 1966–August 1970)
   New Poems 1971–72
   Widening Circles
   Other Rooms
   Sunflower Poems of Celebration, ed. Isabel Gillard, Stafford, Paris Books, 1999.
   Uncollected

1967

'Suppose—' (30 April–1 May 1967)
   Collected: *M, P55–80, P55–87*
'The Making of the Book' (20 May 1967)
   Poetry of the Committed Individual
   Englische Lyrik der Gegenwart (translated into German by the editors).
   Collected: *M, P55–80, P55–87, DLD*

1968

'Motion' (4 June 1968)
   Grosseteste Review, 1:2 Autumn 1968, ed. Tim Longville, Lincs.
   Uncollected
'Cultures' (radial poems) (2 July 1968 and April 1974)
   Cultures (*see* section B)
   The Atlantic Review, new ser., 2, Autumn 1979, ed. Robert Vas Dias,
      London. The cover design of this issue incorporates the text of
      'Cultures' no. 1.
   Uncollected
'Titles' (15 July 1968)
   Titles (*see* section A)
   Consolidated Comedies (plus two additions) (*see* section A)
   Uncollected
Translation of 'Winterreise' by Wilhelm Müller (September 1968–January
      1969)
   Winter Journey (Schubert), LP Nimbus 2131, released 1981. Shura
      Gehrman (vocal), Nina Walker (piano). This recording, and those of
      the translations made in 1969 (*see* below), contains textual alterations
      unauthorised by RF.
   Uncollected

1969

'Epic' (1969)
   Joe Soap's Canoe, 16, 1993, ed. Martin Stannard, Felixstowe.
   It Follows That (*see* section A)
   Collected: *DLD*

Translation of 'Schwanengesang' (texts by Heinrich Heine and Ludwig Rellstab) (February 1969)

The Man Who Steals the Flame (Schubert), CD Nimbus 5022, date of release unavailable. Shura Gehrman (vocal), Nina Walker (piano).

Uncollected

['The Double' (a translation of Heine's 'Der Doppelgänger') appeared in *Festival '81: An Anthology of Art in Britain since 1971*, ed. Joseph Allard and Michael Prochak, Colchester, Ampersand Press, 1981.]

Translation of 'Die Schöne Müllerin' (Wilhelm Müller) (8–16 September 1969)

Fair Maid of the Mill (Schubert), CD Nimbus 5023, date of release unavailable. Shura Gehrman (vocal), Nina Walker (piano).

Uncollected

'Continuity' (6 October 1969)

Stand, 11:1

Poetry of the Committed Individual

Collected: *M, P55–80, P55–87*

1970

'Glenthorne Poems' (1–7 January 1970)

Sad Traffic, 5, 1971, ed. Pete Ball, Roger Hutchinson, et al., Barnsley.

Widening Circles (poem 8 only)

Collected: *M, P55–80, P55–87*

'The Cut Pages' (9–21 January 1970)

Other: British and Irish Poets Since 1970, ed. Richard Caddel and Peter Quartermain. Middletown, Connecticut: Wesleyan University Press, 1999. Contains a section from 'The Cut Pages' ('He paints words...').

Collected: *The Cut Pages* (1971, Fulcrum edition), *The Cut Pages* (1986, Oasis/Shearsman edition).

'The Six Deliberate Acts' (24 January–2 February 1970)

Michigan Quarterly Review, 9:3, Summer 1970.

Collected: *M, P55–80, P55–87*

'Metamorphoses' (February 1970)

Metamorphoses (*see* section B)

The Cut Pages (1971, Fulcrum Press), *The Cut Pages* (1986, Oasis Books/ Shearsman Books) (*see* section A)

Collected: *P55–80, P55–87, DLD*

'Critics Can Bleed' (10 February 1970)
    Collected: *M, P55–80, P55–87*
'Matrix' (25–29 May 1970)
    Stand, 11:1, 1970–71, ed. Jon Silkin, Newcastle upon Tyne.
    Widening Circles (poem 10 only)
    Collected: *M, P55–80, P55–87*
'Correspondence' (16 July 1970)
    Collected: *M, P55–80, P55–87*
'Poem' (10 August 1970)
    Raster, 4 (translation into Dutch).
    Collected: *M, P55–80, P55–87, DLD*
'The Sky, the Sea' (23–26 August 1970)
    Collected: *M, P55–80, P55–87*

1971

'North Wind Harrying the North' (23 January 1971–22 February 1977)
    Palantir, 6, June 1977, ed. Jim Burns, Preston, Lancs.
    Consolidated Comedies (*see* section A)
    Uncollected
'Jim Burns Enters the Seventies' (8–9 April 1971)
    Consolidated Comedies (*see* section A)
    Uncollected
'From the *Town Guide*' (29 April 1971)
    Samphire, 12
    Conference Booklet: British Poetry, Polytechnic of Central London.
    Four Poems (*see* section A)
    Collected: *JS, P55–80, P55–87*
'The Least' (5 July 1971)
    Poetry Review, 62:3, Autumn 1971, ed. Eric Mottram, London.
    The Harvill Book of Twentieth Century Poetry
    Collected: *JS, P55–80, P55–87, DLD*
'Artists, Providers, Places to Go' (7 July 1971)
    Poetry Review, 62:3
    Echinox: 1973 (translated into Romanian by Dimitri Coicoi-Pop).
    Collected: *JS, P55–80, P55–87, DLD*
'The Sign' (8 July 1971)
    Poetry Review, 62:3
    Collected: *JS, P55–80, P55–87, DLD*

'Epitaph: for Lorine Niedecker' (5 August 1971)
   Epitaphs for Lorine, ed. Jonathan Williams. Champaign, IL, Monkeytree
      Press, Jargon Books, 1973.
   Collected: *JS, P55–80, P55–87, DLD*
'In Festival' (*c*. November 1971)
   Birmingham Post, 7, December 1971.
   Uncollected

1972

'Occasional Poem 7.1.72' (12 January 1972)
   A Tumult for John Berryman: A Homage to John Berryman, ed. Marguerite
      Harris. USA, Dryad Press, 1976.
   The Harvill Book of Twentieth Century Poetry in English
   Collected: *JS, P55–80, P55–87, DLD*
'Commuter' (12 January 1972)
   Widening Circles
   Four Poems (*see* section A)
   The Glasgow Herald, 19 February 1998
   Collected: *JS, P55–80, P55–87, DLD*
'One World' (12 January 1972)
   Steaua: 1973 (translated into Romanian by Dimitri Coicoi-Pop).
   Comedies (*see* section A)
   Consolidated Comedies (*see* section A)
   Uncollected
'Also' (31 January–9 February 1972)
   Also (*see* section B)
   Collected: *JS, P55–80, P55–87*
'Inscriptions for Bluebeard's Castle' (10–14 May 1972)
   Bluebeard's Castle (*see* section B)
   Grosseteste Review, 7:1–3, Summer 1974, ed. Tim Longville, Pensnett, Staffs.
   To Dentpo, 20, April 1981, Athens, Greece (translated into Greek by John
      Stathatos).
   Collected: *JS, P55–80, P55–87, DLD*
'107 Poems' (27–29 December 1972)
   Poetry Review, 64:1, Spring 1973, ed. Eric Mottram, London (entitled
      '107 Poems, State Four').
   A Various Art
   Collected: *JS, P55–80, P55–87, DLD*

1973

'On Reading Robert Duncan and Hearing Duke Ellington' (1973?)
   Other Rooms
   Uncollected
'A Grammar for Doctrine' (23 August 1973)
   Collected: *JS*, *P55–80*, *P55–87*
'The Tourists' Window' (23 August 1973)
   Meantime, 1, April 1977
   Uncollected
'Sets' (11 September 1973–5 January 1974)
   Grosseteste Review, 7:1–3
   Collected: *JS*, *P55–80*, *P55–87*, *DLD*

1974

'In the Black Country' (1 January 1974)
   Poetry Supplement compiled by Philip Larkin for the Poetry Book Society,
      Christmas 1974.
   Four Poems (*see* section A)
   Collected: *JS*, *P55–80*, *P55–87*
'Timelessness of Desire' (1–5 January 1974)
   Grosseteste Review, 7:1–3
   Festival Booklet, Malvern Poetry Festival, 26 March 1979.
   Collected: *JS*, *P55–80*, *P55–87*, *DLD*
'The Dream' (1–16 February 1974)
   Comedies (*see* section A)
   Consolidated Comedies (*see* section A)
   Uncollected
'At Once' (26 January–5 April 1974)
   Grosseteste Review, 7:1–3
   A Various Art
   Collected: *JS*, *P55–80*, *P55–87*
'In the Wall' (22 June–1 October 1974)
   Poetry Review, 65:2–3, 1975, ed. Eric Mottram, London (this contains 12
      lines deleted from the version printed in the collections below).
   Collected: *JS*, *P55–80*, *P55–87*
'Emblem' (31 July 1974)

Madeira and Toasts for Basil Bunting's Seventy-Fifth Birthday, ed. Jonathan Williams. Champaign, IL, Jargon Books, 1977.

The New British Poetry, ed. Gillian Allnutt, Fred D'Aguiar, Ken Edwards, Eric Mottram. London, Paladin, 1988.

Artis, 9 (translated into Greek by John Stathatos).

Collected: *JS, P55–80, P55–87, DLD*

'Corner' (26 August 1974)

Curiously Strong, 4:9–10, 1975, ed. Ian Patterson, London.

Artis, 9 (translated into Greek by John Stathatos).

Collected: *JS, P55–80, P55–87*

'On the Open Side' (26–27 August 1974)

Poetry Supplement Compiled by Philip Larkin

On the Open Side (see section B)

The New British Poetry

Thirty Years of the Poetry Book Society 1956–1986, ed. Jonathan Barker. London, Century Hutchinson, 1988.

Four Poems (see section A)

Collected: *JS, P55–80, P55–87*

'It is Writing' (26 August 1974)

Nineteen Poems and an Interview (see section A)

The Firebox: Poetry from Britain and Ireland after 1945

Collected: *JS, P55–80, P55–87, DLD*

'A Poem Not a Picture' (7–28 August 1974)

Poetry Review, 65:2–3

Gargoyle, 24, 1984, ed. Richard Peabody Jr., Washington, DC.

Collected: *JS, P55–80, P55–87, DLD*

1975

'Cut Worm' (12 January 1975)

Nineteen Poems and an Interview (see section A)

Collected: *JS, P55–80, P55–87, DLD*

'Dark on Dark' (7–19 January 1975)

Nineteen Poems and an Interview (see section A)

Dark on Dark (see section B)

Collected: *JS, P55–80, P55–87, DLD*

'The Only Image' (19 January 1975)

Nineteen Poems and an Interview (see section A)

Gargoyle, 24

Borderlines: Contemporary Poems in English

Collected: *JS, P55–80, P55–87, DLD*

'Dusk' (2–3 March 1975)

    Nineteen Poems and an Interview (*see* section A)

    Imprint, 1

    Artis, 9 (translated into Greek by John Stathatos).

    Collected: *JS, P55–80, P55–87, DLD*

'Mouth Talk' (19 March–6 July 1975)

    Nineteen Poems and an Interview (*see* section A)

    Collected: *JS, P55–80, P55–87*

'Wish' (7 April–6 July 1975)

    Nineteen Poems and an Interview (*see* section A)

    Collected: *JS, P55–80, P55–87*

'Handsworth Liberties' (6 May 1975–13 March 1978)

    Nineteen Poems and an Interview (*see* section A) (contains nine of the poems in this sequence, differently numbered than in the collections listed below).

    Windows, 2, February 1977 (poem no. 6)

    Raster, 4 (translation into Dutch of poem given as no. 27–no. 16 in the collections listed below).

    Conference Booklet: British Poetry, Polytechnic of Central London, June 1977 (poems given as nos. 5, 12, 14, 27–nos. 4, 7, 9, 16 in the collections listed below).

    Montemora, 4, 1978, ed. Eliot Weinburger, New York (contains seven of the poems in this sequence, differently numbered than in the collections listed below).

    Artis, 9 (poems 12 and 16 translated into Greek by John Stathatos).

    A Various Art (poems 8 and 13)

    Numbers, 2, Spring 1987, ed. John Alexander, Alison Rimmer, Peter Robinson, Clive Wilmer. Cambridge (poems 10 and 15).

    A State of Independence, ed. Tony Frazer. Devon, Stride Publications, 1998 (poems 1–16).

    Collected: *JS, P55–80, P55–87*

'Without Location' (15 June–6 July 1975)

    Nineteen Poems and an Interview (*see* section A)

    Collected: *JS, P55–80, P55–87*

'Some Loss' (24 June–7 July 1975)

    Nineteen Poems and an Interview (*see* section A)

A Various Art

Collected: *JS, P55–80, P55–87*

'The Poet's Message' (29 June–6 July 1975)

Nineteen Poems and an Interview (see section A)

Collected: *JS, P55–80, P55–87, DLD*

'Of the Empirical Self and for Me' (4 August–4 November 1975)

Poetry Wales, 12:1, Summer 1976, ed. J. P. Ward, Swansea.

Borderlines: Contemporary Poems in English

Contemporary British Poetry: Patterns from the 1950s to the Present Day

Collected: *JS, P55–80, P55–87, DLD*

'Barnardine's Reply' (16–22 November 1975)

Barnardine's Reply (see section A)

Poems for Shakespeare: A Selection, ed. Roger Pringle and Christopher Hampton. London, Globe House Publications, 1978.

Collected: *JS, P55–80, P55–87, DLD*

'Simple Location' (9–11 December 1975)

Meantime, 1

Matieres d'Angleterre: Anthologie bilingue de la Nouvelle Poesie Anglaise, ed. Pierre Joris and Paul Buck. France, Les Trois Cailloux, 1984 (English text, and translation into French).

Collected: *JS, P55–80, P55–87*

'If I Didn't' (11–14 December 1975)

Poetry Wales, 12:1

Poetry Dimension Annual 5, ed. Dannie Abse. London, Robson Books, 1978.

Collected: *JS, P55–80, P55–87, DLD*

'Paraphrases' (14–28 December 1975)

Stand, 19:1, 1977–78, ed. Jon Silkin, Newcastle upon Tyne.

The Penguin Book of Light Verse, ed. Gavin Ewart. London, Penguin Books, 1980.

The Hutchinson Book of Post-War British Poetry

Ord & Bild: Nordisk Kuturtidkrift Grundad 1892, 2, 1997, Göteborg, Denmark (translation into Danish by Gunnar D. Hansson).

Collected: *JS, P55–80, P55–87, DLD*

'Passing Newbridge-on-Wye' (21 December 1975–1 January 1976)

Meantime, 1

Collected: *JS, P55–80, P55–87*

1976

'Diversions' (19 July–August 1976)
  Poetry Book Supplement Compiled by Stuart Montgomery for the Poetry Book Society, Christmas 1976.
  Montemora, 3, Spring 1977, ed. Eliot Weinburger, New York.
  Englische Lyrik der Gegenwart (poem 18 translated into German by the editors).
  Collected: *JS, P55–80, P55–87, DLD*
'Rules and Ranges for Ian Tyson' (19–27 December 1976)
  Other: British and Irish Poets since 1970
  Collected: *JS, P55–80, P55–87*

1977

'Staffordshire Red' (15–21 February 1977)
  Stand, 19:1
  New Orleans Review, 22:2
  A State of Independence
  Collected: *JS, P55–80, P55–87*
'The Dirty Dozen' (22 February 1977)
  Palantir, 6
  Collected: *JS, P55–80, P55–87, DLD*
'Style' (22 February 1977)
  Palantir, 6
  Collected: *JS, P55–80, P55–87*
'Butterton Ford' (6 June 1977)
  Collected: *JS, P55–80, P55–87*
'Forward, the Light Brigade!' (11 September 1977)
  Comedies (*see* section A)
  Consolidated Comedies (*see* section A)
  Uncollected
'3rd November 76' (25 September 1977)
  Angels of Fire, 2, ed. Penelope Toff and Jeremy Silver. London, NoSuch Press, 1983.
  A Year in Poetry, ed. Foster and Guthrie, New York, 1995.
  Collected: *JS, P55–80, P55–87, DLD*
'Discovering the Form' (25 September 1977)
  Samphire, 13:1, Spring 1978, ed. Kemble Williams and Michael Butler.
  Collected: *JS, P55–80, P55–87*

'Stopping the Show' (27 September 1977)

    Night Ride and Sunrise, ed. Edward Lowbury. Aberystwyth, Celtion, 1978 (title misprinted as 'Stopping the Snow').

    Uncollected

'The Trace' (29 November–14 December 1977)

    Lettera, 15, February 1978, ed. John Freeman, Cardiff.

    Poetry in English Now, ed. John Freeman. Cardiff, Blackweir Press, undated (*c.* 1979).

    A Various Art

    Collected: *JS, P55–80, P55–87*

1978

'Five Pilgrims in the Prologue to the Canterbury Tales' (21 May 1978)

    Riders and Horses, ed. Ronald King. Guildford, Surrey, Circle Press, 1982.

    Collected: *P55–80, P55–87, DLD*

'Thank God We Don't Have To . . .' (22 August–22 October 1978)

    JW/50: A Fiftieth Birthday Celebration for Jonathan Williams, ed. Jonathan Greene. Frankfurt, Truck/Gnomon, 1979.

    Uncollected

'Pete Brown's Old Eggs Still Hatch' (22 October 1978)

    New Departures, 13, 1981 ed. Michael Horovitz, Stroud, Glos.

    Consolidated Comedies (*see* section A)

    Collected: *P55–87*

1979

'Releases' (29 May–14 June 1979)

    The Atlantic Review, new ser., 2, Autumn 1979, ed. Robert Das Vias, London.

    Collected: *P55–80, P55–87*

'Just Where to Draw the Line' (27 April 1979)

    The Atlantic Review, new ser., 2

    Consolidated Comedies (*see* section A)

    Collected: *BR*

'The Red and the Black' (18 April–2 May 1979)

    The Atlantic Review, new ser., 2

    Collected: *P55–80, P55–87*

'Wonders of Obligation' (10 July–13 August 1979)
  Wonders of Obligation (*see* section A)
  Rock Drill, 2, n.d. (*c.* 1981), ed. Penelope Bailey and Robert Sheppard, Southsea, Hants. (ll. 124–149).
  A Various Art
  The New British Poetry (ll. 157–279)
  Collected: *P55–80, P55–87, DLD*
'Roller' (23–24 August 1979)
  Roller (*see* section B)
'Rudiments' (9 December 1979)
  Lettera, 19, February 1980, ed. John Freeman, Cardiff (entitled 'My Father').
  Collected: *P55–87*
'The Open Poem and the Closed Poem' (9–12 December 1979)
  Lettera, 19
  Local Colour, Spring 1982, ed. Peter Higginson, Norwich.
  Collected: *P55–87*

1980

'The Supposed Dancer' (22 January 1980)
  Aggie Weston's, 17, Summer 1981, ed. Stuart Mills, London.
  The Harvill Book of Twentieth Century Poetry in English
  Collected: *P55–80, P55–87, DLD*
'Days of the Lyric' (22 January 1980)
  New Departures, 13
  Uncollected
'In the Earliest Stages' (8–24 February 1980)
  Megaphone, 1, Summer 1980, ed. John Ash, Paul Edwards, Richard McGann, Manchester.
  Uncollected
'Irreversible' (24 February 1980)
  Megaphone, 1
  Consolidated Comedies (*see* section A)
  Collected: *P55–87, DLD*
'The Home Pianist's Companion' (7 June 1980–5 August 1980)
  Palantir, 18, September 1981, ed. Jim Burns, Preston, Lancs.
  Arc, Summer/Fall 1984, ed. Christopher Levenson, Ontario.

Running Changes (*see* section A)
Collected: *P55–87, DLD*
'The Whale Knot' (4–5 August 1980)
Whales: A Celebration, ed. Greg Gatenby. Boston and Toronto, Little, Brown & Co., 1983.
Settling the Score: Twenty East Midlands Writers
Collected: *P55–87, DLD*

1981

'The Burning Graves at Netherton' (2 March 1981)
Moz-Art, October 1981, ed. Alan Mahar, Birmingham.
Poetry Review, 71:1, October 1981, ed. Roger Garfitt, London.
Arc, Summer/Fall 1984
Running Changes (*see* section A)
A State of Independence
Other: British and Irish Poets since 1970
Collected: *P55–87*
'Magritte Imitated Himself' (9 April 1981)
Poetry Supplement Compiled by Andrew Motion for the Poetry Book Society, Christmas 1981.
Collected: *P55–87*
'Provision' (14 September 1981)
Poetry Durham, 1, Summer 1982, ed. Michael O'Neill and Gareth Reeves, Durham (entitled 'At Cinderhill').
Collected: *P55–87*
'A Poem to be Watched' (14 September 1981)
Grosseteste Review, 14, ed. Tim Longville, Matlock, Derbyshire.
Arc, Summer/Fall 1984
Collected: *P55–87, DLD*
'A Modern Story' (28 September 1981)
West Midlands Arts News Report, April 1982
It Follows That (*see* section A)
Collected: *DLD*
'The Running Changes' (27 November 1981)
Presences of Nature: Words and Images of the Lake District
Arc, Summer/Fall 1984
Running Changes (*see* section A)
Collected: *P55–87*

1982

'New Diversions' (June 1982–February 1987)
>   *The Powys Review*, 14, 1984, ed. Belinda Humfrey, Lampeter, Dyfed (poem 19).
>   *Infolio*, 36, 19 August 1986, published by Tom Raworth, Cambridge (poems 15 and 21).
>   *From Diversions Second Series* (*see* section A) (this contains eight poems from the sequence).
>   Collected: *P55–87* (this contains passages originally published in *The Half-Year Letters*—*see* section B).

'Don't Ask' (31 July 1982)
>   *Poetry Supplement Compiled by Alan Brownjohn for the Poetry Book Society*, 1982.
>   *Running Changes* (*see* section A)
>   Collected: *P55–87*

'The Lesson in Composition' (18 December 1982)
>   *Credences*, new ser., 3:2, Spring 1985, ed. Robert J. Bertholf, Buffalo, NY.
>   Collected: *P55–87*

'The Passive Partner' (21 December 1982)
>   *Credences*, new ser., 3:2
>   Collected: *P55–87*

'Self-Portraits and Their Mirrors' (21–23 December 1982)
>   *Credences*, new ser., 3:2
>   Collected: *P55–87*

1983

A Furnace (30 March 1983–29 April 1985)
>   *Stand*, 26:3, Summer 1985, ed. Jon Silkin, Lorna Tracy and Michael Blackburn, Newcastle upon Tyne ('Introit').
>   *A Dog's Nose: Basil Bunting 1900–1985*, ed. Michael Farley. Leicester, Taxus Press, 1986 (section vi, 'The Many').
>   *Ninth Decade*, 6, 1986, ed. Tony Frazer, Ian Robinson and Robert Das Vias, London (section i, 'Calling').
>   *The Poetry Book Society Bulletin 128*, Spring 1986 (a passage from section ii, 'The Return').
>   *Aquarius*, 17/18, 1986–87, ed. Eddie Linden; guest editor this issue A.T. Tolley (a passage—here entitled 'Coleman Hawkins'—from section iv, 'The Core')
>   Collected: *F, DLD*

'Mystery Poems' (6 April 1983)
  Grosseteste Review, 15, 1983–84, ed. Tim Longville, Matlock, Derbyshire.
    Collected: *P55–87*.
'Stop' (– November 1983)
  The Poetry Book Society Anthology 3, ed. William Scammell, Hutchinson,
    London, 1992.
    Collected: *DLD*

1985

'They Come Home' (18–19 March 1985)
  Numbers, 5, Spring 1989, ed. John Alexander, Alison Rimmer, Peter
    Robinson, Clive Wilmer, Cambridge.
    Collected: *BR*
'The Elohim Creating Adam' (27 May 1985)
  With a Poet's Eye: A Tate Gallery Anthology, ed. Pat Adams. London, The
    Tate Gallery, 1986 (entitled 'The Elohim').
    Collected: *P55–87*
'News for the Ear' (2 June 1985)
  Conjunctions, 8, 1985, ed. Bradford Morrow.
    Collected: *P55–87, DLD*
'The Left-Handed Punch' (2 June 1985)
  The Left-Handed Punch (*see* section B)
'The Nation' (30 July 1985)
  Bull, 1, 1985, ed. Keith Lindsay, Birmingham (entitled 'The National
    Poem' and arranged as prose)
    Collected: *P55–87, DLD*
'On the Neglect of Figure Composition: A Prelude and an Exhibition'
    (30 July–22 September 1985)
  Poetry Review, 76:1–2, June 1986, ed. Mick Imlah, London.
    Collected: *P55–87, DLD*
'The Toy' (14–20 September 1985)
    Collected: *P55–87*

1987

'A Sign Illuminated' (18 January 1987–27 March 1988)
  First and Always: Poems for Great Ormond Street Children's Hospital, ed.
    Lawrence Sail. London, Faber & Faber, 1988.

The Hutchinson Book of Post-War British Poetry
Emergency Kit: Poems for Strange Times, ed. Jo Shapcott and Matthew
    Sweeney. London, Faber & Faber, 1996.
Collected: *BR*
'Near Garmsley Camp' (19 January 1987)
    Near Garmsley Camp (*see* section A)
    A State of Independence
    Collected: *P55–87*.
'Three Stone Lintels at Eleven Steps' (30 July–2 August 1987)
    Collected: *BR*

1988

'English 88' (15 March 1988)
    High on the Walls: A Morden Tower Anthology, ed. Gordon Brown.
        Newcastle upon Tyne, Morden Tower/Bloodaxe Books, 1990.
    Collected: *BR*
'Going' (26 March 1988)
    The Poetry Book Society Anthology 1989–90, ed. Christopher Reid. London,
        Hutchinson, 1989.
    Collected: *BR*

1989

'The Ticket-of-Leave Man' (24 February 1989)
    Catgut and Blossom—Jonathan Williams in England. London, Coracle Press,
        1989.
    Collected: *BR*
'Freelance' (27 March 1989)
    Bête Noire, 8/9, Autumn 1989/Spring 1990, ed. John Osborne, Hull.
    Collected: *BR*
'Hypnopaedia' (27 March 1989)
    The Poetry Book Society Anthology, 1989–90
    The Forward Book of Poetry. London, Forward Press, 1995.
    Collected: *BR*
'Our Own' (11 May 1989)
    One for Jimmy, ed. Matthew Sweeney, Hereford and Worcester, 1992.
    Collected: *BR*

'Top Down, Bottom Up' (15–19 May 1989)
  Top Down, Bottom Up (*see* section B)
  Collected: *BR*
'The Solution: After Brecht' (8 November 1989)
  Bête Noire, 8/9
  Other Rooms
  Uncollected

1990

'The Sidings at Drebkau' (4 January 1990)
  Bête Noire, 8/9
  Collected: *BR*
'The Collection of Things' (7–8 January 1990)
  Bête Noire, 8/9
  Valentina Polukhina, *Brodsky through the Eyes of his Contemporaries*. New
    York, St Martin's Press, 1992.
  Zrezda, 1, St Petersburg 1997, (translated into Russian by Viktor Kulle).
  Collected: *BR*
'Homage to Edwin Morgan' (7–8 March 1990)
  Felt-Tipped Hosannas. Glasgow, Third Eye Press, 1990.
  Collected: *BR*
'The Poetry of Place' (29 March 1990)
  The Poetry Book Society Anthology, 1, ed. Fraser Steel. London, Hutchinson,
    1990.
  Collected: *BR*
'The Host' (15 May 1989–29 March 1990)
  The Poetry Book Society Anthology, 1
  Collected: *BR*
'Every Man His Own Eyebright' (1 April 1990)
  New American Writing, 8/9, Fall 1991, ed. Maxine Chernoff and Paul
    Hoover, Chicago, IL ('26 New British Poets' section, ed. Richard
    Caddel).
  Collected: *BR*
'The Mark' (18 September–5 December 1990)
  New American Writing, 8/9
  Collected: *BR*

1991

'Hollywood Legend' (8–10 January 1991)
New American Writing, 8/9
Uncollected
'Upright' (10–11 January 1991)
New American Writing, 8/9 (entitled 'Upright Drawing')
Collected: BR
'According to Clocks' (13–20 January 1991)
New American Writing, 8/9
Peacock Blue, ed. Nicholas Johnson. Newcastle under Lyme, Heron Press, 1994 (revised and retitled 'The Time, Saturday').
Other Rooms (entitled 'The Time, Saturday').
News for the Ear: A Homage to Roy Fisher, ed. Peter Robinson and Robert Sheppard. Exeter, Stride Publications, 2000 (entitled 'The Time, Saturday').
Uncollected
'Six Texts for a Film' (23 March–10 May 1991)
Oasis, 50, November 1991, ed. Ian Robinson, London ('The Repair Shop').
PN Review, 83 (18:3), January/February 1992, ed. Michael Schmidt, Manchester ('Birmingham River', 'Abstracted Water').
Stand, 33:2, Spring 1992, ed. Jon Silkin, Newcastle upon Tyne ('Talking to Cameras').
New Writing 2, ed. Malcolm Bradbury and Andrew Motion. London, Minerva, 1993 ('Town World').
Collected: BR
'Six Texts for a Film' is read by Roy Fisher in Birmingham is What I Think With, a film on Roy Fisher and his work, directed by Tom Pickard and distributed by Arts Council Films (1991).
'Anansi Company' (7–24 August 1991)
Other Rooms
Anansi Company (see section B)
Collected: BR
'Promenade on Down' (14–22 September 1991)
PN Review, 83
Collected: BR
'The House on the Border' (11–13 October 1991)
Oasis, 50
Collected: BR

1992

'Poem Beginning with a Line by Josephine Clare' (2 February–7 April 1992)
  Joe Soap's Canoe, 16, 1993
    Collected: *BR* (revised version)
'Photographers' Flowers' (22–23 March 1992)
    The Poetry Book Society Anthology, 3, ed. William Scammell. London, Hutchinson, 1992.
    Collected: *BR*
'Stop' (28 March 1992)
    The Poetry Book Society Anthology, 3
    It Follows That (*see* section A)
    Collected: *DLD*
'For Ian Tyson at 60' (July 1992)
    It Follows That (*see* section A)
    Uncollected
'The Mouth of Shade' (26 October 1992–18 January 1993)
    Shearsman, 14, 1993, ed. Tony Frazer, Plymouth.
    Collected: *BR*
'A Working Devil for the Birthday of Coleman Hawkins' (21 November 1992)
    Collected: *BR*
'Day In, Day Out' (30 November 1992–18 January 1993)
    Shearsman, 14
    Collected: *BR*

1993

'A Song' (11–15 January 1993)
    Collected: *BR*
'In the Visitors' Book' (11–15 January 1993)
    What Poets Eat, ed. Judi Benson. London, Foolscap, 1994.
    Collected: *BR*
'Witness' (1993)
    What Poets Eat
    Uncollected
'Bing-Bong Ladies from Tongue Lane' (May 1993)
    It Follows That (*see* section A)
    Uncollected

'Envoi' (August 1993)
  The Rialto, Summer 1993, ed. John Wakeman, Rhiannon Wakeman and
    Michael Mackmin, Norwich.
  Collected: *BR*
'Hand-me-Downs' (August 1993)
  Klaonica: Poems for Bosnia, ed. Ken Smith and Judi Benson. Newcastle
    upon Tyne, Bloodaxe Books, 1993.
  The Independent (no. 3482), Monday, 24 November 1997.
  Other Rooms
  Collected: *DLD*
'It Follows That' (30 November 1993–15 January 1994)
  Settling the Score: Twenty East Midlands Writers (poem 12 only)
    It Follows That (*see* section A)
  Collected: *DLD*

1994

'The Pitch' (15 January 1994)
  Other Rooms
  Uncollected
'Flyposter' (19 March 1994)
  Other Rooms
  Uncollected
'The Dow Low Drop', 1–5 (25–29 March 1994)
  Sharp Study and Long Toil (Durham University Journal Special Supplement), ed.
    Richard Caddel, University of Durham, 1995.
  Collected: *DLD*
'When I'm Sixty-Four' (10 June 1994)
  Alive in Parts of this Century: Eric Mottram at Seventy, ed. Peterjon
    and Yasmin Skelt. Twickenham and Wakefield, North and South,
    1994.
  Uncollected
  'And on that Note: Jazz Elegies' (4 October 1994–25 March 1999)
    New Poetry for the New Century, ed. Don Patterson and Jo Shapcott,
    London, Picador, 1999.
  Uncollected

1995

'The Slink' (25–27 June 1994)
> *Angel Exhaust*, 12 Autumn 1995, ed. Andrew Duncan, Cambridge.
> Collected: *DLD*

1996

'On Not' (15–20 March 1996)
> *A Journey*, Svava Barker, Deirdre Cameron, *et al.* (The Word Hoard Writers). Huddersfield, West Yorkshire, Spout Publications, 1997.
> Uncollected

'Last Poems' (27 May 1996)
> *CCCP 8*, Programme and Anthology of the Eighth Cambridge Conference of Contemporary Poetry, 24–26 April 1998.
> *News for the Ear: A Homage to Roy Fisher*
> Uncollected

'Item' (27–29 May 1996)
> *New Writing*, 6, ed. A. S. Byatt and Peter Porter. London, Vintage, 1997.
> *News for the Ear: A Homage to Roy Fisher*
> Uncollected

'At the Grave of Asa Benveniste' (11 August 1996)
> *Poetry Review*, 86:3, Autumn 1996, ed. Peter Forbes, London.
> *News for the Ear: A Homage to Roy Fisher*
> Uncollected

1997

'Four Songs from the Camel's Coffin' (24 August–12 September 1997)
> *A Gathering for Gael Turnbull*, ed. Peter McCarey. Glasgow, Au Quai, 1998.
> Uncollected

1998

'The Fisher Syndrome Explained, with How to Stay Succumbed' (29 July 1998)
> *Sneak's Noise: Poems for R. F. Langley*, ed. Peter Riley. Cambridge, Infernal Histories, 1998.
> Uncollected

1999

'Processional: For Lee' (22 March 1999)
  Birthday Boy: A Present for Lee Harwood, ed. Patricia Farrell and Robert
    Sheppard. Liverpool, Ship of Fools, 1999.
  Uncollected

D. Interviews with Roy Fisher

Sad Traffic, 5, Barnsley, 1971, pp. 31–34. 'A Tuning Phenomenon: An
    Interview with Roy Fisher'. [The interviewer is not identified.]

Nineteen Poems and an Interview, Pensnett, Staffs., Grosseteste Press, June
    1975, pp. 12–38. Jed Rasula and Mike Erwin, 'An Interview with
    Roy Fisher'. The interview is dated 19 November 1973.

Saturday Morning, 1, London, Spring 1976, unpaginated. 'Conversation with
    Roy Fisher'. Transcript of a conversation between RF and Eric
    Mottram, 22 January 1973.

Granta, 76, Cambridge, June 1977, pp. 17–19. 'Roy Fisher Talks to Peter
    Robinson'.

Hack, 1, Madeley College of Education, Crewe, 1980, pp. 16–34. John
    Gallas, 'Interview with Roy Fisher'. The interview took place in
    November 1980.

Gargoyle, 24, Washington DC, 1984, pp. 75–96. Robert Sheppard, 'Turning
    the Prism: Interview with Roy Fisher'. The interview took place on
    7 June 1982.

Arts Report: The Arts Newspaper of the West Midlands, 53, June 1986, p. 10.
    David Hart, 'And then back to Sparkbrook'.

Robert Sheppard, *Turning the Prism: An Interview with Roy Fisher*, London,
    Toads Damp Press, January 1986, pp. 5-26. A reprint, in booklet
    form, of the interview published in *Gargoyle*, 24 (*see above*).

'Interview: Roy Fisher by Helen Dennis', University of Warwick, 1987.
    Transcript of a conversation that took place on 9 May 1984.

'John Tranter Interviews Roy Fisher'. Published in two parts on the
    Internet by *Jacket* magazine, at http://www.jacket.zip.com.au./
    jacket01/fisheriv.html. The interview took place on 29 March 1989.

Disclaimer, 2, Keele University (no date, but published early 1990),
    unpaginated. Jonathan Roper, 'An Interview with Roy Fisher'. The
    interview took place on 27 September 1989.

Staple, 18, Mickleover, Derbyshire, Summer 1990, pp. 41-46. Donald Measham and Bob Windsor, 'Talking to *Staple*: Roy Fisher'. The interview took place on 5 April 1990.

Valentina Polukhina, *Brodsky Through the Eyes of his Contemporaries*. St Martin's Press, 1992, pp. 292–307. This contains 'A Noble Quixotic Sight', an interview with RF by Valentina Polukhina about Joseph Brodsky. The material was reprinted, translated into Russian, in *Zrezda*, 1, St Petersburg, 1997.

Prop, 2, Bolton, Lancs., 1997, pp. 28-30. Ra Page, 'People Who Can't Float'.

Poetry News: The Newsletter of the Poetry Society, London, Spring 1998, pp. 8–9. Siân Hughes, 'The Cost of Letters'.

Interviews Through Time, and Selected Prose, ed. Tony Frazer. Kentisbeare, Devon, Shearsman Books, 2000. This contains selections from the interviews by Mottram, Robinson, Tranter, Rasula and Erwin and Sheppard listed above, together with a new interview with Peter Robinson, entitled ' "They Are All Gone Into the World": Roy Fisher in Conversation with Peter Robinson'. This interview was conducted *via* e-mail from April to June 1998.

News for the Ear: A Homage to Roy Fisher, ed. Peter Robinson and Robert Sheppard. Exeter, Stride Publications, 2000. This contains ' "Come to Think of It, the Imagination": Roy Fisher in Conversation with John Kerrigan'. The interview was conducted *via* e-mail between 24 September 1998 and 20 February 1999.

E. Critical and other Prose by Roy Fisher

Mermaid, 18:1, Birmingham, October 1951, pp.1–2. Editorial.

Tlaloc, 13, n.d. (*c.* 1966), Leeds, unpaginated. Review of *Twenty Words: Twenty Days* by Gael Turnbull.

'Style and Narrative Viewpoint in the Later Novels of Norman Mailer', MA thesis, University of Birmingham, 1970.

The Cut Pages; London, Fulcrum Press, 1971, pp. 6–7. 'Note'.

Language and Style, 6:2, 1973. 'The Mind of Marion Faye: Stylistic Aspects of Norman Mailer's *The Deer Park*'.

Vole, 4, 1977, ed. Richard Boston, pp. 38–39. 'Brum Born'.

Journal of American Studies, 12:2, August 1978, pp. 254-56. Review of *An Autobiographical Novel* by Kenneth Rexroth.

Poetry Book Society Bulletin, 99, Christmas 1978, unpaginated. 'Roy Fisher writes . . .' (brief commentary on *JS*).

Journal of American Studies, 14:2, August 1980, pp. 325–26. Review of *Robert Creeley's Poetry: A Critical Introduction* by Cynthia Dubin Edelberg.

Powys Review, 11, Lampeter, Dyfed, 1982/83, pp. 86–87. Review of *Englishman's Road* by Jeremy Hooker.

Stand, 25:1, Newcastle upon Tyne, Winter 1983–84, pp. 51–3. Review of *Dada and After* by Alan Young.

The Beau, 3, Dublin, 1983/1984, pp. 6–10. Three extracts from *Talks for Words* (*see* section A).

1985 Prizewinners, Poetry Society, London, 1985. Includes an account by RF of his experience of judging (with Tom Paulin and Carol Rumens) the 1985 Poetry Competition.

A Birmingham Dialogue, Birmingham, Protean Pubs, 1986. By Paul Lester and Roy Fisher. This pamphlet contains 'The Poetry of Roy Fisher' (pp. 5–20), an undergraduate dissertation by Paul Lester written in 1974, and 'Reply to Paul Lester by Roy Fisher' (pp. 21–9) written in 1985.

The Cut Pages, London, Oasis Books/Shearsman Books, 1986. Prefatory note (unpaginated).

A Furnace, Oxford, Oxford University Press, 1986, pp. vii–viii. 'Preface'.

Numbers, 2, Cambridge, Spring 1987, pp. 24–8. 'Handsworth Compulsions'.

Beat Dreams and Plymouth Sounds: An Anthology, ed. Alexis Lykiard. Devon, Plymouth Arts Centre, 1987, unpaginated. 'Note on Variations'.

The Independent (no. 520), Friday, 10 June 1988. 'The Power of Speech'.

The Jazz Rag, 10 September 1989, p. 21. Review of *Beat Goes Poetry*, a recording of the Cellar Jazz Quintet with readings by Kenneth Rexroth and Lawrence Ferlinghetti.

Contemporary Authors (Autobiography Series), 10, Detroit, New York, Fort Lauderdale, London, Gale Research Inc., 1989, pp. 79–100.

Spleen (2nd edn) by Nicholas Moore; London, Menard Press, 1990, pp. 8–10. Foreword.

High on the Walls: A Morden Tower Anthology, ed. Gordon Brown. Newcastle upon Tyne, Morden Tower/Bloodaxe Books, 1990, p. 57. Note on reading at Morden Tower.

Poets on Writing: Britain, 1970–1991, ed. Denise Riley. London, Macmillan, 1992, pp. 272–75. Chapter 35, 'Poet on Writing'.

The Jazz Anthology, ed. Miles Kington. London, Harper and Collins, 1992, pp. 29–32, 48–9, 105–09, 210–11. Contains five sections from 'Remembrance of Gigs Past' (*see* section F). Date of broadcasts wrongly given as 1970; correct year 1988.

What Poets Eat, ed. Judi Benson. London, Foolscap, 1994, p. 23. 'The Heavy Spinach Soup' (recipe).

Brief comment on back jacket of *Secret Files*, collection of poems by Eleanor Cooke, published in 1994 by Jonathan Cape.

Sons of Ezra: British Poets and Ezra Pound, ed. Michael Alexander and James McGonigal. Amsterdam, Rodopi, 1995, pp. 41–42.

Contemporary Poets (6th edn), ed. Thomas Riggs. Detroit, St James Press, 1996, p. 345. Commentary on his procedure as a poet.

The Rialto, 35, Autumn 1996, Norwich, pp. 30-32. 'Roy Fisher Reviews Roy Fisher' (review by RF of *DLD*). This was also published in the Bloodaxe 1997 catalogue (pp. 34–35).

Stand, 38:2, Newcastle upon Tyne, Spring 1997, pp. 44–46. Review of *Collected Poems and Translations* by A. C. Jacobs.

Brief comment on flyer for *The London*, poem by David Rees, published 1997 by West House Books and Gratton Street Irregulars (reproduced on back cover of the poem).

Poets on Poets, ed. Nick Rennison and Michael Schmidt. Manchester, Carcanet Press, 1997. Brief essay on the work of Thomas Campion, p. 60, and a selection of Campion's poetry, pp. 61–62.

When Suzy Was, Kelvin Corcoran. Kentisbeare, Devon, Shearsman Books, 1999. Afterword.

Interviews Through Time, and Selected Prose, ed. Tony Frazer. Kentisbeare, Devon, Shearsman Books, 2000. The prose pieces included in this book are the autobiographical essay published in *Contemporary Authors*, five of the *Talks for Words* (number four is excluded), and the self-review published in *The Rialto*.

News for the Ear: A Homage to Roy Fisher, ed. Peter Robinson and Robert Sheppard, Exeter, Stride Publications, 2000. 'Licence my Roving Hands', a revised version of 'Remembrance of Gigs Past' (*see* section F).

F. Radio broadcasts and recorded readings

1   Radio broadcasts

Signature, Western Region Service, 13 July 1955. 'The Moral' and 'La Magdalena', read by actors.

New Poetry, Third Programme, 23 August 1959. RF read 'The Intruder'.

Midland Poets, Midland Region Service, 30 March 1960. 'The Entertainment of War', read by an actor.

Midland Poets, Midland Region Service, 6 November 1960. 'Necessaries', read by an actor.

Midland Poets, Midland Region Service, 24 November 1961. 'The Tidings', read by an actor.

Poetry Now, Third Programme, 14 March 1967. RF read from *The Ship's Orchestra*.

New Worlds, Radio Four, 17 November 1967. RF interviewed by Derek Parker.

The Arts This Week, Third Programme, 17 December 1969. George Melly read 'The Wrestler'.

Poetry Now, Radio Three, 8 June 1970. RF read and discussed work from *The Cut Pages*.

The Poet Speaks, Radio Three, 20 February 1973. RF read 'The Least', 'From the Town Guide', 'Occasional Poem 7.1.72', 'The Sign', 'Artists, Providers, Places to Go', 'The Thing about Joe Sullivan', 'A Debt for Tomorrow', 'One World', 'Abraham Darby's Bridge', 'As the White Chalk Cliff'.

Poetry Cambridge, Radio Three, 5 May 1975. RF contributed.

Poetry Cambridge, Radio Three, 21 April 1977. RF contributed.

Poetry Now, Radio Three, 29 July 1977. RF read 'Staffordshire Red'.

A Word in Edgeways, Radio Four, 27 November 1977. Contribution by RF to unscripted conversation; other contributors were Brian Redhead, Stanley Ellis and Bernice Rubens.

Words, Radio Three. A series of six talks by RF, broadcast on 27 November, 4, 11, 18, 25 December 1977 and 1 January 1978. The talks were published as *Talks for Words* (*see* section A).

Poetry Cambridge, Radio Three, 17 August 1979. RF read from *City*.

Sounding Off, Radio Four, 8 September 1979. Talk by RF: 'Whenever You Hear a Piano Played in a Club or Pub, Complain Instantly to the Management'.

One Pair of Ears, Radio Three, 4 January 1980. Talk by RF.

Kaleidoscope, Radio Four, 21 February 1980. Review by RF of *Duet for One* by Tom Kempinski with Dizzy Gillespie, and *Dizzy*, autobiography of Dizzy Gillespie.

A Word in Edgeways, Radio Four, 20 September 1980. Contribution by RF to unscripted conversation; other contributors were Brian Redhead, Angela Carter and Chris Bonnington.

Poetry Now, Radio Three, 2 January 1981. RF read 'The Whale Knot'.

Poetry Now, Radio Three, 1 May 1981. RF read 'The Burning Graves at Netherton'.

All That Jazz, Radio Four, 24 October 1981. Talk by RF on the career of Earl Hines.

The Living Poet, Radio Three, 20 November 1981. RF read 'Seven Attempted Moves', 'The Memorial Fountain', 'Irreversible', 'The Home Pianist's Companion', 'Poem', 'Handsworth Liberties' poems 11 and 15.

Take the Money and Run, Radio Four, 29 July 1982. Talk by RF.

Just after Four, Radio Four, 1 March 1983. Talk by RF on 'Handsworth Liberties'.

Just after Four, Radio Four, 14 February 1984. Talk by RF, 'The Anxiety of Influence'.

Just after Four, Radio Four, 15 February 1984. Talk by RF, 'Recollections of the Gas Buggy'.

Just after Four, Radio Four, 16 February 1984. Talk by RF, 'Portrait of the Artist as a Young Man'.

Just after Four, Radio Four, 17 February 1984. Talk by RF, 'Slimy Things with Legs'.

Faces, Radio Four, 9 February 1985. Feature, compiled and presented by RF.

A Word in Edgeways, Radio Four, 5 May 1985. Contribution by RF to unscripted conversation; other contributors were Brian Redhead, Rabbi Lionel Blue and Gillian Tindall.

Poetry 85, Radio Three, 12 December 1985. RF contributed as one of the judges of the 1985 National Poetry Awards.

New Premises, Radio Three, 1 June 1986. RF contributed to discussion on contemporary arts.

Poetry Now, Radio Three, 11 July 1988. RF read 'A Sign Illuminated'.

Remembrance of Gigs Past, Radio Four, 7 August 1988. Talk by RF, 'The Lure of the Function Room'.

Remembrance of Gigs Past, Radio Four, 14 August 1988. Talk by RF, 'The Thing about Bass Players'.

Remembrance of Gigs Past, Radio Four, 21 August 1988. Talk by RF, 'Early Retirement'.

Remembrance of Gigs Past, Radio Four, 28 August 1988. Talk by RF, 'The Leader of the Band'.

Remembrance of Gigs Past, Radio Four, 4 September 1988. Talk by RF, 'De Profundis: The View from the Crevasse Club'. A revised version of *Remembrance of Gigs Past* is published as 'Licence my Roving Hands' in *News for the Ear: A Homage to Roy Fisher*, ed. Peter Robinson and Robert Sheppard (*see* section G).

Time for Verse, Radio Four, 14 March 1990. RF read 'The Entertainment of War', 'As He Came Near Death', 'The Memorial Fountain'.

Time for Verse, Radio Four, 21 March 1990. RF read 'Quarry Hills', 'The Only Image', 'Dusk', 'The Poet's Message', 'In the Black Country', 'It is Writing'.

Time for Verse, Radio Four, 28 March 1990. RF read 'The Thing About Joe Sullivan', first two sections of *The Ship's Orchestra*, 'Core' (from *F*).

Time for Verse, Radio Four, 4 April 1990. RF read 'Passing Newbridge-on-Wye', 'Diversions' poem 16, 'Staffordshire Red', 'Discovering the Form', 'The Passive Partner', 'In Touch'.

Time for Verse, Radio Four, 11 April 1990. RF read 'The Nation', 'English 88', 'Our Own', 'Top Down, Bottom Up', 'Near Garmsley Camp', 'Hypnopaedia'.

The Fortunate Cat, Radio Three. A series of five conversations between RF and Mel Hill on the relationship between jazz and poetry in RF's work, broadcast 25–29 December 1995. These programmes were repeated on Radio Three, 2–6 September 1996.

Fine Lines, Radio Four, 26 July 1998. A conversation, chaired by Christopher Cook, between RF and Linda France. RF read 'The Making of the Book', 'Of the Empirical Self and for Me', 'The Slink'. This programme was repeated on Radio Four, 9 January 1999.

Music You Can't Forget, Radio Cuillin, Portree, Isle of Skye, September 1998. 'Why They Stopped Singing', read by the presenter.

(2) Recorded readings

City: Poetry and Prose by Roy Fisher read by the Author. A long-playing record, AMBER 7102, produced by Nimbus Records, Monmouth, 1977. RF reads the whole of *City*.

Roy Fisher: Readings at Coracle Press no. 4. A cassette, produced by Audio Arts,

London, 1982. It is a recording of a reading given by RF on 4 December 1981. Contains 'A Modern Story', 'The Home Pianist's Companion', 'Magritte Imitated Himself', 'Handsworth Liberties' poems 1–16, 'Pete Brown's Old Eggs Still Hatch', 'Jim Burns Entering the Seventies', 'Titles', 'North Wind Harrying the North', 'Irreversible', 'Wonders of Obligation', 'The Trace', 'Let the Flute be Silenced' (listed thus on cassette sleeve: collected as 'Chirico'), 'The Intruder'.

City Poems. A cassette published by the Department of English, University of Keele, Staffs. The reading was recorded at the University of Keele on 6 January 1988. Contains 'After Working'; three prose-paragraphs from *City*; 'In the places...' (from *F*, section I); '12 November 1958' (from *F*, 'Introit'); a passage from 'Wonders of Obligation'; 'The Hospital in Winter'; 'For Realism'; 'In the Black Country'; 'The Memorial Fountain'; 'Once invented...' (from *F*, section III); 'The Burning Graves at Netherton'; 'Mansions of prosperity...' (from *F*, section v); 'Handsworth Liberties' poem 15; 'The Sun Hacks'; 'In an afternoon...', 'The Park', 'The City asleep...', 'I come quite often now upon a sort of ecstasy...' (all from *City*); 'Late at night...' (from *F*, section I); 'Lullaby and Exhortation for the Unwilling Hero' (from *City*); 'If only the night...' (from *F*, section III); 'This age...' (from *F*, section v).

G. On Roy Fisher

Kulchur, 2:6, Summer 1962, pp. 3–9. Denise Levertov, 'An English Event': review of *City*.

Kulchur, 2:7, Autumn 1962, pp. 23–29. Gael Turnbull, 'Some Resonances and Speculations on Reading Roy Fisher's *City*'.

Ambit, 27, 1966, pp. 40–42. Jim Burns, 'Retrospect 16: *Migrant*', an essay on *Migrant* magazine containing references to, and quotation from, RF.

The Spectator, 219:7270, 27 October 1967, pp. 502–03. John Horder, 'Physical Responses', review of *The Ship's Orchestra*.

Tarasque, 3, n.d. (*c.* 1968), unpaginated. Stuart Mills, 'Hors d'Oeuvres'.

Grosseteste Review, 1:2, Autumn 1968, pp. 14–16. Gael Turnbull, 'Notes on *The Ship's Orchestra*'.

Times Literary Supplement, 3517, 24 July 1969, p. 828. 'Midland Fantasy', unsigned review of *CP68*.

London Magazine, 9:7, October 1969, pp. 92–95. Julian Symonds, 'Sensational Journalism', review of *CP68*.

Tarasque, 5, n.d. (*c.* 1969), pp. 5–15 and 29–31. Stuart Mills, 'Musique d'Ameublement', an essay on RF's work as represented by *Interiors*; a review of *The Ship's Orchestra*.

Poetry Review, 60, Autumn 1969, pp. 208–09. Robert Garioch, 'Battles Won': review of *CP68*.

New Statesman, 78:2018, 14 November 1969, pp. 700–01. Alan Brownjohn, 'Subways', review of *CP68*.

Children of Albion: Poetry of the 'Underground' in Britain, ed. Michael Horovitz. Harmondsworth, Penguin, 1969, pp. 319–20. Commentary on RF.

Stand, 11:1, 1969-70, pp. 9–18. Eric Mottram, 'Roy Fisher's Work'. Also, pp. 70–71, review by Robin Fulton of *CP68*.

Encounter, 34:2, February 1970, pp. 84–91. Ronald Hayman, 'The City and the House', review of *CP68*.

Contemporary Poets of the English Language, ed. Rosalie Murphy. London, St James Press, 1970, pp. 373–74. Brief biography, selected bibliography and brief critical account by Edward Lucie-Smith.

The Guardian, 12 August 1971, p. 12. Peter Porter, 'Virtuoso on Orkney', review of *The Cut Pages* and *M*.

The Times, 12 August 1971, p. 8. Robert Nye, 'Magic is Not Enough', review of *M*.

Tribune, 35:36, 3 September 1971, p. 14. Jim Burns, 'Personal Explorations', review of *M* and *The Cut Pages*.

New Statesman, 82:2115, 1 October 1971, p. 447. Alan Brownjohn, 'Awesome Fragments', review of *M*.

The Guardian, 12 November 1971, p. 10. Raymond Gardner, 'Man about Town'.

Stand, 13:1, 1971–2, pp. 72–3. Review by Anne Cluysenaar of *M*.

Lines, 11, February/March 1972, unpaginated. Review by Adrian Philpott of *M* and *The Cut Pages*.

Revolt into Style, George Melly. Harmondsworth, Penguin, 1972, pp. 210, 214.

The Private Library, 6:1, Spring 1973, pp. 29–35. Jim Burns, 'Migrant Press'.

Thomas Hardy and British Poetry, Donald Davie. London, Routledge & Kegan Paul, 1973, pp. 152–79. Chapter 7, 'Roy Fisher: An Appreciation'. This book was reprinted, together with other essays by Donald Davie, in *With the Grain*, ed. Clive Wilmer. Manchester, Carcanet, 1998.

Pelican Guide to English Literature: The Modern Age (3rd edn), ed. Boris Ford.

Harmondsworth, Penguin, 1973, pp. 479–80. Commentary on RF by Charles Tomlinson.

Poetry of the Committed Individual: A 'Stand' Anthology of Poetry, ed. Jon Silkin. Harmondsworth, Penguin, 1973, pp. 34–37. Commentary on RF by Jon Silkin.

Poetry Nation, 5(3:1), 1975, pp. 74–87. J. D. Needham, 'Some Aspects of the Poetry of Roy Fisher'.

Widening Circles: Five Black Country Poets, ed. Edward Lowbury. West Midlands Arts, 1976, pp. 6–8. Editorial introduction contains commentary on RF.

Tribune, 40:42, 15 October 1976, pp. 6–7. Jim Burns, 'An English Craftsman and other Novelties': review of *Nineteen Poems and an Interview*.

Perfect Bound, 2, Winter 1976–77, pp. 79–82. Peter Robinson, 'Roy Fisher's "Body Sensations"'.

Windows, 2, February 1977, pp. 25–26. Robert Hampson, 'Roy Fisher: Propositions and Explorations'.

Stoneferry Review, 2, Winter 1978, pp. 51–65. John Osborne, 'The Incredulous Eye: Craig Raine and Post-Modernist Aesthetics', essay containing various references to RF.

Tribune, 42:49, 8 December 1978, p. 8. Martin Booth, 'Chronicles of Sensibility', review of *JS*.

The Observer, 7 January 1979, p. 10. Martin Dodsworth, 'Abysses and Avenues': review of *JS*.

Encounter, 52:3, March 1979, pp. 61–64. Alan Brownjohn, 'Fascination of What's Difficult', review of *JS*.

Poetry Review, 69:1, July 1979, pp. 66–68. John Cassidy, 'Energy and Shape': review of *JS*.

Stand, 20:3, 1979, p. 71. Review by Anne Cluysenaar of *JS*.

PN Review, 12 (6:4), 1979, pp. 27–28. Peter Robinson, '2 or 3 Things about Roy Fisher', review of *JS*.

Atlantic Review, new ser., 2, Autumn 1979, pp. 39–50. John Ash, 'A Classic Post-Modernist'.

The Cambridge Quarterly, 1979, pp. 274–76. Review by John Freeman of *JS*.

Contemporary Authors, 81–84, ed. Frances Carol Locher. Michigan, Gale Research Co., 1979, p. 175. Biographical/bibliographical entry.

Palantir, 14, April 1980, pp. 57–59. Review by Lawrence Freeman of *JS*.

'Career Patterns of Contemporary British Poets', Michael Peter Ryan. Thesis submitted for PhD University of London, 1980. Answers by RF to questionnaire, pp. 62, 85–89, 91–92, 232–45, 271–72. A copy of this thesis is held by the Arts Council Poetry Library, South Bank, London.

Kudos, 6, 1980, pp. 50–52. Robert Sheppard, 'The Thing about Roy Fisher', review of *JS*.

Montemora, 7, 1980, pp. 225–28. Review by Martin Dodman of *JS*.

Stand, 21:2, 1980, p. 80. Review by Desmond Graham of *Comedies*.

British Poetry Since 1970: A Critical Survey, ed. Peter Jones and Michael Schmidt. Manchester, Carcanet New Press, 1980, pp. 125–28. Deborah Mitchell, 'Modes of Realism: Roy Fisher and Elaine Feinstein'.

'Responsibilities and Distances: the Moral of the Poet in the Work of Donald Davie, Roy Fisher and Charles Tomlinson', Peter Robinson, PhD dissertation, University of Cambridge, September 1980. A copy is lodged in the University Library, Cambridge.

Grosseteste Review, 13, 1980/81, pp. 83-92. Peter Robinson, 'Liberties in Context', review of *P55–80*.

London Review of Books, 19 February–4 March 1981, pp. 19–20. Stephen Brook, 'The Pain of Living', review of *P55–80*.

Gehenna, 1, n.d. (*c.* 1981), pp. 26–31. Robert Sheppard, 'British Poetry 1960–80: Roy Fisher and Lee Harwood'.

PN Review, 20 (7:6), 1981, pp. 61–63. Glen Cavaliero, 'Simply the Known', review of *P55–80*.

Moz-Art, 3, February–May 1981, pp. 32, 34. Review by Alan Mahar of *P55–80*.

Quarto, March 1981, p. 10. George Szirtes, 'The Innocence of the Eye', review of *P55–80*.

Tribune, 45:16, 17 April 1981, p. 7. Jim Burns, 'The Rest of the World', review of *Talks for Words*.

London Magazine, 21:1–2, April/May 1981, pp. 112–15. Michael Hulse, 'Dirty Dramas', review of *P55–80*.

Encounter, 57:3, September 1981, pp. 62–69. Laurence Lerner, 'Wrestling with the Difficult', review of *P55–80*.

Ambit, 87, 1981, pp. 66–67. Review by Jim Burns of *P55–80*.

The Observer, 22 November 1981, p. 27. Peter Porter, 'Laundromat Lyrics', review of *P55–80*.

Times Literary Supplement, 20 March 1981, p. 314. Phillip Gardner, 'A City of the Mind', review of *P55–80*.

Delta, 62, 1981, pp. 23–29. David Punter, 'Metal on Stone', review of *P55–80*.

Rock Drill, 2, n.d. (*c.* 1981), pp. 18–20. Review by Robert Sheppard of *P55–80*.

Iron, 33, September/November 1981, p. 42. Review by Keith Turner of *Talks for Words*.

Shearsman, 5, 1982, pp. 77–81. 'A Strenuous Art': review by Philip Crick of *P55–80*.

A Guide to Twentieth Century Literature in English, ed. H. Blamires. London and New York, Methuen, 1983, p. 84. Entry on RF.

The British Dissonance, A. Kingsley-Weatherhead. Columbia, University of Missouri Press, 1983, pp. 29–55. Chapter 3: 'Roy Fisher'.

The Full Note: Lorine Niedecker, ed. Peter Dent. Devon, Interim Press, 1983, p. 40. Quotation of a letter from Lorine Niedecker to Kenneth Cox in which she writes appreciatively of a Roy Fisher book (probably *CP1968*).

Credences, new ser., 3:2, Spring 1985, pp. 173–79. Review by Janet Somerville of *P55–80*.

British Poetry 1964 to 1984: Driving Through the Barricades, Martin Booth. London, Routledge & Kegan Paul, 1985, pp. 54–56, 83, 90, 96. Commentary on RF's involvement with small presses and little magazines.

Poetry Today: A Critical Guide to British Poetry 1960–1984, Anthony Thwaite. London, Longman, 1985, pp. 91–92.

Contemporary Poets (4th edn), ed. James Vinson and D. L. Kirkpatrick. London, St James Press, 1985, pp. 267–68. Biographical/bibliographical details, plus critical account by Anne Cluysenaar.

Dictionary of Literary Biography, 40, *Poets of Great Britain and Ireland since 1960*, Part 1: A–L, ed. Vincent B. Sherry. Michigan, Gale Research Co., 1985, pp. 136–43. Select bibliography plus critical account by Deborah Mitchell (including photograph of hand-corrected draft typescript of 'Colour Supplement Pages', at this stage entitled 'Little Scene').

Books and Bookmen, 366, April 1986, pp. 23–24. 'A Shared Shame': review by Paul O'Prey of *F*.

The Observer, 27 April 1986, p. 27. 'Soliloquies on the City': review by Peter Porter of *F*.

Arts Report: The Arts Newspaper of the West Midlands, 53, June 1986, p. 11. Mary Cutler, 'In Search of a Place', review of *F*.

British Book News, June 1986, p. 365. Review by Raymond Tong of *F*.

Times Literary Supplement, 20 June 1986, p. 677. Robert Sheppard, 'Timeless Identities', review of *F*.

English Studies: A Journal of English Language and Literature, 67:3, Lise, Netherlands, June 1986, pp. 234-49. Peter Barry, 'Language and the City in Roy Fisher's Poetry'.

Sunday Times, 6 July 1986, p. 46. David Sexton, 'Tact and Tenderness', review of *F*.

The Powys Review, 19 (5:3), 1986, pp. 71–73. Review by Jeremy Hooker of *F*.

Ambit, 105, 1986, p. 87. Review by Jim Burns of *F*.

London Magazine, 26:5–6, August/September 1986, pp. 132–35. Simon Rae, 'Prayer and Privacy', review of *F*.

The Green Book: a Quarterly Review of the Visual and Literary Arts, 2:5, n.d. (*c.* late 1986), pp. 54–55. Review by Fred Beake of *F*.

Temenos, 8, 1987, pp. 272–76. Brian Merrikin Hill, 'A Just Celebration', review of *F*.

Roy Fisher—A Bibliography, Derek Slade. London, January 1987.

Crafts, 84, January/February 1987, pp. 22–23. George Szirtes, 'Playing Games', article on Ronald King and Circle Press, with various references to RF.

Stand, 28:2, Spring 1987, p. 72. Review by Terry Eagleton of *F*.

The Poet's Voice, 3:3, n.d. (1987), pp. 21–24. Brian Merrikin Hill, 'A Notability', review of *F*.

The Many Review, 5, Summer 1987, pp. 3–5. John Lees, 'Section through a Double Spiral', review of *F*.

Dutch Quarterly Review of Anglo-American Letters, 18:1, 1988, pp. 1–19. Peter Barry, ' "Fugitive from all Exegesis": Reading Roy Fisher's *A Furnace*'.

New Statesman and Society, 1:18, 7 October 1988, p. 34. John Lucas, 'Country of Fallen Dreams', review of *P55–87*.

Sunday Times, 30 October 1988, p. G10. Dannie Abse, 'Fascinatin' Rhythms and Stormy Weather', review of *P55–87*.

Poetry Review, 78:3, Autumn 1988, pp. 51–52. Douglas Houston, 'Not the Royal Society of Literature', a review of *A Various Art*, ed. Andrew Crozier and Tim Longville. Singles out RF for particular mention.

Bête Noire, 6, Winter 1988, pp. 186–96. Ian Gregson, ' "Music of the Generous Eye": Roy Fisher's *Poems 1955–1980*'.

Times Literary Supplement, 10–16 March 1989, p. 257. Robert Sheppard, 'Commitment to Openness', review of *P55–87*.

Verse, 6:1, March 1989, pp. 60–66. Ian Gregson, 'Roy Fisher: *A Furnace* and Before'.

Poetry Review, 79:2, Summer 1989, pp. 27–28. John Mole, 'The Innovative Flicker of the Piano Player', review of *P55–87*.

Nutshell, 6, October 1989, pp. 41–42. Sian Hughes, 'Roy Fisher's Birmingham'.

Powys Review, 23 (6:3), 1989, pp. 77–78. Review by Douglas Houston of *P 55–87*.

Poetry Durham, 22, 1989, pp. 24–27. Michael Hulse, 'Roy Fisher and the Weight of Attribution'.

Contemporary British Poetry: Patterns from the 1950s to the Present Day, Francesco Dagosei, Milano, 1989. Contains five poems by RF (*see* section C) together with an introduction, commentaries and questions for students.

Bête Noire, 8/9, Autumn 1989/Spring 1990. James Keery, 'Nature, Flowers and the Night Sky: a Review of *A Various Art*'. References to RF on pp. 44–47, 51–52.

Stand, 31:3, Summer 1990, pp. 41–42. Review by Lawrence Sail of *P 55–87*.

PN Review, 74, 16:6, 1990, p. 60. Dennis Keene, 'Withering', review of *P 55–87*.

Textual Practice, 3:3, 1989, pp. 413–25. Andrew Lawson, 'Life after Larkin: Post-Modern British Poetry'.

Ariel: A Review of International English Literature, 22:3, Calgary, AB, Canada, July 1991, pp. 7–24. Bert Almon, ' "If I Didn't Dislike Mentioning Works of Art": Roy Fisher's Poems on Poetics'.

PN Review, 83 (18:3), January/February 1992, pp. 25–32. Andrew Crozier, 'Signs of Identity: Roy Fisher's *A Furnace*'.

Cultural Revolution?: The Challenge of the Arts in the 1960s, ed. Bart Moore-Gilbert and John Seed. London and New York, Routledge, 1992, pp. 162–65. Chapter 8, Robert Sheppard, 'British Poetry and its Discontents'.

English: The Journal of the English Association, 41:169, spring 1992, pp. 49–70. Robert Sheppard, 'De-Anglicizing the Midlands: The European Context of Roy Fisher's *City*'.

New British Poetries: The Scope of the Possible, ed. Robert Hampson and Peter Barry. Manchester, Manchester University Press, 1993; chapter 1, Eric Mottram, 'The British Poetry Revival 1960–75', pp. 36–37, chapter 7, David Miller, 'Heart of Saying: The Poetry of Gael Turnbull', pp. 186–89. Other references to RF in the book, *passim*.

English Poetry since 1940, Neil Corcoran. London and New York, Longman, 1993, pp. 164–79. Chapter 12, 'Varieties of Neo-Modernism'.

Iron, 74, November 1993–February 1994, p. 49. David Stephenson, 'Poetry Live': review of a reading by RF at Morden Tower, Newcastle upon Tyne.

Yearbook of English Studies, 24, 1994, pp. 117–45. Mary Ellison, 'Jazz in the Poetry of Amiri Baraka and Roy Fisher'.

Oxford Companion to Twentieth Century Poetry in English, ed. Ian Hamilton. Oxford and New York, Oxford University Press, 1994, p. 164. Entry on RF by William Scammell.

Independent on Sunday, 21 August 1994, p. 28. William Scammell, 'Capping the Psychic Gushers', review of BR.

Sunday Times, 25 September 1994. Alan Brownjohn, 'Variety Acts': review of BR.

Poetry Review, 84:4, Winter 1994/5, pp. 55–56. Lawrence Sail, 'Weights and Measures', review of BR.

Poetry in the British Isles: Non-Metropolitan Perspectives, ed. Hans-Werner Ludwig and Lothar Frietz. Cardiff, University of Wales Press, 1995, pp. 85–88. Chapter 4, Jeremy Hooker, 'Place in Modern English Poetry'.

Poetry London Newsletter, 5:1, May 1995, p. 19. Review by Peter Daniels of BR.

Ambit, 141 1995, p. 71. Review by Jim Burns of BR.

The Reader's Companion to Twentieth Century Writers, ed. Peter Parker. Oxford and London, Fourth Estate/Helicon, 1995, pp. 239–40. Entry on RF and selected bibliography.

Iron, 76, July–October 1995, p. 35. Michael McCarthy, 'Poetry Live', review of a reading by RF at Colpitts, Durham on 10 March 1995.

PN Review, 107 (22:3), January/February 1996, pp. 28–30. Jeremy Hooker, 'Roy Fisher: Magician of the Common Place'.

PQR (Poetry Quarterly Review), 3, Spring 1996. Review by Tony Charles of DLD.

Contemporary Poets (6th edn), ed. Thomas Riggs. Detroit, St James Press, 1996, pp. 344–46. Entry on RF, containing selected bibliography, comments by RF, and critical commentary by Anne Cluysenaar.

Ambit, 145, London, 1996, pp. 21–22. Review by Vernon Scannell of DLD.

New Relations: The Refashioning of British Poetry, 1980–1994, David Kennedy. Seren Press, Wales, 1996, pp. 103–06, 126, 134, 237.

The North, 18, 1996, pp. 34–40. Sean O'Brien, 'Roy Fisher: A Polytheism with No Gods'.

Contemporary Poetry and Postmodernism: Dialogue and Estrangement, Ian Gregson. London, Macmillan, 1996, pp. 170–91. Chapter 10, 'Music of the Generous Eye: The Poetry of Roy Fisher'.

Sunday Times, 19 May 1996, section 7, p. 11. Alan Brownjohn, 'Thoroughly Modern', review of *DLD*.

The Observer, 26 May 1996, p. 16. Helen Dunmore, 'A Few Dolours More', review of *DLD*.

Times Literary Supplement, 28 June 1996, p. 25. Sean O'Brien, 'A New Kind of City', review of *DLD*.

The School Librarian, August 1996. Review by Norton Hedges of *DLD*.

Cambridge Paperback Guide to Literature in English, ed. Ian Ousby. Cambridge, Cambridge University Press, 1996, p. 144. Entry on RF.

Oxford Companion to Twentieth Century Literature in English, ed. Jenny Stringer. Oxford, Oxford University Press, 1996, p. 218. Entry on RF.

NATE News, Sheffield, Autumn 1996. Review by John Lancaster of *DLD*.

Poetry Review, 86:3, Autumn 1996, p. 88. Elaine Feinstein, 'Margin Allies', review of *DLD*.

Waterstone's Guide to Poetry Books, ed. Nick Rennison. Middlesex, Waterstone's Booksellers, 1996, p. 46. Entry on RF.

Contemporary British Poetry: Essays in Theory and Criticism, ed. James Acheson and Romana Huk. New York, State University of New York Press, 1996, pp. 35–62. Chapter 2, John Matthias, 'The Poetry of Roy Fisher'.

PN Review, 111 (23:1), September–October 1996, p. 79. Ra Page, 'The Finished Picture': review of *DLD*.

London Review of Books, 19:1, 2 January 1997, pp. 30–31. John Kerrigan, 'Rooting for Birmingham': review of *DLD*.

The Life of Metrical and Free Verse in Twentieth-Century Poetry, Jon Silkin. London, Macmillan, 1997, pp. 303–09. 'Roy Fisher: Language, or What It Refers To?'

Stand, 38:4, Autumn 1997, p. 53. Review by Rodney Pybus of *DLD*.

Times Literary Supplement, 14 November 1997, pp. 16–17. John Kerrigan, 'England of the Mind', review of three books on contemporary British poetry; contains various references to RF.

The Independent, 19 November 1997, p. 3. Article on the Paul Hamlyn Awards for Artists 1997 (RF was the recipient of an award.)

The North, 22, 1998, p. 22. Ian McMillan, 'Poets I Go Back To . . .'.

The Deregulated Muse, Sean O'Brien. Newcastle upon Tyne, Bloodaxe, 1998, pp. 112–22. Chapter 10, 'Roy Fisher: A Polytheism with No Gods'.

'The Aesthetics of History in the Modern English Long Poem: David Jones's *The Anathemata*, Basil Bunting's *Briggflatts*, Geoffrey Hill's *Mercian Hymns* and Roy Fisher's *A Furnace*', William Wootten, PhD dissertation, University of Durham, 1998. A copy is lodged in the University of Durham Library.

Lives of the Poets, Michael Schmidt. London, Weidenfeld and Nicolson, 1998, p. 876.

The Poet as Spy: The Life and Wild Times of Basil Bunting, Keith Alldritt. London, Aurum Press, 1998, pp. xiv, 151, 185, 197, 201.

Fishing by Obstinate Isles: Modern and Postmodern British Poetry and American Readers, Keith Tuma. Illinois, Northwestern University Press, 1998, pp. 239–43.

Far Language: Poetics and Linguistically Innovative Poetry, 1978–1997, Robert Sheppard. Exeter, Stride Publications, 1999. This contains 'Timeless Identities', Sheppard's *TLS* review of *F*, pp. 18–20, and 'Commitment to Openness', which includes his *TLS* review of *P55–87*, pp. 32–34.

News for the Ear: A Homage to Roy Fisher, ed. Peter Robinson and Robert Sheppard. Exeter, Stride Publications, 2000. Contains poems and/ or prose connected with RF by Edwin Morgan, Thom Gunn, John Matthias, Gael Turnbull, Tony Baker, Lee Harwood, Jeremy Hooker, Richard Caddel, Robert Sheppard, Fleur Adcock, Maurice Scully, Peter Robinson, Elaine Feinstein, Peter Riley, Ken Edwards, August Kleinzahler, Sean O'Brien, Charles Tomlinson, Carol Ann Duffy, and John Tranter.

General Index

Page numbers in bold indicate references to the Bibliography

Wordsworth, William 164, 226
  The Prelude 99–100

Yeats, William Butler 56, 61, 63, 68, 71,
  75, 154, 204, 300, 305

'Blood and the Moon' 293
'Leda and the Swan' 61, 62
'Sailing to Byzantium' 80 n.30, 291

Zukofsky, Louis 150, 153, 189

Index of Works by Roy Fisher